CHIASMUS IN THE NEW TESTAMENT

Manufactured in the United States of America

Originally published in 1942, under the title *Chiasmus in the New Testament: A Study in Formgeschichte*, by the University of North Carolina Press. Published in 1992, under the title *Chiasmus in the New Testament: A Study in the Form and Function of Chiastic Structures*, with a new preface, by Hendrickson Publishers, Inc. University of North Carolina Press Enduring Edition published in 2012.

Library of Congress Cataloging-in-Publication Data
Lund, Nils Wilhelm, 1885–1954.
Chiasmus in the New Testament: a study in the form and function of chiastic structures / by Nils Wilhelm Lund.
p. cm.
Originally published: Chapel Hill: University of North Carolina Press, 1942.
Includes bibliographical references and indexes.
1. Bible. N.T.—Criticism, Form. 2. Bible. N.T.—Language, style.
3. Chiasmus. I. Title.
BS2377.L86 1992
225.6'6—dc20 92-35
CIP

ISBN 978-1-4696-0851-8

To

MY WIFE

For she herself also hath been a helper of many and of mine own self.—Rom. 16.2.

PREFACE TO THE 1992 REPRINT OF NILS W. LUND, *CHIASMUS IN THE NEW TESTAMENT*

This year is the fiftieth anniversary of the publication of Nils Wilhelm Lund's *Chiasmus in the New Testament: A Study in Formgeschichte* (Chapel Hill: University of North Carolina Press, 1942). This reprinting of Lund's classic work is a celebration of that anniversary as well as an attempt to call attention to a volume long out of print for its importance for today's concern for rhetorical and literary analysis of the New Testament. George A. Kennedy, undoubtedly the premier scholar today of Graeco-Roman and early church rhetorical studies, refers to Lund's book as an important work, noting that chiasmus is an example of one of " . . . a few devices commonly found in ancient texts and given labels by modern critics [that] are not identified at all in handbooks of the classical period."[1]

Chiasmus (or chiasm) is a term based on the Greek letter *chi* (χ) which refers to an inverted parallelism or sequence of words or ideas in a phrase, sentence, or any larger literary unit. For example, Mark 2:27 contains a chiasmus which may be represented as follows:

A The sabbath
B was made for man
B′ and not man
A′ for the sabbath.

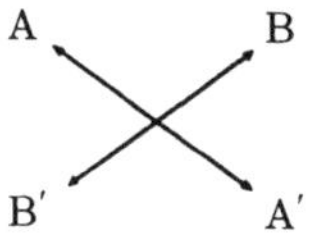

A B
B′ A′

Chiasmus involves fundamentally two elements: inversion and balance (as shown above). Often this leads to a third basic feature: climactic centrality, when the inversion has a middle element (see, for example, the illustration of the Prologue of John below with the climactic centrality expressed in line H).[2]

[1] G. A. Kennedy, *New Testament Interpretation through Rhetorical Criticism* (Studies in Religion; Chapel Hill and London: University of North Carolina Press, 1984), p. 10 for the mention of Lund; p. 28 for the quotation.

[2] For this basic understanding see Augustine Stock, "Chiastic Awareness and Education in Antiquity," *Biblical Theology Bulletin* 14 (1984), 23–27, especially p. 23. See also John W. Welch, "Introduction," in John W. Welch, *Chiasmus in Antiquity: Structures, Analyses, Exegesis* (Hildesheim: Gersten-

Nils W. Lund and the Development of the Book

Nils Wilhelm Lund was born in Gävle, Sweden, on March 6, 1885. His father, a sea captain, went to Argentina in 1885. As part of an extensive Swedish emigration to Argentina and Brazil, the rest of the family, including Nils, emigrated to Argentina in 1889. Nils later came to the United States in 1903, where he settled in Boston. He studied at North Park Theological Seminary in Chicago from 1907 to 1910, graduating in 1910. He served the North Park Covenant Church in Chicago, 1910–1911. He was married in 1912 in Boston to Signe Fagerholm, who died in 1943. (He married Hannah Anderson in Boston in 1946; Lund was fond of noting that the name Hannah was chiastic in structure.) He served the Covenant Church in Lindsborg, Kansas, 1911–1916, during which time he received the A.B. in 1915 from Bethany College in Lindsborg. He then served the Swedish Congregational Church in Lynn, Massachusetts, 1916–1920, during which time he received the S.T.B. in 1919 from Andover Theological Seminary. He next served the Covenant Congregational Church in Boston, 1920–1922, during which time he received the S.T.M. in 1921 from Harvard University. In 1922 Lund came to North Park Theological Seminary as a teacher; he served on the faculty until his death on January 2, 1954. From 1925 to 1948 Lund was the Dean of the Seminary. During this time his works on chiasmus were published, and on December 19, 1941, he received his Ph.D. from the University of Chicago. Lund was a member and former vice-president of the Chicago Society of Biblical Research.

Lund's book was the publication of his Ph.D. thesis at the Divinity School of the University of Chicago: "Chiasmus in the New Testament: A New Approach to 'Formgeschichte.'" It was the culmination of work he had begun in 1908, while a student

berg, 1981), 9–16, especially p. 9. Many other terms are used for the chiastic concept; Welch (p. 10) lists nine others (e.g., introverted parallelism; concentrism). He also notes the term *hysteron proteron* (the latter first) in his essay "Chiasmus in Ancient Greek and Latin Literature," in the same volume, pp. 250–68, especially p. 251. Charles H. Talbert refers to the concept as "the principle of balance" in his *Literary Patterns, Theological Themes, and the Genre of Luke–Acts* (Society of Biblical Literature Monograph Series 20; Missoula: Society of Biblical Literature and Scholars Press, 1974), p. 67.

at North Park Theological Seminary, which found expression in seven articles he published between 1930 and 1934. Lund submitted his thesis to the University of Chicago on July 12, 1934, recording in his diary for that day: "Today I handed in the dissertation on chiasmus in the New Testament. It has been on my mind constantly for years, and it is with a sense of great relief that I come to an end. I hope it will be accepted."[3] It is not clear what led to a delay, but Lund's thesis oral examination was not held until December 6, 1941, more than seven years later. He records the following in his diary for December 6:

> Slept till 7 A.M. — of all mornings! Arrived at Dean [Ernest Cadman] Colwells [*sic*] office at 8:55, the first to arrive. Dr. [Harold R.] Willoughby came at 9.05, [Allen Paul] Wikgren at 9.10, and [William A.] Irwin at 9.15. They began to examine & later Dean Colwell came directly from Denver & Dr. [Donald W.] Riddle my advisor at 9.40. For two hours & 40 min. the exam went on, with never a dull moment. I learnt a few things, about my own research. Willoughby was the most strenuous objector to my "projections" in Rev. [Revelation]. The meeting was most cordial. I was admitted by vote to the doctorate. Now all is over but the fanfare & flag-waving Dec. 19. Signe & children share my joy. I am very happy and very weary. I thanked the five examiners for their fine consideration & friendship during intermittent and sporadic studies.

The seven articles Lund published between 1930 and 1934 are listed here chronologically:[4]

"The Presence of Chiasmus in the Old Testament," *American Journal of Semitic Languages and Literatures* 46 (1929/30 [46:2, January 1930]), 104–26;

"The Presence of Chiasmus in the New Testament," *Journal of Religion* 10 (1930), 74–93;

"The Influence of Chiasmus upon the Structure of the Gospels," *Anglican Theological Review* 13 (1931), 27–48;

"The Influence of Chiasmus upon the Structure of the Gospel according to Matthew," *Anglican Theological Review* 13 (1931), 405–33;

[3] Lund's diaries are in the Covenant Archives and Historical Library at North Park Theological Seminary, Chicago, Ill. This and the following diary citations are transcribed from his 1934 and 1941 diaries respectively.

[4] In some cases the data listed here correct the listing of these articles in Lund's book (pp. 417–18).

"The Literary Structure of Paul's Hymn to Love," *Journal of Biblical Literature* 50 (1931), 266–76;

"Chiasmus in the Psalms," *American Journal of Semitic Languages and Literatures* 49 (1932/33 [49:4, July 1933]), 281–312; and

"The Literary Structure of the Book of Habakkuk," *Journal of Biblical Literature* 53 (1934), 355–70 (with H. H. Walker).

Lund's work displays considerable interest in the book of Revelation,[5] for which he had already written a lesson book for the Covenant Church in 1935.[6] His full-scale commentary on Revelation, however, was not published until the year after his death.[7]

Lund published two further articles on chiasmus after his book appeared, each of which is basically a summary of his book:

"The Significance of Chiasmus for Interpretation," *Crozer Quarterly* 20 (1943), 105–23; and

"Chiasmus i Nya Testamentet," *Svensk Teologisk Kvartalskrift* 25 (1949), 299–320.

What contacts and negotiations Lund undertook to have his book published are not clear, but he made an agreement with the University of North Carolina Press, which acknowledged receipt of his manuscript on March 19, 1940, a little over a year and a half before his oral examination on his thesis. Lund received his first copies of the book on March 27, 1942, just over three months after his University of Chicago graduation.[8]

The Reception of the Book

In spite of limited distribution, Lund's *magnum opus* received significant attention at the time of its original publica-

[5] See *Chiasmus*, chapters 17–21, pp. 321–411.

[6] *Outline Studies in the Book of Revelation* (Covenant Graded Lessons. For Senior Young People's and Adult Departments, School Year 1935–36—Second Term; Chicago: Covenant Book Concern, 1935) [136 pp.].

[7] *Studies in the Book of Revelation* (Chicago: Covenant Press, 1955 [256 pp.]. Lund's introduction is dated All Saints Day, 1953, just two months and a day prior to his death. Lund states in the introduction that the original contribution of his work on Revelation is the chiastic structures he proposes for Revelation.

[8] This information is taken from Lund's personal files in the Covenant Archives and Historical Library.

tion and has continued to enjoy recognition and use by later scholars working with chiasmus as the pioneering work in the field.

Lund's *Chiasmus* received meaningful reviews by at least six prominent scholars, four of whom wrote in rather well-known journals: Henry J. Cadbury,[9] Floyd V. Filson,[10] Sherman E. Johnson[11] and Thomas S. Kepler.[12] In addition, Ovid R. Sellers reviewed the volume in the Presbyterian Seminary [now McCormick Theological Seminary] *Alumni Review*,[13] and George F. Hall published a review article, "Dean Lund's Study in Formgeschichte," in the *Augustana Quarterly*.[14] An unsigned notice also appeared in the *Christian Century*.[15] Among many personal letters Lund received, perhaps attention could be called to the April 1, 1942 letter from the famous New Testament scholar, Frederick C. Grant. Grant said in part: "I am sure that the book will be for many years to come *the* standard treatise on the subject."[16]

All the reviewers gave considerable praise to the achievement of Lund, although most also expressed significant reservations. Kepler noted that Lund " . . . has really done a very patient, disciplined bit of research. . . . The book is scholarly; it is written in a most edifying fashion; its thesis regarding *chiasmus* as a form is sound."[17] Johnson calls the book " . . . solid, scholarly and beautifully printed . . . " and concludes by observing that " . . . Lund has made many brilliant suggestions. . . . We can only hope that every commentator from now on will take full account of this lucid and helpful book."[18] Sellers concludes his summary of the book by noting that " . . . there is no doubt that his book is an original and important contribution to Biblical study."[19] The *Christian Century* note

[9] *Journal of Religion* 23 (1943), 62–63.

[10] *Journal of Near Eastern Studies* 2 (1943), 92–94.

[11] *Anglican Theological Review* 24 (1942), 266–67.

[12] *Journal of Bible and Religion* 10 (1942), 165–66.

[13] 18:1 (July 1942), 46–47.

[14] 21 (1942), 349–57.

[15] 59 (1942), 664–65 (May 20 issue).

[16] The Frederick C. Grant letter is in Lund's personal files in the Covenant Archives and Historical Library.

[17] Kepler, p. 166.

[18] Johnson, p. 266; p. 267.

[19] Sellers, p. 47.

states that "it is difficult to escape the impression that he has found too much of it [chiasmus]. However, . . . his work will not be superseded; the book is a marvel of patience and completeness."[20] Cadbury notes that Lund was anticipated by only one or two scholars and that he " . . . has succeeded in selecting the best evidence and in finding the most effective visual way of presenting it." Cadbury further observes that not all of Lund's evidence is of equal cogency and that he sometimes emends the text in order to make his theories work. Cadbury concludes by noting that " . . . the reader should be warned neither to accept nor to reject the author's sober contention without faithfully pondering what he has laid before us and subjecting it to every alternative explanation that is conceivable."[21] Filson makes several positive observations. He notes that "this book challenges widely held ideas that many biblical authors wrote in a non-literary atmosphere and without literary training or intention." Thus, Lund has shown " . . . that there is more use of chiastic patterns in the Bible than we usually realize." Filson states that " . . . Lund's conclusions are revolutionary."[22] Filson, however, " . . . is unable to accept the sweeping claims for the existence of large numbers of extensive chiastic structures." He thus concludes that Lund's work is " . . . a scholarly but overzealous argument which no doubt will remain the standard publication of the case for chiasmus in the Bible."[23] Hall is perhaps most cautious; he wonders whether or not Lund's theses about chiasmus will have much influence or be very convincing. He does, however, state that the work deserves praise and careful scrutiny.

In more recent years, especially in the 1970s and 1980s, there seems to have been a revival of interest in chiasmus, focusing often but not exclusively on the New Testament. Lund's importance is often noted in these more recent studies. For example, R. Alan Culpepper refers to Lund as the one " . . . who might be called the father of modern studies of chiastic structures."[24] John W. Welch identifies Lund as " . . . the

[20] P. 665.

[21] Cadbury, p. 63.

[22] Filson, p. 93.

[23] Ibid., pp. 93, 94.

[24] R. Alan Culpepper, "The Pivot of John's Prologue," *New Testament Studies* 27 (1980/81), 1–31; the quotation is from p. 6.

scholar who has probably done more than any other to bring the study of chiasmus to life in the twentieth century. . . . "[25] Ronald E. Man refers to Lund's work as " . . . an epoch-making work in the study of New Testament chiasm. For the first time a major, systematic treatment of the subject was undertaken."[26]

Among the more important broad studies of chiasmus in the last twenty years are those of Charles H. Talbert, David J. Clark, John W. Welch, Ronald E. Man and Augustine Stock. Talbert attempts a brief, general survey of what he calls the "patterns reflecting the principle of balance" in classical, Israelite-Jewish and early Christian literature.[27] Clark's work is an attempt to develop criteria by which chiasmus can be identified.[28] John W. Welch edited a somewhat remarkable volume of essays on chiasmus in a broad range of ancient literatures (Sumero-Akkadian; Ugaritic; Hebrew Bible; Aramaic contracts and letters; Talmudic-Aggadic narratives; Greek and Latin literature and the New Testament). The volume contains Welch's introduction to chiastic studies, a bibliography and indexes to specific texts in ancient literature for which a chiastic structure has been suggested. This includes a detailed list of references, in canonical text order, for the Old Testament and the New Testament (pp. 297–352) along with bibliographic references locating discussions of these chiastic texts in the secondary literature.[29] Man provides a brief survey of the study of

[25] Welch, "Introduction," *Chiasmus in Antiquity*, 9–16; the quotation is from p. 9.

[26] Ronald E. Man, "The Value of Chiasm for New Testament Interpretation," *Bibliotheca Sacra* 141 (1984), 146–57; the quotation is from p. 147. See also his "Chiasm in the New Testament" (unpublished Th.M. thesis, Dallas Theological Seminary, 1982). For some additional references to Lund see R. N. Soulen, *Handbook of Biblical Criticism* (2d ed.; Atlanta: John Knox, 1981), p. 41 (Lund's book is " . . . an overzealous but helpful analysis. . . . "), and N. Turner, *Style* (J. H. Moulton, *A Grammar of New Testament Greek* [volume 4; Edinburgh: T. & T. Clark, 1976]), pp. 97–99.

[27] Talbert's chapter 5, "The Patterns in the Light of the Lucan Milieu," in *Literary Patterns*, pp. 67–88 (with considerable bibliography).

[28] David J. Clark, "Criteria for Identifying Chiasm," *Linguistica Biblica* 35 (1975), 63–72. Additional articles on chiasmus were subsequently published in this journal: Angelico di Marco, "Der Chiasmus in der Bibel," *Linguistica Biblica* 36 (1975), 21–97; 37 (1976), 49–68; 39 (1976), 37–85; 44 (1979), 3–70.

[29] Welch, *Chiasmus in Antiquity*. For some additional bibliography on chiasmus in the Old Testament, see Talbert, *Literary Patterns*, pp. 85–86, and Man, "The Value," p. 155, n. 11.

chiasmus in the New Testament, with representative bibliography.[30] Stock provides important perspectives for setting chiasmus in the context of education and thought in the Graeco-Roman world.

The Importance of Chiasmus

Lund almost single-handedly drew attention to chiasmus and to its importance for interpretation. The examples Lund identified often are not convincing, and at times he clearly forced texts to fit his desired pattern. For example, the suggested arrangement of Romans 11:33–36[32] or Matthew 23[33] would not excite anyone about the significance of chiasmus. Lund himself admitted that his arrangement of Colossians 1:24–2:1 was less convincing.[34] Also, even after arguing that chiasmus did not require perfect symmetry,[35] Lund did not hesitate to excise expected glosses that did not fit a chiastic pattern.[36] Most interpreters would admit that subjectivity on the part of an interpreter is an unavoidable reality and would expect occasional unconvincing examples. What lies at the foundation of this "slipperiness" are numerous methodological questions that deserve more adequate discussion than they have so far received.

Despite Lund's admitted excess, his focus on chiasmus has placed biblical scholarship forever in his debt. Chiasmus is of unquestioned significance for interpreting texts.[37] Examples exist, of course, in which the identification of a chiasmus is merely interesting and does not contribute significantly to

[30] Man, "The Value."

[31] Stock, "Chiastic Awareness."

[32] Lund, *Chiasmus*, p. 222.

[33] Ibid., p. 283.

[34] Ibid., pp. 212–13.

[35] Ibid., p. 213.

[36] Note his argument that Ephesians 5:29a and 6:16a are glosses (pp. 200 and 205, respectively) and that for Matthew 23 verse 15 is placed before verse 14 and that verses 16–22 are excluded from the original construction (although they, too, are given a chiastic arrangement).

[37] For general discussions see Man, "The Value"; John Breck, "Biblical Chiasmus: Exploring Structure for Meaning," *Biblical Theology Bulletin* 17 (1987), 70–74; and Welch, "Chiasmus in the New Testament," in *Chiasmus in Antiquity,* 211–49. Again, however, those who focus on chiasmus tend to cite examples that are debatable.

understanding (e.g., the chiasmus in Romans 2:7–10 is clear, but has little impact on meaning[38]). Other examples, however, radically alter the way texts are perceived. If the chiasmus is longer than four elements, the center of the structure is emphasized and the corresponding parallels provide commentary on each other.

One of the most striking and important uses of chiasmus occurs in the Prologue of the Gospel of John. Lund had identified a chiasmus in 1:1–18 centered around 1:13, even though he omitted parts of the text.[39] Several other scholars have noticed the chiastic structure as well, but the most convincing analysis of the Prologue is that by Alan Culpepper, who shows that the center of this chiasmus is 1:12b: "He gave them authority to become the children of God."[40] The arrangement of the Prologue is as follows:

A The Word as *theos* with God 1:1–2
  B Creation came through the Word 1:3
    C We have received life from the Word 1:4–5
      D John was sent to testify 1:6–8
        E Incarnation and the response of the world 1:9–10
          F The Word and his own (Israel) 1:11
            G Those who accepted the Word 1:12a
              H He gave authority to become the children of God 1:12b
            G′ Those who believed the Word 1:12c
          F′ The Word and his own (believers) 1:13
        E′ Incarnation and the response of the community 1:14
      D′ John's testimony 1:15
    C′ We have received grace from the Word 1:16
  B′ Grace and truth came through the Word 1:17
A′ The Word as *theos* with God 1:18

[38] See Eberhard Jüngel, "Ein paulinischer Chiasmus: Zum Verständnis der Vorstellung vom Gericht nach den Werken in Röm 2,2–11," *Unterwegs zur Sache* (Munich: Chr. Kaiser, 1972), 173–78; and Kendrick Grobel, "A Chiastic Retribution-Formula in Romans 2," *Zeit und Geschichte: Dankesgabe an Rudolf Bultmann zum 80. Geburtstag* (ed. Erich Dinkler; Tübingen: Mohr-Siebeck, 1964), 255–61, who argued that in this section Paul is adapting an originally Jewish statement.

[39] N. W. Lund, "The Influence of Chiasmus upon the Structure of the Gospels," *Anglican Theological Review* 13 (1931), 42–46.

[40] See Culpepper. See also Man, "The Value," p. 151; and Jeff Staley, "The Structure of John's Prologue: Its Implications for the Gospel's Narrative Structure," *Catholic Biblical Quarterly* 48 (1986), 241–64.

If parallels within the chiasmus are based on language, concepts, and content, all the parallels in this section evidence at least two of the three except for E and E′, which are based on content alone. The implications of this structure are significant. Suddenly the Prologue makes sense, and the attempts to remove the statements about the testimony of John the Baptist to discover an earlier hymn are shown to be futile. Also the chiastic structure strengthens the already strong argument for the reading of *theos* in 1:18 (evidenced by P^{66} and P^{75}) instead of *huios*. Theological and exegetical insight is gained as well, for the parallel between 1:9–10 and 1:14 shows that 1:9 is referring to the incarnation instead of to general revelation. The structure underscores the importance of 1:12 as the climax and of 1:1 and 1:18 as the theological basis of the whole section.

Suggestions of chiastic structure have been made for numerous other passages as well, although some are not convincing. For example, 1 John 1:6–7 can be viewed as chiastic, but only at the cost of not considering the rest of the sentence in 1:7b.[41] Other suggestions of chiasmus are helpful, however, and the exegete must give careful consideration of such structures without imposing a pattern on the text. Three other suggestions that merit attention are Galatians 4:1–7,[42] Ephesians 2:11–22[43] and Ephesians 5:5.[44]

[41] See Breck's suggestion ("Biblical Chiasmus," p. 72):

A If we say we *have fellowship with* him
  B and (yet) *walk in the darkness,*
    C we lie and do not the truth
  B′ If we *walk in the light* as he is in the light,
A′ *we have fellowship with* one another. . . .

Breck recognizes that the sentence in verse 7 continues by saying "and the blood of Jesus his Son cleanses us from all sin," but says "the chiastic pattern concludes with a central doctrinal affirmation." Consideration must be given to the structure of 1:5–2:2 as a whole.

[42] See Welch, *Chiasmus in Antiquity,* p. 214, who suggests:

A The *heir* remains a *child* and *servant* 4:1
  B Until the time appointed of the *father* 4:2
    C When that time came, *God* sent forth his *Son* 4:4
      D Made under the *law* 4:4
      D′ To redeem those under the *law* 4:5
    C′ Because you are sons, *God* sent forth the Spirit of his *Son* 4:6
  B′ That you cry Abba, *Father* 4:6
A′ That you are no more a *servant* but a *son* and *heir.* 4:7

Obviously, verse 3 is omitted on this explanation. A better suggestion is to see the parallels much more straightforwardly: verses 1 and 7; verses 2 and 6

Just as intriguing as the suggestions of chiasmus for individual passages are the chiastic arrangements of large sections or of entire books. A surprising number of such suggestions have been made. Lund argued that the books of Revelation and Philemon were in toto chiastic and that large sections of Matthew (4:12–14:12; 5–7; 10; 15:1–20; and 23) and 1 Corinthians (7 and 11:34b–14:40) were as well.[45] Kenneth Bailey arranged the travel narrative in Luke 9:51–19:48 as a long chiasmus.[46] Several people have found chiasmus in Mark, especially in 2:1–3:6.[47] John Welch argued for chiastic structures (or adaptations

---

(with verse 6 showing the time set by the Father); verses 3 and 5 (enslaved; redeemed); and the whole of verse 4 as the climax.

[43] See the suggestions of J. C. Kirby, *Ephesians: Baptism and Pentecost* (London: SPCK, 1968), pp. 156–57; Giovanni Giavini, "La structure littéraire d'Eph. II.11–22," *New Testament Studies* 16 (1969/70), 209–11; and Kenneth Ewing Bailey, *Poet and Peasant: A Literary-Cultural Approach to the Parables in Luke* (Grand Rapids: William B. Eerdmans, 1976), p. 63. None of these suggestions is convincing as a tight chiasmus. A better suggestion of chiasmus might be:

A Gentiles in the flesh, at that time without Christ, alienated from God, his people, and his purposes 2:11–12
  B In Christ the "far ones" are made near by the blood of Christ 2:13
    C Christ is our peace who unites people and destroys the enmity 2:14
      D He destroyed the law of commandments and ordinances 2:15a
    C′ He creates unity, making peace, reconciling to God, having killed the enmity 2:15b–16
  B′ He preached peace to the far and near to give access to God 2:17–18
A′ You [Gentiles] are no longer strangers, but belong to God's people and his family and are joined to Christ to serve God 2:19–22

Bailey, Giavini, and Kirby all identify verse 15a as the turning point. The passage is at least "loosely chiastic." This raises the question as to whether a chiasmus must be perfect (see discussion later in this essay).

[44] See S. E. Porter, " ἴστε γινώσκοντες in Ephesians 5,5: Does Chiasm Solve a Problem?" *Zeitschrift für die neutestamentliche Wissenschaft* 81 (1990), 270–76. Further, on Paul in general see Joachim Jeremias, "Chiasmus in den Paulusbriefen," *Zeitschrift für die neutestamentliche Wissenschaft* 49 (1958), 145–56.

[45] Lund, *Chiasmus*, passim. See also his *Studies in the Book of Revelation.*

[46] Bailey, *Poet*, pp. 80–82. Also on Luke–Acts see Donald R. Miesner, "The Missionary Journeys Narrative: Patterns and Implications," *Perspectives on Luke-Acts* (ed. Charles H. Talbert; Special Studies Series 5; Danville: Association of Baptist Professors of Religion/Edinburgh: T. & T. Clark, 1978), 199–214; Donald R. Miesner, "Chiasm and the Composition and Message of Paul's Missionary Sermons," S.T.D. thesis, Lutheran School of Theology at Chicago, 1974; and Kenneth R. Wolfe, " The Chiastic Structure of Luke–Acts and Some Implications for Worship," *Southwestern Journal of Theology* 22 (1980), 60–71.

[47] M. Philip Scott argued that Mark's whole Gospel is a chiasmus; see "Chiastic Structure: A Key to the Interpretation of Mark's Gospel," *Biblical*

of chiastic structures) for James, Galatians, 1 Corinthians, Hebrews, Colossians, Philemon, 2 Timothy, Jude, Matthew, John, and Revelation.[48] Peter Ellis likewise viewed the Gospels of Matthew and John and the seven Pauline letters he analyzed as chiastic.[49] The degree to which these suggestions are convincing varies considerably. The most plausible are those relating to the Gospel of Matthew, parts of the Gospel of Mark, the travel narrative of the Gospel of Luke, sections of 1 Corinthians, and the letter to Philemon, but none of the suggestions can escape critique.

A modern reader surely will ask, "Could chiasmus have been that prevalent in the ancient world?" How people in the ancient world functioned will always be difficult to determine. It is doubtful that as many books are chiastic as has been suggested, but the presence of chiasmus in the ancient world is unquestioned. The very way that learning occurred may have contributed to chiastic structures and awareness.[50] In all probability chiasmus was used for mnemonic purposes to assist in the dissemination of material in an oral culture.[51] It was a way for a hearer or reader to keep track of the sequence of

---

Theology Bulletin 15 (1985), 17–26. Joanna Dewey found chiasmus in 2:1–3:6; see *Markan Public Debate: Literary Technique, Concentric Structure, and Theology in Mark 2:1–3:6* (Chico: Scholars Press, 1980), pp. 109–23. She also found chiasmus in 1:1–8 (pp. 145–47); 4:1–34 (pp. 147–52); and 12:1–40 (pp. 159–63). See also her earlier "The Literary Structure of the Controversy Stories in Mark 2:1–3:6," *Journal of Biblical Literature* 92 (1973), 394–401. John Edward Phelan argued that Mark 6:30–8:10 is a chiasmus; see "Rhetoric and Meaning in Mark 6:30–8:10," unpublished Ph.D. dissertation, Northwestern University, 1985, pp. 207–28. On Mark see also Augustine Stock, "Hinge Transitions in Mark's Gospel," *Biblical Theology Bulletin* 15 (1985), 27–31.

[48] Welch, *Chiasmus in Antiquity,* passim. In fact, Welch included Ephesians and 1 Timothy as well, but the patterns were not strictly chiastic.

[49] See Peter F. Ellis, *Matthew: His Mind and his Message* (Collegeville: Liturgical Press, 1974), p. 12; idem, *Seven Pauline Letters* (Collegeville: Liturgical Press, 1982), passim; and idem, *The Genius of John* (Collegeville: Liturgical Press, 1984), pp. 13–15. Charles H. Talbert also argued that most of John, especially 1:19–5:47, was chiastic; see "Artistry and Theology: An Analysis of the Architecture of Jn 1,19–5,47," *Catholic Biblical Quarterly* 32 (1970), 341–66.

[50] See the discussion by Augustine Stock, "Chiastic Awareness," who is dependent on H. I. Marrou, *A History of Education in Antiquity* (New York: Sheed and Ward, 1956), who reports (p. 151) that children in Roman times had to learn the alphabet forward, backwards and then both ways at once (i.e., alpha-omega, beta-psi, etc.).

[51] Welch, *Chiasmus in Antiquity,* p. 12; H. Van Dyke Parunak, "Oral Typesetting: Some Uses of Biblical Structure," *Biblica* 62 (1981), 153–68.

ideas. Therefore, chiasmus was rhetorical, artistic, and functional both for the author in arranging material for emphasis and for the reader in remembering that material.

Methodological Questions

The identification of chiasmus in ancient texts has become an increasingly popular venture. However, the subjectivity of scholars, unfounded and competing chiastic arrangements, and the slipperiness of the whole process of identifying chiasmus point to a number of methodological questions that deserve more careful discussion than they have received. Lund was aware of most of these issues, but while giving implicit and explicit answers, he did not actually discuss the questions. If scholarship is to move past the exuberant fascination with chiastic possibilities to a clear and objective understanding, the following questions will need substantive discussion.

1. *To what degree is chiasmus a way of thinking as opposed to a literary structure?* Sometimes humans think in linear fashion and move logically to a final conclusion. At other times the thought process goes into and out from a primary idea, resulting in a chiastic pattern. If ancient educational methods promoted chiastic thinking,[52] does there need to be a distinction between a habit of thought and a literary structure? Is such a distinction possible?

2. *To what degree is chiasmus conscious or unconscious?* Lund knew that chiasmus is a "very natural mode of expression" and often represents the unconscious workings of the mind.[53] If a chiasmus could be identified as unconscious, would it be less important?

3. *Is perfection required before a pericope is labeled a chiasmus?* Most writers on chiasmus—admittedly persons biased toward the identification of chiasmus—would say perfection is not required. Charles Talbert, in fact, argues from comments on style from ancient writers that perfection in structure was avoided. Asymmetrical structures are what one would

[52] See note 50.

[53] Lund, *Chiasmus*, p. 128. See the discussions by Stock, "Chiastic Awareness," and by Clark, "Criteria," pp. 71–72.

expect.[54] If so, how does one know whether a particular passage should actually be identified as chiastic? The tendency of scholars to summarize long sections of scripture in their own words only compounds the problem. If perfect symmetry was avoided, how much imperfection is allowed for something still to be considered chiastic in structure, and what is the significance of those portions of the text omitted from the structure?[55]

4. *Given that the center of an extended chiasmus is the climax, are the beginning and the end of a chiasmus also emphasized?* The example of the Prologue of John would suggest that this is so.

5. *What are the legitimate bases for the identification of chiasmus?* The use of identical words or cognates and similar constructions in inverted parallelism is easy enough to identify. But can chiasmus legitimately be based on parallel ideas?[56] Most scholars assume so. Do the lengths of the parallel sections need to be approximately the same, or could one be much longer than the other? Talbert argued that the lengths do not need to be similar.[57]

6. *What is the relation between chiasmus and inclusio?* The danger of forcing *inclusio* into chiasmus is real, but the use of one does not preclude the other. For example, the Prologue of John is clearly a chiasmus, but surely John 20:28 joined with John 1:1 is an example of *inclusio*.

7. *What is the difference between chiasmus and recurring themes in a text?* If themes recur in a text, one can almost certainly push them into a chiastic structure, but is this always a genuine chiasmus?

No suggestion is made that simple answers exist for these questions. As an artistic form, chiasmus would not allow simple solutions. Furthermore, human language is infinitely com-

[54] See Talbert, "Artistry," pp. 361–62. Lund also argued that perfection was not necessary (*Chiasmus*, p. 213) and that an irregularity in the pattern of Psalm 90 was a deliberate departure. Welch, *Chiasmus in Antiquity*, p. 231, suggested that imperfection in Jude was intended.

[55] Parunak ("Oral Typesetting," p. 159) argued that structures that are partially chiastic are also effective and that deliberate breaks in a structure sometimes appear for emphasis (pp. 166–68).

[56] See discussions by Clark, "Criteria," pp. 65–66, and Dewey, *Markan Public Debate*, pp. 132–34.

[57] Talbert, "Artistry," p. 362.

plex and variable, and numerous possibilities exist in relation to the issues raised here.

Even though answers are not easy, the questions must be carefully addressed, for the abuses of chiasmus are frequent. The fact of the matter is that if a person wants to find chiasmus, he or she probably will. Even those persons who discuss criteria for identifying chiasmus often make unjustified identifications of chiasmus.[58]

Ultimately, one can do only what Lund himself did—carefully analyze the text and identify the structures that are revealed in the text. No value is to be found in forcing texts to conform to structures with which one is enamored. Chiasmus is a functional and artistic literary device and a frequent method of human expression. One will understand texts only where the text reveals structure, not where it is imposed.

Appreciation

We want to express our appreciation to Timothy J. Johnson, Director of Archives, Covenant Archives and Historical Library (housed at North Park Theological Seminary), and Philip J. Anderson, Professor of Church History, North Park Theological Seminary, for their help in finding and interpreting material on Nils W. Lund in the Archives, and to Norma S. Sutton, Seminary Librarian, North Park Theological Seminary, for her help in locating material. We also would like to express our thanks to the family of Nils W. Lund for their cooperation in allowing this book to be published again.

David M. Scholer, Distinguished Professor of
New Testament and Early Church History

Klyne R. Snodgrass, Dean of the Faculty and
Paul W. Brandel Professor of New Testament Studies

North Park Theological Seminary
Chicago, Illinois
January 2, 1992 (the thirty-eighth anniversary of Lund's death)

[58] Note the confusing suggestion by Clark, "Criteria," pp. 66–71, or the overemphasis on chiasmus by Welch.

PREFACE

The studies contained in the following pages were begun in 1908 while I was a student at North Park Theological Seminary, Chicago, Illinois. My attention was then called to certain peculiarities in the style of Biblical writers designated as "the inverted order." These stylistic features consisted of an orderly arrangement of ideas in a sentence or paragraph up to a certain point, after which the ideas were repeated in the inverted order until the sentence or paragraph was completed. Although I was at that time frankly skeptical as to the actual existence of any literary arrangement of such nature and could see very little, if any, practical value in studying its forms, the impulse to investigate led me into a more careful examination of the whole subject. I had worked intermittently at my task for several years, when I came upon John Forbes's *The Symmetrical Structure of Scripture*. Through this book I learned that a group of English writers over a hundred years ago had devoted themselves to similar studies. Although their contributions were never quite forgotten, John Jebb's *Sacred Literature* in 1820, and Thomas Boys's *Key to the Book of Psalms* in 1825, had apparently not aroused any greater interest. J. A. Bengel in Germany had observed the same phenomena in the New Testament, and had made some use of them in exegesis in his work *Gnomon novi testamenti*, published at Tübingen in 1742. Bengel uses the old rhetorical term *chiasmus* to designate these inversions, and for several reasons this term has been used in the following pages.

The general impression one gets from attempting to trace the results of these early investigations is that such literary analysis received at the time very little attention among scholars. The pioneer work of Jebb is usually recognized in reference works, but his own book is only rarely found. The copy that is in the Andover-Harvard Theological Library is the only one I have been able to find in this country. Even those writers who at all allude to Jebb give only very brief illustrations of what he called "introverted parallelism." I am convinced, however, that Jebb's discovery is of even greater significance than that of his more famous countryman Robert Lowth, Lord Bishop of London. For Lowth's work in the parallelisms deals with lines only, whereas the principle of chiasmus is applied far more extensively by the Biblical writers, at times influencing longer sections of the text. The reappearance of chiastic structures in the New Testament is due to the blending of two separate cultures, the Semitic and the Greek. In the chiastic principle we have one of the most important literary factors that shaped the structure of many of its writings. It is a cultural heritage from the Semites, the gift of the East to the West.

Although these studies are based on the original text, no attempt has been made to print the text because of prohibitive costs. For our purposes, therefore, the text and the verse notations of the American Standard Bible have generally been used, through the permission of its copyright owner, the International Council of Religious Education. Since the argument in some cases depends on a close reproduction of the sentence order in the original, I have in such instances felt free to violate English usage. I have received numerous helpful suggestions from *The Old Testament, An American Translation*, edited by the late Dr. J. M. P. Smith, and from *The Holy Scriptures, According to the Masoretic Text, A New Translation*, issued by The Jewish Publication Society of America. Reasons for preferring one of several readings are usually discussed when textual problems occur in the text. In such cases arguments drawn from the *form* of the passage have, in the nature of the case, received considerable attention. The text of Westcott and Hort has usually been followed, but some suggestions from Tischendorf's *Editio Octava* have been helpful.

The method of presentation employed perhaps would require a word of explanation. In brief passages the lines are indented and parallel terms are printed in italics. Later on the italics are eliminated, since the reader no doubt by that time has formed the habit of detecting the parallel ideas in a structure without further aid. A system of lettering has been used for easy reference. In a longer structure consisting of many sections which are parallel, the letters A B C are used for the first sections and A′ B′ C′ for their counterparts. Groups of such sections are often placed within brackets and designated X Y Z and their counterparts X′ Y′ Z′. Longer passages are divided into Parts I, II, III, IV, etc., and their contents are usually expressed in an outline. In order further to facilitate references to the text the usual verse notations of the American Revised Version are placed at the right of the page.

The suggestion is here made that the reader from the beginning form the habit of proceeding from the opening line of a structure to the centre, and there begin to make his line-to-line comparisons as he reads the latter half of the chiastic units. The reader should not dip into the middle of the book without reading the opening chapters, for these contain matters that are essential to the understanding of the whole presentation. Under no circumstances should it be assumed that I am under the impression that the ancient manuscripts were written in some such form as are the structures here presented. The graphic method of presentation employed in this book is merely a device adopted in order to eliminate unnecessary explanations and to render a complicated subject easy to grasp with a minimum of time and effort. We have no direct knowledge of the appearance of the original manuscripts. All the copies that have reached us are of a much later date, and they all indicate that a certain degree of standardization of size and script had already taken place. We are therefore now in no position either to affirm or deny the presence in the original manuscripts of any guides to their chiastic structure. Any conclusion along these lines must therefore be reached only on the basis of inherent probabilities. I have reached the conclusion that much of these symmetries was altogether subconscious, and that it was felt rather than seen. This is merely another way of saying that the writers had learned their forms so thoroughly that they had forgotten them as forms. For the more extensive symmetries, however, I must postulate some degree of conscious effort on the part of the writer. Whether or not these longer divisions were in some graphic manner indicated in the original manuscript is impossible to say, though I should not consider it altogether unlikely.

Some of the passages included in this book have already appeared in print in various journals, namely, *The American Journal of Semitic Languages and Literatures; The Journal of Religion; Journal of Biblical Literature;* and *Anglican Theological Review.* I wish to thank the editors of these journals for their unfailing kindness and for many valuable suggestions. I also feel indebted to Dr. W. C. Graham of the Oriental Institute, who first suggested the possibility of using this material as a dissertation and has often encouraged me in the work. To Dr. O. R. Sellers of the Presbyterian Seminary, Chicago, who has never failed me when I have consulted him, to the various members of the faculty in the New Testament Department of the University of Chicago from whose instruction I have profited, to Dr. Edgar J. Goodspeed and Dr. Donald W. Riddle, who have advised me and encouraged me during the work I owe a debt of gratitude. Finally I wish to express my deep appreciation to my colleague, Professor E. Gustaf Johnson, who carefully read the proofs, and to those generous friends and alumni of North Park Theological Seminary whose financial support has made the publication of the manuscript possible.

The material for this dissertation has been collected during a period of over twenty-five years. Every part of it has been worked over more than once, and many parts have been rewritten many times. The difficulties in such work are divided between the analysis of the forms themselves and the attempt to give the results to the reader in acceptable form. Even though I have not succeeded altogether in making the book readable, this is due more to the nature of the material discussed than to any lack of effort. Whatever the deficiencies of the book may be, however, I hope they may not seriously detract from the argument itself. In the nature of the case many of my conclusions must be regarded as tentative rather than final, or what the Germans call a *Versuch.* Conclusions in such matters as these can, in many instances, only approximate the truth. For in all study of form much consideration must be given to the personal factor, which is about equally distributed between the original writer of a passage and the student who attempts an analysis of its form. I trust, however, that the evidence will be sufficient to support the affirmations I have made, and that the reader, after examining the material, will feel inclined to accept what I have ventured to call the laws of chiastic composition.

N. W. LUND

North Park Theological Seminary
Chicago, Illinois
February, 1941

CONTENTS

The Book of Revelation

INTRODUCTION

CHAPTER I

THE STUDY OF FORM

Thomas Edison, before turning his attention to any major invention, is reported to have set his assistants to work to discover what others had attempted and achieved along the same lines. The wisdom of such a procedure is evident. It produces a necessary perspective; it makes for economy of effort; and it is likely to kindle the enthusiasm of the worker. The history of the study of form is a long one, and the men who have been engaged in this study are many. We cannot within a limited space give an exhaustive account of these scholars and their work, but we may indicate briefly some of their achievements—a historical sketch in which certain very well defined groups are prominent. With reference to the subject matter there are two distinct groups of scholars, namely, those who are interested in the Pauline epistles and those who are attracted by the gospels. Concerning the method of approach we discover one group, by far the larger, whose approach is classical and another whose approach is through the Hebrew forms of the Old Testament. Historically, we may distinguish three periods in the study of form, namely, the early fathers, the writers of the Reformation period, and the modern writers. It is in the modern period only that we find any scientific method in the study of form. These modern attempts are divided between Germany and England.

In describing the writing of the Old Testament Josephus[1] says that the songs of Moses in Exodus, Chapter 15, and Deuteronomy, Chapter 32, were written "in hexameter verse," and that the psalms of David were written "in several sorts of metre," trimeters and pentameters. Similar statements are found in Eusebius[2] and Jerome.[3] Jerome not only quotes the two preceding

[1] *Antiquities*, Bk. II, 16:4; Bk. IV, 8:44; Bk. VII, 12:3. English translation by H. St. John Thackeray in *Loeb's Classical Library*.

[2] *Praeparatio Evangelica*, 11:5.

[3] *Preface to Job.*

authors but also adds as a personal contribution to the subject that he himself had been able to verify these statements when he heard the Hebrew Scriptures read by the Jews in Palestine. These statements, however, are not considered by modern scholars as a true description of the forms of Hebrew poetry, but are regarded rather as an attempt to describe to men of Greek and Roman culture the comparatively unknown Hebrew Scriptures in terms of their own familiar literature.

Augustine,[4] who for years had been a teacher of rhetoric, had also made some observations as to the style of the Scriptures. The prophetic writings of the Old Testament and the epistles of Paul have engaged his attention. He rebukes those who boast of the eloquence of their own writings and disparage the Scriptures. In the latter he finds "an eloquence peculiarly their own," so modestly applied "that it is not conspicuous either by its presence or its absence." "And," he adds, "in those passages where the learned do note its presence, the matters spoken of are such, that the words in which they are put seem not so much to be sought out by the speaker as spontaneously to suggest themselves; as if wisdom were walking out of its house—that is the breast of the wise man—and eloquence, like an inseparable attendant, followed it without being called for." Augustine supplies several interesting examples from Paul with which to illustrate the rhetorical skill of the apostle. In Romans 3:5 he discovers the Greek κλῖμαξ which the Latins call *gradatio:*

> Knowing that tribulation worketh patience,
> and patience, experience,
> and experience, hope.

In addition he finds in this passage another literary figure called περίοδος, "the clauses of which are suspended on the voice of the speaker till the whole is completed in the last clause":

> And hope maketh not ashamed,
> because the love of God is shed abroad in our hearts,
> by the Holy Spirit which is given unto us.

Modern writers have devoted some attention to the rhetorical forms in 2 Cor. 11:16-20, and we are not surprised that the quality

[4] *On Christian Doctrine*, Bk. IV, cc. 6, 7, 20.

of this passage should have attracted the attention of Augustine. In a long and detailed treatment of the passage he sets forth the κῶλα and κόμματα, which are called *membra et caesa* by the Latins. It is evident, on the one hand, that Augustine is himself interested in proving the rhetorical quality of these passages and, on the other, that he will not admit that the Pauline rhetoric has been learned in the schools. He would rather have it that Paul's was "wisdom naturally produced, accompanied by eloquence." The rhetorician and the churchman are obviously at conflict in Augustine. Though the rhetorical qualities of these passages did not fail to impress a man of his literary training, yet he feels himself unable to admit that Paul was indebted to the schools for his skill. Two centuries later Pope Gregory the Great[5] exclaimed: "I am strongly of the opinion, that it is an indignity that the words of the oracle of heaven should be restrained by the rules of Donatus." And two hundred years earlier than Augustine, Tertullian[6] had written: "What indeed has Athens to do with Jerusalem? What concord is there between the Academy and the Church? . . . Away with all attempts to produce a mottled Christianity of Stoic, Platonic, and dialectic composition."

Jerome had a thorough knowledge of the classical writers and such a taste for them that only after much fasting and many tears did he succeed in breaking himself of the habit of reading them.[7] That he should be interested in matters of form is natural. In one of his letters to Pope Damasus[8] he explains the meaning of the word "Hosanna," but also observes that Luke "among all the evangelists was most learned in Greek" and therefore refrained from using foreign words. When taken to task by Magnus, a Roman orator, for his habit of quoting the classics, Jerome defends himself by pointing out how Paul had quoted the classics (Tit. 1:12, 1 Cor. 15:33; Acts 17:28) and how the fathers of the church had modeled their writings after such writers.[9] Evidently no amount of fasting could make him shed his early literary training.

On the whole, the attitude of the fathers of the church seems

[5] Quoted by E. P. Cubberley, *The History of Education*, p. 95.
[6] Tertullian, *Against Heretics*, Chap. VII.
[7] Epistle XXII, 30.
[8] Epistle XIX.
[9] Epistle LXX.

to be that the gospel has been victorious over paganism not because of any perfection in rhetorical form but because of its simplicity. According to Origen[10] "it was not any power of speaking, or any orderly arrangement of their message, according to the arts of Greek dialectics or rhetoric, which was in them the effective cause of converting their hearers." Origen suggests that if Jesus had selected as his messengers men with rhetorical training "he would most justly have been suspected of employing artifices, like those philosophers who are leaders of certain sects, and consequently the promise respecting the divinity of his doctrine would not have manifested itself."

In Chrysostom[11] this attitude is exaggerated to the extent that it becomes ridiculous. He tells an anecdote of a dispute between a Christian and a Greek which he himself heard. The Greek was trying to prove that Paul was "unlearned and ignorant" (Acts 4:13), and the Christian endeavored to show that he was more eloquent than Plato himself. This is a wrong procedure in such disputes.

> Rather, says Chrysostom, let us charge the apostles with want of learning; for this same charge is praise. And when they say that the apostles were rude, let us follow up the remark and say that they were also untaught, and unlettered, and poor, and vile, and stupid, and obscure. It is not slander on the apostles to say so, but it is even a glory that, being such, they should have outshone the whole world.

An utterance like this, however, is not to be taken as a sober estimate of Paul as a writer, but as oratory and propaganda. In another passage Chrysostom is expressing appreciation of Paul's use of the rhetorical question.[12] Lactantius,[13] a western writer, who by his style has earned the title, "the Christian Cicero," takes the same position in regard to the Scriptures as Chrysostom. "With the wise and the learned, and the princes of this world, the sacred Scriptures are without credit, for the prophets spoke in common and simple language, as though they spoke to the people." It is not that God could not produce eloquence but rather that he

[10] *Against Celsus*, Bk. I, chap. lxii. [11] Homily III on 1 Cor. 1:10.

[12] Homily XIII on 2 Cor. 6:11, 12; *On the Priesthood*, Bk. IV, chaps. 5-7.

[13] *The Divine Institutes*, Bk. I, chap. i; Bk. VI, chap. xxi.

wished divine things to be presented "without adornment, that all might understand the things which he himself spoke to all." With the exception of Augustine, who finds in the New Testament a natural eloquence not of the schools, and of Jerome, who thinks he has discovered metre like that of the classics in the Old Testament, the fathers as a rule deny the presence of rhetoric in the Scriptures. While they recognized here and there passages that seemed to move on a higher plane than the rest and here and there detected a suggestion of the rhetoric which was in vogue in their own day, they were also well aware of the fact that these writings did not measure up to the requirements of the schools. There must have been on their part a certain hostility to the writings of the literary men of the times who freely brought forth ideas and references to a mythology which was offensive to the taste of the teachers of the church. When, in the age of Constantine, the church had assimilated, at least to some extent, Greek culture, the dogmatic interest had begun to overshadow the literary. This tendency prevailed until the Renaissance awakened new interest in literary pursuits.

The stimulus for literary studies given by the Renaissance in Germany largely resulted in a new interest in the study of the Scriptures. Reuchlin's contributions to the study of Hebrew were important. Luther's admiration for the Greek learning of his friend Melanchthon is well known. With these new interests in cultural pursuits it was natural that scholars also should seek to determine the relations of the New Testament writers to Greek culture. In regard to Paul, who of all is the most prominent, there existed two schools of opinion. One considered Paul a universal scholar, well versed in the philosophies of the ancient world, and the other held that he was limited in worldly knowledge.[14] Erasmus, who by his editions of the Fathers and of the Greek New Testament did so much to make the writings of the early church accessible to scholars and who by his letters and personal contact with prominent men, both educators and princes, created a new interest in this literature, also had considered the question of

[14] Eduard Norden, *Die antike Kunstprosa* (Berlin: 1918), Vol. II, pp. 494-495, notes.

rhetoric in the New Testament. In his own picturesque way he has given a vivid description of Paul as a writer.[15]

> Much toil is bestowed by learned men in explaining the devices of poets and rhetoricians. But in this rhetorician (Paul) there is need of much more toil in order to detect what he urges, whither he tends, what he prohibits, so full is he of artifices everywhere, it may be said without boasting. So great is his artfulness that you would not believe that the same man was speaking. Now like some clear spring he wells up gently, soon like a torrent he rolls down with a mighty crash, snatching many things with him on his way, now placidly and smoothly he flows, then expands broadly, as if spreading out into a lake. Again he hides himself somewhere, and then springs forth from another direction, when he appears, like the wonderful Meander, bathing, now these, now those banks; now and then making a digression far away, he doubles back on himself by a returning bend.

There are several interesting factors which are revealed in this quotation. Erasmus, himself a humanist with a deep interest in the forms of discourse, had studied Pauline style and had there discovered considerable stylistic versatility. He had also found in his epistles some features which were disturbing to one who was imbued with classical models; for however wonderful Meander might have been, meandering in writing and doubling back on oneself Erasmus could not condone. Evidently he found it difficult to reconcile himself to a certain diffusiveness and repetitiousness in the Pauline epistles. This critical attitude is born of the Renaissance, and its conclusions are similar to those of modern writers. Whenever the purely classical standards are employed in appraising the New Testament, its style is found wanting. Modern classicists agree in this respect with the conclusions of the early fathers of the church. We shall now mention some of the most prominent modern writers in this field and give a brief account of their different lines of approach.

When the critical interest which received its impulse from the Renaissance had begun to make itself felt, a new attitude and a new method of approach appeared in more than one field of investigation with the result that the Christian religion could no longer

[15] Erasmus, *Paraphrases*, quoted by Meyer, in *Second Corinthians*, American Edition, Paragraph 1, Remark 1 of the Introduction.

be studied apart from other religions but became a chapter in a general "Religionsgeschichte." Likewise, the Christian literature must be surveyed from the viewpoint of "Literaturgeschichte." These are only two examples of a general leveling process the object of which was to take Christianity out of its former exclusiveness and to place it without reserve in the stream of general history. Thus it could become subject to investigation in accordance with methods used in dealing with other historical phenomena.

But should the writings of the New Testament be regarded as literature at all? Franz Overbeck[16] in his essay on *The Beginnings of Patristic Literature* takes the position that the writings of the New Testament cannot properly be included in the history of literature; for they do not themselves employ the forms of literature proper nor do they constitute the basis for the later Christian literature, which took the forms of the Greeks and Romans for its pattern. At the time when the canon had been determined and Christianity had made its way into the more cultural and educated strata of pagan society, Christian literature proper may be said to begin with the Apologies. Yet, he feels some hesitation in including even these writings, since they were written for outsiders, and Christian literature proper may include only writings by Christians for Christians. For a similar reason the Gnostic writings are excluded. Overbeck would begin with Clement of Alexandria.

The general judgment of Overbeck is confirmed by Eduard Norden[17] with respect to the gospels and the epistles. "The gospels stand altogether apart from artful literature. Viewed in a purely external fashion as literary monuments they bear the stamp of something absolutely new." The closest analogy to them that is to be found in Greek literature is the eight books of Philostratus on the life of Apollonius of Tyana. The introduction to the Gospel of Luke is, next to the introduction to Hebrews, the best written sentence in the New Testament. A comparative study of the Synoptists proves that Luke's many improvements in the struc-

[16] "Über die Anfänge der patristischen Literatur," *Hist. Zeitschr.* N. F. XII (1882), pp. 417 ff.; and summary by Norden, *op. cit.*, Vol. II, pp. 479, 480.
[17] *Op. cit.*, pp. 479-510.

ture of the sentence have been made by one who was acquainted with principles of style. Yet, with all this said, Norden cannot find a place for the gospels in any category of Greek literature. They represent something absolutely new, even though Justin calls them "memoirs."

The Pauline epistles have no more right to be regarded as literary productions, for they were merely "artless and occasional substitutes" for the spoken word. Paul wrote to his churches only what he would have said to them, had he been there in person. Since, however, the writing of letters on every conceivable subject was common among the Greeks, the epistles of Paul stand somewhat closer to Greek conceptions than the gospels and Acts. Norden quotes 2 Cor. 11:6 and 1 Cor. 2:1 ff. in which Paul confesses himself to be "rude in speech" and reminds the Corinthians that he did not come to them "with excellency of speech and of wisdom." What is the exact relation between these utterances in which Paul appraises his own spoken words and the actual style in which he wrote his epistles? Norden answers this question by saying that only with great difficulty does he understand Paul. His method of argumentation is strange, and his style is not Greek. The defects of his Greek style are best seen in comparison with the Epistle to the Hebrews, with the periodic structures in the Epistle of Barnabas, and with the First Epistle of Clement which, at least in the method of argumentation, is Greek. Norden evidently finds himself in accord with Renan's description of Paul's style, when he likens it to "a rapid conversation taken down in shorthand and reproduced without corrections."[18] The favorable judgments on Paul's effectiveness as a writer given by such men as Chrysostom and Jerome can therefore be used only with great care in view of the general impression produced by the epistles themselves.

One must not conclude because of the total impression of the epistles of Paul on ancient and modern readers alike that they lack artfulness in every detail. One will often find in the midst

[18] M. Goguel, *Life of Jesus*, English trans. Alice Wyon (New York: 1933), p. 106.

of the passages which are written only in the rhetoric of the heart, old, well-known forms which belong strictly to the artful prose of the Greeks. Paul has made abundant use of the antithesis, a prominent device in the language of controversy. In passages like Romans 8:31 ff. and 1 Cor. 13, where Paul brings back to the Greek language the fervor of earlier days, the form rises to that of Plato at his best.

After this summary of Norden's very interesting chapters one hardly knows whether Paul did write *Kunstprosa* or not. The difference between an uncorrected transcript of a rapid conversation, on the one hand, and a style like that of Plato at his best, on the other, is indeed extreme. The origin of such artful writing as is found in Paul's epistles Norden will not ascribe to any acquaintance with the Greek classics but rather to the Asianic Sophists, who altogether ignored the literature of the past. This derivation of Paul's style is not without its difficulties, since, according to Norden himself,[19] "softness and empty feeling is the characteristic of the Hellenistic Asianites and their eloquence." It is probably not in that respect that Paul is related to Asianism, but rather in the two special literary forms developed by this school, namely, the diatribe and the Asianic rhythm. To these two forms we must now give some attention inasmuch as they have figured in recent studies of the New Testament.

The period about 300 B.C. was one of decline, coinciding with the destruction of the Attic spirit and the Hellenistic originality as a whole. It seems that what the Greek language gained in extent it lost in content, for the cosmopolitan idea itself is decidedly un-Greek. Yet there were in this period influences that became of the greatest importance for the development of Greek prose in imperial Rome. Cicero and Quintilian connect these influences with the person of Demetrios of Phaleros, an obscure rhetorician. He did not present in his teaching the great Attic masters. Instead of the strength and austerity of Demosthenes, whom he criticized, he substituted an enervated and pleasing form of address. Cicero says that this type of public speech "flowed

[19] *Op. cit.*, pp. 126-155.

down from the fountain of the Sophists into the forum," and it certainly corresponds with his own descriptions of the eloquence of Thrasymachos, Gorgias, and Isocrates.

The diatribe, originally a school declamation, was developed from the dialogue. Instead of two speakers, as required by the dialogue, one speaker would introduce an imaginary character with whom he would carry on the argument. As a result of such a procedure long periods in the discourse would be changed into brief sentences. Questions and answers were frequent. Personification was common. Virtue and Nature, etc., were personified and appeared as speaking in the discourse. The diatribe was rhetorical in construction, having parallelisms, especially of the antithetic variety. The beginning and the end of the lines of a couplet frequently had a similar sound (*Anaphora* and *Epiphora*). These various characteristics combined to make a breezy and lively discourse which was likely to catch and hold the attention of the crowd for which it was designed.

In recent years this form has attracted a great deal of attention chiefly through the work of Bultmann,[20] who has demonstrated the similarity between the forms of the diatribe and some of the forms found in the epistles of Paul. In many sections in which the dialogue and its characteristic catchwords occur, in the rhetorical turn of the sentence, in the disposition of the material, in those forms of argumentation which cannot be traced directly to Rabbinical influence, and in the whole temper of the epistles, Bultmann finds close parallels between Pauline style and the popular diatribe.

Another approach to the study of the Pauline epistles was made by Blass,[21] who undertook to show the presence of rhythm. His attempt, however, is less convincing than that of Bultmann. In the first place, there is no complete unanimity between the classicists themselves in regard to the nature of the Asianic rhythm.[22] Secondly, Blass finds rhythm only in certain patches.

[20] Rudolf Bultmann, *Der Stil der paulinischen Predigt und die kynisch-stoischen Diatribe* (Göttingen: 1910).

[21] Friedrich Blass, *Die Rhythmen der asianischen und römischen Kunstprosa* (Leipzig: 1905).

[22] *Op. cit.*, pp. 1, 2; 41-43.

Thirdly, he must resort to a great many doubtful textual emendations in order to carry out his scheme.

Another extensive and penetrating study of form in the Pauline epistles is that of Johannes Weiss.[23] He discusses a variety of the most common Greek and Roman rhetorical forms and in many of his results agrees with Bultmann. Both writers assume that the epistles of Paul have their present form because they represent speech rather than writing. Bultmann concludes that we may safely argue from the nature of Paul's writings to the nature of his sermons. Weiss thinks that Paul in dictating his letters developed a kind of spoken prose and that the Pauline epistles were written largely for the *ear*. Paul does not possess a good prose style; he uses short coördinated sentences paired off by some kind of a copula. Yet, Weiss goes on to say,

> What Paul is lacking in prose style he makes up for somewhat in his carefully written letters by a sure rhetorical movement, which is definite, stirring, frequent, and, because of symmetry, rhythmic swing, and fulness of sound does appear artful.

An extraordinary element of Paul's speech is parallelism of members, which Weiss traces to Hebrew influence. Strange to say, the Wisdom of Solomon is particularly mentioned as the source of parallelism, although the whole Old Testament is full of it. Parallelism, however, is no sign of elevated speech, for it is found even in the more business-like sections. In those parts where Paul has made use of parallelism with greater art and swing, Weiss is led to think of Greek rather than of Hebrew models! The antithetic parallelism is to Weiss much more than a dialectic mannerism. It is an essential form of Paul's religious and theological thought. The character of his conversion had left traces in Paul's preaching and writing. That Paul forms parallelisms, however, is no proof of any real rhetorical art. Weiss's judgment, even in regard to 1 Cor. 13, the most famous of Paul's works, is as follows: "About this chapter I do not maintain that the apostle has used reflexion concerning the form. The whole swing is too strong

[23] Johannes Weiss, *Beiträge zur paulinischen Rhetorik* (Göttingen: 1897), in *Theologische Studien* in honor of Bernhard Weiss, pp. 167-9.

for this, and the feeling is too direct." We recall how Norden held that Paul in this chapter reaches the height of Plato in the Phaedo. This judgment, however, Weiss modified somewhat in his commentary on First Corinthians and in his *Urchristentum*, where he seems to include in his more favorable estimate the Pauline letters in general. In this passage he is quoting and commenting on a statement of von Wilamovitz-Moellendorff,[24] which contains such an interesting view of Paul from a recognized classical scholar that it is worth quoting in full:

> Hellenism is surely a preliminary condition for him. He read only the Greek Bible, and he even thought in Greek. He certainly became the executor of Alexander's testament in that he brought the gospel to the Greeks, but he is also carved out of an altogether different kind of wood. He is a Jew, as Jesus is a Jew. Yet this Jew, this Christian, thinks and writes Greek for all the world, though more immediately for his brethren to whom he speaks. Since his Greek has nothing to do with any school, and with any model, but wells forth directly and unaided out of his heart, and yet is Greek—no Aramaic translation (as the words of Jesus)—it makes him into a classical Hellenist. At last, at last, we read something in Greek springing from a fresh and living experience, that is, from his faith. In this faith is his hope secured, and his warm love embraces humanity. In order to bring it healing he gladly threw away his life. A fresh life of the soul, however, sprouts forth wherever he sets his foot. In place of his work he writes his letters. The style of these letters is Paul's, and none but Paul's. They are neither private nor literary letters, but rather an inimitable though also an ever after imitated middle-type.

Commenting on this passage, Weiss[25] shows how often in a crisis great personalities impress their stamp even on the language they use in expressing their ideas. Luther and Rousseau are such examples. Only in such instances, when formal restraint is shaken off, does language really become the expression of personality. Weiss goes on to say:

> Especially the shedding of rhetorical conventions is a great step forward compared with antiquity. In this respect Paul is still a man of antiquity, and even his spontaneity is not as free, as indicated by our first impressions. Even in the personal and more intimate sections of his letters

[24] *Die Kultur der Gegenwart*, Teil I, Abteilung viii, p. 157.
[25] Johannes Weiss, *Das Urchristentum* (Göttingen: 1917), p. 304.

we find a rhetorical element of form, which we do not any more feel as such, since we are so little accustomed to it. This is due to the fact that Paul has spoken his letters, and in doing so, always had in mind the limited public in his churches.

Though the modern man may boast of what he calls individual style, antiquity knew nothing of it. To be a writer then meant to conform to some kind of style. Difficult though it may be to fit Paul into any of the Greek schools of style, there are traces of Greek form in his epistles, and in the passages in which he seems furthest removed from the accepted Greek forms of his day, we may do well to remember that, to use the words of von Wilamowitz-Moellendorff, he also was "carved out of an altogether different kind of wood." His Jewish antecedents have not as yet been sufficiently considered in recent discussions of his style.

It was inevitable that the same efforts that had been made to find a place for the Pauline epistles in the history of Greek literature should be made with reference to the gospels. When Justin Martyr applies to them the term "memoirs," he is merely attempting to explain the nature of the gospels as distinct from the epistles in terms of the current Greek literature. If he had at all interested himself in problems of style, however, he must have felt, as some of the later fathers of the church did, the great difference between the gospels and Greek memoirs. The attempt to treat the gospels as a chapter in Greek literature was doomed to be even less successful than a similar attempt with the epistles. After New Testament scholarship had wrestled for a century with literary analysis of the component documents of the gospels, an entirely new chapter opened in gospel criticism by the arrival of "form-history." All exponents of this new theological discipline are agreed as to the sharp distinction that should be maintained between history of literature and history of form. Martin Albertz,[26] in referring to attempts already made to incorporate the writings of the Old and New Testaments as specific chapters in a general history of the world's literature, says that even if the Bible as such holds a place in literature, its several books can hardly be included among literary works with the exception, possibly, of the

[26] *Die synoptischen Streitgespräche* (Berlin: 1921), p. 1.

Epistle to the Hebrews. "To undertake a 'literary' investigation of Jesus' spoken words is a misleading way of speaking," he says. We should avoid this terminology and speak of a "form-historical" investigation instead.

The fundamental principles that underlie the new approach to the study of form in the gospels had already been developed in the Old Testament field. Hermann Gunkel had earlier looked for extra-biblical sources in the Apocalypse,[27] and in his commentary on Genesis[28] he had traced the similarities of Babylonian and Old Testament lore. In the Scandinavian countries Moltke Moe of Norway and Axel Olrik of Denmark have gathered around themselves an enthusiastic group of younger scholars who have given themselves to the study of folklore. The published results of these studies are to be found in the *FF Communications for the Folklore Fellows,* several volumes in all, and numerous monographs. The folklore of Scandinavia, Finland, Bohemia, and Hungary has been collected and classified, its distinctive types studied, and the laws of its formation ascertained. At a conference of historians in Berlin in August, 1908, Olrik himself made a brief statement of these laws which he later published.[29] He mentions several of the laws governing such lore, as the law of repetition, the law of three, the law of contrast, the restriction to only two speakers on the scene, etc. A new application of this method of study is made by Gunkel,[30] in which he also touches upon gospel stories. All this is "form-history," and does not belong to the history of literature proper. These stories have no known author.[31] They were not written, but were handed down by word of mouth through centuries, and, like stones on the beach, slowly assumed a somewhat similar character. Seeking the explanation of the laws of *two* or of *three,* Olrik warns against operating merely with religious concepts, for in folklore the number three is not merely something that has to do with deity but has a much wider

[27] *Schöpfung und Chaos,* 1894.

[28] *Genesis übersetzt und erklärt,* 3te Auflage (Göttingen: 1910).

[29] *Folkelige Afhandlinger,* edited by Hans Ellekilde, p. 177 ff. A summary in Erich Fascher, *Die formgeschichtliche Methode,* p. 40.

[30] *Das Märchen im Alten Testament* (Tübingen: 1921).

[31] K. L. Schmidt, *Die Stellung der Evangelien in der allgemeinen Literaturgeschichte.* In *Eucharisterion* (Göttingen: 1923), part 2, pp. 50-132.

application: animals, birds, fish; earth, heaven, sea; earth, heaven, and the nether world, etc. He concludes by saying:

> It is a question whether both epic and religious triads do not rest upon an age-old psychological basis. Here are new problems to solve. Every epic law is to be followed in its full scope, through all humanity, if necessary, and then only the meaning of these forms for the development of the human spirit will be made clear.

The task, therefore, is to find general laws that operate similarly in all lore.

On the basis of such principles the analysis of the gospel material is now to be undertaken. Dibelius[32] in a now famous book announces the program of the new study of the gospels. Form-history is a preliminary study to history of literature. Its center of interest is not the gospels as they now exist but in the small component parts of the gospels. These parts have had a long history before they entered the written gospels. The writer of the gospel does not create these sections; they were the work of the folk-spirit operating unconsciously in the shaping of the material. The writer acts merely as an editor. These parts are not now in their pure form, for they have been supplied with introductions and conclusions by the gospel editor. It is possible, however, to peel off these additions and to obtain the pure forms by a process of criticism. In the gospel of Mark, Dibelius has recovered only seven such sections, or *paradigms*.

A word must be said in describing these small parts. All have a stereotyped form. They are short. Each is complete in itself. They are compact, and this feature is obtained by stripping them of all unnecessary details. They are made to converge in a point. Often a saying of Jesus clinches the point of the story and makes a universal application of the particular truth that is taught. In other words, they resemble the illustrative anecdote used by modern speakers, historical or biographical, as the case may be, but always shaped so as to serve some specific purpose. These *paradigms*, or models, were created to serve the need of missionary

[32] Martin Dibelius, *Die Formgeschichte des Evangeliums* (Tübingen: 1919), English trans. from Second German Edition (1933), entitled, *From Tradition to Gospel*, by Bertram Lee Woolf (London: 1934).

preaching, and Dibelius specifies that the preaching was to Gentiles, not to Jews.

At a later stage the second form, *the story* (die Novelle) arose. In Mark there are eight of this type. They vividly describe Jesus as a worker of miracles, and have three specific characteristics: (1) They sketch broadly the situation. (2) The worldly relations of the disciples (hunger, danger, etc.) enter in. (3) Edifying motives and any word of Jesus for general application, which are prominent in the paradigm, are absent. These stories served a twofold purpose, namely, to please the audience and to serve as a guide to early Christian workers of miracles.

The third type is called *parenesis;* it consisted of sections that were designed to instruct early Christians in the moral code of their religion. There are such passages not only in the epistles of Paul but in all the epistles. They are of such nature that we must presuppose an early common Christian teaching. The most important part of this teaching was made up of words of Jesus, but to these words were added whatever new sayings the situation required. These new sayings were drawn freely from Jewish and Greek sources. There are other forms in Dibelius, like legend, epiphany, myth, but the paradigm, the story, and the parenesis are the most important.

To ascertain the present form of the component parts of the gospels, however, is only the first step of the analytical process. The next step is to discover how and when they assumed this particular form. This may be done by a study of the historical situation out of which each one arose, or, "der Sitz im Leben." This naturally involves an extensive historical reconstruction of many different situations by the aid of such written records as may be at our disposal, or by the aid of a creative historical imagination controlled by known historical facts. The sum total of the completed investigation is that while the gospels give at best a very meager information of the times they purport to describe, namely, the first three decades of the first century, they do give us, nevertheless, a very good picture of the times in which they themselves were composed. Though the consistent application of the method to New Testament criticism is new, the method itself has been in vogue for decades in Old Testament criticism. The modern historical scholar has used Chronicles and Kings only after stripping these books of the Deuteronomic framework.

The second great exponent of form-history is Bultmann.[33] In his book he describes in the first chapter the problem and the means of solving it. The researches of Wrede, Johannes Weiss, Wendling, and Wellhausen have proved, to use the latter's own words, that even in the earliest written gospel there are "secondary accretions in the tradition." Form-history, therefore, must take up the task where the literary analysis left it and attempt to determine by a study of the component parts of the Synoptic gospels their historical position, what is primary or secondary material, and what is editorial additions. While Dibelius undertook to analyze only a limited material, Bultmann's work is more inclusive, for he uses all available material. He also treats as one of the main problems the relations between Palestinian and Hellenistic Christianity, for these relations are of greatest importance to the history of the gospel tradition.

As to the means of solving the problem Bultmann has three ways of procedure: (1) By observing the use made of the Marcan material in Matthew and Luke and by a similar study of the other material, it is possible to ascertain certain laws of development in the tradition. These laws being ascertained, it should be possible to read them back into an even earlier tradition and make use of them there with some degree of certainty. (2) To recognize the original form of a story or a saying of Jesus is the goal of form-history. With this recognition comes also a recognition of secondary accretions. Together with the previous literary observations these are important in ascertaining the history of the tradition. (3) For the study of the several parts of the tradition as well as for the history of the tradition there are analogies available from Rabbinism and Hellenism. The study of folklore is especially valuable, for it offers a similar line of development as that of the gospel tradition. It is obvious from Bultmann's preliminary statement of method, that though he recognizes the limits of a

[33] Rudolf Bultmann, *Die Geschichte der synoptischen Tradition* (Göttingen: 1921), ed. 2, 1931.

purely literary analysis of the gospels, he will not dispense with this kind of work, but will supplement it with form-history.

The most important of Bultmann's classifications is the *apothegm,* a thing uttered. It is a term used to describe short and pithy sayings, but also includes some doings of Jesus which have a historical frame. They are classified into controversial discourses, school-discourses, and biographical apothegms. In some respects the term covers both the paradigm and the story in Dibelius' classification; this with some justification, perhaps, for it would seem as if these two classes of his overlap at times. The line of demarcation is therefore not always distinct. After a minute analysis of the material, there is a sketch of the form and history of the categories. (1) The *controversial* discourses arise from a situation or act which provides the occasion. The opponent, a Pharisee or someone else, puts the question, dealing with fasting, cleansing, or the sabbath, and Jesus answers, usually with a question, an illustration, or a proverb. This form of discourse is so typically Rabbinical that one must refrain from designating it as an example for preaching. Several Rabbinical examples are given. (2) The difference between the controversial and the *school-discourse* is the absence in the latter of any act that provides occasion for asking the question. The master is asked merely from curiosity. In some instances Bultmann suspects that originally independent words of Jesus have been provided with a historical setting. Both of these types of discourses can be Palestinian in origin, although they may have been modified somewhat in a Hellenistic environment, while some of them may have originated there. (3) The difference between the two preceding forms and the *biographical* apothegm is much greater. Nearly all of these are ideal constructions, with the exception of Lk. 13:31-33 and Mk. 14:1-9. Some are of pure symbolical or ideal nature, like Mk. 13:1-2; Lk. 19:41-44; 23:27-31. Yet others may give a historic occasion; that is true of the cleansing of the temple (Mk. 11:15-19). There, however, the incorporated saying of Jesus has lifted the narrative into the realm of the ideal. Whenever the person of the Master or the community is in the foreground, we are dealing with a case in which an illustrative scene is used to express a truth. Bultmann sees good reasons for assuming a Palestinian origin of these also, since there are many Rabbinical examples.

The next great group in the classification of the material consist of "words of the Lord" (Herrenworte). In this class are included only those words of Jesus which are, or could have been, a part of an independent tradition. Moreover, words in direct discourse in a narrative, such as the words to Judas in Lk. 22:48, are not included. These sayings of Jesus are divided into three groups: (1) Logia proper, or Wisdom sayings; (2) prophetic and apocalyptic sayings; (3) sayings giving laws and rules for the community. In each of these classes there are several subdivisions, each expressing some phase of the person of Jesus as it was conceived in the early church; to the first subdivision there are closely corresponding Old Testament examples. The form and the history of each class are treated separately. To these classes are added two more groups of material, namely, (4) the I-words, or sayings of Jesus in the first person singular, and finally, (5) the parables. The remaining part of the book deals with the narrative materials in the gospels, their form and their history.

Bultmann's conclusion is a summary of his results. The motive for the gospels is found in apologetics and polemics in the early church. The collection of the traditional material began in the Palestinian church. With all the various forms of this traditional material there was nothing that the church did not already find fully developed in Judaism.

That such forms already were present certainly favors the relatively rapid deposit of a unified settled tradition. For all that, the gospel type was not yet created, but only prepared for. In this fashion only separate parts had been preserved. And when these finally were fixed in writing and thereby also underwent redaction—as the case was presumably with the discourse material in Q, and with briefer collections of apothegms and miracle stories used by Mark—then it was only a question of arrangement, of summarizing. The idea of a unified, well-knit presentation of the life of Jesus evidently lay far beyond the Palestinian community. This corresponds both to the picture we must make of the character of this eschatological community and to the analysis of our oldest gospel, that of Mark.

The gospel type Bultmann regards as the creation of the Hellenistic church, a type depending largely on two distinct factors: (1) the taking over by the Hellenistic church of the Palestinian tradition; (2) the appearance of new motives and interests in the Hellenistic community, which brought about a modification of the traditional material. The taking over of the tradition is hardly intelligible if we merely think of Jewish missionaries; it is, if we postulate communities with a high percentage of Gentiles together with the Jews. Some elements of the tradition must have caused great difficulties; yet it is certain that even the Pauline churches knew of a tradition of the words of Jesus (cf. 1 Cor. 7:25; 9:14).

The differences between Bultmann and Dibelius are not found in the ruling principles of their works, but are due mostly to method of procedure and historical outlook. Bultmann treats all the extant material; Dibelius, only a part. Bultmann adopts literary analysis of the documents as part of his technique, whereas Dibelius evidently considers such procedure unnecessary or unprofitable. Bultmann discusses the history of each group of material in his classifications separately; Dibelius treats them as a whole. Finally, Bultmann gives much attention to the influence of the Jewish Christian community in Palestine and its contribution to the development of the tradition, an influence which is largely discounted by Dibelius, who, on the other hand, ascribes the greater influence to the Gentile Christian communities. This last-mentioned point seems to be the most important feature in which the two scholars differ. No presupposition could be more vital, and influence the results more effectively, than that of excluding, or even minimizing, early Palestinian influences in the shaping of the gospel tradition.

Among the exponents of form-history we must also include Weidinger.[34] A disciple of Dibelius, he has applied the master's method to certain sections of the Pauline epistles, which he classifies as *parenesis*, or instruction in the moral code of early Christianity. For the practice of compiling lists of sins and virtues and groups of exhortations designed to meet the needs of the various classes in the church, literary models are discovered in the writings

[34] Karl Weidinger, *Die Haustafeln* (Leipzig: 1928).

of Hellenistic Judaism and Stoicism. To these sections the general name of "Haustafeln" is given, a term which owes its familiarity to the fact that sections compiled for a similar purpose in the Smaller Catechism of Luther were known by the same name. Among the sections listed as early *parenesis* we find Eph. 5:22-33; in this passage, however, the chiastic structure should be traced to Old Testament sources, as will be seen presently.

The various writers that have from time to time appraised the epistles and the gospels in regard to style have made their approach through the Greek classics. When Josephus and Jerome described Hebrew poetry in terms of trimeters, pentameters, and hexameters, their approach was through Greek and Latin literature. Even when Justin Martyr called the gospels "memoirs," he had the same point of view. It was natural that these new types of writings should be described in terms of the old types by those who first interested themselves in a comparison because the unknown is always described in terms of the known. Nevertheless, the procedure was misleading, since it set up Greek rhetoric as the only standard by which these writings were to be judged. The result of this mistake is seen clearly in the writings of the church fathers. They can only partly identify the marks of Greek rhetoric. Whatever does not fall into its categories is either described as the natural eloquence of the heart or is dismissed as crude and unfinished. There is a strange unanimity on this point even among modern writers. Paul writes some artistic passages in his epistles, to be sure, but they are not *Kunstprosa*, taken as a whole. Blass[35] has given the reasons why they are not to be so considered, when he states that the writer has not been trained in the Greek schools. He does not aim to please but only to produce an impression when he writes. Only in the Epistle to the Hebrews does Blass find something that fits his definition of artistic prose, though he admits that "in Matthew there really is some artistic sense of style," but that "it is mainly drawn from ancient Hebrew, and not from Greek."[36]

[35] Friedrich Blass, *Grammar of New Testament Greek*, trans. Henry St. John Thackeray, M.A. (Second ed.; London: 1905), p. 305, n. 2.

[36] *Op. cit.*, p. 302.

The recognition of possible Hebrew literary models in the Greek of the gospel of Matthew is important. Not only Blass, but other modern scholars have of late given considerable attention to Jewish antecedents and their influence upon the writings of the New Testament. Our reference is not to scholars who have labored along linguistic lines to prove that some of our gospels are translations from the Aramaic language into Greek,[37] for there seems to be among them considerable disagreement as to what constitutes Aramaisms in the gospels. Indeed, some of the Aramaisms which are regarded as assured are discovered to be common in such a decidedly Greek writer as Epictetus.[38] The Jewish influence to which we have reference is not primarily of a linguistic nature, though some such influence may be admitted, but rather one of literary style. Men like von Wilamovitz-Moellendorff, though assuming that Paul read the Old Testament only in the Greek, do not forget that Paul was a Jew, and Johannes Weiss frequently calls attention to the presence of *parallelismus membrorum* in the epistles of Paul. More recently Bultmann[39] has expressed Paul's indebtedness to the Hebrew in matters of style, and indicated this as an important field for future research:

> A difficulty arises as the result of the complicated character of these letters. Not one species of letters only (the diatribe) has influenced them, for the style of Paul may not at all be explained by the Greek alone, but is moulded just as much by the Old Testament, or the Semitic style. When both these elements, the Greek and the Jewish, are acknowledged and displayed, then for the first time will the correct literary personality of Paul present itself. But this ideal cannot at present (in 1910) be realized, since the necessary preliminary work has not been completed.

The frank recognition of two literary traditions, the Greek and the Semitic, in the writings of Paul, and, we may add, in the New Testament as a whole, is of primary importance for the understanding of characteristic New Testament forms. When Bultmann

[37] C. F. Burney, *The Aramaic Origin of the Fourth Gospel* (Oxford: 1922); *The Poetry of Our Lord* (Oxford: 1925); C. C. Torrey, *The Aramaic Origin of the Gospel of John*, in *Harvard Theological Review*, XVI (1923), pp. 305-344; *The Four Gospels, A New Translation* (New York: 1933).

[38] E. C. Colwell, *The Greek of the Fourth Gospel* (Chicago: 1931).

[39] R. Bultmann, *Der Stil der paulinischen Predigt* (Göttingen), pp. 3, 4.

wrote these words, some preliminary work had already been done by his famous countryman J. A. Bengel and by several English scholars whose works will be described in the next chapter. These men were steeped in the classics, but they did not forget that the Old Testament was an influential factor in the development of a literary tradition in the early church. Among modern students of form-history, Bultmann more than anyone else has emphasized the influence of Palestine and the Old Testament upon the history of the gospel tradition. Though his attention had been directed to the Palestinian community, yet he, in common with all modern German writers on style, has paid no attention to the English predecessors in the field. In all the works which are devoted to penetrating and scholarly observations of Greek rhetorical forms in the New Testament, there is no trace of any attempt to study a literary form commonly known as *chiasmus*, which was used extensively in the Old Testament.

This particular form has been studied by a few English writers. That early scholarly tradition has not been lost completely, however, for the Bible Dictionaries, as a rule, give an example or two of what is called "introverted parallelism." The works of Briggs[40] and of Moulton[41] also make mention of this particular species of parallelism. Johannes Weiss now and then points out a chiasmus of four or six members (cf. Rom. 14:7 ff; Phil. 4:11-13; 1 Cor. 7:1-7; 9:19-22). Horne[42] gives several pages to it in later editions of his famous work. Except for these sporadic references and a few examples given in books dealing with the literary aspects of the Scriptures,[43] there seems to be no scientific study of this form since the days of John Forbes in 1854. Writers who are at all interested in the study of form have made their approach through the classical literature, and are more or less agreed in judging the New Testament to be deficient in matters of form. This attitude still prevails among modern German writers on the subject, even though some of them recognize a

[40] C. A. Briggs, *Biblical Study* (New York, 1883).

[41] R. G. Moulton, *The Literary Study of the Bible* (Boston: 1889).

[42] T. H. Horne, *An Introduction to the Critical Study and Knowledge of the Holy Scriptures*, 3 vols. (London: 1818, 11th ed. 1860).

[43] Louise Seymour Houghton, *Hebrew Life and Thought* (Chicago: 1906).

Hebrew literary heritage which has left deposits in the New Testament. On the whole, it may be said that the early English writers have exercised no influence in Germany, with the exception of Lowth, whose work was translated and annotated by Michaelis,[44] a learned orientalist.

There may be good reasons for the predominant classical interest in Europe and the resultant approach to the study of form in the Scriptures. The classical interest dominated the Renaissance, and the impetus given to intellectual pursuits in Europe was largely determined by this interest. It may be seen in the type of education that developed in the German Gymnasium and the English Grammar School. There even the study of *oriental* history was pursued through such sources as were provided by the ancient Greek historians. Only with the archeological discoveries of the nineteenth century did new material come to the attention of the historian. A long time passed, however, before the new point of view, resulting from the study of the new material, made itself felt in the modern historiography of the Orient. It is not at all surprising, then, that under such circumstances the study of literary forms also should have been dominated by classicism. The brilliancy of the Greek civilization, brought to the attention of Europe through the Renaissance, obscured the fact that this civilization was younger by millenniums than the culture of Egypt and Babylonia. Only in comparatively recent times have we learned to think in terms of the characteristic cultures of these ancient countries, cultures which were not Greek, but Semitic. Modern archeology has now given us some vivid glimpses of how old and rich these ancient civilizations really were. We may, even here, speak of a literary heritage.[45] In the writings of the Old Testament we have the remains of only one branch of this Semitic culture, that of Israel.

If we possessed the literary remains of the Aramaic language, we would be assured of another substantial body of writings which now has perished. Collections like the Elephantine Papyri, however, show us how widely distributed Aramaic writing was, and

[44] Göttingen, Vol. I, 1758; Vol. II, 1761.

[45] J. H. Breasted, *Ancient Records of Egypt* (Chicago: 1906-7); D. D. Luckenbill, *Ancient Records of Assyria* (Chicago).

where writing is common there must be a reading public as well. With reference to this lost literature we are at present where we were before the cuneiform and hieroglyphic inscriptions had been found and decoded. It may be a fantastic dream to expect some of this Aramaic literature to come to light in the future, but as to its previous existence there can be little doubt. The Aramaic was for centuries the *lingua franca* of the Ancient East, and was even in the first century of our era a living language in Palestine.[46] A large part of our New Testament was written by or among a people who spoke and wrote Aramaic.

It is therefore reasonable to postulate that the literary forms of the ancient Semitic culture should have influenced the writings of the New Testament as well. There is, to be sure, as the result of modern German scholarship, definite evidence available of Greek rhetorical forms in the writings of the New Testament. No one would for a moment deny the Greek literary influence, for most of these writings were produced in the midst of the Greek civilization which had spread over the eastern Mediterranean world through Alexander and his successors for three centuries before the Christian era. There exists, however, when all allowances for Greek influence have been made, a residue of form in the New Testament, which may not under any circumstances be derived from the Greek schools, and which is also of such definite literary character that it may not, as has sometimes been done, be explained as resulting from haphazard attempts of non-literary Christians. This residue of form is Semitic. For we must not be unmindful of the fact that the disciples of Jesus and a large percentage of the earliest membership of the Christian church, not only in Palestine but also in the Mediterranean countries and in the Orient, were Jews. They were heirs to a Semitic culture, centuries older than the Greek. It was their native culture, the separation of which from the Greek civilization they were never permitted to forget and the literary monument of which is found in the Old Testament. These sacred writings were

[46] Theodor Nöldeke, *Aramaic Language*, E. B. cols. 280-6; Theodor Zahn, *Introduction to the New Testament*, Vol. I, pp. 1-33; Gustaf Dalman, *Jesus-Jeshua*, Eng. trans. P. P. Levertoff, pp. 1-35; Flavius Josephus, *Wars of the Jews*, Preface 1; *Against Apion*, Bk. I, 9.

used in the liturgy of the temple and the synagogue, and soon came to be used for a similar purpose in the church.

Under such circumstances, not only the religious and ethical conceptions, but also the vocabulary and literary style of the community as well, came to be influenced by its liturgical writings. Among members of the Christian community who did not write and, perhaps, did not even read, the frequently recurring liturgical readings would impress themselves unconsciously upon the memory and tend to develop a definite style of religious speech. Among writers the forms of the Old Testament would be the literary models nearest at hand. When the growing Christian community for pedagogic reasons, and quite early in its history, found it necessary to produce writings teaching its own characteristic truths, these would be cast in the mould already made congenial through familiarity with the Old Testament. Since the first members of the Christian community were Jews, and therefore may be supposed to have been familiar with the Old Testament from Judaism, we need not even assume that any length of time was required for the church to assimilate these literary forms. Long before there was any liturgical reading of the Old Testament in Christian assemblies, the Christians themselves were modeling their religious language after the Old Testament. This process must have begun with Jesus himself and his earliest followers. When the time came for a more definite organization of the public worship, the Old Testament became a part of the formal worship, and later the characteristic Christian writings were added. These writings, from the very time of their production, were intended for the purpose for which they were later used. Johannes Weiss has insisted that the Pauline epistles were written for the *ear* and has deduced considerable evidence to prove his contention. To this evidence must be added all those indications in the epistles and the gospels which show the influence of the liturgical style of the Old Testament.

The following pages, therefore, are devoted to the tracing of the Hebrew literary influence on the Greek text of the New Testament; more definitely, they discuss one particular Hebrew form, namely, the extensive use of the inverted order commonly called chiasmus. Since no satisfactory preliminary work exists dealing with the Old Testament material, a study of characteristic passages from the law, the prophets, and the psalms will be made in order to establish the laws governing chiastic structures. A survey will then be made of the epistles and the gospels in order to ascertain how far the chiastic arrangement of ideas recurs in the writings of the New Testament. The scope of our investigation will be restricted to that residue of form which has resisted all attempts to find a place for it in any of the Greek categories, but which, nevertheless, is of a literary character and therefore may not be dismissed as being merely poor Greek or careless writing. The writings of the New Testament constitute a middle-type, a mixture of Greek and Hebrew forms, created by the mingling of two distinct cultures, which had become an accomplished fact three hundred years before the New Testament was written.

The deposit of Greek rhetorical forms has already been investigated by several writers with good results. The Semitic angle of the problem has hitherto been approached partly as a study of language, in the study of Aramaisms in the gospels, and partly as a study of literature, in the attempts to link the gospels with the forms of Hebrew poetry.[47] Our own task, though somewhat related to the latter, should not be identified with it. For the chiasmus as a literary form is not any more characteristic of poetry than it is of prose. In fact, it would be hazardous to say that it is more prevalent in the one field of literature than in the other. The chiasmus seems to be part of Hebrew thought itself, whether expressed in poetry or in prose, and to this factor we may look for the explanation of the readiness with which the extensive application of this literary principle of structure has passed over into the Greek writings of the New Testament.

[47] C. F. Burney, *The Poetry of Our Lord* (Oxford: 1925); J. M. Crum, *The Original Jerusalem Gospel* (London: 1927).

CHAPTER II

PRELIMINARY SURVEY

Every attentive reader of the Bible has, at some time, been more or less conscious of the variations in the literary style of its several books. Much has been written by able scholars about the literary charm of the Scriptures, and no one who has made regular use of the Scriptures has been altogether insensitive to this charm. There is, however, another aspect to the literary appreciation of the Bible. While there are undoubtedly many passages of high literary quality and lofty moral sentiment, there are also passages which appear to suffer from a monotonous and repetitious style. Writers who have devoted their attention to the technicalities of Hebrew and Greek style have not failed to point out these apparent defects, when they have compared the writers of the Bible with the best writers of Greek and Roman antiquity. Works devoted to a literary study of the Bible are so numerous and so ably written by masters widely approved in their respective fields that the well-informed reader may have every reason to feel that another book is not needed. The present writer, however, has devoted his attention to a comparatively small area of the vast field and has dealt with matters that somehow seem to have escaped the attention of modern writers on the subject. When the nature of the *chiasmus* as a literary principle has been grasped and its wide application in the writings of the Old and New Testament ascertained, the reader will find that some passages commonly regarded as verbose and loose in construction are really specimens of an altogether different literary style; he will also discover that these passages conform rigidly to patterns that were fully recognized by the original writers and their first readers. If he should also consider it worth while to familiarize himself with the chiastic style and the many combinations and nuances of which this apparently rigid form of literary expression is capable, he will discover, to his great surprise, that some passages, which have formerly seemed monotonous, have now taken on a literary charm the presence of which he formerly did not suspect. Should he finally become so interested that he is willing to live with these forms, until they become familiar to his mind and experience, he will discover that they are not rigid, but plastic, and that they have a fascination all their own. The purpose of this treatise, then, is to uncover and describe the literary and cultural heritage of the Semites, which has not as yet been sufficiently studied, but has left clear traces in the style of the writings of both the Old and New Testament.

At this point it may be necessary to describe the *chiasmus* itself. According to its Greek origin the term designates a literary figure, or principle, which consists of "a placing crosswise" of words in a sentence. The term is used in rhetoric to designate an inversion of the order of words or phrases which are repeated or subsequently referred to in the sentence. The simplest application of the principle is found in structures of only *four* terms; of this form there are many instances in ancient as well as modern poetry. The following examples will illustrate the principle:

If e'er to bless thy sons,
My *voice* or *hands* deny,
These *hands* let useful skill forsake,
This *voice* in silence die.
(Dr. T. Dwight)

The chiasmus is here obtained by the arrangement of the terms "voice" and "hands" in the inverted order. The Old Testament abounds in examples of chiastic constructions of four lines; this may be seen by examining the following lines, in which the chiasmus consists, not of identical terms, but of similar ideas. If these couplets are compared, it will be found that the *last* part of the first line is parallel to the *first* part of the second line, etc.; the oblique line indicates the break in the sentence:

He shall send thee help/from the sanctuary,
And from Zion/he shall hold thee up.
He shall remember/all thy offerings,
And thy burnt-sacrifice/he shall accept as fat.
He shall give thee/according to thy heart,

And all thy counsel/he shall fulfill.
We will shout for joy/in thy salvation,
And in the name of our God/we will set up our banners.
(Ps. 20:2-5)

Thoroughly wash me/from my iniquity,
And from my sin/cleanse me.
(Ps. 51:7)

These forms abound on the pages of the Old Testament, but they are not infrequent in the New Testament:

The sabbath/was made for man,
And not man/for the sabbath.
(Mk. 2:27)

Many commentators have recognized in the following words of Jesus a chiastic structure, for only so do they become intelligible.

Give not that which is holy unto the *dogs*,
  Neither cast your pearls before the *swine*,
  Lest haply they (the swine) *trample* them under their feet,
And they (the dogs) turn and *rend* you.
(Mt. 7:6)

This passage becomes clear at once, if we connect the two central and the two extreme lines, for swine trample and dogs rend. These examples are sufficient to illustrate the chiasmus of four terms, which is the simplest form of expressing the principle of inversion. We observe that there are inversions of *identical terms* (cf. Mk. 2:27), but more often of *similar ideas* (cf. Ps. 51:7), and not infrequently the inversion consists in the proper arrangement of *nouns* and *verbs* in couplets (cf. Ps. 20:2-5). It matters little in what manner the inversion is obtained. In this field the only limit is found in the ingenuity and inventiveness of the authors. But whenever the principle of inversion is employed by the writers, it is usually easily detected, and should be recognized by the interpreter. There is really no good reason why the chiastic couplets in Ps. 20:2-5 printed above should not be rendered in our English versions so as to preserve the original pattern of the poet.

Very little attention, if any, has been given to this problem by translators, and yet there is considerable charm hidden away in the rhythmic movement of the ideas in such passages.

Were these and similar minor examples of chiasmus the only instances, we might dismiss them as less significant instances of literary ornamentation which should not be considered of any greater importance in the study of style. Such passages were observed and described by Robert Lowth in his work *Isaiah, A New Translation, etc.* London, 1778, 13th Edition 1842 in the Preliminary Dissertation xiv, but neither he nor the students that followed up his researches seem to have grasped their full significance, nor the *extensive use of chiasmus.* The simpler form in four terms frequently occurs in both classical and modern literature, but of more extensive chiastic systems there is no trace, except in so far as they are found in Scripture. The following instance from Augustine[1] is one of the rare examples of the more extensive use of chiasmus outside of the Scriptures. It is a fine specimen, entirely worthy of Augustine, who was for many years a professor of rhetoric.

Ibi est *aurum,*
Ibi est *palea,*
Ibi *ignis* in angusto operatur.
Ignis ille non est diversus, et diversa agit,
Paleam in cinerem vertit,
Auro sordes tollit.

We have in this passage an inversion, not only of four, but of six terms and, in addition, a play upon the word *ibi,* which is placed at the beginning of the first three lines. The three terms which make up the structure show a tendency to gravitate from the *end* of the first three to the *beginning* of the last three lines of the system.

Although such structures may be rare in other writers, they frequently occur in the Scriptures, specimens having been found without difficulty both in the Old and in the New Testament:

[1] *Enarr. in Ps. XXI,* quoted by R. C. Trench, *Notes on the Parables,* Revell's ed., p. 62, note. *Martyrium Petri et Pauli,* 2, in *Acta Apostolorum.* Editors, Lipsius and Bonnet (Leipzig, 1891), p. 118.

Save me,
 O my God,
  For thou hast smitten
   All my enemies
    On the cheek-bone;
    The teeth
   Of the wicked
  Thou has broken.
 To Yahweh
The salvation. (Ps. 3:7, 8)

For languishing am I
 Heal me, O Yahweh.
  For have been troubled
   My bones;
   And my soul
  Has been troubled greatly.
 And thou, O Yahweh,
How long? (Ps. 6:2, 3)

O God,
 Break
  Their teeth in their mouth;
  The great teeth of the young lions
 Break out,
O Yahweh. (Ps. 58:6)

Shall turn
 His mischief
  Upon his own head;
  And upon the crown of his head
 His violence
Shall descend. (Ps. 7:16)

We have in these passages examples of six, eight, and even ten members in a chiastic system. In the commentaries such passages, usually arranged as quatrains or couplets, are treated as ordinary parallelisms. But although they may conform to the rules of parallelism and rhythm, it is clear that these do not exhaust the formal features of such passages. We have here a *thought-pattern*, which is quite distinct from parallelism and rhythm. A study of these patterns is, therefore, of great significance in the analysis of individual psalms and in determining the strophe in Hebrew poetry.

In the Greek of the New Testament we frequently find similar structures:

For ye died,
 And your life
  Is hid
   With Christ
    In God;
   When Christ
  Is manifested,
 Your life,
Then shall ye also with him be manifested in glory. (Col. 3:3, 4)

Neither do they put new *wine* into old wine-skins:
 Else burst
  The skins,
   And the *wine* is spilled,
  And the skins
 Are destroyed;
But they pour new *wine* into new wine-skins, and both are preserved. (Mt. 9:17)

These two passages clearly show an inversion of the ideas. They differ in this respect only, namely, that they have a *single* line at the centre. But there are many such examples in the Old Testament.

We have thus seen that the chiasmus as a principle of literary construction is applied far more extensively than the ordinary four-lined specimens would lead us to believe. We shall find, presently, that even these examples, striking as they are, do not at all convey an adequate picture of the presence of chiasmus in the Scriptures, for at a later stage we shall present evidence to show that even longer passages have been moulded in these forms. Before we enter upon an analysis of longer sections, it may be well to give a review of the works of those men who pioneered in this field. The present writer had, quite independently and through other influences, entered upon this line of research, when he discovered predecessors. Of these writers we shall now give an account.

Though the chiasmus in its simplest form of four members was well known and cultivated in classical literature, no use seems to have been made of the principle in exegesis until J. A. Bengel called attention to it and employed it, to some extent, in his exposition of the New Testament.[2] Bengel, however, used the term to designate not only passages in which there is an inversion of the ideas or terms, but also some passages, such as Hebr. 12:18-19; vss. 22-24, in which no inversion is found. Here Bengel observed not less than seven parallel ideas, though without inversion of their order. In accordance with the practice of the early English writers we shall designate these *alternating* parallelisms and reserve the term chiasmus only for those instances in which there is an inversion of the terms or ideas. We shall have frequent occasion to refer to both forms of parallelism, alternating and chiastic, for they are often found in combination, as many of the following examples will prove. To Bengel, then, belongs the credit of having first grasped the significance of chiastic forms in the writings of the New Testament and of having applied the principle to

[2] *Gnomon novi testamenti* (Tübingen: 1742), American trans. C. T. Lewis and M. R. Vincent, 2 vols. (Philadelphia: 1860-2).

exegesis. He arranges Rom. 3:9-6:12 in a series of seven sections, which are treated as being parallel in an inverted order, thus placing Faith (3:22) in the fourth, or central, section. Whether we agree in detail with Bengel's conclusions or not, to him belongs the honor of having discovered the significance of chiasmus for interpretation. His own countrymen, however, were not so impressed by his observations along these lines as they were by his other researches, for among those Germans who have written extensively on the style of the New Testament not one seems to have followed his lead. The scholarly succession was taken up by English writers, who made valuable contributions to the study of chiastic forms.

In the year 1753 Jean Astruc published his epoch-making conjectures as to the origin of the Pentateuch, printing on the title page the following quotation from Lucretius IV. 1, "Free through the Muses' pathless haunts I roam, where mortal feet have never strayed"—words which indicate the mood in which the writer issued his book. On the other side of the channel Robert Lowth, Lord Bishop of London, in the same year delivered his first lecture on the sacred poetry of the Hebrews at Oxford.[3] With Lowth the modern study of parallelism begins, and to him we are indebted for the accepted division of Hebrew parallelism into *synonymous*, *antithetic*, and *synthetic*. In the Middle Ages some observations on the form of Hebrew poetry had been made, but Lowth's lectures put the study of Hebrew poetry on a scientific basis. He was a great classical scholar and master of a finished Latin style, but his knowledge of orientalism was deficient. The defects in his book, which were due to this limitation, were corrected by his German editor and translator, J. D. Michaelis, who was a learned orientalist. Michaelis visited England and was much impressed as he heard Lowth deliver his second lecture. The German edition of Lowth's lectures was published in Göttingen, Vol. I in 1758 and Vol. II in 1761, with copious notes by the editor. The results arrived at by Lowth have, as a whole, been

[3] *De sacra poesi Hebraeorum praelectiones academicae*, Am. ed. *Lectures on the Sacred Poetry of the Hebrews* by Robert Lowth, D.D., Lord Bishop of London, trans. from original Latin by G. Gregory, F. A. S. A new ed. by Calvin E. Stowe, A.M. (Andover: 1829).

accepted by modern scholars. They form the basis of all subsequent studies in this field.[4]

The next English writer of note is John Jebb, Bishop of Limerick.[5] In Jebb's extensive correspondence with Alexander Knox[6] one finds from time to time references to Jebb's studies in parallelism. These studies led to the publication of his *Sacred Literature*, a book rarely found in America. In this book Jebb offered a criticism of Lowth's work. He suggested, as a substitute for synonymous parallelism, the term *cognate* parallelism, since the second member of a series always diversifies and generally enhances the first member. The word *synonymous* implies mere repetition. Jebb's most important contribution, however, was his treatment of what he designated as the *introverted parallelism.* Jebb's definition follows:

> There are stanzas so constructed, that, whatever be the number of lines, the first shall be parallel with the last; the second with the penultimate; and so throughout, in order that looks inward, or, to borrow a military phrase, from flanks to centre. This may be called *introverted parallelism.*[7]

From the many examples given by Jebb one is here reproduced:

> The idols of the heathen are silver and gold:
> The work of men's hands;
> They have mouths, but they speak not;
> They have eyes, but they see not;
> They have ears, but they hear not;
> Neither is there any breath in their mouth;
> They who make them are like unto them:
> So are all they who put their trust in them. (Ps. 135:15-18))

Wright[8] has criticized Jebb's use of the term *introverted parallelism* on the ground that it is really not a new type of parallelism but only a group of ordinary parallelisms forming a strophe. Jebb had not been altogether unmindful of this fact, for his definition deals with "*stanzas* so constructed," etc. On the whole, it seems

[4] George Buchanan Gray, *The Forms of Hebrew Poetry* (London: 1920).

[5] *Sacred Literature* (London: 1820); and *Correspondence with Alexander Knox*, edited by C. Forster (Philadelphia: 1834), 2 vols.

[6] *Op. cit.*, Vol. II, pp. 54, 78, 87, 90, 191-198, 263, 266, 269, 271, 274, 306, 368. The reception of *Sacred Literature* is mentioned on pp. 298, 303, 306.

[7] John Jebb, *Sacred Literature*, p. 57.

[8] Smith's *Dictionary of the Bible*, "Hebrew Poetry."

best to abandon altogether Jebb's term, and to use the term *chiasmus* which emphasizes the principle, rather than any of its manifold variations. This term is also broad enough to include the most extensive passages as well as those brief examples which do not even contain lines. The term, moreover, is non-committal, since it may apply equally well to poetry and prose, whereas *parallelism*, *stanza*, and *strophe* are terms which invariably have a stricter application to poetry. By the use of such terms the reader is led to assume that he is dealing with poetry, and he will, consciously or unconsciously, impose upon the material those formal limitations which are associated with poetry in his own mind. His own attitude will hamper his investigations and prevent him from tracing *to the fullest extent* the symmetries of any given passage. We shall therefore make use of the term *chiasmus*. It is the earliest term used; it has a cognate adjective and adverb which are often needed in our discussions; it is more flexible and inclusive; and it is already in use in general literature.

The Rev. Thomas Boys of London, a soldier under the Duke of Wellington in the Peninsular Wars and a translator of the Bible into Portuguese, is the author of two books which are devoted to a study of the inverted order in both the brief passages and in the longer sections.[9] The first of these books is *Tactica Sacra*, which seems to be entirely unknown in America. Allusions to it in later writers indicate that it dealt with passages in the New Testament. The second book, which discusses the psalms, was issued in a new edition by E. W. Bullinger, London, 1890, who has this to say of the *first* edition:

> It contained only sixteen examples, with a full dissertation on the principles involved, and many illustrations, some of which, with his remarks, we have given above. He lived to complete nearly the whole book of Psalms, but it is not until now that they have been published.[10]

Boys abandons Jebb's term *introverted parallelism* and prefers to speak of *correspondence*, since the phenomena to be described include, not only lines, but also paragraphs and whole books in

[9] *Tactica Sacra* (1824); and *Key to the Book of Psalms* by Rev. Thomas Boys, M.A., of Trinity College, Cambridge, Curate of St. Dunstan's in the West, author of *Tactica Sacra* (L. B. Seely & Sons, Fleet Street, London: MDCCCXXV).

[10] *Op. cit.*, p. xx.

the Bible. The first edition is well written, all the evidence being carefully chosen and clearly presented. The edition by Bullinger suffers from some defects, for it is based on the incomplete notes left in Boys's Hebrew Bible after his death. While Boys must be given credit for having uncovered many facts concerning chiastic structures in the Psalms, he failed to make the most of the principle with which he worked. He often observed terms and phrases which recur in a psalm, and rightly concluded that they had something to do with the literary structure of the psalm. He did not, however, subject each psalm to a minute analysis and made no attempt whatsoever to ascertain the principle of the Hebrew strophe. What he found of chiastic structures is, as the reader may suspect from the brief passages already presented, only a small part of what may be discovered in the Psalms by a minute analysis. The literary artistry of the Psalms is much more minute and intricate than Boys's method reveals.[11] But later we shall deal with this subject more fully.

In Scotland at least two writers have manifested an interest in this form of research. One of them, John Forbes, has written two works which apply the principle of inversion to both Old and New Testament.[12] In the first of these works[13] Forbes refers to Bengel as a predecessor, but in such a manner that one is left uncertain whether he received his inspiration from him. To Boys and Jebb he refers frequently.

The other Scottish writer interested in this particular field was Professor William Milligan, whose important work on the Book of Revelation gives clear evidence of the author's acquaintance with the inverted order of certain sections of the Apocalypse. Professor Milligan, however, does not use the terminology of Jebb and Boys or make any reference to predecessors,[14] but it is clear that he attaches great importance to his own conclusions with ref-

[11] "Chiasmus in the Psalms," *AJSL*, Vol. XLIX, pp. 281-312.

[12] Rev. John Forbes, LL.D., *The Symmetrical Structure of Scripture*, or The Principles of Scripture Parallelism Exemplified, in an analysis of the Decalogue, The Sermon on the Mount, and other passages of sacred writings (Donaldson's Hospital, Edinburgh, T. & T. Clark: 1854). Also *Analytical Commentary on the Epistle to the Romans* (T. & T. Clark: 1868).

[13] *Op. cit.*, p. 214, note.

[14] *Lectures on the Apocalypse* (3rd ed.; London: 1892), pp. 94, 95.

erence to plan and structure in the book and that these conclusions are partly based on evidence of the inverted order. In the preface to the second edition he declares that the correct view of the plan of the book is as fatal to the source hypothesis held by Völter as it is to that held by Vischer.

In recent years the Oxford University Press has published *The Companion Bible* under the editorship of the late Doctor E. W. Bullinger. The work is prepared on a generous scale and embodies many interesting and useful features, the most important of which is the application of Jebb's principle of the inverted order. Were it not for certain glaring defects of the work, its publication would be gratifying, since it embodies a sound literary principle which has waited too long for recognition. The defects are largely the same as those found in Boys's *Key to the Book of Psalms*, edited by Bullinger. Blocks of material are loosely arranged and described as "correspondences," receiving as proof only a word or phrase which is common to two sections. A single line is at times balanced against a whole paragraph because a certain catchword appears in both. The hypothesis is overworked to the extent that the order of the books in the Hebrew Canon is said to be determined by the inverted order. The editor's "dispensational" views protrude everywhere and become, at times, quite fantastic. The disastrous results of the editor's method can be avoided only by a scrupulous attention to details, by a thorough grasp of fundamental laws of chiastic structure, and by a careful observation of varieties of form in poetry and prose.

After this brief survey of the literature devoted to the study of chiastic forms, we shall now attempt to describe the laws governing chiastic structures. In the work of attempting to ascertain and classify these laws the present writer has had no help from his predecessors. The fact remains, however, that when a great many passages have been studied and compared, certain recurring features impress themselves upon the reader. They are so definite and recur in so many different combinations, that one is justified in calling them the laws of chiastic structures. These laws are the following: (1) *The centre is always the turning point.* The centre, as we shall see, may consist of one, two, three, or even four lines.

(2) At the centre there is often a change in the trend of thought, and an antithetic idea is introduced. After this the original trend is resumed and continued until the system is concluded. For want of a better name, we shall designate this feature *the law of the shift at the centre.* (3) Identical ideas are often distributed in such a fashion that *they occur in the extremes and at the centre* of their respective system, and nowhere else in the system. (4) There are also many instances of ideas, occurring at the centre of one system and recurring in the extremes of a corresponding system, the second system evidently having been constructed to match the first. We shall call this feature *the law of shift from centre to the extremes.* (5) There is a definite tendency of certain terms to gravitate toward certain positions within a given system, such as the divine names in the psalms, quotations in central position in a system in the New Testament, or such terms as "body" when denoting the church. (6) Larger units are frequently introduced and concluded by *frame-passages.* (7) There is frequently a mixture of chiastic and alternating lines within one and the same unit.

Examples illustrating these laws will be introduced in order to familiarize the reader with them, and references will be made to them from time to time as occasion arises. The reader is asked to accept these attempts to formulate a law *tentatively,* in the light of such evidence as is here briefly presented, awaiting supplementary data which from time to time will be introduced and discussed. We shall then first give a few examples which show clearly how *the centre was regarded as a turning point.*

> *Ashkelon* shall see it and fear;
>   *Gaza* also and be very sorrowful;
>   And *Ekron:*
>   For *her* (i.e. Ekron's) expectation shall be ashamed,
>   And the king shall perish from *Gaza;*
> And *Ashkelon* shall not be inhabited. (Zech. 9:5)

Boys has given this passage as an example of how these forms occur in passages "where poetry, according to our ideas of it, is out of question." The chiastic form of the passage is clear, but it shows just as clearly how the centre becomes the turning point. Three statements predict the fate of the Philistine cities, but when the centre is passed, the fourth line, introduced by "for," begins an *elaboration* of the prediction. This is continued until the end of the system is reached. In whatever way one chooses to describe the difference between the first and the last half of the system, the difference is clearly marked.

We may now take another example, showing similar characteristics, except that there is a *single central line*.

> *Seek* ye me, and ye shall *live*.
> But seek not after *Bethel*,
> Nor enter into *Gilgal*,
> And pass not to *Beer-sheba:*
> For *Gilgal* shall surely go into captivity,
> And *Bethel* shall come to naught.
> *Seek* Yahweh, and ye shall *live*. (Amos 5:4b-6a)

The first line of this system Harper unites with the words that precede, in order not to make "the prophet give two exhortations in practically the same language."[15] He also suggests the removal of the central line to some place before the second line, so as not to interrupt the chiasmus formed by the names Bethel and Gilgal. Neither of these changes is needed, nor is it necessary to assume that a line parallel to that dealing with Beer-sheba has fallen out of the centre, for the system runs true to form as it now stands in our arrangement. There are many instances of chiastic systems with single lines at the centre. We observe, however, that while the first and last lines carry an invitation and a promise, the intervening five lines are of a different nature. Of these five lines, the first three give a warning, but the last two, introduced by "for," as in Zech. 9:5, carry a threat. Consider also the following passage:

> And Yahweh said unto Moses:
> He shall surely be put to death, the man,
> They shall stone him with stones,
> All the congregation without the camp.
> And they brought him,
> All the congregation without the camp,
> And stoned him with stones
> To death,
> As Yahweh commanded Moses. (Num. 15:35-36)

[15] W. R. Harper, *Amos and Hosea* (I. C. C.), *in loco.*

In this passage the first four lines are devoted to the command, and the last five to its execution. In the previous passage from Amos, including seven lines in all, the first four formed the first half and the next three the last half of the system. It is not impossible that we are touching a subtle system of *numerical* symmetry in such arrangements to which we shall have occasion to call the reader's attention in other passages. The present writer is convinced from his observation of a great number of passages that the Hebrew writers have certain numerical designs woven into their writings. These are found not only when numerical adjectives, like three, seven, etc., are expressed, but also where conspicuous words are grouped in clusters in an artistic fashion so as to express designs. Of this we shall see more presently. The three passages already discussed illustrate one way in which the centre is marked off as the turning-point of a system.

The following passages will show another way in which the centre is emphasized for the same reason. The following verse reads like an inventory but is, nevertheless, chiastic in form, a fact which shows how wrong it would be to relate these forms to poetry only.

And he had sheep and oxen,
And he asses,
And men servants,
And maid servants,
And she asses,
And camels. (Gen. 12:16)

This passage, simple as it is, illustrates a principle of construction which frequently occurs in such systems, namely, *a sudden shift from one subject to another* when the centre is reached, after which the former subject *is resumed* and adhered to until the end of the system. In the inventory of Abraham's wealth we observe that the first two and the last two lines enumerate *animals,* while the two central lines enumerate *human beings.* There are, of course, much more elaborate and artistic expressions of the law of the shift—if we may call it so for want of a better name—as may be seen from the following passage:

Arise,
Shine,
For thy light is come,
And the glory
Of Yahweh
Upon thee is risen.

For, behold, darkness shall cover the earth
And gross darkness the peoples.

But upon thee will arise
Yahweh,
And his glory upon thee be seen,
And nations shall come to thy light,
And kings to the brightness
Of thy rising. (Isa. 60:1-3)

In the first two and last two lines, as well as in the two central lines, we have a parallelism of *ideas*, but not of words. This condition our English versions do not reveal. In all the other lines of the system, however, there exists, not only a parallelism of ideas, but also a parallelism of *words*. And yet the most striking feature is that the system opens with a beautiful description of the future light and glory of Israel, that the scene suddenly shifts from light and glory to darkness and gross darkness when the centre is reached, and that finally the note of hope and joy is heard once more, amplified now to include all the nations. One who is thinking merely in terms of *parallelismus membrorum* and rhythm, would proceed to arrange such a passage in a strophe of four couplets, or eight lines. However acceptable such an arrangement might be, it is clear that we have in this passage something more than ordinary parallelism and rhythm; here there is a *thought-pattern*, which is chiastic in form and obeys the laws of such constructions.

Under the discussion of the law of the shift at the centre one may include all those passages which show an artistic and closely knit combination of *chiastic* and *alternating* lines. These systems are of two kinds. One kind begins with chiastic order, shifts to alternating at the centre, then resumes the chiastic order once more, maintaining this order until the end of the system is reached. The other kind, beginning with a series of alternating lines, shifts to chiastic order at the centre; then it resumes the original alternating order after the centre is passed, retaining this order till the system is completed.

Let the wicked forsake his *way*,
And the unrighteous man his *thoughts;*

And let him return to Yahweh,
And he will have mercy upon him;
And to our God,
For he will abundantly pardon.

For my thoughts are not your *thoughts,*
Neither are your ways my *ways,* saith Yahweh. (Isa. 55:7-8)

This passage is a sample of the first kind of combination of chiastic and alternating lines. How spontaneous such forms are may be gathered from the last two lines of the structure, in which an extra chiastic feature is discovered in the forms, "my—your and your—my," a minor piece of ornamentation, a final flourish. The next passage, far more elaborate and extensive, is the exact reversal of the former passage; here we have chiastic lines in the centre and alternating lines in the extremes.

Because ye have said, 15
We made a covenant with death,
And with Sheol are we at agreement;
A When the overflowing scourge shall pass through,
It shall not come unto us;

B For we made lies our refuge,
And under falsehood have we hid ourselves.

Therefore, thus saith the Lord Yahweh, 16
C Behold, I lay in Zion { a stone, a stone tried,
a corner precious
a foundation well founded

D He that believeth shall not be in haste. 17

C′ And I will make justice the line,
And righteousness the plummet.

B′ And hail shall sweep away the refuge of lies,
And the waters shall overflow the hiding-place;

And your covenant with death shall be annulled, 18
And your agreement with Sheol shall not stand;
A′ When the overflowing scourge shall pass through,
Then shall ye be trodden down by it. (Isa. 28:15-18)

The lines printed in italics in this structure represent introductory statements designating as speakers the rulers, on the one hand, and the Lord, on the other. What is vital for our present purpose is the observation that, while the *extremes* of this passage describe the plans by which the rulers intended to obtain security for Zion (AB) and the frustration of these plans (B′A′), the *centre* carries by way of contrast a description of the refuge provided by the Lord himself. In C the laying of the corner stone is described in a line which branches off into a triplet (of this more will be said presently); in C′ the references to the "line" and the "plummet" also point to building operations. The very core of the message is found in the central line, "He that believeth shall not be in haste." Thus, the climax is at the centre, not at the end, where we should expect it. It is remarkable also that it is the centre which is quoted in the New Testament where we often meet with the "corner stone" and the demand for belief in Him. How consciously and minutely the sense of contrast between the centre and the extremes is maintained may be seen in a comparison between the "justice" and "righteousness" with which the Lord himself builds, and the "lies" and the "falsehood" in which the rulers seek their security (BB′). It will not be necessary to point out in detail the parallelisms which every reader may be trusted to discover for himself. One new feature, however, calls for some brief remarks. The reader who has observed the alternating order of the lines in AB and passed over the centre (CDC′) feels disturbed, when he encounters the couplet B′ in its present position. He would perhaps attempt to obtain regularity by moving B′ from its present position and by placing it after A′.[16] The puzzle will be solved for him in a much simpler way, since in many passages there are *lines* which are alternating, while the *clusters* into which these lines are gathered often follow the chiastic order with

[16] A suggestion has been made by Dr. Kemper Fullerton of Oberlin in an article in AJSL, Oct., 1920. The central material (CDC′) he treats as extraneous, a deposit of a later "lithic theology," which prevailed at some period in Israel's history. Lines 3, 4 in section A, he thinks, originally *preceded* lines 1, 2; this would shape the statement of the protasis (AB) and the apodosis (B′A′) into the following chiastic order: "scourge-covenant-lies-covenant-scourge." Neither the interpolation nor the transposition need be invoked, for the passage is perfectly regular as it stands.

reference to one another. In this particular case the clusters ABB'A' form a chiastic structure, but their lines alternate. Although our present plan does not call for an extended treatment of the whole section of the Book of Isaiah in which this passage occurs, it may be of interest to the reader to notice that the passage we have analyzed seems to be a part of a far-flung symmetrical pattern which begins in 28:9 and ends in 28:22. There are three preceding and three following sections with characteristic phrases and parallel content. Their relationship may be briefly described by the following outline:

A "Understand the message", vss. 9-11: The Assyrians.
  B "This is the rest", vss. 12-13.
    C "Ye scoffers", vs. 14.
      D The Rulers of Jerusalem and the Lord, vss. 15-18 (cf. above)
A' "Understand the message", vs. 19: The Assyrians.
  B' "For the bed is shorter", vss. 20-21.
    C' "Ye scoffers", vs. 22.

The passages already discussed may serve as a brief introduction to a more extended discussion of the chiastic forms in the Old Testament. In the following chapter we shall attempt to show how deeply such forms have determined the structure of some of the ancient laws of the Hebrews.

THE OLD TESTAMENT

CHAPTER III

THE LAW

Any reader of the legal portions of the Pentateuch has observed how repetitious its language is in many sections. He has probably explained the nature of the laws by references to modern legal documents which are also repetitious. A closer examination of the structure of some of these laws will show, however, that the reiterations follow certain verifiable literary patterns, and that mere legal formality is not sufficient to explain their form.

A And by these ye shall become *unclean*.

Whosoever *toucheth* the carcass of them shall be *unclean* until even;
B And whosoever *beareth* aught of the carcass of them shall *wash* his clothes,
And be *unclean* until even.

C Every *beast* which parteth the *hoof*, and is not clovenfooted, nor cheweth the cud, is *unclean* unto you.

D Every one that *toucheth* them shall be *unclean*.

C′ And whatsoever goeth upon its *paws*, among all the *beasts* that go on all four, they are *unclean* unto you.

Whosoever *toucheth* their carcass shall be *unclean* until even,
B′ And he that *beareth* the carcass of them shall *wash* his clothes,
And be *unclean* until even.

A′ They are *unclean* unto you. (Lev. 11:24-28)

Like the preceding passage in Isa. 28:15-18 this passage has seven sections, and its lines are alternating while the groups of lines are chiastic. The passage shows how necessary it is to ascertain the chiastic structure, for the references in A and B are hardly intelligible until the contents of C are considered. We read of "these" and "them," but do not know what is meant thereby until we have read the enumeration of the unclean animals in C. The seven sections are well balanced. There are two degrees of ceremonial uncleanness, depending on whether the carcass is merely touched or carried, and the penalty is merely to remain unclean until even, or, in addition, to undergo a washing of the clothes

(BB′). The beasts that render a person unclean are now described in sections CC′ with renewed emphasis on their uncleanness. In the seven sections comprising the passage there are two series, those bearing the odd numbers (1, 3, 5, 7), which emphasize the uncleanness of the animals (ACC′A′), and those bearing even numbers (2, 4, 6), which mention the manner in which man is rendered unclean. The verb "touch" is found only in the even sections (BDB′). Although these facts so far stand unsupported, we shall find presently that there is much evidence to support the hypothesis that in series of seven the odd and the even sections are made to carry distinctive contents.

In the preliminary discussion of the chiasmus we saw that in the structure contained in Matt. 9:17 the word "wine" occurred in the first, last, and central lines, and *nowhere else* in the system. In the following passage we have more evidence of the method of distributing *parallel ideas and terms at the extremes and the centre of a structure*, for the references to the "house" are found in AA′ and toward the centre of B.

And he shall take to *cleanse* the *house* two birds and cedar wood,
A and scarlet, and hyssop:
And he shall *kill one of the birds* in an earthen vessel over *running water*,

And he shall take the *cedar wood*, and the *hyssop*, and the *scarlet*
And the *living bird*,
And dip them into the blood of *the slain bird*, and in the *running water*,
And sprinkle the *house*
B Seven times;
And he shall cleanse the *house*
With the blood of *the bird* and with the *running water*,
And with the *living bird*,
And with the *cedar wood*, and the *hyssop*, and the *scarlet*,

A′ And he shall take the *living bird* out of the city into the *open field*,
And make an atonement for the *house*, and it shall be *clean*. (Lev. 14:49-53)

In the treatment of this passage the present writer has been anticipated by Boys, who, strange to say, has not included the material in the sections marked AA′ in our arrangement. These lines, however, should be included, for they contain the formal introduction and conclusion to the law, and they are as much a part of the chiastic structure as section B is. Seldom does one find this much symmetry packed into so brief a passage. The passage opens with a statement of the things required for the cleansing and gives directions for the killing of one of the birds (A). It ends with the concluding act of the cleansing when the living bird is let out into the open field (A′). Presumably the act of cleansing ends in the same locality in which it begins, for the "running water" is located in "the open field." The cedar wood, hyssop, and scarlet are terms that form a *triplet* in the first and last lines of B. The climax of the act of cleansing is to be looked for, when the house is sprinkled *seven times;* this climax is found in the centre and not at the end of the system. In other laws concerning leprosy we shall find a similar arrangement of balanced triplets, as well as references in a central position to the sevenfold sprinkling. The other symmetries of this passage do not need further comment, since they become clear when the words printed in italics are compared.

We are now to give an arrangement of two laws governing the cleansing of *persons* from leprosy. These laws deal with the same subject as the preceding, but they are somewhat different since one is the law pertaining to ordinary cases and the other is the law relating to the poor. Both of these laws show an elaborate combination of chiastic and alternating lines with traces of numerical symmetry; they also illustrate the law of distribution of related ideas at the extremes and at the centre. For all the labor that has been expended on the analysis of the Pentateuch in the last hundred years, the present writer is not acquainted with any analysis which has taken account of the features we are discussing in this treatise. Such symmetries certainly must have far-reaching implications for the literary investigation of the Pentateuch. Their strictly objective character renders them a particularly useful check on much of the subjective theorizing which has followed in the wake of the critical studies of the Pentateuch.

And on the eighth day he shall take 10
Two he-lambs without blemish,
And one ewe-lamb a year old without blemish,
And three tenth parts of an ephah of fine flour
for a meal-offering mingled with oil,
And one log of oil.

And the priest that cleanseth him shall set the man that is to be cleansed, 11
And those things, before Yahweh, at the door of the tent of meeting.

A And the *priest* shall take one of the he-lambs, 12
And offer him for a trespass-offering,

And the log of *oil*, 13
And wave them for a wave-offering *before Yahweh:*
B And he shall kill the he-lamb in the place where they kill the *sin-offering*,
And the *burnt-offering*,
In the place of the *sanctuary* (omit 13b as a gloss).

C And the priest shall take the blood of the *trespass-offering*, 14

(that is to be cleansed,
upon the tip of the right *ear* of him
D And the priest shall put it and upon the thumb of his right *hand*,
and upon the great toe of his right *foot*,

E And the priest shall take the log of *oil* 15
And pour it into the palm of his own left *hand*,

(his left *hand*, 16
And the priest shall dip his right finger in the *oil* that is in
F And shall sprinkle of the *oil* that is his *hand* seven times
before Yahweh

E′ And the rest of the *oil* that is in his *hand* 17

(to be cleansed,
upon the tip of the right *ear* of him that is
D′ Shall the priest put and upon the thumb of his right *hand*,
and upon the great toe of his right *foot*,

C′ Upon the blood of the *trespass-offering*,

And the rest of the *oil* that is in the priest's hand 18
he shall put upon the head of him that is to be cleansed,
And the priest shall make an atonement for him *before Yahweh.*
And the priest shall offer the *sin-offering*, 19
B′ and make an atonement for him that is to be cleansed, because of his un-
And afterward he shall kill the *burnt-offering*, (cleanness;
and the priest shall offer the burnt-offering and the meal-offering
Upon the *altar*. 20

A′ And the *priest* shall make an atonement for him,
And he shall be clean. (Lev. 14:10-20)

The first group of lines enumerates the materials needed for the cleansing, and the next two lines indicate the *place* where the act of cleansing is to take place. Beginning with A the various steps of the cleansing sacrifice and its application are enumerated and described until the conclusion is reached in A′. The section marked B in our arrangement contains the following terms: "oil," "before Yahweh," "sin-offering," "burnt-offering," and "the place of the sanctuary." Though section B′ is nearly twice as long as B, it is not difficult to see that these sections were constructed to correspond item for item. All the terms already enumerated recur, all following the same order except the last one; it is clear, however, that "the place of the sanctuary" and "the altar" refer to the same locality. The cleansing is achieved by the application of both *blood* and *oil,* and the detailed description of the two acts is found in CDE and E′D′C′ respectively. As was the case in the previously discussed law governing the cleansing of the house, the climax of the act, the moment in which the oil is sprinkled seven times before Yahweh, is described in the centre of the passage. The triplet which we found in the former law, consisting of the cedar wood, the hyssop, and the scarlet, is also a feature in this law, where we observe the balanced position in the structure of the triple reference to the ear, the hand, and the foot. The only difference in this case seems to be that the triplet is made more elaborate and pronounced than in the former law. The phrase *before Yahweh,* occurring in BFB′ and nowhere else in the structure, is symmetrically distributed in accordance with the law of distribution at the extremes and at the centre of chiastic systems.

The following law is identical in purpose and in form with the preceding, except that it is a little more elaborate, having certain special provisions relating to the poor, whose economic status did not permit them to carry out the full provisions of the regular law.

And if he be poor, and cannot get so much, then shall he take 21
A One he-lamb for a trespass-offering to be waved, to make an atonement for him,
And one tenth part of an ephah of fine flour mingled with oil for a meal-offering,
And a log of oil;

And two *turtle doves,* 22
Or two *young pigeons,*
Such as he is *able to get;*
B And one shall be for *sin-offering,*
And the other for *burnt-offering.*
And on the eighth day he shall bring them for his *cleansing* unto the *priest,* 23
Unto the door of the tent of meeting, *before Yahweh.*

And the *priest* shall take the lamb of the trespass-offering, 24
C And the log of *oil,*
And the priest shall wave them for a wave-offering *before Yahweh.*

D And he shall kill the lamb of the trespass-offering,
And the priest shall take *the blood of the trespass-offering,* and put it 25

Upon the tip of the right *ear* of him that is to be cleansed,
E And upon the thumb of his right *hand*,
And upon the great toe of this right *foot*,

F And the *priest* shall pour of the *oil* into the palm of his own left
hand 26

G And the *priest* shall sprinkle with his finger some of the *oil*
That is in his left *hand* seven times *before Yahweh*. 27

F′ And the *priest* shall put of the *oil* that is in his *hand* 28

Upon the tip of the right *ear* of him that is to be cleansed,
E′ And upon the thumb of his right *hand*,
And upon the great toe of his right *foot*,

D′ Upon the place of *the blood of the trespass-offering*.

And the rest of the *oil* (be cleansed, 29
C′ That is in the *priest's* hand he shall put upon the head of him that is to
To make an atonement *before Yahweh*.

And he shall offer of the *turtle doves*, 30
Or of the *young pigeons*,
Such as he is *able to get*, 31
B′ The one for a *sin-offering*,
The other for a *burnt-offering*, with the meal-offering.
And the *priest* shall make an atonement for him that is to be *cleansed*,
Before Yahweh.

A′ This is the law of him in whom is the plague of leprosy, 32
Who is not able to get that which pertaineth to his cleansing. (Lev. 14: 21-32)

The symmetry of this passage is even more extensive and more pronounced, since section B′ is here better proportioned than was the elaborate section B′ in the former case. In A we find the statement that this is the law of the poor—a fact that is repeated in the conclusion of A′. The reader who has already traced the parallelisms of the previous law will readily discover for himself the parallel features of this law by taking note of the terms printed in italics. The law of distribution at the extremes and at the centre is seen once more in the distribution of the phrase *before Yahweh*, which occurs in five places (BCGC′B′). The objection that AA′ and *not* BB′ are the extremes of the structure may easily be set aside, because in this law, as well as in the former, AA′ may be regarded as the introduction and conclusion of the law—the frame, as it were, within which the law proper is developed. The triplets formed by the references to the ear, the hand, and the foot (EE′) are in this case accompanied by other triple arrangements which refer to the *priest*, the *oil* and the *hand*. All of these are three times repeated *together* (FGF′). The triple reference to the two latter terms is a feature in the centre of the former law (cf. EFE′), but there we find no triple reference to the priest. A careful comparison of these two laws reveals, whatever the reason may be, that the symmetry is more regular in the law pertaining to the poor, than it is in the regular law which precedes it.

Another striking feature that often characterizes the centre of chiastic structures is the *triplet*. The usual form has a couplet or a single line at the centre, but in some instances the centre includes a triplet. The impression of the present writer is that the triplet at the centre is of more frequent occurrence in the writings of the New Testament than in those of the Old; this is an impression, however, which may be due merely to the fact that he has worked with more material in the former than in the latter. Nevertheless, the following examples show that the triplet at the centre occurs in the Old Testament.

And *Yahweh* spake unto *Moses*, saying, 13
Bring forth him that hath *cursed* without the *camp;* 14
A And let all that heard him lay their hands upon his head,
And let all the congregation *stone him:*
And thou shalt speak unto the *children of Israel*, saying 15

B Whosoever curseth his *God* shall bear his sin.

And he that blasphemeth the name of Yahweh, he shall surely be put to (death; 16
C All the congregation shall certainly stone him;
As well the *sojourner*, as the *home-born*,
When he blasphemeth the Name shall be put to death.

And he that smiteth any *man* mortally shall surely be put to death; 17
D And he that smiteth a *beast* mortally shall make it good, life for life; 18
And if a man cause a *blemish* in his *neighbor*, as he hath done so shall (it be done unto him. 19

Breach for breach, 20
E Eye for eye,
Tooth for tooth.

As he hath caused a *blemish* in a *man*, so shall it be rendered unto (him; 21
D′ And he that killeth a *beast* shall make it good;
And he that killeth a *man* shall be put to death.

C′ Ye shall have one manner of law, 22
As well for the *sojourner*, as for the *home-born*.

B′ For I am Yahweh your *God.*

And *Moses* spake to the children of Israel: 23
A′ And they brought forth him that had *cursed* out of the *camp,*
And *stoned him* with stones.
And the *children of Israel* did as Yahweh commanded Moses. (Lev. 24:13-23)

This passage contains two separate laws: the one against blasphemy, which fits into the historical context; the other against violence, which has nothing to do with the historical situation. The preceding verses (24:10-12) tell the story of a son of an Israelitish woman and an Egyptian father who blasphemed the Name and cursed; this event gives rise to the law. The central part of this passage, however, dealing with violence against man and beast (DED′), is a well-knit unit by itself. In the centre we find a triplet stating the law of retaliation (E), while on either side there is a threefold application of the law to man, beast, and man (DD′). We need not discuss in detail the extremely interesting symmetry of this passage in which a great number of parallel terms are found, but it would seem that source criticism of Leviticus would, in this instance at least, receive help from a study of the chiastic form. On either side of this centre are found two sections, one a little more elaborate than the other, but both stating that the law is uniform to both sojourners and home-born (CC′). In BB′ we have the only instances in which the name Elohim occurs in the structure. A introduces the command to stone the offender, while A′ describes how the command was obeyed. For our present purpose the threefold occurrence of a triplet at the centre of a structure is the most interesting feature. There can be no doubt that the frequent recurrence of triplets in the writings of the New Testament looks to such passages as this for their models.

A systematic search for structures of this kind in the legal sections of the Pentateuch would, very likely, be abundantly rewarded and would contribute not a little to our understanding of the disposition of the material. The critical study of the Pentateuch has nearly always taken account of *sequence,* and when there has been little or no sequence in the arrangement of sections, scholars have turned to the hypothesis of dislocation or redaction.

But why should logical considerations alone be permitted to determine the organization of the material in a book, when we have such abundant evidence that its writers were influenced by a well-developed aesthetic interest? May it not be, after all, that blocks of material were arranged in accordance with chiastic or alternating patterns or a combination of both, and that in the mind of the writer and the informed reader similar sections, though far apart in these books, were connected with one another? May it not be also that the language is artistic, although at times it appears to be exceedingly prolix and discursive, the style of "a jurist rather than a historian" in whose interest it is to be "circumstantial, formal, and precise."[1] No doubt legal writings are the least imaginative of all prose, but after a close study of some of these structures we are not ready to deny them certain aesthetic qualities. There is repetition, to be sure, but a measured and orderly repetition acording to fixed literary patterns.

The chiastic structures in the Law are not confined to the legal sections only but are found also in the narrative parts. The third chapter of Genesis, which describes the meeting between the fallen pair and God and relates the meting out of punishment, contains the chiastic order. The participants are introduced as follows: man (vs. 9), woman (vs. 12), and the serpent (vs. 13). The sentence upon them is pronounced in the reverse order: the serpent (vs. 13), the woman (vs. 16), and the man (vs. 17). The same phenomenon is observable in the genealogy of Gen. 10:1, where the order is Shem, Ham, and Japheth; these names are inverted when their descendants are enumerated: Japheth (vs. 2), Ham (vs. 6), and Shem (vs. 21). Likewise in Gen. 14:13 the names Mamre, Eshcol, and Aner occur, but when referred to again at the conclusion of the narrative, their names are given in the reverse order (vs. 24). These passages remind one of the procedure of Josephus in Ant. XVII, 1, 2 ff. where he enumerates the sects of the Jews, Essenes, Sadducees, and Pharisees; in further describing them, however, he follows the opposite order. To find a chiastic order in such cases is not surprising, since almost any

[1] S. R. Driver, *Introduction to the Literature of the Old Testament* (1910 ed., p. 12).

writer who has a series of enumerations will reverse the order when he has occasion to refer back to his own words.[2]

The following passage is the central panel in the story of the flood. It records with great dramatic effect the thoroughness of the destruction wrought by the catastrophe. Even though vs. 23 in our Hebrew text reads, "both man, and cattle, and creeping things, and birds of the heavens," yet consulting the first half of the system and its terms it is easy to detect that the passage originally was chiastic. The words, "and beasts," have evidently dropped out, while "cattle" and "creeping things" have been transposed. In its original form the passage reads as follows:

And all flesh *died* that moved upon the *earth*, 21
 Both birds,
  And cattle,
A And beasts,
   And every creeping thing that creepeth upon the earth,
    And every man:

    B All in whose nostrils was the breath of the spirit of *life*, 22
      Of all that was on *the dry land*

      C *Died;*
        And *was destroyed*

    B′ Every *living* thing 23
      That was upon the face of *the ground*,

    Both man,
   And creeping things,
A′ [And beasts],
  And cattle,
 And birds of the heavens,
And they *were destroyed* from the *earth*. (Gen. 7:21-23)

There are no less than eighteen parallel items in this structure. Up to the first line of A′ everything is in order. This is also true of the last two lines of A′. The one elimination, namely, "and beasts," has been restored within brackets, and one transposition, "creeping things" and "cattle," has been made. This passage is like an arch, most of the material of which lies in order on the ground, with but one stone missing and two other stones a little

[2] Cf. ῞ΥΣΤΕΡΟΝ ΠΡΟΤΕΡΟΝ ῾ΟΜΕΡΙΚΩΣ (Cicero, Att. 1, 16, 1) by Samuel E. Bassett, in *Harvard Studies in Classical Philology*, Vol. XXXI (1920), pp. 39-62.

out of line due to the collapse of the arch. We have the law of distribution at the extremes and at the centre clearly represented, since "died" in A and C expresses the same idea, though with different verbs in Hebrew, while the verb "destroy" is identical in A′ and C. Likewise "the earth" in AA′ is parallel to "the dry land" in B and to "the ground" in B′. The same law of distribution was observed in the terms "unclean" in Lev. 11:24-28, "before Yahweh" in Lev. 14:10-20, and "cleanse the house" in Lev. 14:49-53.

Encountering so much detailed symmetry in the central panel of the story of the flood, one is tempted to look for a continuation of the chiastic structure on either side of the centre. The cycle of narratives in Gen. 4:17-11:9 appears to be a combination of alternating and chiastic sections which may be represented by the following outline:

A The contribution of Cain and his descendants, 4:17-22.
  B A poetic section: the Song of Lamech, 4:23-24.
    C The generations of Adam, 4:25-5:32.
      D The wickedness of mankind; big men; 6:1-8.
        Yahweh saw it and determined their destruction, vss. 5-7.

        E The three sons of Noah, 6:9-12.
          F God's covenant with Noah, 6:13-22.
            G Yahweh declares he will destroy everything, 7:1-5.
              H Noah enters the ark, 7:6-9.
                I The flood continues to rise, 7:10-20.
                  J The central panel: enumerating the results of the flood (cf. detailed structure above), 7:21-23a.
                I′ The flood continues to fall, 7:23b-8:12.
              H′ Noah leaves the ark, 8:13-19.
            G′ Yahweh declares he will not curse the ground any more, (8:20-22.
          F′ God's covenant with Noah, 9:1-17.
        E′ The three sons of Noah, 9:18-19.

A′ The contribution of Noah: a vineyard; his descendants, 9:20-24, 28.
  B′ A poetic section: the Curse of Canaan, 9:25-27.
    C′ The generations of the sons of Noah, 10:1-32.
      D′ The wickedness of mankind: a big tower, 11:1-9
        Yahweh saw it and determined to confound them, vss. 5-9.

The verse that precedes this cycle may properly be regarded as the conclusion to the story of Cain's murder of Abel, while the genealogy beginning in 11:10 and immediately following the cycle, is no part of it but is, without doubt, intended to introduce the family of Abraham. If the reader will take these sections and compare them in pairs, he will discover some remarkable parallelisms of ideas and sometimes of terms. No one can miss the contrast between the earth filled with violence before the flood in 6:10 and the statement after the flood in 9:19, "These were the sons of Noah: and of these was the whole earth overspread." The contrast between the old wicked race that was to be destroyed and the new race, the descendants of the righteous Noah who walked with God, properly opens and closes the story of the flood. It may be interesting for source criticism to observe the distribution of the divine names, Elohim and Yahweh, in the central division, which is chiastic. Yahweh is found in GG′, and Elohim in all the other sections. Yahweh is found also in 7:16b, but this is a lone exception (LXX reads κύριος ὁ θεὸς). We shall have occasion to return to the symmetrical distribution of divine names, when we take up the analysis of certain psalms and again when we come to consider a similar distribution of the titles of Jesus in narrative sections of the gospels. The distribution of the passages dealing with Noah's age (cf. 7:6; 8:13), the seven days (cf. 7:10; 8:10, 12), and the forty days (cf. 7:12, 17; 8:6) seems also to follow a chiastic order of arrangement, though the work of the redactor may have somewhat obscured their original position. Our purpose is not to discuss the problem of source criticism. It is generally agreed that the sources of the Pentateuch have been edited because of a liturgical necessity. Our interest is to point out how this liturgical interest has been satisfied by casting the material in a chiastic mould.

CHAPTER IV

THE PROPHETS

We shall now present some longer and shorter sections from the prophets, the second great division of the Hebrew Canon. We have already described some of the briefer chiastic systems in our preliminary discussion of the several laws of structure, and in one instance we have described a longer passage made up of alternating and chiastic sections in combination (cf. Isa. 28:9-22). The following passage from Isaiah includes chapters 2-4 and may serve as illustration of how the writings of the prophets have been cast in the chiastic mould. There are many problems in these chapters to which commentators have called attention and offered their solutions. These problems are connected with the sequence in the separate sections, the strophic nature of the material, the refrains, and the text. Though our own task is more restricted in scope, it will appear from time to time that observance of the chiastic patterns often sheds light on some of these puzzling problems. A discussion of this kind, however, may easily become occupied with a number of questions, which, though interesting in themselves, have no direct bearing on the main purpose of this treatise. We shall attempt therefore to confine the investigation solely to the structure of these chapters and by means of cross-references to abbreviate the discussion as much as possible.

A Prophecy of Two Cities

Isaiah 2:1-4:6

The word that Isaiah, the son of Amoz, saw concerning Judah and Jerusalem. 1

Part I: 2:2-6a

And it shall come to pass in the end of days, 2
A That the mountain of Yahweh's house shall be established on the top of the (mountains,
And shall be exalted above the hills.

And all *nations* shall flow unto it, 3
And many *peoples* shall go and say,
Come ye, and let us go up to the *mountain* of Yahweh,
To the *house* of the God of Jacob.
B And he will teach us of his *ways*,
And we will walk in his *paths*.
For out of *Zion* shall go forth the law,
And the word of Yahweh from *Jerusalem*.
And he shall judge between the *nations*, 4
And shall decide concerning many *peoples*.

And they shall beat their swords into plowshares,
A′ And their spears into pruning-hooks.
Nation shall not lift up sword against nation,
Neither shall they learn war any more.

O house of Jacob, 5
A′′ Come ye and let us walk in the light of Yahweh; 6
For thou hast forsaken thy people,
The house of Jacob.

Part II: 2:6b-22

For they are filled with sorcery from the east,
A And with soothsayers like the Philistines,
And they strike hands with the children of foreigners.

Their land also is full of silver and gold, 7
B Neither is there any end of their treasures;
Their land also is full of horses,
X Neither is there any end of their chariots.

Their land also is full of idols; 8
A′ They worship the work of their own hands,
That which their own fingers have made.

And the mean man is bowed down, 9
A′′ And the great man is brought low:
Therefore forgive them not.

Enter into the *rock*, 10
And hide thee in the *dust*,
A From before the *terror* of Yahweh,
And from the glory of his *majesty*,
When he ariseth *to shake* mightily the earth (LXX).

The lofty looks of man shall be *brought low*, 11
B And the haughtiness of men shall be *bowed down*,
And Yahweh alone shall be *exalted in that day*.

For Yahweh of hosts hath *a day*, 12
Upon all that is proud and haughty,
And upon all that is lifted up,
And it shall be brought low.
And upon all the cedars of Lebanon, that are high and lifted up, 13
Y C And upon all the oaks of Bashan,
And upon all the high mountains, 14
And upon all the hills that are lifted up,
And upon every lofty tower, 15
And upon every fortified wall,
And upon all the ships of Tarshish, 16
And upon all display of fine ships (LXX).

And the loftiness of man shall be *bowed down*, 17
B′ And the haughtiness of men shall be *brought low*,
And Yahweh alone shall be *exalted in that day*.
And the idols shall utterly pass away. 18

And men shall go into the caves of the *rocks*, 19
And into the holes of the *dust*,
A′ From before the *terror* of Yahweh,
And from the glory of his *majesty*,
When he ariseth *to shake* mightily the earth.

In that day a man shall cast away to the moles and to the bats, 20
His idols of silver and his idols of gold,
A Which he made for himself to worship,
To go into the rifts of the rocks, 21
And into the clefts of the crags,

X′

From before the *terror* of Yahweh,
B And from the glory of his *majesty*,
When he ariseth *to shake* mightily the earth.

Cease ye from man, 22
C In whose nostrils is breath,
For of what account is he?

Part III: 3:1-4:1

For, behold, the Lord, Yahweh of hosts, 1
Doth *take away* from Jerusalem and from Judah,
Stay and staff,
Every stay of bread, and every stay of water:
A The mighty man, and the man of war, 2
The judge, and the prophet,
And the diviner, and the elder, 3
The captain of fifty, and the man of rank,
And the counsellor, and the cunning charmer, and the skilful enchanter.

And *I will give* children to be their princes, 4
And babes shall rule over them.
And the people shall oppress one another, 5
X B Every man his fellow,
And every one by his neighbor.
The child shall behave himself proudly against the old man, 6
And the base against the honorable.

(saying,
When a man *shall take hold* of his brother in the house of his father,
Thou hast a mantle,
Be thou our ruler,
C And let this ruin be under thy hand.
In that day will he swear, saying, 7
I will not be a healer;
For in my house is neither bread nor clothing:
Ye shall not make me ruler of the people.

For Jerusalem is ruined, 8
A And Judah is fallen;
Because their tongue and their doings are against Yahweh,
To provoke the eyes of his glory.

Y

Their respecting of persons doth witness against them, 9
A′ And they declare their sin as Sodom,
They hide it not. Woe unto their soul!
For they have done evil unto themselves.

Happy the righteous! for well shall they fare, 10
A For they shall eat the fruit of their doings.
Woe unto the wicked! ill shall they fare, 11
For the work of his hands shall be done to him.

My *people!* children are their oppressors, 12
B And women rule over them.
My *people!* they that lead thee cause thee to err,
And destroy the way of thy paths.

Z

Yahweh standeth up to contend, 13
B′ And standeth to judge the *people.*
Yahweh will enter into judgment, 14
With the elder of his *people*, and the princes thereof:

It is ye that have eaten up the vineyard,
A′ The spoil of the poor are in your houses.
What mean ye that ye crush my people, 15
And grind the face of the poor?

Y′
It is the oracle of the Lord, God of hosts.
Yahweh said, Because the daughters of Zion are haughty, 16
And walk with outstretched necks,
And ogling with their eyes,
Walking and mincing as they go,
And jingling with their feet; (daughters of Zion, 17
Therefore the Lord will smite with a scab the crown of the head of the
And Yahweh will lay bare their secret parts.

X′

A
In that day the Lord *will take away* the beauty of 18
The anklets and the fillets and the crescents,
The pendants and the bracelets and the veils, 19
The headtires and the armlets and the sashes; 20
And the perfume-boxes and the amulets,
The rings and the nose-jewels; 21
The festival robes and the mantles and the shawls, 22
The girdles and the gauze robes* and the fine linen, 23
The turbans and the capes.

B
And it shall come to pass, that 24
Instead of sweet spices *there shall be* rottenness
And instead of a girdle, a rope,
And instead of curled hair, baldness,
And instead of a robe, a girding of sackcloth;
Branding instead of beauty. 25
Thy men shall fall by the sword,
And thy mighty in the war.
And her gates shall lament and mourn, 26
And she shall be desolate and sit upon the ground.

C
And seven women *shall take hold* of one man in that day, saying, 4:1
We will eat our own bread,
And wear our own apparel:
Only let us be called by thy name,
Take thou away our reproach.

*So the Jewish Version, J. M. P. Smith has "lace gowns."

Part IV: 4:2-6

A′′
In that day will the growth of Yahweh 2
Be fair and glorious,
And the fruit of the land
Will be excellent and comely for them that are escaped of Israel.

A
And it shall come to pass that he that is left in *Zion*, 3
And he that remaineth in *Jerusalem*, shall be called holy,
Even every one that is written unto life in *Jerusalem;*
When the Lord shall have washed away the filth of the daughters of *Zion*, 4
And shall have purged the blood of *Jerusalem* from the midst thereof,

B
By the spirit of judgment,
And by the spirit of destruction.

A′
And Yahweh will create over every dwelling-place of mount Zion, 5
And over her assemblies,
A cloud and a smoke by day,
And the shining of a flaming fire by night:
For over all the glory shall be a canopy.
And there shall be a pavilion for a shade in the day-time from the heat,
And for a refuge and for a covert from storm and from rain.

These chapters contain four great panels depicting Jerusalem. In Part I and Part IV the ideal Jerusalem of the prophet's vision is portrayed. Between these two extremes two more panels, Part II and Part III, are placed, setting forth the real Jerusalem as the prophet saw it in his own day, the victim of idolatry and arrogance, on the one hand, and of oppression and vanity, on the other. The lights are very bright and the shadows very dark in these prophetic paintings. The key to the whole message will be found in the contrast between the day in which Isaiah lived (Parts II and III) and "that day," the day of Yahweh, that was to bring upon Israel both punishment and purification, thus effecting the final realization of the ideal (Parts I and IV). Though our task compels us to discuss the form rather than the content of these chapters, it will be found that a strict attention to the form will also aid us in the analysis of the content.

In Part I (2:1-6a) there would be an almost perfect cluster of parallelisms, were it not for A, which has only one couplet (eliminating the introductory line, "And it shall come to pass," etc.), whereas A′ has two well-balanced couplets. The contents of these two strophes are parallel, because the exaltation of Mount Zion over the other hills is merely a poetic way of expressing the mastery of Yahweh over the nations, the beneficent results of which are set forth in A′. In B the means of establishing this supremacy over the nations are indicated. It is not warfare and might but the Law of Yahweh which will subdue the nations. The chiastic structure is composed of five couplets, of which the central emphasizes Yahweh's "ways" and his "paths." The two couplets enclosing the central one indicate the locality from which the divine influence proceeds, and the two extreme couplets describe the scope of Yahweh's power. It may interest the reader to notice that the terms "nations" and "peoples" occur in the reverse order in Micah 4:1, 2 and vs. 3. Observance of the chiastic structure will show that the punctuation in our English versions is incorrect in both places, since the period must come after "the hills." In A″, which is chiastic and is the connecting link which unites Part I to Part II, we have in the central lines the exhortation, "Let us walk in the light of Yahweh"; this brings us back to the words of the nations, "We will walk in his paths" (B). If the nations are ever to walk in accordance with the divine will, Israel must be first to do so. The following line contrasts this happy condition with the deplorable state of a forsaken people, Israel's present state; thus we are introduced to the real Jerusalem as Isaiah saw it in his day. For the present we shall defer the treatment of Part II and instead discuss the structure of Part IV.

Part IV (4:2-6) opens with a description of the fertility of Palestine "in that day"—the day when Yahweh will have perfected the redemption of his people. The delightful agricultural scene in A″ is introduced abruptly, there being no connection with the preceding or following verses. Though there may be no connection in the immediate context, there is, nevertheless, a parallel idea in Part I, where there was another reminder of agricultural pursuits in the references to the "plow-shares" and the "pruning-hooks." In 2:5, 6 there are references to Jacob and to Yahweh, and in 4:2, to Yahweh and Israel. In the main body of Part IV we discover further references to Zion and Jerusalem (cf. AA′), but the inhabitants are not the nations of the former passage, but the remnant of Israel purified from its sins. Our justification for regarding A′ as parallel to A is that both deal with the same locality, one describing the purity and the other the security of Israel in Zion. The means by which the cleansing has been effected is here, as in Part I, placed in the centre (B). But since Israel did not readily take to instruction, its lessons were learned by judgment and destruction. In Parts I and IV, then, the future glory of Mount Zion is described. There are the following differences: in one the participants are the nations and in the other, Israel; in one the means of realizing the ideal is instruction, in the other, destruction; in one we see a nation forsaken, in the other a nation favored by God. Yet, in both there are peace and security, obtained by the abolition of warfare and by divine protection. Evidently the prophet is recalling the pillar of fire and the cloud of the desert wanderings (4:5). Within this ideal framework we now have the indictment of the nation.

Part II (2:6b-22) contains a strong and well-arranged indictment of the two national sins, *idolatry* and *arrogance*. The former is traced to Israel's foreign affiliations, and the latter to the abundance of her prosperity. In X we find that the idolatry is described in A′ and its accompanying features, sorcery and soothsaying, in A. The central strophe B describes the wealth, and the resulting trust in human means of obtaining security. Trust in handmade idols and forgetfulness of Yahweh can only lead to degradation (A″). The two verbs "bowed down" and "brought low" are significant, since they are woven into the following discourse in a manner which indicates that the writer had in mind a well-defined pattern (cf. Y, 2:11, 17). In X′, which is the counterpart of X, idolatry is discussed once more, but this time to show its utter failure and its rejection by Israel. Once more the fact that idols are made by hand is emphasized, and again the human element is brought in to show its weakness (C). This additional statement, if judged only by the immediate context, may be regarded as a gloss (Skinner), but since the structure as a whole shows a similar section in 2:9, it must be treated as part of the text. By the same judgment the three lines in B appear dubious, for they find no parallel in X. The presence of the three lines in X′B, where they do not belong, may be easily accounted for by observing that the words "rocks" and "crags" occur in the two preceding lines. The similarity of the lines in vs. 21a to vs. 10a and, to an even greater extent, to vs. 19a may have led a copyist to insert the three lines after X′A, a section which is complete without them. Sections X and X′ are parallel; the idolatry, the silver and the gold, the emphasis on idols as being handmade, and the futility of such human effort are common to both sections.

Y is the longest and most striking of the three sections. In A and A′ we have the most minute symmetry, line for line and word for word. The last line of A in our arrangement is added from A′, since it is clear that the Septuagint translators in A also translated from a text that contained this line. In BB′ the same conditions exist, except that no parallel is found in B for the last line of B′. It is tempting to add this line to B, especially since such an arrangement would be in accordance with the law of distribution at the extremes and at the centre. Since idolatry is the subject of X and X′ it is fitting that there should be some mention of it also in Y. There is also a possibility that A and B were written as they now stand in our Masoretic text and that A′ and B′ were each given an extra line by the original writer by way of emphasis. Yet it would seem that the last line of B′ interrupts the context and looks like a gloss, and for this reason the former suggestion seems preferable. In B and B′ the arrogance of Israel is described as expressing itself in "lofty looks" (B), or "loftiness" (B′), and in "haughtiness," which must be "brought low" and "bowed down." These verbs were found together also in 2:9, 11. When they recur in vs. 17 their order is inverted as may also be seen in some psalms. This is another way of applying the chiastic principle. Two lines in a quatrain are often inverted in the corresponding quatrain without arranging all the four lines in a chiastic fashion.

However, when the first half of these lines ("loftiness," "haughtiness") retains the same order in the parallel section, while the second half inverts the order of the verb, as in this case, such an instance is rare. The present writer does not recall any other instance of such an arrangement, except in the Greek text of Matt. 7:16-20, in which the qualities of the respective *trees* follow the order, good-corrupt-good-corrupt, while the qualities of the *fruit* follow the order, good-evil-evil-good.[1]

The central panel of Y is C, consisting of twelve lines which set forth the humiliation of man and all his works. It should be observed that the two ideas, the humiliation of man, and the day of Yahweh, are expressed in B and B′. These two ideas recur in C, where the first four lines set forth in general terms what will take place "in that day," while the next eight lines form four couplets which are more specific in their description of the coming humiliation of man. The last of these lines has been emended with the aid of LXX, which makes better sense than MT. In the third line LXX has two adjectives which make this line more nearly similar to the preceding line. In the fifth line the words, "that are high and lifted up," seem awkward, since they come at the end of the line and, under the present condition of the text, leave the "cedars" and the "oaks" without specific descriptive

[1] *Anglican Theological Review*, Vol. XIII, No. 1 (Jan., 1931), p. 30.

adjectives. The next couplet reveals a distribution of "high" and "lifted up," one of these being found with each member of the couplet. One naturally looks for some similar distribution of these adjectives with the "cedars" and the "oaks."

In Part II we read an indictment against the *idolatry* and the *arrogance* of the nation. In Part III (3:1-4:1) we have an amazingly thoroughgoing indictment of *oppression* and *vanity*. The sections X and X′ are alternating in form; in each the order seems to be: What God will *take away* from Israel (A and A), what he will *substitute* for it (B and B), and finally, what the *result* will be (C and C). These three steps in the discourse are clearly marked, and the connection should not be dismissed as being fanciful.[2]

In comparing the separate sections of X and X′ we observe that they must have been constructed with reference to one another. In X the subject is the *leaders* of the nation, while in X′ their *women* are described. This twofold feature, the leaders and their women, recurs also in the central section Z, where in B the "oppressors" and the "women" are named side by side. The position of these ideas in the structure is in accordance with the law of distribution at the extremes and at the centre to which we have referred on several occasions. Taking up now the sections dealing with the rulers and the women for the sake of comparison, we observe a more detailed symmetry. In XA there is an enumeration of the various types of persons who were included among the leaders of the nation. This enumeration is found in the last five lines of A. The terms occur in pairs, except in the last line, where we have a triplet. All these Yahweh will take away. Turning to X′A, we discover there also something that Yahweh will *take away* from the women. The enumeration of these articles is also perfectly symmetrical. First, there are three triplets; then in the centre, two pairs; after that the triplets are resumed to the end.

[2] J. Skinner, in *The Book of the Prophet Isaiah* (Vol. I, p. 31), who, in comparing 3:6 with 4:1, says in his quotation from Weir and Cheyne, "A companion picture to iii.6—the male population are in search of a ruler; the women in search of a husband—an interesting but misleading fancy! The poem has nothing to do with the scene of anarchy which is the burden of iii.1-12." The alternating form, quite to the contrary, clearly shows that the latter part has very much to do with the former, its literary counterpart.

In the last line, where we would expect a triplet, we have a pair. We need not assume textual corruption, since it is possible that the same love of variation which made the writer conclude with a triplet in XA, which was entirely at variance with the preceding order, could have made him finish with *a pair* in X′A. The uncertainty of the translation of some of the terms included in the dress of the women makes it less desirable to pursue further the analysis of the symmetry of this section. In general it may be said, that the first three lines deal with articles of adornment, whereas the last three lines enumerate articles of the dress.

The general trend of XB is to show what the Lord will *substitute* for what he has taken away. In the first and the last couplet there is parallelism between "babes"* and "the child" and between "princes" and "the honorable." The three intervening lines describe the oppression that will follow the impending anarchy. The substitutes for the established order which was taken away are here described as something the Lord has given the nation. In X′B we find a similar enumeration of substitutes for the articles of finery and dress which were taken away by the Lord. The first half of the list is a series of striking contrasts, suddenly interrupted by a line of different content, namely, "Branding instead of beauty." After this line the description is resumed with a different emphasis altogether, for now the loss is not things, but *men*, and the women's mourning over the slain is described in the last couplet. The central line, which substitutes branding for beauty, is different in content from the four preceding, in which occurs a contrast of more impersonal items. It is significant that this variation should occur at the centre, and that the second half should be made up of two *couplets*. This is not true of the first half. These details are not accidental but show the care with which the passage was written and the many ways in which the writer was able to introduce variation.

The contrast between XC and X′C need not be doubted. The man who "shall take hold" of his brother in order to persuade him to be ruler, and the seven women who "shall take hold" of the one man in order to make him their husband are intended to em-

* Or "caprice," but cf. Isa. 66:4.

phasize *the absence of men* in the state. The references to food and clothing in both sections appear a bit ridiculous, and the unwillingness on the part of the man in either case is not without humor. The invitation, "Let this *ruin* be under your hand," is a bit of sardonic humor which is hard to surpass; this is also true of the implication that a man who is the possessor of a mantle is qualified to be a ruler! Nothing could better set forth the thoroughness of the impending judgment than these descriptions of the fate of the rulers and their women. What the Lord takes away, what he substitutes, and what the final result will be for the leaders and their women—these considerations summarize the content of X and X′.

The same general subject, namely, the leaders and their women, is pursued in Y and Y′, except that it is approached from another angle. While in X and X′ their judgment was described, in Y and Y′ the causes of their judgment are set forth. The leaders were given to words and deeds which were contrary to the will of Yahweh (YA) and in the administration of justice they "respected persons" (A′). In all this they were as brazenly boastful "as Sodom." A similar theme is pursued in Y′. In this section the presence of the divine names Adonai and Yahweh determines the arrangement of the first and the last couplets. There is a contrast between the pride of the daughters of Zion, on the one hand, and their future humiliation, on the other. Their vanity is rather satirically described in the four central lines. Here also we are dealing with *the cause* of the judgment (cf. "Because," etc. in vs. 8 and vs. 16). The two elements, then, that make for social injustice in Israel are the violence of the men and the vanity of the women (YY′).

The central section of this long passage is Z, which is made up of four quatrains that are chiastic with reference to one another. The subject of A is "the righteous" and "the wicked" and their respective ends, whereas in A′ the same parties are again presented. The wicked are here the oppressors; they despoil the righteous, and grind the face of the poor. The subject of oppression is clearly expressed also in XB above, and we may assume that it is implied in the discussion of the vanity of the women in

X′ below, somewhat after the fashion of Amos 4:1. In Z both in A and A′ "eating" is mentioned. The unrighteous men who have "eaten up the vineyard" (A′) shall also "eat the fruit of their doings" (A). We should not consider such far-flung contexts fanciful, for they are a part of the literary structure. In the two central quatrains of Z we have in B the misdeeds of the rulers and their women mentioned, and in B′ Yahweh's judgment over them. Thus this order reverses the order of A and A′, since there we have first the judgment of the wicked, and of the righteous (A), and lastly the deeds that bring upon the wicked the judgment (A′). It should be noticed that the term for "people" is symmetrically distributed on alternate lines in the two central quatrains. Nor should it surprise us that we meet with the term "paths" to designate a life of rectitude, since this is the term employed at the very beginning of this long structure (cf. 2:3). A life in conformity with the divine will is to "walk in his paths," and, by way of contrast, a life of disobedience is to "destroy the way of thy paths." The law of distribution at the extremes and at the centre makes the writer repeat in the centre such references to conformity to the Law with which his discussion began. It is also interesting to observe how in A′ we meet with the designation of the nation as "the vineyard," here the object both of the designs of unscrupulous spoilers and of the divine compassion. In chapter five this idea is wrought into a beautiful song of the vineyard, in which the moral failure of the people itself is set forth and condemned, a song which displays the same chiastic arrangement as the chapters preceding it.

Let us summarize the total impressions of these chapters. The prophet paints a picture of an exalted nation, which ministers to the nations of the world, giving them the knowledge of truth and the ideals of living. This is the first panel of the picture. The nation as a whole will not share in this glorious future, but only those "that remain in Jerusalem," those "that are written unto life in Jerusalem." They will be purified by judgment and destruction and will at last receive divine protection. This is the substance of the fourth panel. We then have the indictment of the nation presented in two panels. The national sins are idolatry and arrogance born of foreign affiliation and national prosperity, and against these the judgment will surely come. "The Lord alone will be high on that day" and the people shall have learned not to trust "in man." This is what the second panel tells us.

Not only idolatry and arrogance, but also violence and vanity are national sins. These sins are distributed among the rulers and their women, who are made conspicuous in the treatment of the subject by the position assigned to these persons in the literary structure. They are all to be judged by Yahweh, who "standeth up to contend," judging not only them but "the people." We have seen the figurative designation of the divine will as "his paths" and that this simile occurred at the beginning and at the centre (cf. Part III, ZB). We should also notice that the idea of judgment which occurs in the same position (cf. B′) is treated in the concluding Part IV, B. An example of the law of distribution at the extremes and in the centre is obvious in an arrangement which has the following features: (1) an emphasis upon the Law of Yahweh and the instruction of the nations therein in the one panel and a reference to the *judgment* based upon this Law in the other panel; (2) a combination of both of these features in the two central quatrains (Part III, ZBB′) of that panel which most fully presents the details of the judgment of the nation. When rightly considered, these facts constitute strong evidence of the literary unity of the whole passage, 2:1-4:6. They also ought to contribute something toward the solution of the problem of the strophic arrangement of these chapters concerning which there is no consensus of opinion among commentators.[3] We now turn to one of the best-known passages in Isaiah.

The Song of the Vineyard, Isaiah 5:1-7

Let me sing a song of my Beloved, 1
A My love-song of his vineyard.
My Beloved had a vineyard,
On a fertile hill-top.

And he trenched it, 2
And cleared it of stones,
B And planted it with choice vines;
He built a watch-tower in the midst of it,
And hewed out a winevat.

[3] Skinner, *op. cit.*, pp. 18, 19.

And he looked for it to yield grapes, 3
C But it yielded wild grapes.
Now, O citizens of Jerusalem,
And men of Judah,

D Judge, I pray, between me
And my vineyard.

What more could have been done for my vineyard, 4
C′ Than that which I have done for it?
Why, then, when I looked for it to yield grapes,
Did it yield wild grapes?

D′ So now, I pray, let me tell you, 5
What I will do to my vineyard:

I will remove its hedge, and it shall be ravaged;
I will break down its wall, and it shall be trampled under foot;
B′ I will make it a waste, unpruned and unhoed. 6
It shall go up in briers and thorns;
And the clouds will I command that they rain no rain upon it.

For the vineyard of Yahweh of hosts 7
A′ Is the house of Israel;
And the men of Judah
Are the plant of his delight.

C′′ And he looked for justice,
But, behold, bloodshed;
For righteousness,
But, behold, a cry.

At an earlier stage the figure of the vineyard has been introduced by the prophet (3:14), but this figurative designation of Israel is now developed into an artistic song of great beauty. The literary merits of this poem and the romantic circumstances of its presentation during the grape harvest have been dwelt on by the commentators and need not further detain us. Our interest centers in the chiastic structure of the poem. Although the poem has a definite strophic structure, it is evident that any attempt to arrange its contents in strophes of an equal number of lines and of equal length must be given up. If, on the other hand, the order of ideas is used as the organizing principle, we shall obtain more satisfactory results. In A the Beloved and his vineyard are introduced without any explanation, and not until the singer is about to take leave of his audience are we told that we are dealing with Yahweh and his people (cf. A′). In B we are informed with utmost brevity of the constructive work of Yahweh for his vineyard in expectation of good results, while B′ more fully describes his destructive work with the vineyard when his expectations have not been fulfilled. These two strophes stand in sharp antithesis to one another. They are also well balanced in content and structure. Only in the *central* lines of each strophe do we find the activities that directly relate to the cultivation of the vine itself: planting, pruning, and hoeing. The reference to the watch-tower in the last couplet of B and the hedge and wall in first couplet of B′ have this in common that they are of a protective nature. The digging of trenches and removal of stones that encumber the field are balanced by the briers and thorns that also are a hindrance to growth and by the rains that should be taken care of by the trenches. Thus there is balance between the first couplet of B and the last of B′. In the first couplet of C and the last of C′ the parallels of the grapes and the wild grapes need no comment. The parallelism between the last couplet of C and the first of C′ is also assured, though it is not fully revealed until the identification of the vineyard and the nation is finally made in A′. The parallelism of the two couplets D and D′ is indicated by the term "I pray" and by their general content; in one the question is raised and in the other the answer is introduced. The analysis of the ideas of the poem indicates that the strophic scheme calls for four strophes that are chiastic (ABB′A′), inclosing four strophes that are alternating (CDC′D′).

The interest is well sustained to the end of the poem. For all that the audience knew the singer is rendering a song of an ordinary vineyard. There is not in the whole song one word of a religious or ethical nature, until the key to the song is placed in the hands of the audience in A′. Even then the whole point is not revealed, for the severe censures of the prophet's message are contained only in the closing words of the song. Then for the first time are we told the meaning of the grapes and the wild grapes (C″).[4] One may well imagine the mingled feelings of the audience in a holiday mood, when it is called upon to exercise some self-examination. The method used to keep the audience uninformed until the end of the poem is similar to that of the writer of the Book of Revelation. After depicting in symbolic

[4] Skinner, *op. cit.*, Vol. I, p. 37.

language the introductory vision of the Lord of the church the key to the symbolism is given the reader in the closing sentences of the passage (cf. Rev. 1:9-19 and vs. 20).

The Burden of Damascus and North Israel
Isaiah, Chapter 17:1-14

Part X: vss. 1-3

Behold, Damascus is taken away from being a city, 1
A And it shall be a ruinous heap
The cities of Aroer are forsaken, 2
They shall be for flocks.

X B And they shall lie down,
And none shall make them afraid.

And the fortress shall cease from Ephraim, 3
A′ And the kingdom from Damascus;
And the remnant of Syria
Shall be as the glory of the children of Israel, saith Yahweh of hosts.

Part Y: vss. 4-11

A And it shall come to pass in *that day*, 4

B That the glory of Jacob shall be made thin,
And the fatness of his flesh shall wax lean.

And it shall be as when the harvestman gathereth the standing corn, 5
C And his arm reapeth the ears;
Yea, it shall be as when one gleaneth ears in the valley of Rephaim,
There shall be left therein gleanings: 6

As at the olive-beating (there are left)
D Two or three berries high up at the *top*,
Four or five in the fruit-tree's branches,
Saith Yahweh, the God of Israel.

In *that day* 7
Shall a man regard his Maker,
And his eyes shall look to the Holy One of Israel.
And he shall not regard the altars, 8
The work
Y E Of his hands;
What his fingers
Have wrought
Shall he not look to,
Either the Asherim,
Or the Hammanim,
In *that day*. 9

(mountain *top*,
His fortified cities shall be like the ruins in the woods and the
D′ Which were cleared before the sons of Israel,
And there shall arise a waste place.

B′ For thou hast forgotten the God of thy salvation, 10
And thou hast not been mindful of the Rock of thy stronghold.

Therefore didst thou plant plants of pleasantness,
C′ And didst set it with slips of a stranger;
In the day of thy planting thou didst make it to grow, 11
And in the morning thou didst make thy seed to blossom—

A′ A heap of boughs in *the day* of grief and of desperate pain.

Part X′: vss. 12-14

Ah, the uproar of many peoples, 12
A That roar like the roaring of the seas;
And the rushing of the nations,
That rush like the rushing of mighty waters!

B The nations shall rush, 13
Like the rushing of many waters.

X′ C But he shall rebuke them.
And they shall flee afar off.

B′ And they shall be chased as the chaff of the mountains before the wind,
And like the whirling dust before the storm.

At eventide behold terror! 14
A′ And before the morning they are not.
This is the portion of them that spoil us,
And the lot of them that rob us.

We have already seen that it is necessary at times to seek a more remote connection when there is none to be found in the immediate context. In the prophecy in Isaiah's seventeenth chapter many commentators regard vss. 12-14 either as part of the following chapter or as an independent oracle of uncertain date. The reason for these divergent views is that these verses seem entirely unrelated to vss. 4-11. The literary connection, however, is to be sought in vss. 1-3, in which we have the counterpart to vss. 12-14. Part X (vss. 1-3) opens with a prophecy of destruction directed against Syria and North Israel, which in Isaiah's days were in alliance (cf. Isa. 7:1 ff.). In X the first quatrain is made up of two couplets setting forth the utter desolation of the cities of Syria; this will result in the turning of the sites of the cities into pastures (vs. 2). There will not be sufficient strength and man power left to shoo the cattle off the premises (B). A fate similar to that which has befallen Syria awaits Ephraim, according to the last quatrain which is chiastic in form (A′).

As a striking contrast to the picture of utter helplessness of the two allies against their foreign foe, which in this case must be Assyria, we have another sketch in X′ of an entirely different situation. In this description neither the coming enemy nor the object of the divine protection is explicitly mentioned, but we have reason to believe that the enemy is none other than Assyria, which is aptly depicted in the "rushing of the nations." The latter must be Zion in the inviolability of which the prophet trusted. The contrast that makes X′ such a fitting antithetic counterpart to X may be briefly summarized as follows: Syria and North Israel were to become so helpless that not even the herds could be driven off the sites of their chief cities, while Zion's divine protector would even put Assyria herself to flight. It is to be noticed that the ideas of weakness (vs. 2b) and of strength (vs. 13b), which are the gist of these two sections, are in the centre of each, as were the lines indicating the *means* by which the nations were to be subdued (Isa. 2:2-6a, central couplet in B) and by which Israel was to be purified (Isa. 4:2-6, B). It is significant that the rushing in of the enemy tide proceeds in the description in X′ until the centre is reached (C) after which the rush is in the opposite direction. This is another of the many instances in which the centre of a system of lines proves to be the turning point. The whole section is exceedingly well balanced, for in B the rush is compared to that of water coming by its own power, while in B′ the flight is likened to that of chaff and dust driven by the wind. The majestic and seemingly irresistible advance of the enemy is depicted in A, but the brief space of his dominion and utter defeat is described in A′. It is difficult to conceive of an artist painting with swifter and bolder strokes two scenes of disaster and of rescue. In these features we rest our contention that there is a literary unity in the two extreme parts of the chapter (XX′).

The middle section Y (vss. 4-11) is both alternating (BCB′C′) and chiastic (ADED′A′) in form. In content it is not less interesting, for it describes the apostasy (B′C′) of Jacob and his punishment (BC). That Israel had forgotten God is stated in one couplet (B′) as an explanation of why the nation should wax lean (B). The figure of a consuming sickness is supplanted by another figure, that of a harvest of corn; this figure pictures the doctrine of a remnant so familiar to readers of Isaiah (C). The doctrine of the remnant is then further elaborated by an entirely new figure, that of the olive harvest (D). It is probably best to separate entirely the figures of the grain harvest from that of the ingathering of olives, by repeating the verb in the first line of D. Once we have accustomed ourselves to the far-flung context of Isaiah, we see how well D′ parallels D. In D the punishment of the nation is described in terms of an olive harvest which leaves a few berries near the top of the trees; in D′ the harvest of the invading enemy is likened to that of Israel centuries earlier, which left only ruins in the woods and at the top of the mountains. Of such ruins there were doubtless still traces in Isaiah's times. We find an unexpected corroboration of our analysis in the Hebrew word אָמִיר. "The Hebrew word," says Skinner, "does not occur again except in vs. 9, where the text is almost certainly wrong." Commenting on vs. 9 he continues, "'Mountain top' is the word rendered 'uppermost bough' in vs. 6 (R. V.). But the LXX gives the clue to the true text, which reads of the Amorite and the Hivvite."[5] The fact that the same word occurring only twice is nevertheless found in parallel positions is strong evidence that we have the original reading.[6] The boldness of comparing the remnant to a few olives left over from the harvest in the top of a tree and to a few ruins left over from the conquest at the top of the hills is characteristic of the prophet. The comprehensiveness of his grasp of Israel's history which enables him to compare the early occupation by Israel with the latter by Assyria, surprises no one who is at all familiar with his versatility. Just as the description of Jacob's punishment moves on from B to C with only a change of figure, so also the account of his apostasy is carried over from B′ to C′. His forgetfulness of God resulted in idolatrous practices, the planting of plants which grow and bloom in honor of strange gods—features which are reminiscent of the grain harvest of the parallel section C.

There remains to be examined the central section E, which is

[5] *Op. cit.*, Vol. I, pp. 143, 144.
[6] F. Delitzsch, *The Prophecies of Isaiah* (T. & T. Clark's ed.), Vol. I, p. 344.

both unique in structure and difficult of elucidation because its position does not seem to fit the context. Again we quote from Skinner:

These verses do not point to a conversion of the few surviving Ephraimites. They rather describe the impression produced by the vindication of Jehovah's righteousness on mankind at large. Both in thought and in structure (!), they interrupt the continuity of the oracle, and may have been inserted later (perhaps by the prophet himself). When they are removed we have three equal strophes, the first two ending with a "saith Jehovah" and the last two beginning with "in that day."[7]

Why the Ephraimites should be excluded from conversion does not appear, for the conception is not strange to Isaiah (cf. 11:12, 13). The inclusion of the Ephraimites certainly does not exclude the possibility that the prophetic horizon is expanded so as to include "mankind at large." The observation that these verses "interrupt the continuity of the oracle" is true only as long as the chiastic nature of the structure is disregarded. For the passage is a splendid illustration of the principle of shifting from one subject to another at the centre, with the resumption of the first subject after the centre is passed—a literary principle of which we have had several examples in the preceding pages. What could be more appropriate in a passage that deals with sin and its punishment than to have a central panel dealing with rejection of the idolatry that brought disaster and return to the God who had been forgotten? In its structure this passage is no more a problem than Isa. 28:15-18, in which the extremes present the schemes of the rulers of Israel in order to obtain national security and their attendant failure, while the centre presents the security provided by Yahweh himself. In neither case will it be necessary to entertain a theory of later redaction, whether by the prophet himself or some one else, for these passages are well-knit literary units. Skinner's objections reveal the underlying causes of much of the suspicion which leads to the rejection of passages, namely, certain accepted

[7] *Op. cit.*, Vol. I, p. 143. The word *hammanim* in vs. 8 can no longer be rendered "sun-images," as in A. R. V. Lev. 26:30; 2 Chron. 14:5; 34:4, 7; Isa. 17:8; 27:9; Ezek. 6:4, 6, since Ingholt's discovery at Palmyra of an altar of incense bearing the inscription *hamman*. The two insignia of the false religion in vs. 8 balance the two names of the true God found in vs. 7, cf. *JPOS* 9, 53 and W. F. Albright, *The Archaeology of Palestine and the Bible*, p. 108.

arbitrary principles in regard to the Hebrew strophe. As long as the strophe is to be determined by assuming that each line is of equal length and each strophe contains an equal number of lines, the result cannot be otherwise than destructive to the text. When we no longer consider the length and number of lines as essential elements in the Hebrew strophe but make *the order of the ideas*, whether alternating or chiastic, the determining factor, then we obtain a principle which is both inclusive and sufficiently flexible to fit the facts in the Hebrew text. The reader who has interested himself in recent discussions on the building of the strophe in Hebrew poetry in general and in the prophets in particular will have discovered for himself what our method of analysis does in this sphere. In part Y we have single lines (AA′), couplets (BB′), triplets (DD′), and quatrains (CC′), not to speak of the central chiastic panel which defies all ordinary classification. Radical as our departure may appear when compared with modern attempts to reduce the writings of the prophets to a system of strophes, it yields results. In our present passage the analysis brings out the fact that there has been a symmetrical disposition of the term *in that day* and of the rare Hebrew word translated *top*. Only in the last line (A′) is the term changed to *in the day*, but it is clear that we are here, as in the other passages, dealing with the day of Yahweh. The words, "in the day of thy planting" (C′), are obviously not in the same class, but neither are they part of the symmetrical scheme of distribution. How necessary it was to the writer to end the passage with a reference to the day of Yahweh may be seen from the fact that the last line has no grammatical connection with the preceding, but is loosely added to complete the structure.

The central system of lines (E) contrasts in two couplets the return to the true God and the rejection of the false idols. "His Maker" and "Holy One of Israel" are parallel in one couplet, and so are the "Asherim" and the "Hammanim" in the other. While the first of the two satisfies our expectations of a *parallelismus membrorum*, the second does not. Nevertheless a glance at the structure should convince us that the two latter terms ought also to constitute a couplet and that they are intended to balance the first couplet. In other words, the order of the ideas, not length of lines, is essential. The intervening six members of the central chiasmus are of such nature that they bear out this principle.

No treatment of this chapter would be complete without some reference to what George Adam Smith has called "the phonetics of the passage" (vss. 12-14):

> The general impression is that of a stormy ocean booming in to the shore and then crashing itself out into one long hiss of spray and foam upon its barriers. The details are noteworthy. In vs. 12 we have thirteen heavy M-sounds, besides two heavy B's to five N's, five H's and four sibilants. But in vs. 13 the sibilants predominate; and before the sharp rebuke of the Lord the great, booming sound of vs. 12 scatters out into a long *yish-sha ʿoon.* The occasional use of a prolonged vowel amid so many hurrying consonants produces exactly the effect now of the lift of a storm swell out at sea and now of the pause of a great wave before it crashes on the shore.[8]

To the student of chiasmus it is an interesting fact that the last booming of the angry waves are heard with the close of the *first half* of the chiastic system, since the rebuke and its effect are placed in the centre of the system. The stylistic effect will not be changed, if we translate with Skinner, "He shall rebuke it (the tumult)" and translate the verbs that follow "as presents and in the singular number." It must always remain an unsolved problem whether these structures were represented graphically in the original manuscripts, but whatever position we take, one thing is certain, namely, that many of these symmetries are of such nature that they may be detected by the ear.

In the Book of Amos there are several passages of great interest which will now be briefly discussed. In Amos 2:14-16 Harper[9] points out certain difficulties in the passage which indicate a defective text. This is also clearly revealed by the chiasmus. When, however, the aid of the Septuagint[10] is enlisted at this point, we obtain a perfect chiasmus:

[8] *The Book of Isaiah,* Vol. I, p. 282.

[9] *Critical and Exegetical Commentary on Amos and Hosea* (I. C. C.), pp. 59-63.

[10] *Journal of Religion,* Vol. X (1930), p. 92 prints the Greek text. αὐτοῦ probably should end the seventh line, as in the second.

And flight shall perish from the runner,
And the strong shall not hold fast his strength,
And the warrior shall not save his life,
And the archer shall not withstand,
And he that is swift of foot shall in no wise escape,
And the horseman shall not save his life,
And the strong shall not find confidence in his power,
(And) the naked shall flee in that day, saith the Lord.

The Greek text of this passage yields a perfect chiasmus of great rhythmic force and beauty. When the Greek is arranged after this pattern, we discover an unusual array of *epiphora,* all the parallel lines in the structure ending in either the same or a similar sound. This strange situation can only imply that the Greek translators were also guided by an aesthetic interest in their rendering of the passage. They were reproducing the form of the passage as well as its content. This discovery is interesting, for when such endings are discovered in the New Testament, they are usually ascribed to a Greek rhetorical influence. Much of this may merely be the influence of the Septuagint. It also raises the important question of how far in other passages such forms in the Hebrew may have influenced the Greek translation. Finally, we may learn from such a passage how easily the Hebrew form may be carried over into a Greek translation. A recognition of this factor is of some importance, particularly to those who hold, with von Wilamovitz-Moellendorff, that Paul read the Old Testament only in Greek.

Another passage with a pronounced chiastic pattern, achieved by an artistic arrangement of couplets, is Amos 9:1-4.

And I saw Yahweh standing by the altar, 1
And he said,

A Smite the capitals, that the thresholds may shake;
And break them in pieces on the head of all of them.

B And the last of them with the *sword* I will *slay;*

C There shall not one of them *flee away,*
And there shall not one of them escape.

D Though they dig into *Sheol,* 2
Thence shall my hand take them.

E And though they climb up to *heaven,*
Thence will I bring them down.

E′ And though they hide themselves in the top of *Carmel*, 3
Thence I will search and take them out;

D′ And though they hide from my sight in the bottom of the *sea*,
Thence will I command the serpent, and it shall bite them.

C′ And though they *go into captivity* before their enemies, 4
* *

B′ Thence will I command the *sword*, and it shall *slay* them

A′ And I will set mine eyes upon them for evil,
And not for good.

In AA′ a general statement is made of the impending destruction of the nation; this constitutes the formal introduction and conclusion to the system. The statement is amplified in the intervening couplets by showing the futility of different means of escape. Whether the flight is downwards (DD′) or upwards (EE′) the avenger, who is none other than Yahweh, will find them. The spirit of this passage is quite similar to that in 2:14-16. There is only one slight irregularity in C′, where we have only a single line to balance the couplet in C. As far as the construction is concerned, B′ could very well be the missing second line in C′; but due to the presence in B′ of the words "sword" and "slay," which are also found in B, it seems best to treat this line as parallel to B. In couplet C there is a twofold emphasis on the futility of escape. In C′ the words "go into captivity" indicate a similar trend of thought, which only needs to be repeated in some form in the second line to make the couplet perfect, say,

And though they go into captivity before their enemies,
(And though they hide in distant lands from their oppressors).

This line is offered only as a suggestion. Were it not for the chiastic form of the passage one would never have detected the need of another line in C′. On the other hand, it would be possible that B and C are intended to be together as three lines and that they are to be balanced by the two lines C′B′. Although this would be a variation from the strict regularity of the rest of the passage, three lines might well be the counterpart of two in such a system.

In Amos also we find that chiastic patterns have been applied to the disposition of material in longer sections. A notable instance meets us at the beginning of the book in the arrangement of the prophecies against Israel's neighbors (1:3-2:15).[11] Seven of these prophecies lead up to the one dealing with Israel, and all of the eight are constructed after the same pattern with regular refrains recurring in each. It is obvious, when we consider the geographical location of these eight nations, that a certain order has determined their selection. The first four form a cross, after which the prophet, facing the east, enumerates the remaining four clockwise until he reaches the prophecy addressed to Israel. A simple diagram will make this clear at once. The numbers before each name indicate the order of the prophecies in the text.

3. Tyre, 1:9.	1. Damascus, 1:3.
8. Israel, 2:6.	5. Ammon, 1:13.
7. Judah, 2:4.	6. Moab, 2:1.
2. Gaza, 1:6.	4. Edom, 1:11.

This geographical arrangement, with four nations on either side of the Jordan represented, proceeds from northeast to southwest and from northwest to southeast, thus making a perfect *chi*. There are many other examples of such chiastic patterns in the prophets, but those already analyzed are fairly representative of both the briefer and the more extensive arrangements. Joshua, Judges, Samuel and Kings (included among the former prophets in the Hebrew canon) offer examples of precisely the same patterns, extending over longer sections—a phenomenon already discussed in the Pentateuch.

The tenth chapter of the First Book of Samuel gives us the beginning of what appears to be a fine example of chiastic order in a narrative section (cf. I Sam. 10:1-16). Samuel informs Saul of what is to happen to him that day. He is to meet first two men, then three, then a whole band of prophets. All this takes place in three specified localities: namely, Rachel's sepulchre, the oak of Tabor, and the Gibeah of God. Samuel's words are written up in perfect conformity to chiastic and alternating patterns, and together make up a very impressive system with a triplet in the centre. Only in the conclusion of the passage does the chiastic

[11] H. H. Walker, "Where were Madmenah and Gebim?" *Journal of the Palestine Oriental Society*, Vol. XIII (1933).

pattern break down, but not so completely that we are unable to discern that the original conclusion corresponded probably step by step to the introduction. Graphically represented, the passage tells its own story with sufficient clearness:

Rachel's sepulchre, two men, asses found, vs. 2.
A The oak of Tabor, three men, supplies, greeting, vss. 3, 4.
The Gibeah of God, a band of prophets, the *Spirit of Yahweh* will fall upon Saul, he shall prophesy with them, vss. 5-6a

B "And thou shalt be *turned* into another man.
And let it be when *these signs* are come unto thee,

C That *thou do* as occasion shall serve thee, for God is with thee,
And thou shalt *go down before me* to Gilgal.

And, behold, I will *come unto thee*
To offer burnt-offerings,
D And to sacrifice sacrifices
Of peace-offerings.
Seven days shalt thou tarry, till I *come unto thee*,

C′ And show thee what *thou shalt do*,
And it came to pass when he had turned his back *to go from Samuel*,

B′ God *turned* him another heart,
And all *those signs* came to pass that day (vss. 6b-9).

The Gibeah, a band of prophets, *the Spirit of God* fell mightily upon him, he prophesied among them, vss. 10-12.
A′ The High-place, probably identified with the oak of Tabor, vs. 13 cf. vs. 3.
Saul's uncle, probably one of the "two men", asses found, vss. 14-16.

The events that were to take place at the Gibeah of God (A) came to pass, and the fulfillment is described in almost the identical words of the prediction (A′). There can be no doubt of the parallelism of these two members. Though Rachel's sepulchre and the two men are not specifically mentioned in the conclusion, we are fairly certain that Saul's uncle was one of the two men. The two items in the conversation, namely, the father's anxiety (vs. 14) and the asses that had been recovered, recur in the conclusion. It remains, then, to identify the oak of Tabor with the same locality as the High-place, but this item should offer no difficulties, since sacred trees at the high-places were not uncommon. One cannot escape the conclusion that A is matched by A′, though the latter probably has been condensed either by the original writer or by an editor. The latter seems the more probable in view of the parallel phrases, "the Spirit of Yahweh" (vs. 6) and "the Spirit of God" (vs. 10). If the supplies enumerated in vs. 3 were intended as offering at Bethel, there might have been a later religious reason for eliminating them (cf. Bethel, vs. 3 with Amos 4:4).

A much longer passage containing a cycle of narratives of remarkable variety and vividness, and apparently built up by the arrangement of its sections in a chiastic pattern, is 2 Sam. 13:1—1 Kings 3:28. Scholars who have studied the text of the Books of Samuel are generally agreed that 2 Sam. 21-24 is an appendix which has been added to the book. They usually explain the present state of these chapters by assuming that into the originally continuous stories of the two calamities (21:1-14; 24:1-25) the two sections dealing with the Philistine wars and the heroes of David (21:15-22; 23:8-38) were inserted, and that finally the two pieces of poetry (22:1-51; 23:1-7) were inserted into the centre of the whole. Thus we would have a wedge within a wedge.[12]

This so-called appendix to the Second Book of Samuel proves to be made up of six sections in a chiastic order. Whatever history the text may have had, the present arrangement is intentional and not the result of an accident in textual transmission. Another important factor is the arrangement of the other material which precedes and follows chapters 21-24. It is admitted by all that the old narrative dealing with David's court is to be traced further into First Kings.[13] When this original connection is laid hold of and followed out to the end, a very remarkable array of sections in chiastic order is discovered—an order in which the parallel sections show a pronounced similarity not only in general content but sometimes in the phraseology that is used and in the personal names that appear in the narrative. In the following outline we shall endeavor to give a graphic representation of the points of contact between the parallel sections without entering into the more intricate problems of redaction. That the original sources have been edited is taken for granted, but only that these sources

[12] B. Stade, E. B. Col. 4276; and G. B. Gray, *Critical Introduction to the Old Testament*, p. 74.

[13] Driver, *An Introduction to the Literature of the Old Testament* (new ed., 1910), pp. 189 ff.

have been cast into a chiastic mould is to be determined by the following outline. Not only the editor but probably also the writer of the history of David's court (2 Sam. 9-20) knew of the chiastic principle of arrangement, as we have already seen in 10:1-16.

Outline of 2 Sam. 13:1—1 Kings 3:28

A Absalom's rebellion; takes ten concubines from David (cf. 15:16; 16:22; 20:3 with 12:8; 2 Sam. 3:6-11). Three men of prominence, namely, Shimei (16:5), Barzillai (17:27), and Joab (18:14), 2 Sam. 13:1-19:15.

B David deals with the three men: Shimei (19:16 ff.), Barzillai (19:31 ff.) and Joab (20:7 ff. cf. 1, K. 2:5), 2 Sam. 19:16-43.

C Sheba's rebellion: Joab is prominent (vs. 10), a woman saves the day (vs. 16), Cherethites and Pelethites (vs. 23), Abiathar and Zadok (vs. 25), 2 Sam. 20:1-26.

D A famine averted by revenge on Saul's house, 21:1-14.
cf. the ending, "*God* was entreated for the land", vs. 14.

E War with the Philistines and David's heroes, 21:15-22.

F A poetic section: Psalm eighteen, 22:1-51.

F′ A poetic section: David's last words, 23:1-7.

E′ War with the Philistines and David's heroes, 23:7-38.

D′ A pestilence averted by sacrifice, 24:1-25.
cf. ending, "*Yahweh* was entreated for the land", vs. 25.

C′ Adonijah's attempted rebellion: Joab is prominent (vs. 7), a woman, here Bath-sheba, saves the day (vss. 1-31), Cherethites and Pelethites (vs. 28), Abiathar and Zadok (vss. 7, 38), 1 Kings 1:1-53.

B′ David advises Solomon concerning the three men: Joab (vs. 5 cf. 2 Sam. 20:10), Barzillai (vs. 7), and Shimei (vs. 8), 1 K. 2:1-12.

A′ Adonijah's renewed attempt at rebellion: tries to take Abishag the Shunammite (cf. 1 K. 1:1-4) for his wife, who was regarded, though erroneously (1:4), as David's concubine. Three men of prominence active in the rebellion are finally disposed of after Adonijah's execution (vs. 25), namely, Abiathar, (vs. 26 ff.), Joab (vs. 28 ff.), and Shimei (vs. 36 ff.), 1 Kings 2:13-3:28.

This somewhat sketchy outline can do no more than call attention to the most outstanding features of the sections. In AA′ there are some clever, though indirect, characterizations of Amnon, Absalom, and Solomon. There can be little doubt that the contrasts are intentional between "the folly" of Amnon in the rape of Tamar (2 Sam. 13:12, 13) and its bloody sequel in the sheep-shearing feast of Baal-hazor (vs. 23 ff.), on the one hand, and the sacrificial feast at Gibeon by Solomon with its sequel in abundant wisdom for the king (1 K. 3:4-15), on the other. Just as the woman of Tekoa employs a tale in which there are two sons (2 Sam. 14:6)—and the tale in the last instance is used in the narrative, not only for the purpose of revealing Joab's cunning in bringing Absalom back to Jerusalem, but also in proving David's penetration and wisdom (vss. 18-20)—so in connection with Solomon we also find a tale of the two harlots and their sons, one of whom had been killed. This tale also has for its purpose in the narrative the revealing of Solomon's wisdom (1 K. 3:28). Again, the reference to Abishag the Shunammite (1 K. 1-4), with the explicit statement that "the king knew her not," appears to be an odd way of introducing the following narrative of the plot to place Adonijah on the throne instead of Solomon. Why the story should come here, and not somewhere near 2:13-25, where its significance is made plain in the attempt of Adonijah to strengthen his chances for the throne by possessing part of David's harem, must remain a puzzle as long as the nearer context alone is made the criterion. But when we find a similar section in the story of Sheba's rebellion, with a similar reference to David's abstinence (2 Sam. 20:3), we may be certain that we have come upon the literary counterpart of the puzzling reference to Abishag the Shunammite. If this story had been placed *after* 2 Sam. 19:43, where it fits better in the account of David's return to Jerusalem, it would not have broken up the continuous story of Sheba's rebellion, as it does in its present position, but would have preceded it. Though we may never be able to explain all these details, one factor stands out clearly, namely, that in connection with both stories of the rebellions there are sections which are connected with each pretender's designs on David's harem.

In the story of Absalom's rebellion, which is one of the most colorful stories in the Old Testament, there are many other persons (cf. AB) who do not appear again in corresponding sections (B′A′). When, however, the three leading men are again mentioned in B′, the order of their names is inverted. To be sure, the account this time is not so full of detail as in B, but completeness is not at all necessary, since this section is obviously intended to be merely a review and a summary of past events. We may compare in 1 Sam. 10:1-16 the sketchy form of A′ (vss. 14-16) with the full account in A. These chiastic structures of paragraphs find their explanation in the liturgical use made of the Old Testament in the Jewish community. The original sources were edited, not for the purpose of conveying items of information concerning the men of the past, but for the purpose of impressing upon the community moral lessons either of warning against evil or encouragement in that which is good. And the lessons themselves are admirably adapted to the purpose for which they were arranged, and therefore have served the purpose well through the centuries, not only in the Jewish synagogue but also in the Christian church. When later we examine the structure of a gospel like that of Matthew, we are not at all surprised to find a similar arrangement of its contents to serve a similar purpose.

CHAPTER V

THE PSALMS

We have already shown how in the Psalms there are chiastic structures in separate strophes which permit of an arrangement of four, six, eight, and even ten members. We shall now give some examples of how the chiastic structure has affected whole psalms. It will not be necessary in this connection to enter into a general discussion of the ordinary *parallelismus membrorum* concerning which there already exists a consensus of opinion, nor of rhythm about which there is less agreement.[1] From over a hundred psalms which have been analyzed the following examples may be given. These psalms are representative of several classes. The arrangement of strophes may be (1) simply chiastic, or (2) alternating, or (3) a combination of both these forms. This simple statement probably includes all the varieties. Yet there may be within these three classes several variations of the arrangement of the strophes; these variations do not introduce any new principle.

There are also *psalms in two parts*, which either (1) stand side by side, thus making their content alone the bond that unites them, or (2) which have their strophes artistically interwoven in accordance with definite patterns. Sometimes we have (3) psalms with a brief prelude introducing the keynote of the main body of the psalm. These introductions may also stand related to the main body only by their content, or they may have their separate parts definitely interwoven with the main body of the psalm. We shall supply one or two examples of each type in order to illustrate these principles of structure.

Beginning, then, with psalms having a purely chiastic arrangement of strophes, we offer the following examples:

[1] "Chiasmus in the Psalms" in *AJSL*, Vol. XLIX (July, 1933), pp. 281-312.

Psalm 58

A Do ye indeed, O *gods*, speak righteousness? 1
Do ye judge uprightly, O ye sons of men?

B Nay, in the heart ye work wickedness, 2
Ye weigh out the violence of your hands in the earth.

C The wicked are estranged from the womb, 3
They go astray as soon as they are born, speaking lies.

Their poison is like the poison of a serpent, 4
D Like the deaf adder that stoppeth her ear,
Which hearkeneth not to the voice of charmers, 5
The most cunning binder of spells.

O *God*, 6
Break
E Their teeth in their mouth;
The great teeth of the young lions
Break out,
O *Yahweh*.

They shall melt away like waters, 7
D′ They shall go away for them,
Like tender grass which wilts away.* 8
Like a snail will melt as it goes along.

C′ Abortions of a woman,
That not have beheld the sun!**

B′ The righteous shall rejoice when he seeth the vengeance, 10
He shall wash his feet in the blood of the wicked.

A′ And men shall say, Surely there is a reward for the righteous, 11
Surely there is a *God* that judgeth the earth.

This poem illustrates several of the laws of structure. (1) The first half of the poem deals with the wickedness of the judges, and the last half with their punishment, showing that the centre is the turning point (cf. Zech. 9:5; Amos 5:4b-6a; Num. 15:35-36, above). (2) The law of the shift (cf. Isa. 60:1-3) is illustrated by the sudden change from a description in the first half to an ejaculatory prayer at the centre, after which the description is once more resumed and continued until the end of the poem. In E we have the only instance of chiasmus within a strophe in the whole poem, and the change is as noticeable as when a musical composition passes from legato to staccato. (3) The law of distribution of similar ideas at the extremes and at the centre is seen in the term Elohim (AEA′).

We have here the first example from the psalms that shows how necessary it is to make the thought-pattern the determining principle in the division of the strophes. Neither length nor number of lines, but only the order of the ideas, can supply us with the clue to the structure of the psalm. In AA′ in addition to the terms Elohim, righteousness and righteous, the psalmist discusses men whose judgment may be questioned and God whose judgment is sure. In BB′ wickedness is parallel to the wicked, hands to feet, violence to blood; the general antithesis between the wicked judges and their just punishment is as pronounced as in AA′. The references to childbirth in CC′ are very striking, since not only these references, but all the other terms enumerated in AA′ and BB′ are to be found only in their respective strophes and nowhere else in the whole poem. This shows that in the structure of the psalm the strophes can have no more than two lines up to this point. Each couplet is a complete whole by itself. If we are to have a quatrain we must look for the second couplet in the other end of the psalm. When we arrive at DD′ we observe a change in this arrangement. The first couplet in either of these strophes is incomplete without the second couplet. This is only one justification for having quatrains at this point. It will also be found that though the parallelism between the serpent and the adder, on the one hand, and the snail, on the other, would not be inapposite, there would be nothing in the two couplets nearest the centre to establish their parallelism. The third line (*) in D′ reads in our Hebrew text, "One who treads his arrows as though they were cut off," which makes no sense in the context. The emendation and translation of the late Doctor J. M. P. Smith, which is obtained by "a transposition of one word and redistribution of consonants," gives good sense and fits admirably both the nearer and the remoter context.[2] In DD′ we have not only references to cold-blooded animal life, but also the use of "like" in comparisons. This shows there is no room in the structure for vs. 9, which must be removed as a gloss; it reads as follows (**):

[2] *The Old Testament: An American Translation* (The University of Chicago Press: 1927), note on Ps. 58:7, p. 1664.

Before your pots shall feel the thorns,
As the green, as the burning, he will take them away with a tempest.

Even though these lines in Hebrew are of about the same length, they do not make a good couplet, whether synonymous or antithetic. In the context the wicked are spoken about, but in vs. 9 they are spoken to. The picture conveyed by the verse is that of a man making a fire of thorns under his pots; the thorns, whether green or burning, are blown away by the storm before the pots have been heated. Interpreters apply the figure to plots that are discovered before they have been matured. Intelligible as this idea is in itself, it is difficult to find a place for it in the context. As a gloss the verse becomes intelligible, for though there is difficulty in finding a place for secret plots in the immediate context in B′, a glance at B supplies the motive for the gloss. The words, "Nay, *in the heart* ye work wickedness," may refer to such secret plots, and the glossator, knowing of the chiastic structure of the psalm, may have added the words in the strophe parallel to B, namely B′.

The following psalm offers an interesting example of how there may be considerable variation in the form of the strophes while the chiastic arrangement, nevertheless, is maintained through the whole psalm:

Psalm 67

May *God* be merciful unto us, and bless us, 1
A May he cause his face to shine upon us. Selah.
That may be known upon the *earth* thy way, 2
Among *all* the nations thy salvation.

B Let the *peoples* give thee thanks, O *God*, 3
Let the *peoples* give thee thanks, *all of them.*

Let the *nations* be glad and sing for joy. 4
C For thou wilt judge the *peoples* with equity,
And the *nations* upon the *earth* thou wilt lead. Selah.

B′ Let the *peoples* give thee thanks, O *God*, 5
Let the *peoples* give thee thanks, *all of them.*

The *earth* hath yielded her increase. 6
May *God* bless us,
A′ Our own *God;*
May God bless us. 7
And *all* the ends of the *earth* shall fear him.

In AA′ occurs a prayer with a statement of its effects in the earth. These two ideas, however, are distributed differently in the two strophes, for in A the first couplet carries the prayer, and the second describes its effect in the earth, while in A′ the central triplet contains the prayer and the outer lines describe its effect. The word "us" in both strophes is expressed by the ending *nu*, which is found three times in each strophe and nowhere else in the whole psalm. "God," "the earth," and "all" are also parallel ideas in AA′. The triplet at the centre of A′ is nothing new. Only its counterpart in A is missing; this indicates that absolute symmetry in such details was not regarded as compulsory by the poet. In BB′ the parallelism is not in need of comment. The similarity in the ending of the two lines is very striking. The most significant feature of this psalm, however, is the artistic distribution of specific terms in accordance with certain definite patterns. Thus Elohim occurs in ABB′A′, but not in C; the earth in ACA′, but not in BB′; the idea of universality, expressed by "all" or "all of them," in ABB′A′, but not in C. The play upon the two terms "peoples" (Heb. ʿammîm) and "nations" (lĕʾ ummîm), besides illustrating the symmetrical distribution of parallel terms in the structure, also displays a certain interest on the part of the poet in numbers. "Peoples" alternates with "nations" in *five* places in such a manner that the odd numbers in the series of five (1, 3, 5) carry the term "peoples," and the even numbers (2, 4) the term "nations." Since "peoples" is repeated twice in the first and the last place, the total number of terms is *seven*. It should be observed that none of these terms occurs in the last line of A, except the Hebrew *gôjîm*, which shows that the term is outside of this scheme. Symmetrical distribution of divine names, and of other terms as well, recurs frequently in the psalms, and there are many examples of this form of literary art in the New Testament. The same may be said of the ending *nu* of the lines in AA′ and BB′, which, if not actually rhymes, at least may be regarded as *epiphora*.

Psalm 29 is another example of the chiastic form determining the structure of a whole psalm. There are some textual changes to be made in this psalm. In vs. 6 Briggs eliminates the word "them," thus obtaining two couplets the first of which deals with the cedars and the second with the mountains (cf. D). The following words in vs. 7, however, would only make a single line, which creates a difficulty in view of the fact that vss. 5, 6 and 8 make perfect couplets. This line in the present arrangement has been moved so as to replace vs. 9a (cf. B′) for reasons which will be given presently. In vs. 9a the commentators have found a problem. Briggs and others solve the problem by a change in vocalization as follows:

> The voice of Yahweh whirleth about (the terebinths);
> (The voice of Yahweh) strippeth bare the forests.

In view of the whole structure of the psalm it seems best to treat vs. 9a as a gloss dealing with the effect of the storm upon the hinds, a gloss which probably originally was added to vs. 6, which is the *only* place in the poem where animal life is alluded to. A copyist would leave out the gloss, discover his omission, and insert it after vs. 8. The presence of the two verbs rendered "maketh to writhe" in vs. 8 would make such an accidental omission of the gloss natural. When, however, the gloss has been placed where it now is in vs. 9a, there would be too much material in this verse thus necessitating some adjustments. The words, "The voice of Yahweh heweth out flames of fire," would then be moved to their present position after vs. 6, where they make vs. 7, and where their position seems justified in the description of the storm in vss. 5, 6. There are good reasons, however, for rejecting this position and for transposing vs. 7 and vs. 9a, as we have done, in view of the structure of the psalm.

Psalm 29

Ascribe unto Yahweh, O ye sons of the mighty, 1
A Ascribe unto Yahweh glory and strength.
Ascribe unto Yahweh the glory due unto his name, 2
Worship Yahweh in holy array.

The *voice* of Yahweh is upon the waters, 3
B The God of glory thundereth,
Yahweh is upon many waters.

C The *voice* of Yahweh is powerful, 4
The *voice* of Yahweh is full of majesty.

The *voice* of Yahweh breaketh the cedars, 5
D And Yahweh breaketh the cedars of Lebanon.
He maketh to skip like a calf/Lebanon, 6
Sirion/like a young wild-ox.

C′ The *voice* of Yahweh maketh to writhe the wilderness, 8
The *voice* of Yahweh maketh to writhe the wilderness of Kadesh.

The *voice* of Yahweh heweth out flames of fire, 7
B′ And strippeth the forests bare,
And in his temple all say, Glory. 9b

Yahweh sitteth at the flood, 10
A′ Yahweh sitteth as king for ever.
Yahweh giveth strength to his people,
Yahweh blesseth his people with peace.

The symmetry of this psalm leaves little to be desired. The majesty and power of Yahweh is the subject of the psalm. In A his people is called upon to give him the honor and worship which are due him, and in A′ he is described as the majestic ruler who gives them strength and peace. In BB′ there is a fine contrast between the "many waters" and "the forests," between the thunder and the lightning (cf. "flames of fire," B′). The two outer lines in B carry the term "waters" with the word "glory" in the centre. In B′ the word "glory" occurs in the last line and has for its parallel "flames of fire" in the first. This is merely another instance of the familiar law of the shift from centre to extremes in parallel sections. Likewise "waters" are in the extremes of B and "the forests" in the centre of B′. Yahweh is the ruler of the sea as well as of the dry land. For the twice-repeated Yahweh in B there is only one divine name in B′, and for Elohim there is no counterpart. Since B′ is the strophe most seriously affected by textual changes, we may assume that these terms originally were perfectly balanced in both strophes. On the other hand, though a symmetrical distribution of the divine names is a frequently recurring feature in many psalms, there are also cases in which such a scheme is not carried out with perfect regularity in all details. In this psalm, however, one has the impression that such a scheme was in the mind of the poet, for Yahweh occurs four times in AA′ and twice in *all* the other strophes with the exception of B′, where the textual changes have occurred.

In C the power and majesty of Yahweh are declared, and in C′ they are portrayed in action upon the wilderness. Yahweh's activity is further described in D as centering upon the mighty cedars and the high mountains. The number of lines in each strophe display a symmetry similar to that of Psalm 67 with two lines in CC′, three in BB′, and four in ADA′. If the content of these be observed more closely, it will be found that AA′ are in the nature of an introduction and conclusion, setting forth the relations of Yahweh and his people, while the intervening five strophes describe Yahweh in action upon nature. In these five strophes we have a symmetrical distribution of the term "voice" which is strikingly similar to the regular recurrence of the terms "peoples" and "nations" in Psalm 67. The term "voice" occurs singly in BDB′ and is twice repeated in CC′. This shows attention to the numerical order, for in the odd numbers of the five strophes (1, 3, 5) we have a single term, and in the even numbers (2, 4) a double. The whole psalm is made up of *seven* strophes, a favorite number in many such structures.

Psalm 101

Of lovingkindness and justice I will sing, 1
A Unto thee, O *Yahweh*, will I sing praises.
I will give heed unto *the perfect way*, 2
How long till thou wilt come unto me?

I will walk in the integrity of my heart
B *Within my house;*
Not I will set *before mine eyes* 3
A base thing.

The work of them that turn aside I hate,
It shall not cleave unto me.
C A perverse heart shall depart from me, 4
An evil thing I will not know.
He that slandereth in secret his neighbor, 5
Him *I will cut off.*

He that hath proud eyes and a proud heart,
Him I will not suffer.
C′ Mine eyes shall be upon the faithful of the land, 6
That they may dwell with me.
He that walketh in *the perfect way*,
He shall minister unto me.

Not shall dwell *within my house* 7
B′ He that worketh deceit;
He that speaketh falsehoods
Not shall be established *before mine eyes.*

Every morning *I will cut off* 8
A′ All the wicked from the land;
Cutting off from the city of *Yahweh*
All the workers of iniquity.

The six strophes that make this psalm are arranged in a chiastic structure. The proof of this will be found in a symmetrical distribution of several phrases. In B it may be a question whether the lines ought not to be arranged as a couplet, since the verb occurs in the third line and not in the fourth, and the fourth without the verb is rather short. The perfect regularity of B′, however, seems to indicate that four lines rather than two is the correct form, and the balancing of the psalm requires a similar arrangement in B. The name Yahweh occurs only in AA′. The first strophe indicates the attitude of the godly man toward Yahweh; the last, his attitude toward the enemies of Yahweh, the wicked. In BB′ the ideal of conduct is set forth, but under two different aspects; in B we are told what the godly man does in regard to himself, and in B′ what he does in regard to the wicked man. We have here a remarkable instance of the law of the shift from centre to extremes in parallel strophes, for the phrases "within my house" and "before mine eyes" which occur in the centre in B are found in the extremes of B′.

Strophes CC′ carry on the discussion of the godly man's attitude, but again under two different aspects. In C′ his attitude toward the godly (cf. with this B). This statement, so far as it relates to C′, is only partially correct, for the opening couplet deals with the wicked, the proud man. At first we should be inclined to group the last couplet of C and the first of C′ in a central strophe, and thus obtain a uniform arrangement of quatrains throughout the psalm, and, in addition, obtain *seven* strophes instead of six. The fact that the second and fourth line of this central quatrain would have the pronoun "him" expressed in Hebrew renders the arrangement still more attractive. And yet, with all these points in its favor, the suggestion must be rejected and the arrangement in our text substituted for it. Again, it is the symmetrical distribution of phrases that provides the needed check. The phrase "I will cut off" in C and "the perfect way" in C′ must balance each other in the two central strophes, the former indicating the godly man's attitude toward wickedness, and the latter his attitude toward righteousness. In other words, the contrast which is sharply presented in AA′ recurs in CC′, but the order is reversed, thus connecting C with A′ and C′ with A. A similar procedure is found to exist with BB′ and CC′. The verb "walk," as applied to the conduct of the righteous man, is found in C′ and in B. The conduct of the wicked man, on the other hand, is described in C as slander and in B′ as speaking falsehoods. It should be noticed that in CC′ these terms (together with the two phrases, "I will cut off" and "the perfect way") occur in the *last* couplet of each strophe; in B the verb "walk" occurs in the first half of the strophe, whereas "speaketh falsehoods" in B′ is placed in the last half.

On the basis of these observations, therefore, we conclude that the present arrangement represents the original plan of the poet. The relations between the strophes may be expressed by two chiastic diagrams. The centre of the poem is indicated by expressing twice in Hebrew the pronoun "him," in the first couplet of C′ and in the last C. This is an emphatic way of serving notice on the reader that the turning point has been reached. The same verbs which are rendered "walk" and "sit" in Psalm 1:1 (and there usually worked up by commentators, though not always convincingly, into some sort of climax) recur in BB′, though "sit" is rendered "dwell" in B′. Again, we observe that the words rendered "work" in C and "worketh" in B′ have the same Hebrew root. This means that ideas from the two extreme couplets in C have been placed in the centre of B′. In the first couplet of C′, we find the words, "Him I will not suffer." A parallel idea, though not expressed in identical terms, is found in B in the words, "Not I will set . . . a base thing." This verb should have been placed in the last line to parallel the verb, "walk," in the first line. Though one hesitates to press such minute details of structure, it is not at all impossible that the verb has been transposed, and that it originally *followed* the phrase, "before mine eyes." If so, the ideas of the first and the last couplet in C′ have also been inverted and placed in the extremes of B, in exact duplication of the process which has been revealed in CB′. Even if the verse has always read as in our text, both the principle of inversion and the law of the shift have been observed, at least to the extent that "walk" occurs in the first couplet and "I will set" in the last.

Also in the two central strophes CC′, which hitherto have been discussed merely in their relation to the psalm as a whole, there are some striking parallels. "A perverse heart" in C and "a proud heart" in C′; the twice repeated pronoun "him" and the general contrast indicated between the godly man's attitude toward the godly and the wicked, justify us in treating CC′ as parallel strophes (cf. "shall depart from me" in C, and "may dwell with me" in C′).

The following psalm is similar to the preceding in the general arrangement of the strophes, in their number, and in the greater length of the two central strophes. The two central strophes, however, offer a minute and intricate pattern that may illustrate such variations as may be found in a literary form which at first may seem very rigid and monotonous.

Psalm 115

Not unto us , O Yahweh, not unto us, 1
A But unto thy name give glory,
Because of thy grace,
Because of thy truth.

Wherefore should the nations say, 2
B Where, now,/is their *God*.
But our *God*/is in *the heavens*, 3
Whatsoever pleased him he *hath done*.

Their *idols* are silver and gold, 4
The *work* of the hands of men.
A *mouth* have they,/but they do not *speak*. 5
Eyes have they, but they do not see.
Ears have they, but they do not hear. 6
C A nose have they, but they do not smell.
They have hands, but they do not handle. 7
They have feet, but they do not walk.
They cannot *make a sound*/with their *throat*.
Like unto them shall all those that *wrought* them be, 8
Every one that trusteth *in them*.

O Israel, trust in Yahweh, 9
Their help and their shield is he.
O house of Aaron, trust in Yahweh, 10
Their help and their shield is he,
O ye that fear Yahweh, trust in Yahweh, 11
Their help and their shield is he.

C′ Yahweh hath remembered us, 12
He will bless.

He will bless the house of *Israel*,
He will bless *the house of Aaron*,
He will bless *them that fear Yahweh*, 13
The small,
And the great.

May Yahweh increase you, you and your *children*. 14
B′ Blessed be ye of *Yahweh*,/who *hath made the heavens* and the earth. 15
The heavens, *the heavens*/are *Yahweh's*,
But the earth he hath given to the *children* of men. 16

Not the dead praise Yah, 17
Nor all they that go down into silence.
A′ But we, we will bless Yah, 18
From this time forth and forever.
Hallelujah.

Psalms 113-118 in our Bible are called the Hallel, or praise; they were sung at the passover meal (Mt. 26:30, Mk. 14:26). Psalm 115 presents in a striking contrast the futility of the idols and the all-sufficiency of the living God to all who trust in him. There is a remarkable literary symmetry in this ancient hymn, which is expressed, not only in separate terms and lines, but in the arrangement of the strophes. In A we are told that glory belongs to God, and not to man, and in A′ we find that the living, and not the dead, are to render God his praise. In B the taunting challenge of the nations, "Where, now, is their God?" is answered with the affirmation that God is exalted in the heavens and that his will is supreme. In B′ the faithful children of God are introduced in contrast to the hostile nations in B, and God's sovereignty is reaffirmed. Observe the parallel terms which are printed in italics, some of which are found in these two strophes only.

The central strophes of the psalm are antithetic: in C the futility of trusting in idols is set forth and in C′, the security given by God. The first of these strophes is *chiastic* in form, while the second is *alternating*. In C there are two introductory lines of a general nature declaring that idols, though made of the best material, silver and gold, are nevertheless "the work of men's hands." The two closing lines again declare the futility of the idols and their makers, but refer to them in the *inverted* order. The intervening *seven* lines are very interesting because of the intricate artistic pattern they display. In six of the seven lines the verb is placed at the *end* of the line; the poet departs from this rule in the seventh line only for a very good reason. The first and the seventh lines form a *chiasmus*, by which the group of lines describing the futility of the idols are knit together in a cluster separated from the two introductory and concluding lines of the strophe. The first four lines begin in Hebrew: "Mouths to them," "eyes to them," etc. This structure continues till the centre is reached, when it changes to "Their hands," "their feet." In this cluster of seven lines, it should be further observed, features of the body that usually come in pairs (like eyes and ears, hands and feet) appear in couplets. This arrangement gives us a pattern in which single lines alternate with couplets.

In strophe C′ we have Israel's great confession of trust in Yahweh. The futility of trusting in other gods is the closing note of the previous strophe. Its opposite is now stated emphatically in three different ways, and is followed by a triple refrain, "Their help and their shield is he." The first half of the strophe ends in the words, "Yahweh hath remembered us, he will bless." The idea of the divine blessing is again taken up in the last half of the strophe and gone over in a triple statement, "He will bless," in which the terms of address from the first half of the strophe are repeated. But whereas the first half of the strophe carries these terms in the beginning of each line where they occur, the second half carries them at the end; and whereas the first half of the strophe is made up of couplets, the last half consists of single lines. Thus we find that the principle of mingling single lines with couplets, which is utilized in one way in C, is expressed in another manner in C′. There is an infinite tenderness in the short closing lines of the two halves of strophe C′. There are no divine names in C, but in C′ they are placed mostly in the first half of the strophe. The psalm ends in jubilant peal of praise, and with a profusion of divine names in strophes B′A′, not less than three in each. This feature finds its explanation in the desire to make the affirmation of faith in the living God against the idolatry of the nations more effective. Eighteen times a year during the continuance of the temple and twenty-one times during the exile was the Hallel repeated at the Jewish feasts in conformity to the law, and at the new moons also according to custom (cf. Sopherim, XVIII. 2).

After all these details have been discussed, there still remains an indefinable something, a mood which comes through the reading of the psalm. This mood must be felt rather than expressed. The contrasts of the psalm are overwhelmingly strong. On the one hand we have the biting satire on idolatry and the idol makers, which reminds us of passages in Isaiah 44:9-20; 40:19, 20; 41:6, 7; 46:6, 7; on the other hand, we have the deeply emotional appeal to trust in Yahweh. When Israel was oppressed by the empires and surrounded on all sides by idolatry, the hope of the faithful remnant found expression in the words of this psalm. Through the liturgical use of such forms they became familiar in the early church, and were carried over, almost unconsciously, into the early Christian writings.

The chiastic arrangement of strophes is only one of the typical structures in the psalms. There are also several instances in which the alternating arrangement prevails. The following is typical.

Psalm 126

A When *Yahweh* turned back the captivity of Zion, 1
We were like dreamers.

B Then was filled with laughter/our mouth, 2
And our tongue/with singing.

Then said they among the Gentiles,
C *Yahweh* hath done great things for them.
Yahweh hath done great things for us; 3
We are glad.

A′ Turn back, O *Yahweh*, our captivity, 4
Like the brooks in the Negeb.

B′ They that sow/with tears, 5
With singing/shall reap.

He that goeth forth and weepeth, 6
C′ Bearing his measure of seed,
Shall surely come again with joy,
Bearing his sheaves.

In this poem the principle of an equal number of lines in each strophe would lead us to arrange the lines in four quatrains. Such a procedure, however, would hide from the reader some important symmetries in the psalm. The two strophes AA′ are obviously parallel, and should be treated as strophes, though they contain only two lines. They both carry the divine name, the verb "turn," the "captivity," and a comparison (cf. "like") in the second line. The jubilant strains of B are only partially repeated in B′, for a note of sorrow here mingles with the joy. That the two are to be regarded as parallel, however, is indicated, not only by the common idea of joy, but by the chiastic arrangement of the two. While the laughter and singing occupy the extremes of the chiasmus in B, their counterparts are placed in the centre in B′. We have already observed another instance of such a shift from centre to the extremes of two phrases in strophes BB′ in Psalm 101. There is a similar distribution of the ideas of joy and sorrow in CC′; in C there is only a joyful mood described among Gentiles as well as among Israelites because of the "great things" done by Yahweh, while in C′ joy and weeping are distributed in alternating lines. In regard to CC′ the ideas are so definitely set off from the rest of the lines, that there can be no possible way of treating them except as parallel quatrains. The ideas of the psalm seem to be evenly divided between the two halves. The first half describes the return from the captivity, and is an occasion for unmixed joy; the second sets forth the missionary task of Israel among the nations, progressing amidst hardships and weeping, but with the assurance of a joyous termination in a harvest. What Yahweh has done is the message of C. What Israel is about to do is the content of C′.

Psalm 121

I will lift up mine eyes unto the mountains: 1
A From whence shall my help come?
My help is from *Yahweh*, 2
Who made heaven and earth.

He will not let thy foot be moved, 3
B He that keepeth thee will not slumber.
Behold, neither will he slumber nor sleep, 4
He that keepeth Israel.

Yahweh is thy keeper, 5
A′ *Yahweh* is thy shade upon thy right hand.
By day/the sun shall not smite thee, 6
Nor the moon/by night.

Yahweh will keep thee from all evil, 7
B′ He will keep thy soul.
Yahweh will keep thy going out and thy coming in, 8
From this time forth and for evermore.

The symmetry of this brief psalm is simple but effective. There are no chiastic forms in the whole psalm, except the last couplet in A′, and yet in each strophe the poet is on the verge of breaking into chiastic strophes but stops short of it. This is so regularly repeated that one suspects a deliberate planning throughout the poem. The reader may compare the two central lines in each strophe. When the first couplet is concluded, the next line takes up the same thought, or a similar one as in A′, and one is led to expect that the last line will finish up in a perfect chiasmus. But this does not materialize. There is a suggestion of parallelism in "the mountains" and "the shade" and in "the heavens" and "the sun and the moon" (cf. AA′). Likewise in the repeated references to the fact that Yahweh "keeps" his own, twice repeated in B and thrice in B′. A departure from this arrangement appears in the first line of A′, "Yahweh is thy keeper"; this, however, may be brought under the rule which has already been observed. This line introduces the second half of the psalm. Therefore, as the first half concludes with the words, "He that keepeth Israel," it is appropriate that the second half should open with a similar sentiment. The poet is merely working out, with reference to the two halves of the psalm, the same scheme which he has already applied to the two halves of each strophe. Finally, there is a parallelism in the references to "the foot" which shall not be moved, that is to say, by slipping or by compulsion (B), and the "going out" and "coming in" alluded to in B′. Thus there seems to be a good deal of care exercised in the structure of this apparently artless poem. The symmetrical distribution of the divine names, which is part of the structure of other psalms, does not appear to have been a part of this psalm.

We have described psalms that are in their structure either chiastic or alternating. We shall now give some examples of psalms whose structure is a combination of these two forms. The following psalm is perhaps one of the clearest examples of such a combination of forms; in addition, it is a good illustration of the futility of insisting upon an arrangement in quatrains. Each couplet in this psalm is a separate strophe, and only such an arrangement will bring out the literary pattern used by the poet.

Psalm 114

A When Israel went forth out of Egypt, 1
The house of Jacob from a people of strange speech,

B Judah became his sanctuary, 2
Israel his dominion.

C The sea saw it, and fled, 3
The Jordan turned back.

D The mountains skipped like rams, 4
The little hills like lambs.

C′ What aileth thee, O sea, that thou fleest? 5
Thou Jordan, that thou turnest back?

D′ Ye mountains, that ye skip like rams? 6
Ye hills, like lambs?

B′ At the presence of *Adon* tremble, thou earth, 7
At the presence of the *God* of Jacob,

A′ Who turned the rock into a pool of waters, 8
The flint into a fountain of waters.

This psalm is composed of eight equal parts, four of which are alternating (CDC′D′), and four chiastic (ABB′A′). In the construction of these eight strophes a regular scheme is followed, introducing a verb in the first line but not in the second. The result is that the second line becomes a sort of echo to the first, which by continued repetition becomes very effective. There are two exceptions to this rule, for in CC′ the second line also carries a verb. The two verbs in C change the effect of this strophe, making it different from the two preceding. Thus the reader is made aware of the fact that he passes now from one part of the poem to another part in which a different literary structure prevails. When he has read through D, he is again arrested by the same kind of change, for C′ also carries two verbs. Thus the arrival at the centre of the poem is signalized. In addition, the question, "What aileth thee?" etc., serves further to emphasize this fact. The sudden changes from "sea" and "Jordan" to "mountain" and "hills," and the recurrence of these in the following questions (C′D′), are too striking to be missed by any reader; they serve to set off the four central strophes from the rest of the psalm. A new line of thought is introduced but not concluded in B′ but is carried to its completion in A′. In other words, the performance in AB is repeated in B′A′. All other strophes in the psalm bring the thought they contain to a conclusion within the strophe (cf. Ps. 58).

A word may now be said in regard to the content of the psalm. Commemorating the Exodus and the settlement of Israel in Canaan, it is a festival psalm sung on the eighth day of the Jewish passover ritual. The psalm begins with the time of the Exodus and concludes with a reference to an event of the Exodus (cf. Ex. 17:6; Num. 20:11). The next strophe takes us to the settlement in Canaan and the establishment of Yahweh's dominion (B). It is to be observed that the *name* of the deity is nowhere introduced until we reach B′. To speak of the chief actor in the psalm long before he has been introduced would be a fault under ordinary circumstances, but becomes very natural, perhaps even conducive to suspense, once the scheme of the poet is understood. That BB′ really are parallel is seen first of all in "Israel" and "Jacob," but also in the fact that "the presence" is naturally expected in his "sanctuary" and in his "dominion" (cf. Pss. 33:8; 96:9; Hab. 2:20).

It would not be beyond the ingenuity of the poet to take a final glance at the four alternating strophes in the centre as he closes the poem. These deal with water and with land, and it may be this fact that prompts him to place in sharp contrast in A′ rock and flint, on the one hand, and pool and fountain, on the other. The psalm is a combination of the chiastic and the alternating patterns. The ingenuity with which the poet acquaints the reader with the change of the pattern, namely, by the introduction of double verbs in CC′ and by the striking question, "What aileth thee?" when the centre is reached, is an exhibition of the finest art. To write so artistically that one achieves an impression of simplicity is, after all, the highest art.

The following psalms represent a strophic arrangement which has not hitherto been considered. These psalms are in two parts, each distinct from the other and at the same time related in various ways to the other. There is, of course, a great variety of such psalms, but only a few of the typical examples may be given.

Psalm 74

Why, O *God*, hast thou cast us off for ever? 1
Why doeth thine anger fume against the sheep of thy pasture?
A *Remember* thy congregation, which thou hast gotten *of old*, 2
Which thou hast redeemed to be the tribe of thine inheritance.
The mountain of this Zion,
Thou hast dwelt in it.

Lift up thy feet unto the perpetual ruins. 3
All the evil that the enemy hath done in the *sanctuary!*
B Thine adversaries have *roared* in the midst of thy *meeting-places*, 4
They have set up their own *signs* for signs.
It seemed as when men wield upwards axes in a thicket of trees; 5
And now its carvings also together they strike down with hatches and
X (hammers. 6

They have set on fire the *sanctuary*, 7
To the earth they have profaned the tabernacle of thy name.
B′ *They said* in their heart, Let us make havoc of them altogether, 8
They have burned all the *meeting-places* of *God* in the earth.
We see not our *signs*, there is no more any prophets, 9
Neither is there any among us that knoweth how long.

How long, O *God*, shall the adversary *reproach*? 10
Shall the enemy *blaspheme* thy name for ever?
A′ Why drawest thou back thy hand, even thy right hand? 11
From the midst of thy bosom consume them.
And *God* is my king from *of old*, 12
Working salvation in the midst of the earth.

* * *

Thou didst break the sea in pieces by thy strength, 13
A Thou didst shatter the heads of the *sea-monsters* in the waters,
Thou didst crush the heads of *Leviathan*, 14
Thou didst give him for food to the people inhabiting the wilderness.

Thou didst cleave fountain and brook, 15
B Thou didst dry up ever-flowing rivers.
Thine is the day,/yea, thine the night, 16
Thou hast prepared the luminary/and the sun.

Thou hast set/all the borders of the earth, 17
C Summer and winter/thou hast made.
Remember this, the *enemy* hath *reproached*, O *Yahweh*. 18
And a foolish people hath *blasphemed thy name.*

X′ *Not* give unto the *wild beast* 19
A′ The soul of thy *turtle dove;*
The life of thy poor
Not forget thou for ever.

Look unto the covenant, 20
B′ For the dark places of the earth are full of the habitations of violence.
Not let the oppressed return ashamed, 21
Let the poor and the needy praise thy name.

Arise, O *God*, plead thine own cause, 22
C′ *Remember* thy *reproach* from the fool all the day,
Not forget the voice of thine *adversaries*, 23
The tumult of those that rise up against thee which ascendeth continually.

There appear to be two strands of thought intertwined in this psalm, namely, the memories of the past and the demands of the present situation. In the first half of the psalm, X (vss. 1-12), there are but few phrases that look back upon the past (cf. "remember" (A) and "of old" (AA')). In the intervening strophes the present activities of the enemies call for divine help (BB'). The first half of the psalm has a chiastic arrangement of the strophes. In the second half, X' (vss. 13-23), the same two strands of thought recur, but in equal proportions and distributed differently over the structure which here is alternating and not chiastic. The memories of the past, most of them of a comforting nature (except vs. 18), are first enumerated (ABC). These strophes evidently are intended to present a firm basis for the prayers of Israel which immediately follow (A'B'C'). Strophes AA' in X' are the only chiastic strophes in the whole psalm.

Considering in detail the first half (X) we find that AA', aside from the reminiscences already mentioned, also have references to "redemption" and "salvation." The divine wrath, which in A is turned against Israel, is to be directed against the enemies to consume them (A'). In B the destruction of the sanctuary is effected by wrecking, in B', by burning. Several terms common to both strophes occur in the same sequence.

In the second half (X') strophes AA', the only chiastic strophes in the psalm, carry references to animals such as the sea-monsters, the Leviathan (A), "the wild beast" and "the turtle dove" (A'). In the first their flesh is given for food to the people of the desert; in the second the plea is made that Israel be *not* given over to her enemy. In B the first couplet contains references to events of the Exodus and entrance into Canaan (cf. Ex. 17:5, 6; Josh. 3:13); these are in turn balanced in B' by the prayer that the oppressed of the poet's own generation need not return ashamed. The references to God as the maker of day and night may properly be regarded as parallel to the prayer that he look to his covenant in accordance with Jer. 33:20. It would seem as if the order of the couplets carrying these references in BB' is inverted. In CC' there is no inversion of couplets, for both strophes conclude with the enemies of Yahweh in rebellion. There is, however, an inversion of terms; "remember" and "reproach" occur in the *last* couplet of C but in the *first* of C′. A divine name is common to both. The pronoun "thou" is expressed in Hebrew twice in A, thrice in B, and twice in C. The occurrence of the negative is indicated by italics in A′B′C′.

There seems to be a symmetrical distribution of other terms that frequently recur in the psalm. Thus "remember" and "reproach," which in X occur apart (AA′), in X′ are brought together in the same line (CC′). In other words, the two extremes of X are brought together in the two end strophes of X′. Again, the terms "enemy" and "adversary," which in X are found in the same strophes (BA′), recur in X′ separated ("enemy" is found in C and "adversary" in C′). In either case there are two opponents to Yahweh which occur together, but the second term is either "a foolish people" (C) or "those that rise up" (C′). Finally, "reproach" and "blaspheme" are found together in XA′, and they are also found together in X′C, that is to say, in the *beginning* of the last strophe in X and at the *end* of the first half of X′. The allocation of these terms and phrases seems too regular to be regarded as merely accidental. Ps. 74 is an example of a psalm in two halves, of which the first is chiastic and the second alternating in the arrangement of its strophes. In the following psalm the first half is alternating and the second chiastic:

Psalm 77

With my voice unto *God*, I will cry, 1
With my voice unto *God*, and he will give ear unto me.
A In the day of my trouble *Adonai* I sought, 2
My hand at night was stretched out and ceased not.
It refused to be comforted my soul. 3

I remember God, and I am disquieted,
I meditate, and *my spirit* is faint. Selah.
Thou holdest fast the lids of mine eyes, 4
B I am troubled and cannot speak.
I have considered the days *of old*, 5
The years of ancient times.
I remember my song at night with my heart, 6
I meditate, and *my spirit* maketh diligent search.

X

Will *Adonai* cast off for ever? 7
And will he be favorable no more?
A′ Is his lovingkindness clean gone for ever? 8
Doth his promise fail for evermore?
Hath *God* forgotten to be gracious? 9
And hath he in anger shut up his tender mercies? Selah.

And I said, This is my infirmity, 10
The years of the right hand of the Most High.
B′ *I will remember* the works of *Yah* 11
For *I will remember* thy wonders *of old.*
I will *muse*/upon all thy work, 12
And upon thy doings/I will *meditate.*

* * *

O God, in the sanctuary is *thy way*, 13
Who is a great god like God?
A Thou art the God that doest wonders, 14
Thou hast made known among the peoples thy strength.
Thou redeemed with thine arm *thy people*, 15
The sons of *Jacob* and *Joseph.* Selah.

The waters saw thee, O God, 16
B The waters saw thee, they were in pain.
Yea, the depths trembled,
The clouds poured out water. 17

X′

The skies gave forth their voice,
B′ *Yea*, thine arrows went abroad.
The voice of thy thunder was in the whirlwind, 18
The lightnings lightened the world.

The earth trembled and shook,
In the sea is *thy way*. 19
A′ And thy paths are in the great waters,
And thy footsteps were not known.
Thou leddest, like a flock, *thy people*, 20
By the hand of *Moses* and *Aaron.*

Both in form and in content Ps. 77 is the counterpart of Ps. 74. Whereas in Ps. 74 the first half of the poem consisted of strophes arranged in accordance with a chiastic pattern, and the last half showed an alternating pattern, the order in Ps. 77 is completely reversed. There are a number of phrases and terms that are found in both psalms, like "remember," "meditate," "of old," "cast off for ever," "redeem," "the right hand," etc. The general conception of Israel as Yahweh's flock which he himself leads is also common to both psalms (cf. 74:1 and 77:20). Another important point of contact is the general procedure of the writers, who find in the reminiscences of the past deeds of Yahweh the assurance that he will also help them in their present afflictions. Whether all these similarities indicate a common authorship is hard to say. They do at least prove the presence of definite literary conventions in the poetic guilds of Israel, a certain common phraseology, and probably a similar liturgical function.

The first half of Ps. 77 is X (vss. 1-12) consisting of four alternating strophes, which end with a chiastic couplet in vs. 12, the only chiastic couplet in the whole poem. In AA′ the prayers of the poet bring him no consolation, for the actions of the deity do not conform to what he is led to expect by the past history of his people. In BB′ the emphasis is on reminiscences of the past, which lead to the conclusion that even the present affliction must be from God (vss. 4, 10). The last half of the poem, X′ (vss. 13-20), sets forth the resurgence of the faith that had temporarily been in eclipse. Strophes AA′ state fully the results of the poet's previous meditations upon "the years of ancient times" (vs. 5). God's "way" stands fully revealed in Israel's past history. Strophes BB′ deal with cosmic accompaniments, storm and rain (B), and lightning and thunder (B′). In the majesty and faithfulness of God faith finds its assurance.

Psalms 42-43

As the hart panteth for the brooks of water, 1
So my soul panteth for thee, O God.
A My soul thirsteth for God, for *the living God.* C′ 2
When shall I come and appear before God? 3
My tears have been my food *day* and *night,*
While they say unto me all the day, Where is thy God?

These things *I remember,* 4
And pour out *within me my soul.*
B For I went with the throng, B′
I led them to the house of God;
With the *voice* of joy and praise—
A multitude keeping holiday.

Why art thou cast down, O my soul? 5
And why art thou disquieted within me?
X C Hope thou in God! AA′
For I shall yet praise him,
The salvation of my countenance (and my God).

O God, *within me my soul* is cast down, 6
Therefore do *I remember* thee,
B′ From the land of Jordan, and the Hermons, B
From the hill Mizar.
Deep unto deep is calling at the *voice* of thy waterfalls, 7
All thy waves and thy billows over me have passed.

By *day* Yahweh will command his lovingkindness, 8
And in the *night* his song shall be with me.
A prayer unto *the God of my life,* 9
A′ I will say unto God my rock, Why hast thou forgotten me? C
Why go I mourning because of the oppression of the enemy?
As with the crushing of my bones reproach me mine adversaries, 10
While they say unto me all the day, Where is thy God?

Why art thou cast down, O my soul? 11
And why art thou disquieted within me?
A Hope thou in God! C
For I shall yet praise him,
The salvation of my countenance, and my God.

Judge me, O God! 43:1
B And plead my cause/against an ungodly nation, B′
From the deceitful and unjust man/deliver me. 2
For thou art the God of my strength.

Why hast thou cast me off?
Why go I mourning because of the oppression of the enemy? A′
X′ C O send out thy light, and thy truth! 3
Let them lead me, let them bring me,
Unto thy holy hill, and to thy tabernacles. A

And I will go unto the altar of God, 4
B′ Unto God the gladness of my joy. B
And I will praise thee upon the harp,
O God, my God.

Why art thou cast down, O my soul? 5
And why art thou disquieted within me?
A′ Hope thou in God! C
For I shall yet praise him,
The salvation of my countenance and my God.

Psalms 42-43 were originally one poem. For some reason a division of the poem was made so that the two parts ended with the same refrain. Neither this division, nor a division into three parts, each ending with the same refrain, represents the original plan of the poet. The two psalms 74 and 77 have shown the poet's technique in balancing parallel phrases in the two halves of the psalm. In Psalms 42-43 we shall find this technique employed more artistically than in any of the previous poems. In order to facilitate a comparison between the two halves of the poem, the letters in the right margin of one half should be compared with those of the left margin in the other half.

The original poem was in two parts, as indicated by the letters XX′. The central refrain C in X recurs twice in X′ in the two extreme strophes AA′. This procedure is merely another application of the law of the shift from centre to the extremes, which we have often observed in these studies. The refrain has a central line, "Hope thou in God!" On either side of this line is a couplet, the first of which indicates a depressed spirit in its two questions, and the last expresses a hope of better times in the future. In 42:5 the words "and my God" should probably be added to the Masoretic text, for the refrain, no doubt, was originally the same in all three places where it occurs.

Turning to the central strophe C in X′ we discover a similar structure. A central line contains a prayer for light and truth, and on either side of this line there are two couplets. The first couplet is, once more, made up of two questions which again indicate a depressed spirit, and the second couplet anticipates better things in the future. Closer examination will reveal that the central strophe in both content and form is definitely related to strophes AA′ in X. The words that express the prayer for guidance to the sanctuary (43:3) are parallel to the longing for the opportunity to "appear before God" (42:3); for the latter phrase is a technical term in the Old Testament for visiting the sanctuary. More striking is the first couplet with its two questions (43:2b), for it has for its parallel two questions, the last of which is *identical* in every word (42:9). This identical line in strophe A′ in X represents a plus in the strophe, giving it an extra line, so that A′ has seven lines, while the parallel strophe A has only six lines. Doubtless this extra line is to be explained with reference to the scheme of interweaving the strophes which is in the poet's mind.

A similar relationship exists between the remaining strophes of the two halves of the poem. In strophe B in X the poet reminiscences about the joy he formerly experienced in the festive assembly, and in B′ he contrasts his present hardships during a life in exile. The voice of joy and praise is now exchanged for the voice of the waterfalls, whose waves and billows are emblematic of his sufferings among strangers. These two sentiments are again expressed in X′, but in the inverted order; for strophe B describes the deceit and injustice visited upon the defenseless stranger by an "ungodly nation," while B′ sets forth the joy and praise of the festive assembly. With all these similarities of *content* between the two halves of the poem, there is, nevertheless, an important difference. The strophes in X carry identical terms, phrases, and even one line which is in every word parallel (cf. AA′). This is not the case in X′ with the exception of strophes AA′ which are identical.

There remains to be discussed the psalm with a prelude. Psalms that belong to this type are of two kinds: either the prelude merely introduces the theme of the psalm, but has no further structural connection with the main body of the poem, or its several couplets are interwoven in a more or less intricate fashion with the psalm itself. The literary principle involved seems to be the same as the one which we have had occasion to observe already in the relations between the two halves of psalms like 74, 77, and 101. For our present purpose the following three psalms have been selected, for they not only represent a similar principle of construction, but also offer some comparisons as to the subject matter. Together they show the influence of a very definite and well-established literary tradition in ancient Israel.

Psalm 30

A I will extol thee, O *Yahweh*, for thou hast drawn me up, 1
And hast not made my foes to rejoice over me.

B *Yahweh*, my God, I cried unto thee, 2
And thou hast healed me.

A′ O *Yahweh*, thou hast brought up my soul from Sheol, 3
Thou hast kept me alive from among those who go down to the pit.

* * *

A Sing praise unto *Yahweh*, O ye his godly ones, 4
And give *thanks* to his holy name.

For a moment lasteth his anger, 5
B For a life-time his favor.
In the evening may tarry weeping,
But in the morning joy (vss. 6, 7 eliminated).

C Unto thee, O *Yahweh*, did I call, 8
And unto thee, O *Yahweh*, I made supplication.

What profit is there in my blood, 9
D When I go down to the crypt?
Shall the dust *thank* thee?
Shall it declare thy truth?

C′ Hear, O *Yahweh*, and be gracious unto me, 10
O *Yahweh*, be thou my helper.

Thou hast turned my mourning 11
B′ Into dancing for me;
Thou hast loosed my sackcloth,
And hast girded me with gladness.

A′ So that my glory may sing praise to thee, and not be silent, 12
O *Yahweh*, my *God*, for ever I will give thee *thanks*.

In the prelude to the psalm the central strophe has reference to a cry for healing which was heard by God. As the result thereof the poet was saved from death and from having his enemies rejoice over his destruction. In A, "thou hast drawn me up" is parallel to "thou hast brought up" in A′; and the rejoicing of the enemies, from which he was saved, was due, no doubt, to their anticipation of his going down to the pit. We have, then, a reference to prayer in the centre, and two references to death and the realm of the dead in the extreme strophes. When we examine the three central strophes of the psalm, we shall find this arrangement completely reversed. In C his call and his supplication are mentioned, the substance of which is quoted in C′. The references to death and the grave, however, are placed in the centre (D). This is the well-known law of the shift from extremes to centre in parallel strophes of which we have already observed so many examples.

The main body of the psalm consists of seven strophes, of which those with even numbers in the series (2, 4, 6) are quatrains and those with odd numbers (1, 3, 5, 7) are couplets. The idea of "thanks" occurs in the two extremes (AA′) and in the centre (D), but in no other place in the psalm. This is the familiar law of distribution of parallel ideas at the extremes and at the centre of a structure. This law seems also to have been in operation, though not perfectly applied, in the distribution of the divine names, for Elohim is found only in the centre of the prelude and in one of the extremes of the psalm proper (A′), though not in A, as would have been expected. The term "godly ones" may not be drawn upon to complete the pattern, since it is represented by another Hebrew word. The name Yahweh, however, has been symmetrically distributed in the whole psalm. It is found in each of the three strophes of the prelude, and in *odd* numbers of the series of seven strophes in the psalm proper, occurring twice in CC′; in other words, the name "Yahweh" occurs twice in the strophes that stand in a definite literary relation to the prelude. In all the other strophes the name Yahweh occurs singly. The central strophe (D) is of a different structure from the other quatrains in the psalm because of its array of questions. The other quatrains (BB′) are also striking in that sorrow and joy alternate from line to line, and in that each of the words that express these sentiments occurs at the end of every line. The only exception is "for me" (B′), which may have been added at this point from a consideration of the rhythm of the line.

The symmetry of the psalm is perfect, but only if vss. 6, 7 be eliminated. These verses read as follows:

> And I said in my prosperity,
> Not shall I be moved forever.
> Yahweh, in thy favor thou hast established my mountain as a stronghold.
> Thou didst hide thy face,
> I was troubled.

These verses do not look like anything else that we find in the psalm. They are not easily made into couplets with the exception of the last two lines which have a close parallel in Ps. 104:29a. This material represents a gloss, or, more specifically, a later adaptation of the psalm made for "the dedication of the house." Beginning with Pss. 23, 24, 29 the psalms carry the superscription, "A Psalm of David," which is abbreviated to "Of David" in Pss. 25, 26, 27, 28. The lengthy superscription of Ps. 30, therefore, "A Psalm (A Song at the Dedication of the House) of David," looks inflated. In reading the psalm through, we find nothing that even remotely refers to a dedication, with the exception of vss. 6, 7, and in these the long central line referring to the mountain as a stronghold comes closest. Since these verses are the only ones that disrupt the otherwise perfect literary structure of the psalm, we are justified in treating them as extraneous. Their insertion adapted a general psalm of thanksgiving to a psalm of dedication, and this was made known by a parenthetic remark in the title as well. For there are three tests that vouch for the correctness of our present analysis of the psalm, namely, the definite literary relation existing between the prelude and the central strophes (CDC′); the recurrence of "thanks" in extremes and centre (ADA′), and the symmetrical distribution of the names of the deity. All of these features, which are characteristic of the psalm, would be disrupted by the inclusion of vss. 6, 7.

Psalm 88

C O *Yahweh*, *God* of my salvation, 1
I have *cried day* and *night before thee*.
C′ Let come before *thy face my prayer*, 2
Incline thine ear unto *my cry*.

D For it is full of troubles/my soul, 3
And my life/unto *Sheol* draweth nigh.
A I am reckoned with them that go down into the *pit*, 4
I am as a man that hath no help;
D′ Among the dead cast away, 5
Like the slain that lie in the *grave;*
A′ Whom thou rememberest no more,
And they from thy hand are *cut off*.

* * *

Thou hast laid me in the lowest *pit*, 6
A In the dark places, in the deeps.
Upon me lieth hard/*thy wrath*, 7
And with all thy waves/thou hast *afflicted* me. Selah.

Thou hast put *mine acquaintance far from me*, 8
B Thou hast made me abominations unto them.
I am *shut up*, and I cannot come forth,
Mine eye wasteth by reason of affliction. 9

I have *called* unto thee, O *Yahweh*, *all the day long*,
C I have spread forth unto thee my hands.
Wilt thou to the dead show wonders? 10
Shall the shades arise and praise thee? Selah.

Shall it be declared in the *grave*/thy lovingkindness, 11
D Thy faithfulness/in *destruction*?
Shall they be known in the darkness/thy wonders, 12
And thy righteousness/in the *land of forgetfulness*?

But I myself unto thee, O *Yahweh*, have *cried*, 13
C′ And in the *morning my prayer* shall come before thee.
Why, O *Yahweh*, dost thou cast off my soul? 14
Wilt thou hide *thy face* from me?

I myself am *afflicted* and ready to die from my youth up, 15
A′ I suffer thy terrors, I am distracted.
Over me has passed/thy fury, 16
Thy terrors/have *cut me off*.

They came round me like water all the day long, 17
B′ They *compassed me about* altogether.
Thou hast put *far from me* lover and friend, 18
Mine acquaintance into darkness.

The prelude opens with two couplets dealing with prayer, a persistent and agonized prayer (vss. 1, 2). Then follow four couplets giving the reason for the prayers. The present afflictions are overwhelming and the poet is brought near death (vss. 3-5). It should be observed that the transition from the prayer to its reasons is marked by the chiastic couplet in vs. 3, the only chiastic couplet in the whole prelude. There are definite literary relations between the terms in italics in the prelude and the several strophes in the main body of the poem. The letters in the left margin will make clear these connections.

In strophes AA′ we are told how the wrath of God has brought the poet near death. The doubling of terms in the second line of A has a parallel in the second line of A′. The strophes end in chiastic couplets of which there are none except in the central strophe D. The references to "wrath," "fury" and "affliction" are common to both strophes.

In strophes BB′ the separation of the righteous man from his fellows is described. "Mine acquaintance" and "far from me" are found in both strophes, but in the first couplet in one (vs. 8) and in the last of the other (vs. 18). The fact that he is "shut up" in the one (vs. 8b) and "compassed about" in the other (vs. 17) also indicates parallel ideas, and inversion of the couplets. Strophes AB and A′B′ are arranged in an alternating pattern, and they enclose the three central strophes CDC′ which are arranged in a chiastic pattern. It should be observed that BB′ are the only strophes that do not figure in the terminology of the prelude.

In CC′ the persistent prayers are described in verbs of praying and crying. Just as strophes AA′ ended in chiastic couplets, so CC′ terminate with two questions. In these strophes only does the divine name appear. The recurrence of terms found in vss. 1, 2 is very clear and striking. It also shows how necessary it is to translate "thy face" in vs. 2 and not "thy presence" or "before thee," as in our English versions. We recall how the plea (vss. 1, 2) and the reason for it (vss. 3-5) were strictly separated in the prelude; they are also separated in the body of the poem. For the plea is found in CDC′ and the afflictions that prompt him to pray in ABA′B′.

The central strophe D sets forth the hopelessness of the hereafter. With vs. 11 Job 26:6 should be compared. "Destruction" (Hebr. *Abaddon*), and "land of forgetfulness" are both references to Sheol. The sequence of thought is this: save me from death, for the dead are not able to praise the Lord.

The parallels in content and form between Ps. 88 and Ps. 30 are no less striking than those already observed in Pss. 74 and 77. Both poems have preludes which are in a definite literary relationship to the main body of the poems they introduce. In the poem itself there are in each case seven strophes, although Ps. 30 is a true chiastic poem while Ps. 88 has a combination of chiastic and alternating strophes. In each case the three central strophes deal with prayer and supplication, based on the hopelessness of the hereafter. And the point is made by means of a series of questions in either case. There is also a definite order discernible in the symmetrical distributions of the divine names, for these occur in some strophes but not in others. In Ps. 30 the "thanks" to God occurs in the two extremes and in the centre (Ps. 30:4, 9, 12), and in Ps. 88:6, 12, 18 the references to "darkness" are distributed in the two extremes and in the centre of the poem. With so many similarities of content, terminology, and structure we must again raise the question whether we have identity of authorship or merely more evidence of rather rigid literary conventions in the poetic guilds.

Psalm 90

O *Adonai*, 1
A dwelling-place *Thou* hast been to us
In generations and generations.
Before the mountains 2
Were brought forth.
Or ever thou gavest birth to
The earth and the world,
From everlasting to everlasting
Thou art
God.

* * *

Thou turnest man to destruction, 3
And sayest, *Return*, ye *children* of men.
A For a thousand years in thy sight 4
Are but as yesterday when it is past,
And as a watch in the night.

Thou carriest them away as with a flood; a sleep they will be. 5
B In the *morning* they are like the grass which *groweth up;*
In the *morning* it flourisheth and *groweth up;* 6
In the evening it is cut down and withereth.

For we are *consumed*/in thine *anger*, 7
And in thy *wrath*/are we troubled.
C Thou hast set our iniquities before thee, 8
Our secret sins in the light of thy face.
For all our days are passed away in thy *rage*, 9
We *consume* our years as a sigh.

The days of our years are threescore years and ten, 10
D And even by reason of strength fourscore years;
Yet is their pride but labor and sorrow,
For it is soon gone, and we fly away.

Who knoweth the power of thine *anger*, 11
And, according to the fear that is due thee, thy *rage*,
C′ So teach us to number our days, 12
That we may get us a heart of wisdom.
Return, O Yahweh, how long? 13
And let it repent thee concerning thy servants.

Oh, satisfy us in the morning with thy lovingkindness, 14
B′ That we may rejoice and *be glad* all our *days*,
Make us *glad* according to the *days* thou hast afflicted us, 15
The years wherein we have seen evil.

Let appear unto thy servants/thy work, 16
And thy glory/upon their *children*.
A′ And let the favor of Yahweh our God be upon us, 17
And the work of our hands do thou establish upon us,
Even the work of our hands establish thou it.

Psalm 90 is one of the grandest poems in the Psalter. In the prelude (vss. 1, 2), which is a well-balanced chiastic structure of ten members, God is described as the eternal home of the soul in all the generations of mankind. To arrange such a strophe in *lines* would be to destroy an exceedingly well-balanced unit.

The body of the poem consists of seven strophes. Strophes 2, 4, and 6 in the series are quatrains, but 1, 3, 5, 7 are longer. This arrangement should be compared with that of Psalm 30. In these strophes the quality of man's life is compared with that of the deity. Even the longest of human lives are brief when compared with eternity. This contrast is especially stressed in the central strophe D and in the two extreme strophes AA′, for in vs. 10a the brevity of man's life is treated, which is never fully understood unless contrasted with strophe A (vs. 4). In vs. 10b man's life is said to be full of labor and sorrow, which statement should be read together with strophe A′ (vs. 17). Only divine favor can make man's labor a success. Thus the two extreme strophes are made to converge in the central strophe. The *children* of men are mentioned in AA′.

Strophes BB′ show a chiastic arrangement of their lines as indicated by the terms in italics. It will be observed that the word *morning* is found in BB′ only, just as *children* was found only in AA′. Strophes CC′ are a little more elaborate, having a chiastic arrangement of *couplets*. Man's iniquity and sin (vs. 8) and the divine anger, manifested in human suffering (vss. 7, 9), are related to each other as cause to effect. The parallel terms in vss. 7, 9 are indicated by italics. In strophe C′ we find a similarity of content and form, but with this difference: Whereas C is devoted to a description of the visitation of divine wrath upon men, C′

sets forth how the wrath is to cease. Again the cause of the removal, i.e., man's acquisition of wisdom, is placed in the central couplet (vs. 12), while the effect, i.e., the knowledge, the power of God's anger and the giving of due reverence to him (vs. 11), as well as the ultimate return of divine favor (vs. 13), are set forth in the extreme couplets of C′. The words "anger" and "rage" which occurred in parallel couplets in C (vs. 7, 9) recur side by side in the same couplet in C′ (vs. 11). Why C′ should make this departure in structure from the pattern of C does not become clear until another feature of the poem is observed. We have already seen how the two couplets in D were definitely related in content to strophes AA′. Likewise the last couplet of C′ (vs. 13) carries the verb "return," which must be connected with vs. 3, the only two places in the psalm where the verb is found. This also sheds light on another feature which also occurs twice in the psalm. The first couplet of C (vs. 7) is chiastic, and this is also true of vs. 16. This may, for want of a better name, be called a species of literary cross-stitching with parallel terms or forms. There are several examples of this method of arrangement in the Psalms. When we have observed the perfect balance of terms in strophe C (vss. 7, 9), we naturally look for a similar balance of terms in C′. But we find the two terms describing the divine wrath in vs. 11, and none in vs. 13. This apparent irregularity, however, is a deliberate departure made by the poet in order to introduce another literary pattern which has been superimposed upon the regular pattern of the poem.

We must bring our observations on the psalms to a close. Our analysis indicates that the chiastic and alternating patterns were approved literary methods in the poetic guilds of Israel. The occurrence in the centre of the structure of references to the realm of the dead (Pss. 30, 88) also indicates a conventional disposition of certain ideas in the writing of poetry. There are, in the New Testament as well, many examples of the tendency of certain terms to gravitate toward the centre of a system, as it were, and to recur in this position again and again. The term "body" when meaning the church, is a notable instance of this tendency in the Pauline epistles. There are also New Testament examples of cross-stitching with terms. Such rigid rules governing both form and content are not likely to find much favor with men of the twentieth century, who are given to what they call self-expression. It is evident, however, that much beauty and charm can live in the most rigid forms. Whether in music, or art, or poetry, an artist appears now and then who has so thoroughly mastered the technique of expression that he is able to infuse life into all forms. He uses his forms so skilfully that the public is deceived by the apparent spontaneity of his productions, and assumes that the works of genius are artless, whereas in reality the apparent artlessness is the result of perfect mastery of the forms of expression. Much has been written, for example, on the mechanical rigidity of the acrostic psalms. Yet the restrictions they impose on the poet are not to be compared with the restrictions of symmetrical distributions of the divine names in strophes or the intricate interweaving of parallel ideas, phrases, or terms in ever-shifting alternating and chiastic patterns. That the poetic spirit of the ancient Hebrews could conquer these rigid forms which to us appear to be so inflexible and forbidding is the highest tribute to their genius.

Before we conclude our discussion of the material in the Old Testament a few remarks with reference to the origin of the chiastic forms may not be without interest. As far as we have progressed we have been analyzing and describing purely objective facts; in the discussion of origins, however, a large element of conjecture must enter. For the origin of the chiasmus, like all other origins, is shrouded in obscurity. It is doubtless safe to postulate at the outset that the chiasmus is a primitive form of expression. It appears to be, in its simplest form, a very natural mode of expression. A speaker or writer, who in the presentation of facts enumerates several items, will often find that in taking up these items later for further treatment in his discourse he will refer to them in the inverted order. Such occurrences are so common that any person who is in the habit at all to observe his own mental processes will have little need of illustrations. At this stage, however, the inverted order could hardly be classified either as literature or art, for such forms represent altogether the unconscious workings of the mind.

In the folksongs of all nations and in the spontaneous jingles recited by children in all lands there are frequent inversions. A well-known example is the opening lines of Old King Cole:

Old King Cole/was a merry old soul,
And a merry old soul/was he.

More elaborate constructions of the same order may be found in the literature for children. The following specimen came from the lips of a little boy, who recited these lines with great gusto. The present writer has never seen them in print and has not been able to find anyone who has traced them to their source. They are possibly part of a purely "oral tradition" which has been in existence a very long time. Both the spelling and the meaning of the first and the last lines must remain an unanswered riddle. In addition to the chiastic order of the ideas this specimen also has meter and rhyme:

Dansity, didity, popity, pin,
  Had a new dress,
    When summer comes in;
    When summer goes out,
  It's all worn out.
Dansity, didity, popity, pin.

The evident delight with which such lines are recited by children indicates that they belong to the nature of things. Yet in the jingles we have some degree of conscious elaboration, for they have been put into shape by some one person who possessed some degree of appreciation of literary form.

In the Greek and Latin literatures the chiasmus attains the status of an accepted literary device. The grammarians, both ancient and modern, are aware of its existence and have observed and discussed the passages in which it occurs. Few writers, however, have been aware of the great role the chiasmus has played in the poetry of Homer. Professor Samuel E. Bassett of the University of Vermont[3] has shown conclusively that Homer has used the chiasmus extensively in the disposition of his material in the Odyssey. Especially in the manner in which Homer introduces questions and answers is the chiasmus prominent. This is due, no

[3] *Op. cit.*

doubt, to the difficulty of carrying on a dialogue in an epic poem. Homer solves this literary problem by introducing his questions in volleys; the answers follow invariably in the inverted order. One of the instances cited by Professor Bassett is of particular interest. Odysseus is represented in one of the scenes of the poem as meeting his mother who has returned to him from Hades. He asks her a series of seven questions relative to his home and his friends; these questions are then taken up in the inverted order and are answered by his mother. There are many such situations in the Odyssey, which are discussed with fine appreciation in Professor Bassett's interesting monograph.

Cicero was familiar with this mannerism of Homer and refers to it in a letter to his friend Atticus as ὕστερον πρότερον ὡμηρικῶς. (Att. I. 16, 1). The ancient grammarians have also made references to this particular feature in the Homeric poems. Professor Bassett suggests that the chiasmus may have determined the disposition of more extensive sections of the Homeric poems, and that after enumerating various items the poet may have felt free to discuss these items, not always in the chronological order in which the events themselves transpired, but taking up the description with what at the time was "in his mind." That type of Homeric criticism which seeks to obtain a better sequence in the epic by rearranging some of the sections may, after all, have missed a very important point of the poet's art. Be this as it may, even in Homer the chiastic form has not been brought to that highly artistic development which we have found in the Old Testament. That the chiasmus was employed by Homer as a conscious literary device which was just as much part of his poetic technique as were all the other Homeric mannerisms, Professor Bassett has shown beyond doubt. In view of these facts one cannot help speculating as to the extent to which Homer, a native of Ionia and living on the fringe of the ancient Semitic world, might have been indebted to the old Semitic culture for some of his impulses and literary patterns. Much has been written in modern times on the Hellenization of the Orient by the conquest of Alexander, for of this chapter in ancient history we know a great deal. But cultural influences never flow in only one direction. There can be little doubt that the Semitic world also left its imprint on the Greek mind, and that the cultural influences that flowed from East to West were at work many centuries before Alexander's conquest of the Orient.

The view of the Ancient Near East which has been prevalent until quite recently, namely, that the East had everything to receive and little, if anything, to impart to the West, must, in view of recent discoveries, be considerably revised. The ancient civilizations of the Euphrates and Nile valleys, and the culture of ancient Syria are now attracting the attention of the orientalist as never before, and recent discoveries are compelling a new attempt to write the history of these ancient countries. Among the more recent discoveries are the Ras Shamra Inscriptions, which have added considerably to the history of the Hebrew language and the religious institutions of the Old Testament world. Professor James A. Montgomery of the University of Pennsylvania has recently called attention to the strophic structure of the Ras Shamra texts.[4]

The Conflict of Baal and the Waters.

Kuthar-of-the-Bands (?) descends and scolds them by name:
"Thy name, thou!"
   Surges, surges,
A The surge of the sea,
   The surge of the sea,
      To his throne the River,
      To the seat of his rule.

Advances/the congregation of Baal,
Like an eagle with his fingers/*he smote*
B *The shoulder* of Zebul-of-the-Sea,
On the breast the Ruler-of-the-River.

Advances/the band of the congregation of Baal,
Like an eagle with his fingers/*he smites*
C *The shoulder* of Zebul-of-the-Sea,
On the breast the Ruler-of-the-River.

— — — — — — — — — — — —
— — — — — — — — — — — —

Kuthar-of-the-Bands descends and scolds them by name:
"Thy name, thou!"
   Aymr, Aymr,

[4] "The Conflict of Baal and the Waters," *The Journal of the American Oriental Society*, Vol. LV, Number 3 (Sept., 1935), pp. 268-277.

A′ Mr of the Sea,
Mr of the Sea,
To his throne the River,
To the seat of his rule.

Advances/the congregation of Baal,
Like an eagle with his fingers/*he smote*
B′ *The skull* of Zebul-of-the-Sea,
On the forehead the Ruler-of-the-River.
He suppresses the sea,
And he raises the earth.

And advances/the band of the congregation of Baal,
Like an eagle with his fingers/*he smites*
C′ *The skull* of Zebul-of-the-Sea,
On the forehead the Ruler-of-the-River.
He suppresses the sea,
He raises the earth.

— — — — — — — — — — — —

— — — — — — — — — — — — — —

At the present stage of scholarly investigation of the Ras Shamra texts many details of this poem must necessarily remain uncertain. Hence no attempt has been made in the present arrangement to reproduce the last two lines in strophes CC′, nor the disputed words *mr* in A′. We venture to suggest that the introductory couplet in BC and in B′C′ should be treated as chiastic. One immediately raises the question why the last half of the poem should go over the same ground as the first half in nearly the same language, but a closer scrutiny of the second half shows several clear indications of a climactic arrangement. Climax is indicated already in the shift of tenses from "he smote" to "he smites" (cf. BC), as noted by Professor Montgomery, but more so in the advance from "the shoulder" and "on the breast" (cf. BC) to "the skull" and "on the forehead" (cf. B′C′), the latter being more vital parts than the former. Further evidence of climax will be found in the description of the two additional lines found in B′C′, which indicate the *results* of the battle. Of a similar nature is the shift from two *jussive* verbs in the last two untranslated lines of C to the two verbs in the *indicative* in the two parallel lines in C′, which detail is fully noted by Professor Montgomery.

Parallelism, chiasmus, strophic arrangement, and alternating couplets in the strophe, together with climax—these are a surprisingly great number of features corresponding to those found in Hebrew poetry to be found within the compass of a few lines of a fragment. Whatever conclusions may yet be reached with reference to the as yet obscure details of the Ras Shamra texts, their discovery has shown beyond doubt that the literary characteristics of the Old Testament have antecedents that may now be traced to the middle of the second millennium before Christ in Syria.

The chiasmus was not altogether unknown to the poets of ancient Babylonia, for there are traces of it in some of their writings. In a poem commonly called "Babylonian Job"[5] there occurs a central section which is clearly a chiastic construction. The hero of the poem is meditating upon the relations between men and the gods, but his conclusions are not very hopeful. The first line refers to measures previously taken in order to propitiate the gods.

Would that I knew that with a god are agreeable such things:
What seems good
 To oneself,
A To a god is worthlessness;
  What to his mind is despicable,
 Before his god.
Seems good.

Who the will of God in the midst of heaven
 Comprehends?
B The counsel of a god is full of knowledge,
  It understands who?
 Where have comprehended
The way of a god human beings?

Who yesterday/was alive,
Is dead/to-day.
C Quickly he is saddened,
  Suddenly he is crushed.
In a moment he sings a hymn,
In a pace he wails like a mourner.

[5] S. Langdon, *Babylonian Wisdom*, has been used for the text. For the translation I am indebted to Dr. F. W. Geers of the Oriental Institute, Chicago, who by request reproduced the order of the sentence in the original. For other translations consult the works of Lehmann-Haas, *Textbuch zur Religionsgeschichte* (2nd ed., 1922), pp. 311 ff.; H. Zimmern (in Reitzenstein, *Das iranische Erlösungsmysterium*), pp. 253 ff.; for the general subject consult Fr. Stummer, *Sumerisch-Akkadische Parallelen zum Aufbau alttestamentlicher Psalmen* (in *Studien zur Geschichte und Kultur des Altertums*, XI 1/2 1922).

Like day and night their will changes:

They are *hungry*, they are like a *corpse*,
D They are *sated*, they rival their *god*.
In *prosperity* they talk of ascending to *heaven*,
They are in *trouble*, they talk about descending to *hell*.

The tale of ancient Babylonia from which this text is taken was discovered by Layard at Koyunjik in 1849. The poem must have been popular, for several copies of it were found in the ruins of Ashurbanipal's palace. The fact that the text in some cases is supplied with a commentary indicates that the poem must have attained the status of a classic. For our purpose the form of the poem rather than its religious and philosophical implications is of interest.

The poem begins with a hymn to Marduk, and the mutilated last tablet indicates that the poem also ends with a hymn of thanksgiving. The central section, which is printed above with a view of presenting its peculiar chiastic form, contains the hero's futile attempts to rationalize the relations between gods and men. What his difficulties are may be seen in the four strophes. In the first place there seems to be no common moral denominator existing between gods and men (A). Such being the case the attempt to understand the gods must be given up (B). Man's life is of too short duration (C) and his mind is altogether too fickle and lacking in constancy (D) to enable him to reach certain conclusions.

The form of these strophes are the usual forms found in the Hebrew psalms. Several examples like strophes A and B have already been discussed. Strophe C is more intricate, for it is made up of three couplets. The first of these is chiastic, and is parallel to the third. For to be alive, or dead, is matched by the singing and wailing in the third couplet. The central couplet merely emphasizes the suddenness with which man passes from life to death. A glance at Ps. 90:7-9 will show a strophe that is exactly alike in structure.

Strophe D is introduced by a single line which indicates in general the subject of the following strophe, but has no structural relations to it. This mannerism of the poet is also found in strophe A above. Strophe D contains two antithetic couplets with the antithetic terms expressed both in the first and second half of the two lines of each couplet. The contrast is between the fortunes and misfortunes of men, but the order of these ideas is inverted in the second couplet, thus producing a quatrain which is chiastic. The inversion of these ideas is maintained in the last half as well as in the first. For the hungry are those in trouble, and the sated are those in prosperity. Likewise a corpse is associated with hell (the Babylonian "Irkallu"), and the god is in heaven. The most striking feature of the quatrain, however, is the abruptness of the statements. They stand side by side in each line without conjunctions or any other grammatical connection. This striking abruptness is found also in Ps. 104:28, 29.

Thou givest unto them, they gather;
Thou openest thy hand, they are satisfied;
Thou hidest thy face, they are troubled;
Thou takest away their breath, they die.

The Hebrew poet has not seen fit to introduce inversion into this strophe, but by the simple device of placing the third line first he would have produced a chiastic strophe which would have been the exact counterpart of the one produced by the Babylonian poet. The literary principle that has been expressed in these strophes has found a more intricate expression in Matt. 7:17, 18, which is discussed in the chapter on the Sermon on the Mount.

From this brief comparison it will be seen that the similarity between the Babylonian poem and the Hebrew psalms is more than a superficial one. Not only are the ordinary features, like parallelism, chiasmus, and strophe present, but an unusual structure as Ps. 90:7-9 with only one couplet chiastic, may be duplicated in the Babylonian poem. Whether these similarities prove interdependence or a common dependence on some other cultural source in the ancient Semitic world may be difficult to determine. Evidence of this nature, however, leads to the conclusion that the late dating of most of the Hebrew psalms is less necessary now than it formerly seemed to be. The literary climate in which such productions usually grow existed in Syria two millenniums before the Christian era. With the spread of the Semitic culture as the result of imperial conquests by Babylonia and Assyria there was an infiltration of thought and literary forms as well. There can be no doubt that a search for such literary forms in the liturgical texts of the ancient world will reveal among other things the use of the chiasmus much more extensively than has been suspected. For the Greek idea of climax is expressed by the ladder (Greek, κλῖμαξ), but the Hebrew idea of climax, which seems to be the general Semitic idea, is that of two ladders. Whatever the origin and spread of this form may be, one thing is certain: it has shaped to a very great extent the writings of the Old Testament, and it has passed over to the Greek New Testament as a sacred heritage of early Jewish Christianity.

THE EPISTLES OF PAUL

CHAPTER VI

THE STYLE OF PAUL

The earliest literary deposit of the Christian tradition consists of the epistles of Paul. Even if it is conceivable, or even probable, that some of the sources from which the evangelists drew their material for their gospels existed in written form before the year 50 A.D., the gospels themselves had not as yet been written. Paul of Tarsus was born in a centre of Greek culture. We recall how a new Greek style was developed by the Asianic rhetoricians at the period of decline in the classical Attic style after 300 B.C., and how this new development assumed two definite forms, namely, the diatribe and the Asianic rhythm. Paul, however, was much more than a Greek; he was also a Hebrew of the Hebrews, who in Jerusalem acquired the training given to scholars of his own race. If, therefore, we should discover in his writings a residue which may not under any circumstances be made to conform to the patterns prevalent in the Greek rhetorical schools, this is merely what we should expect from a writer of his training and circumstances. Unless we feel free to assume that Paul took his Jewish training less seriously than his Greek education, we should naturally expect to find some traces of this training in his writings. Strange to say, these traces have been sought in his Rabbinical method of argument, of Scripture quotation, of allegorization, and the like, but rarely in his literary style. Whenever Paul does not measure up to Greek rhetorical standards, it has been assumed either that he is not interested in or that he is unable to write a literary style. Few students of his style have made the most of the observation, that his writings represent a "middle-type."

Now, the epistles of Paul have always presented a great many problems to the interpreter. Not only are they full of allusions to situations with which we are little acquainted, and they present modes of thought which seem strange to us, but they suffer also from a diffuse and repetitious style, which, at times, makes it difficult to construe his sentences. Even when there is no difficulty in following his thought, his literary style appears heavy and cumbersome. From the earliest times to our own days, we meet with writers who find Paul difficult to follow. In the early church we find one who discovers in the epistles of Paul "some things hard to be understood" (2 Pet. 3:16). Erasmus observes how Paul often "making a digression far away, doubles back on himself." Norden, in spite of his warm admiration for Paul as a man, admits that only with great difficulty does he understand his writings, for the Apostle's method of argumentation is strange, and his style is not Greek. Therefore, as the first step in our study of the Pauline epistles we shall give a few appraisals of Paul as a writer by men who have devoted themselves to such studies. These criticisms will give us a view of the real problem before us. We shall then through observation of the structure of a great number of passages in the Pauline epistles attempt to show how a comparatively simple solution is found in the application of the chiastic principle to these passages.

Archdeacon Paley long ago made some remarks concerning the style of Paul. They refer to "a species of digression, which may be properly denominated *going off at a word.* It is turning aside from the subject upon the occurrence of some particular word, forsaking the trend of thought then in hand, and *entering upon a parenthetic sentence* in which that word is the prevailing term." Among such cases Paley quotes Eph. 4:8-11, of which passage we shall hear more presently.[1] In a sermon entitled "Transformation by Beholding," on 2 Cor. 3:18, Alexander Maclaren, while quoting these words of Paley makes the following remarks of his own on Paul's style:

> This whole section of the epistle in which our text occurs is a remarkable instance of the fervid richness of the apostle's mind, which acquires force by motion, and like a chariot wheel catches fire as it revolves. One of the most obvious peculiarities of his style is his habit of "going off at a word." Each thought of his is, as it were, barbed all around, and catches and draws into sight a multitude of others, *but slightly related to the purpose in hand.* And this gives at first sight the appearance of confusion to his writings. But this is not confusion, it is richness.

[1] William Paley, *Horae Paulinae,* Chap. VI, No. III.

The luxuriant underwood which this fertile soil bears, as some tropical forest, does not choke the great trees, though it drapes them.

Though the famous English preacher is inclined to hide the apparent confusion of Paul's style by calling it richness, other writers have been less lenient in their criticism. Referring to the first two chapters of Colossians, Samuel Davidson[2] does not hesitate to call their style "loose and tautological," and Jülicher[3] can allude to the "unwonted stiffness" of the same two chapters as being in Ephesians "substantially exaggerated and multiplied." Cumbrous sentences, full of participles and relative pronouns, are the rule. Many other scholars concur in this rather unfavorable estimate of the style in the epistles of Paul. No less an authority than Friedrich Blass, while discussing the accumulation of participles in some of the sentences of Luke, whom he pronounces "never devoid of a certain amount of stylistic refinement," takes a side-glance at Paul, and observes that this refinement differs "from the instances of accumulation in the epistolary style of Paul, which consists rather of a mere stringing together of words." Blass, in comparing the periodic sentence of artistic style with the loose sentence of the oldest, less sophisticated writings, finds that the latter is, on the whole, the style of the New Testament, agreeing with the manner of Semitic models on which the narrative is based. This method of stringing together many sentences with a καὶ is found in the gospels and appears tedious:

> Another class of continuous style is that where the opening sentence is developed by appending to it a participle, or a clause introduced by ὅτι, or a relative sentence or in some similar way, since in this case also *there is no end or termination in view;* this manner of writing, which is freely employed by Paul in large portions of the Epistles to the Ephesians and Colossians, is indeed still more tedious and presents still greater obscurity than the simple linking together of the sentences by means of καὶ.[4]

There seems to be unanimous agreement among scholars that the style of Paul is exceedingly verbose and repetitious, and that his sentences are loosely put together and hence difficult to under-

[2] Samuel Davidson, *An Introduction to the New Testament*, Vol. II.
[3] A. Jülicher, *An Introduction to the New Testament*, p. 142.
[4] Friedrich Blass, *Grammar of New Testament Greek*, pp. 251, 275-276.

stand. Blass, however, emphasizes the central point of the whole matter by directing our attention to the Semitic models of Paul. But neither Blass nor any other scholar has questioned whether it is fair to judge the style of writings, which for their models have Semitic patterns, by the canons of classical Greek writers. Much of the Pentateuch is likewise verbose and repetitious, but, as we have already seen in the leprosy laws, the repetitiousness may easily be reduced to a system, to a literary style, which is just as fixed and determinable as any style of the Greeks or the Romans, and which has just as much claim to our appreciation as any other forms that may come before us in the literatures of the human race. The literary patterns which were followed by the writers of the New Testament have not been known, and modern writers on the style of the New Testament have measured it altogether by Greek standards. Though all these writers have more or less correctly described the facts to be found in the epistles of Paul, they have all gone astray when called upon to explain these facts. To some "a digression far away," to speak with Erasmus, has offered clear evidence of interpolations. The difference between passages in the same epistle which remind us of "the clear spring" and "the torrent" would be used as evidence of Paul's nervous disposition or of his irascible temper. Other writers seem inclined to apologize for Paul, and they remind us of the difficulty of maintaining a good style while dictating, or while leaving a large share of the details to an amanuensis. The sincerity and ardent nature of the apostle together with the rush of his thought, as in the quotation from Maclaren, have been made to condone for his style. The picture of a man so occupied with his ideas that he had neither time nor inclination to consider the form of his message has been presented to explain why his epistles are what they are. With reference to The Second Epistle of Paul to the Corinthians, A. Robertson has observed that "the order is emotional rather than logical; a subject is not taken up, dealt with, and disposed of, but, like some strain in a piece of impassioned music, occurs, is lost in a maze of crowding harmonies, *and recurs again and again.*"[5]

These quotations from various writers might be multiplied.

[5] *Hastings Dictionary of the Bible*, Vol. I, p. 497.

They all emphasize the same points, namely, digression, recurrence, and the indefinite termination of the sentence. The criticism is just, provided we agree that Paul's style is to be judged solely by our own Greek and Roman principles of rhetoric. As soon as we approach his epistles with the standards provided for us by the *chiastic* and *alternating* order of ideas, so conspicuous a feature of Hebrew style, we have a new instrument for the investigation and appraisal of Paul's style.

The late Johannes Weiss, though he is comparing Paul with the Greek rhetoricians, has, nevertheless, given some attention to two features which prove helpful in the understanding of Paul's style: (1) that the epistles are written for the *ear* and are not to be interpreted by logic only, and (2) that we have in them frequent examples of the Hebrew *parallelismus membrorum.*

What Paul is lacking (!) in prose style he makes up for in his carefully written letters by a sure rhetorical movement which, decisive, stirring, and frequent as it is through symmetry, rhythm, buoyancy, and fulness of sound, does appear artful.[6]

Speaking of parallelisms he says, "In no way are these parallelisms a sign of an elevated speech by the apostle, for they occur also in the more sober and business-like parts of the epistles. But besides he has in some parts of his epistles made use of it with greater art, buoyancy, and grace. Often one would not think of the Hebrew parallelism at all, for the Greek rhetorical model seems to lie nearer. But even in this territory the parallelism in several varieties is a well-liked form of expression.[7]

Johannes Weiss has observed that parallelism is found not only in passages containing lofty thought, but also in passages dealing with routine matters of church administration. This does not surprise us, for parallelism of some kind is found also in the most prosaic of all prose, the Levitical laws of the Old Testament. Less acceptable is the observation of Weiss that Paul should have approached the Greek rhetorical models in the more artful of his passages. There is no more artful passage in the epistles of Paul than the thirteenth chapter of First Corinthians and this chapter is one of the finest specimens of chiasmus in the New Testament.

[6] Johannes Weiss, *Beiträge zur paulinischen Rhetoric*, p. 167.
[7] *Op. cit.*, p. 169.

The most surprising factor in this long and interesting treatise by Weiss is that he nowhere betrays any knowledge of the extensive use of chiasmus in the New Testament. To be sure, he will occasionally call attention to an ordinary chiasmus of four or six lines,[8] but he is not aware of the longer structures in the epistles of Paul. It is merely symptomatic of modern tendencies that such an eminent writer who is interested in matters of style has not made use of the chiastic principle to any greater extent in his investigations of Paul's style.

We intend to call attention to the cultural heritage of the Hebrews, as it stands revealed in the style of Paul, and to show that Paul's style, when judged in the light of this heritage, is not deficient from a literary point of view. It is merely *a new type* of Greek style which has its cultural roots in the Old Testament. The apostolic age was a creative age in more ways than one, and to the student of church history there is nothing surprising in the fact that a new religious movement like Christianity should have been creative also in the forms through which it expressed its distinctive truths.

[8] Johannes Weiss, *Das Urchristentum*, p. 310, on 1 Cor. 9:19-22.

CHAPTER VII

THE FIRST EPISTLE TO THE CORINTHIANS

We have already given an example of chiasmus from Col. 3:3-4, but there are many more in the epistles of Paul. We shall give a number of these together with a discussion of the most outstanding features of their arrangement and style. The following passage from 1 Cor. 6:12-14 shows a combination of chiastic forms with the ordinary couplet:

All things are lawful for me; 12
But not all things are expedient.
All things are lawful for me;
But I will not be brought under the power of any.

Meats 13
A For the belly,
And the belly
For the meats.

B And the Lord both it
And them shall bring to naught.

But the body not for fornication,
A′ But for the Lord,
And the Lord
For the body.

B′ And God both raised the Lord, 14
And will raise us up through his power.

The trend of thought in this passage becomes clear by the literary analysis. In vs. 12 Paul opposes certain misapplications of his own principle of the Christian's freedom from the Law. The Corinthian church had undoubtedly misused Paul's statement, "All things are lawful for me." In his answer Paul shows that some things are not expedient and that others are of an enslaving nature to man. In vss. 13, 14 the nature of the misunderstanding is made clear. The Pauline disregard for meats had been given an unwarranted application to other functions in which the body was involved, and the Corinthians had begun to treat fornication as of no consequence. In A Paul mentions this principle about meats, and in B he agrees to it on the ground that both belly and meat will be brought to naught (Col. 2:22). In A′, on the other hand, Paul sets forth the misuse of the former principle and in B′ he corrects their mistake on the ground that the body is to be raised. Two chiastic structures carry the statement of the principle (AA′), and two couplets (BB′), alternating with the former, contain Paul's own comment on the principle.

In 1 Cor. 5:2-6 the following structure is to be found which deals with Paul's advice in regard to fornication.

A And ye are *puffed up*, and did not rather mourn, 2

That might be taken away from you he that hath *done this thing*. 3
B For I, indeed, being absent in body, but *present* in spirit,
Have already judged, as though I were *present*.
Him that hath so *wrought this thing;*

In the *name* of the *Lord Jesus*, 4
C *Ye* being gathered together
And *my spirit*,
With the *power* of our *Lord Jesus*,

To deliver such a one *to Satan*, 5
For the *destruction*
B′ Of the *flesh*,
That the *spirit*
Might be *saved*
In the day of *the Lord*.

A′ Your *glorying* is not good. 6

Paul reproves the attitude of the Corinthians in making light of the offender (AA′). What might have happened to the offender, had the church acted in accordance with Christian principles, is set forth in B, and what will happen, when they so act, is described in B′. The authority on which this action is based is that of the Lord, made evident in the accord of Paul and the church (C). The structure of the central system indicates that the reading of some manuscript in the first line, "*our* Lord Jesus," is probably the correct one. The only difference between this passage and the previous one is that the former has alternating sections while in this the chiastic form is permitted also to shape the order of the sections. This is a clear example of how a sentence that would fall under the criticism of Blass because of apparently interminable additions to the main sentence, may not be without termination; the sentence hastens with steady steps toward its termination. Not for one moment is the end lost sight of, as may be seen in the additional, "Your glorying is not good," which terminates the structure at the point where it began in A. Such a sentence can only be considered chiastically.

In 1 Cor. 9:19-22 we have a passage which contains a personal confession of Paul, yet even this autobiographical section of the epistle is wrought in literary form. This has not escaped Weiss,[1] although he does not observe the alternating order of the ideas in the chiastic form of the whole passage.

For though I was free from all, 19
A I brought myself under bondage to all,
That I might gain the more.

I became 20
B To the Jews,
As a Jew,
That I might gain Jews.

To them that are under the law,
C As under the law,
Not being myself under the law,
That I might gain them that are under the law.

To them that are without law, 21
As without law,
C′ Not being without the law of God,
but under the law of Christ,
That I might gain them that are without law.

I became 22
B′ To the weak,
Weak,
That I might gain the weak.

To all
A′ I have become all things,
That I might by all means save some.

This is a good example of passages in which the sections are chiastic while the lines are alternating. Paul shows how in dealing with his converts he has always adapted himself to the stage of maturity in which he found them. The purpose, which in all six instances is expressed in the last line of each section, was to gain

[1] Johannes Weiss, *Das Urchristentum*, p. 310.

them for Christ. Only in A′ is the verb "save" substituted for "gain," but the meaning remains unchanged. Line by line the same ideas recur without variation until the passage is completed, unless it be in C′ where the reference to "the law of Christ" is made, probably to save Paul from the charge of being a lawless person. This passage is of the same type as Isa. 28:15-18; Lev. 11:24-28; 14:21-32.

Even in a passage of such practical content as 1 Cor. 11:8-12 the literary form is observed with great care. Paul is setting forth the reasons why women should be veiled in public assemblies.

For the man is not 8
A Of the woman,
But the woman
Of the man.

For neither was the man created 9
B For the woman,
But the woman
For the man.

C For this cause the woman ought to have authority 10
upon her head because of the angels.

Nevertheless, Neither is the woman 11
B′ Without the man,
Nor the man
Without the woman, in the Lord.

For as the woman is 12
A′ Of the man,
So is also man
By the woman; but all things are of God.

In this passage we find an interesting play upon the terms "man" and "woman." In AB man is found in the extremes and woman in the centre of the two chiastic structures, while in B′A′ this order has been reversed. The division between the two kinds of structures is marked by C which contains the statement of what ought to be done, but in this statement there is no chiastic form. The former order is deliberately interrupted before the latter is introduced. In meaning there seems to be some parallel between BB′; the preposition ἐκ, which appears in A, recurs once in A′. In AA′ there is also a parallel meaning. The whole structure is the central panel of the passage 11:2-16.

In Ps. 89:30-34 we have what may have been the model of this passage. The whole poem is a splendid specimen of chiastic structure, but only the section which offers similarities to our passage will be introduced here.

If his sons forsake 30
A My law,
And in my judgments
Do not walk;

If my statutes 31
B They profane,
And do not keep
My commandments;

C Then will I visit with a rod their transgression, 32
And with stripes their iniquity.

But my lovingkindness 33
B′ Not I will utterly take away from him,
And not I will be false
In my faithfulness.

Not I will profane 34
A′ My covenant,
And what is gone out of my lips
Not I will change.

In this passage there is a play upon the nouns and the verbs, the nouns appearing at the centre and the verbs in the extreme lines in AA′. This order is completely reversed in BB′. There is also a play upon the possessives, "my," which follow the order of the nouns. Finally we have the negatives, "not," which are double in B′A′ but occur singly in AB. The central couplet C stands in a class by itself, since there is no chiasmus in these lines. By beginning the sentence with the words, "Then their transgression I will visit," etc., these lines also could have been made chiastic, but they are left as an ordinary couplet, and the reason is that they serve as a dividing line between the two halves of the structure. The only irregularity is found in the third line of A′, where the circumlocution, "what is gone out of my lips" probably means, "my statutes," or "my promise." Thus the order of nouns and verbs, of negatives and possessives, are made to contribute to the artistic form of the passage. Paul, who, like so many of his race, knew the psalter by heart, would, almost unconsciously, find his literary models in its hymns.

The following passage from 2 Cor. 1:3-5 is not only perfectly symmetric, but is written with unsurpassed spontaneity. The parallelisms seem to trickle from the pen of the writer with unconscious ease, and they testify to his perfect mastery of form. The words of Weiss with reference to 1 Cor. 9:19-22 may be applied to this passage with still greater propriety. "Such things do not originate by themselves but only through meditation or through masterly training."[2]

Blessed the God 3
And Father
A Of our Lord Jesus Christ,
The Father of mercies,
And God

Of all comfort, who comforteth us 4
In all our afflictions,
B That we may be able to comfort them that are
In any affliction
Through the comfort wherewith we ourselves are comforted of God.

For as abound the sufferings 5
Of Christ
A′ Unto us,
Even so through Christ
Aboundeth also our comfort

There are several interesting features in this passage. The symmetrical distribution of the names of the deity in A is conspicuous, as is the name of Christ in A′. In the central section (B) there is a double parallelism of "comfort" and "comforteth" in the first and the last lines, and this double parallelism is found also in the extreme lines of A′. In B the parallelisms are synonymous, but in A′ they are partly synonymous and partly antithetic (cf. "sufferings" and "comfort"). The meaning of affliction is explained in the central line, "that *we* may be able to comfort." Whether Paul is administering reproof to those that have been remiss in any Christian duty, or bringing comfort to his brethren, he observes the same careful literary style. Never were form and freedom more beautifully blended than in this passage.

[2] *Das Urchristentum*, p. 310.

We need not continue to give any greater number of the briefer passages, which may be found almost anywhere in the epistles of Paul, but shall proceed to analyze some of the *longer sections* into whose structure the chiastic and alternating parallelisms have entered. The seventh chapter of Paul's First Epistle to the Corinthians is long; it deals with some social problems which arose when Christians attempted to apply the ideals of Christianity in a pagan society. We shall first give a general outline of the main parts of this chapter and later give the separate parts. This is done with a view of helping the reader to grasp the main features of the chapter from the start before we enter into the details.

A Literary Analysis of Chapter Seven

I. Introduction: A man is not to touch a woman, vs. 1.
II. The Sexual Problem in the Married State and its Solution, vss. 2-5.
III. Rules Governing Married Couples and some Unmarried, vss. 6-17.
IV. Circumcision or Uncircumcision, vss. 18-20.
V. Bond or Free, vss. 21-24.
VI. Rules Governing Virgins and some Married Couples, vss. 25-35.
VII. The Sexual Problem in the Virgin State and its Solution, vss. 36-39.
VIII. Conclusion: A woman is happier as she is, vs. 40.

It will be seen at a glance that the first three parts and the last three deal with the sexual problem, while parts IV and V deal with classes in the church, and what their attitude ought to be. No one can read through the chapter without sensing the radical change of subject at the centre (vss. 18-24). This is nothing else than the law of the shift at the centre, of which several instances have been noticed in the Old Testament. We shall now give a detailed arrangement of Part II (vss. 2-5):

Part II, vss. 2-5

A But because of fornications, 2

B Let each man have his own wife,
And let each woman have her own husband.

C Let the husband render unto the wife her due; 3
And likewise also the wife unto the husband.

C′ The wife hath not power over her own body, but the husband; 4
And likewise also the husband hath not power over his own body, but
(the wife.

B′ Defraud not one the other, except it be by consent for a season, 5
That ye may give yourselves unto prayer, and may be together again,

A′ That Satan tempt you not because of your incontinence.

This passage does not contain Paul's preference in regard to marriage, which he has expressed in the introduction and conclusion of this chapter (cf. vs. 1 with vs. 40), but rather his concessions because of weak human nature (cf. vs. 6). The members of the church were confronted with temptations because of fornications (A) and because of incontinence (A′). They should live in monogamy (B) and they should have marital relations, unless by consent they denied themselves for a season and for specific reasons (B′). The rights of each party are stated in CC′. Paul follows the principle of expediency in the face of human weakness. We shall see later how precisely the same principle is invoked with reference to the virgins in Part VII.

Part III, vss. 6-17

But this I say by way of concession, 6
Not of commandment.
X Yet I would that all men were even as myself; 7
Howbeit each man hath his own gift from God,
One after this manner.
And another after that.

But *I say* to the unmarried and to the widows, 8
A It is good for them if they abide even as I.
But if they have not continency, let them marry: 9
For it is better to marry than to burn.[3]

But to the married I give charge, *not I* but the Lord, 10
That the wife depart not from the husband—
But should she depart, 11
Y B Let her remain unmarried,
Or else be reconciled to her husband—
And that the husband leave not his wife.
But to the rest *say I*, not the Lord: 12

If any brother hath an unbelieving wife,
And she is content to dwell with him,
A′ Let him not leave her.
And the woman that hath an unbelieving husband, 13
And he is content to dwell with her,
Let her not leave her husband.

For is sanctified 14
A The unbelieving husband
In the wife;

And is sanctified
B The unbelieving wife
In the brother.

Else your children were unclean,
But now they are holy.
Y′ C Yet if the unbelieving departeth, 15
Let him depart.
The brother and sister is not under bondage in such cases:
But God hath called us in peace.

For how knowest thou, O wife, 16
A′ If thy husband
Thou shalt save?

Or how knowest thou, O husband,
B′ If thy wife
Thou shalt save?

Only as the Lord hath distributed to each man, 17
X′ As God hath called each,
So let him walk;
And so I ordain in all the churches.

This part of the chapter contains two frame-passages (XX′) which are made to carry the general message: (1) that men differ in accordance with the gift of God, or his call of each, and (2) that this difference has determined the apostle's advice. What he says is a concession and not a commandment (X), and is not ordained for the Corinthians alone, but uniformly for all the churches (X′). The two couplets in X′ correspond in thought with the first two in X, but the third in X has no counterpart in X′. Between this framework are placed two sections (YY′). The first

[8] Vss. 8, 9 are not parallel in content to vss. 12b-13. They do not appear to belong to YB at all. If they were placed between vss. 5 and 6 they would come *last* in Part II and form a good counterpart to vs. 39. Part III would then close with a reference to widows and Part VII, its counterpart, close with a similar reference in vs. 39.

of these (Y) advises that each Christian should remain as he is and seek no change in his status, but there is a difference in the statements, for in A and A′ we have merely the advice of Paul himself (cf. "I say," in A and in last line of B), while in the central section (B) we have the command of the Lord (cf. "not I, but the Lord"). While the structure of B indicates that the line introducing the advice in A′ really belongs to B, this does not change the fact that the contents in A and A′ correspond in one respect; for they are Paul's own advice, as distinguished from that of the Lord. That the social relations shall remain as they are, unless for grave reasons there is a necessity for changing them, is the burden of both sections. The command of the Lord is in line with the words of Jesus (Mt. 5:31, 32; 19:9), with these exceptions: (1) that the passages from the gospels contemplate the husband's "putting away" his wife, whereas Paul is thinking of one party leaving the other; and (2) that *both* parties are addressed and not the man only, as in the gospel. It is clear that in B Paul is addressing *Christians only* who were under his care and for whom the words of Jesus would be binding. This is significant, for in the central section C of Y′ we are not dealing with believers only, but with unbelievers also (cf. central lines). The verb "depart" is used in both cases, and nowhere else in Part III. Does not this fact prove the significance of the centre in such structures, and that the passage is constructed with a definite plan in view?

In Y, then, the advice is given to maintain things as they are, as far as possible, and in Y′ the reason for this request is given. Again we have in Y′ a remarkable instance of how the centre is the turning point of the system. For beginning with A and B and including the first couplet in C, we are contemplating a situation in which either party in the marriage is *willing* to remain in marriage. At the centre the *unwilling* parties are introduced, at least as a possibility; the advice that follows after the centre is passed is directed to either party in a marriage in which *one* wishes to terminate the relations. Yet, though the contents are the opposite to those of the first half, the *forms* are identical. We need not here ascertain in what sense one of the parties may be said to "sanctify" the other, although this is the reason given for maintaining the relations. Likewise, the inability of one party to "save" the other is given as the reason for not continuing the relations with an unwilling party. If a comparison be made between A and B, on the one hand, and A′ and B′, on the other, it will be found that though the *groups* of lines alternate, the *lines* themselves are chiastic. Had not the necessities of the case required a change of one term from "sanctified" to "save" in A′B′ we should have had a perfect chiasmus of three members, but, even as it is, "save" is a good parallel to "sanctify."

Part IV, vss. 18-20

Wast any man called being circumcised? 18
A Let him not become uncircumcised.
Hath any man been called in uncircumcision?
Let him not be circumcised.

Circumcision is nothing, 19
A′ And uncircumcision is nothing;
But the keeping of the commandment of God. 20
Let each man abide in the calling wherein he was called.

There were two classes in the church, Jews and Gentiles, whose chief difference was whether they were circumcised or uncircumcised. Neither should attempt to change its status, for such an external feature as circumcision was nothing. The keeping of the commandment of God alone was essential. Therefore, let each remain as he is.

Part V, vss. 21-24

Wast thou called being a bondservant? 21
A Care not for it;
But if thou canst become free,
Use it rather.

For he that was called in the Lord being a bondservant, 22
B Is the Lord's freedman;
Likewise he that was called being free,
Is Christ's bondservant.

Ye were bought with a price; 23
C Become not bondservants of men.
Brethren, let each man, wherein he was called, 24
Therein abide with God.

Having shown how the chasm between Jew and Gentile may be bridged, the apostle directs his attention to another cleavage in ancient society, that between bond and free. He advises against brooding over the situation, when one is a slave, but if there is an opportunity offered to become free, one should seize it (A). For the two classes which are so far apart on the social scale are, nevertheless, equalized in Christ. The slave is set free, with Christ's freedom, and shares in his opportunities. The free man, on the other hand, assumes the obligations of a Christian and enters the servitude that Christ imposes upon him (B). Both bond and free were bought by Christ and are free from all men, i.e., in a religious and moral sense. They should therefore be satisfied to remain as they are, but *with God*. There is a wealth of meaning compressed in these two words (C). We are at once conscious of the different nature of the two problems of Parts IV and V, for the problems are religious and racial, in one, and economic or social, in the other. As soon as we are done with the two central parts, however, we are back to the same subject with which the chapter began, that of marriage, in which both the married and the unmarried states are considered.

Part VI, vss. 25-35

X Now concerning virgins I have no commandment of the Lord, 25
But I give my judgment, as one that obtained mercy of the Lord to be trustworthy.

Y
A I think therefore that it is good by reason of the distress that is upon us, 26
that it is good for a man to be as he is.

Art thou bound to a wife? 27
B Seek not to be loosed.
Art thou loosed from a wife?
Seek not a wife.

But shouldest thou marry, 28
B′ Thou hast not sinned,
And if a virgin marry,
She hath not sinned.

A′ Yet such shall have tribulations in the flesh,
And I would spare you.

Z
A But this I say, brethren, that the time is shortened henceforth, 29

That both those that have wives
May be as though they had none;
And those that weep, 30
As though they wept not;
B And those that rejoice,
As though they rejoiced not;
And those that buy,
As though they possessed not;
And those that use the world, 31
As not using it to the full.

A′ For the fashion of this world passeth away.

Y′

A But I would have you free from cares. 32

B He that is unmarried is careful for the things of the Lord,
How he may please the Lord;
But he that is married is careful for the things of the world, 33
How he may please his wife,

C And is divided. 34

B′ Also the woman[4] that is unmarried, and the virgin, is careful for (the things of the Lord.
That she may be holy in body and in spirit;
But she that is married is careful for the things of the world,
How she may please her husband.

A′ And this I say for your own profit; 35

X′ Not that I may cast a halter upon you, but for that which is seemly,
And that ye may attend upon the Lord without distraction.

Part VI (vss. 25-35) is the counterpart of Part III. We therefore have a right to expect many similarities in the two, and in this we are not disappointed. We find the first striking parallel in the opening line of each part where the apostle disavows any "commandment." The term is not found elsewhere in the whole epistle, and its presence in the opening statement (vss. 6, 25) of the two parallel parts is due only to a deliberate design on the part of the writer. But the relation between the two parts is much more organic than one of similarity of terms. In both parts the desire to maintain the present status is the basis of the apostle's advice. He deals with the same groups of people, the married and the unmarried. The married people are dealt with in greater detail, and the unmarried, only incidentally. The permission to marry granted to the unmarried and the widows, who have not continency (Part III, YA), is balanced in the counterpart by a

[4] This line we expect to be similar in structure to the first line of Y′B, as are the third and fourth lines, and to read: "She that is unmarried is careful for the things of the Lord." Tischendorf's digest of readings indicates great confusion in the text in vs. 34.

ἡ ἄγαμος μεριμνᾷ τὰ τοῦ κυρίου

This is the reading of Tischendorf, Griesbach, and Alford, who make καὶ ἡ γυνὴ καὶ ἡ παρθένος subject of the preceding verb μεμέρισται. Alford quotes Jerome to the effect that the reading in Latin codices is: *Divisa est virgo et mulier.* Jerome adds, however, *tamen non est apostolicae veritatis,* i.e. not in Greek codices. In Y the *man* is considered in B and the *virgin* in B′. This would be repeated in Y′ if καὶ ἡ παρθένος is retained in the first line of B′. The words καὶ ἡ γυνὴ were either added by a scribe who sought another subject for the preceding verb or were originally subject of the verb.

similar permission to the unmarried and the virgins (Part VI, YB′). In one respect Part VI is fuller than its counterpart, for it supplies the *reasons,* or rather some new reasons for maintaining the present status, namely, the present distress, the short time and the passing of the world, and the distractions of the married state. With these preliminary remarks of comparison between the two parts we may now enter upon a detailed analysis of Part VI.

In the two frame-passages (XX′) we have a statement of a more personal nature, in which the apostle's intentions are made clear. In the frame-passages of Part III similar statements occur. In the two sections Y and Y′ the advantages of the unmarried state under the present circumstances are discussed, but in the first the emphasis is on the escape from distress, while in the second the reason given is the avoidance of distractions. In Part III the marriage problem is discussed with reference to the married and the unmarried state, the chief factors in the problem. In addition, *the widows* are mentioned. In Part VI the same major parties occur in the discussion of the marriage problem, and a new factor, *the virgins,* is added. Nothing more is said about the virgins in this part, but in the following verses, 36-38, they are fully discussed. Judging from the opening words, "Now concerning virgins," one would expect them to be the main topic of Part VI, but they are not dealt with fully until we reach Part VII. This fact would at first incline us to include vss. 36-39 in Part VI, were it not for the presence of the two frame-passages (XX′) which definitely establish the extent of Part VI. We shall also find a justification of our arrangement in the *theme* of Part VII and Part II, for both argue the permissibility of the married state on the grounds of expediency. As the arrangement shows, we have in Y the three groups concerned in the marriage problem, the married, the unmarried, and the virgins. The virgins are to be considered as a special class, whose unmarried status had a religious significance and is therefore dealt with separately. How necessary the *balance* of the parts was felt to be in the opinion of the writer, may be seen from the manner in which the virgins are introduced in Y′. They had been mentioned in Y, with a word of advice appended, and they are introduced again in Y′B′, if only by the brief words, "and the virgin . . . ." To anyone who is inclined to doubt the correctness of our theory of "frame-passages" a study of Y′ is recommended. In B the married *man* is discussed, and in B′ the married *woman*. Each quatrain is complete in itself and well balanced even in minute details, the words, "and the virgin" being the only exception due to the remoter symmetry of Y. There is no way of connecting A either with the preceding or the following, and the same may be said of A′, which sums up the message of Y′. Frame-passages of the same distinctive type are found also in Y and Z, and their peculiar function in the literary structure is proved (1) by the similarity of content, (2) by the fact that they may not be woven into the quatrains that they encase in any other way, since these are perfect in structure without them. Of a similar nature is C, "and is divided." The conjunction and verb may not be attached to B without destroying a symmetry which is already perfect without it, and though it could go with "the woman" in the first line of B′, the symmetry of this quatrain would then be destroyed. No, the words, "and is divided," are *central*, because they were designed to be so by the original writer of the passage. Because they give the gist of the whole matter they are intended to occupy the position between the two quatrains which deal with the man and the woman and the *distractions* of marriage.

At first sight one may feel that when the reference to the wives in Z has been read, the rest is irrelevant matter which has been introduced without sufficient reason in the context. This central section, however, has a definite function assigned to it, for it elaborates the principle of the Christian's detachment from the world. The reason for his detachment is not to be sought in any ascetic view of the world, but in the three reasons already alluded to, namely, the present distress, the shortness of time, and the distractions connected with the "use of the world." There is a great gulf fixed between the ascetic who uses not the world, because he finds it inherently evil, and the Christian who knows how to "use the world," though not "using it to the full." The world, as Paul sees it, is not an end in itself, but merely a means to an end. This principle which is basic also in the Christian conception of marriage is very appropriately introduced and elaborated in a central position in Z.

Part VII, vss. 36-39

But if any man thinketh that he behaveth himself unseemly toward his virgin, 36
if she be passed the flower of her age,
And if need so requireth,
A Let him do what he will.
He sinneth not,
Let them marry.

But he that standeth stedfast in his heart, 37
Having no necessity,
B But hath power as touching his own will,
And hath determined this in his own heart
To keep his own virgin,
Shall do well.

So then both he that giveth his own virgin in marriage 38
C Doeth well;
And he that giveth her not in marriage
Shall do better.

A wife is bound for so long time as her husband liveth; 39
D But if the husband be fallen asleep,
She is free to be married to whom she will;
Only in the Lord.

Part VII in common with its counterpart II has no frame-passages. This establishes definitely a certain order in the presence or absence of frame-passages. They alternate, being absent in II and VII, present in III and VI, and, again, absent in IV and V. Parts I and VIII are themselves two frame-passages which inclose the whole structure. For a clear understanding of vss. 36, 37, we must determine what is meant by "virgin." Does the term mean simply *daughter*, or does it imply the existence already in the apostolic church of a group of religious "virgins," dedicated to a life of virginity, perhaps from childhood? If the former view is accepted, with most of the older interpreters, the "man" in the case is the father of a daughter, who is concerned about his daughter's marriage to a suitor. The "need" which would require marriage would then refer either to the pressure of social custom or to the sexual desire of the virgin. Now this view fits best with the conditions imposed upon the interpreter by the contents of vs. 36. If, on the other hand, we assume that Paul is speaking of an early practice of virginity, which permitted a maiden and a man to enter into friendly relations without contemplating marriage, the interpretation of the details will materially differ. The words, "any man" and "his virgin" would there refer to the man and to the maiden he has chosen for "his virgin." The words "behaveth himself unseemly" would then imply lack of sexual restraint on the part of the man, and so would the "need" which "requireth" marriage for its satisfaction. The words "let them marry" would under any view refer to the two parties that enter into marriage, but in this case *both* subjects of the verb would be expressed, whereas under the former view the marrying man would have to be introduced as subject of the verb without having been previously mentioned. If we assume that we are here dealing with a man and his maiden, we shall have no difficulty with vs. 37 in which the same order of ideas prevails: the man, the need (or necessity), his will, marriage (or keeping his virgin). To assume that we are dealing with a father and his daughter in vs. 36 and with a man and his maiden in vs. 37, as the words there seem to require, will make the whole passage uncertain. We shall therefore assume that the man is the *same* man throughout the whole passage, and that he is not the father, but the man who keeps a virgin. This gives the most natural explanation of such details as, "thinketh that he behaveth himself unseemly toward his virgin," "if need so requireth," "let him do what he will," "let *them* marry," and the corresponding details in B. The discussion in vs. 36 contemplates a man who has need of marriage, and that in vs. 37 one who has not. Both have freedom to do what they wish, but Paul's preference is with the latter and not with the former. So far we have encountered no difficulty for a consistent interpretation along the lines indicated. When we reach vs. 38, however, we encounter an obstacle in the verb rendered "give in marriage." For *ex hypothesi* the man *marries* his virgin, and does not "give her in marriage," as required by vs. 38. Nor may we here bring in the *father*, for the phrase "his own virgin" means in vs. 38 what it meant in vs. 37. This difficulty may be avoided if we postulate that Paul has not been discussing a marriage between a young man and his maiden in the preceding, but marriage of virgins in general, or the principle of such marriages. If such alliances which the whole theory of religious virginity presupposes actually existed in Paul's time, and if they were settled early in the maiden's life, or at least before her maturity (cf. "if she be passed the flower of her age"), and if such an arrangement related definitely one maiden to one man, may it not be supposed also that the man would have something to say in case of an eventual marriage of the maiden, even though she did not marry *him?* With such an assumption of a man *in loco parentis* in vs. 38 we would be able to give a consistent and satisfactory interpretation of this difficult passage, while relating it to a man and his maiden rather than to a father and his daughter. On this assumption we can also see the reason for introducing the widows in this connection. The relations of religious virginity may be dissolved upon agreement, but that of marriage only by death of the husband. In either case it is the marriage of the *woman* which is contemplated. The opening words of this chapter indicate that Paul wrote by direct request and presumably about local issues of a dubious nature.

But are we not stressing the parallelism of Parts II and VII unduly? The former deals with married couples and the latter with virgins and widows, and there seems to be no closer relationship between the two. Aside from the *persons* discussed in the two parts, however, there is a very close parallelism between the two. In both Paul's preference is the unmarried state, and his advice to marry is merely a concession to weak human nature. In both the presence of *temptation* in the preferable course is clearly brought out. And, finally, we may inquire whether the words, "Defraud ye not one the other, except it be by consent for a season, that ye may give yourselves unto prayer, and may be together again," etc., do not take us into the same realm of religious practices as those contemplated by a life of virginity. To these striking parallels one would wish to add something with reference to widows in order to balance the last section (D) of Part VII. If vss. 8, 9 had preceded vss. 6, 7 instead of following them, that is to say, if in Part III the material designated YA had been on the other side of the frame-passage X, it could have been incorporated into Part II, and we should have had a section there also dealing with widows. Since, however, vss. 8, 9 fit fairly well into the place assigned to them in our arrangement, and since there is no evidence in the MS of dislocation at this point, we shall have to satisfy ourselves with the sufficiently close relationship which we have succeeded in establishing between the two parts II and VII.

Finally we must say a word about Parts I and VIII. Throughout this long chapter, with the exception of IV and V, the central parts, we have dealt with the sexual problem in which both man and woman have been involved. We are not surprised, therefore, to find that the opening words read, "It is good for a *man* not to touch a woman," and that the closing words read, "But *she* is happier if she abides as she is." These words bring before us the two sexes involved, and also the negative and positive aspects of the problem of maintaining the present status. Thus the whole long chapter is found to be one well-knit whole in accordance with the chiastic and alternating arrangements which we have found in the Old Testament. Not only our literary interest will be satisfied by these observations, but the logical consistency of Paul's presentation will be seen in a clearer light by such an analysis.

In Paul's First Epistle to the Corinthians there is another long section the literary unity and symmetry of which is assured; this section consists of chapters 12 to 14 which contain a full discussion of the spiritual gifts in the church and some problems which had arisen in the use of these gifts. There are three distinct divisions: the *first* enumerates the gifts of the Spirit and sets forth the necessity for unity in diversity; the *second* shows the only thing that will effect unity, namely, love; and the *third* describes how the principle of unity will operate in a practical way in regard to the spiritual gifts. These three divisions correspond broadly to the three chapters. The material is distributed in accordance with the literary patterns already discussed in chapter seven. We have here the same type of frame-passages and of chiastic and alternating systems of lines which are balanced with reference to one another. In the treatment of such structures it may be advantageous at times to bring the extreme parts together for purposes of immediate comparison and to defer the discussion of the middle parts.

The discussion of parallel sections together will save us from much needless repetition and spare the reader the inconvenience of referring back to pages which he has already read. We shall first give a general outline, which later will be discussed in detail:

Concerning Spiritual Gifts, 11:34b-14:40

A *Introduction:* The gifts and those that have them: the Spirit, 11:34b-12:3.

B *The diversity and unity of the spiritual gifts:* the principle, 12:4-30.

C *The gifts and the graces:* 12:31-14:1a.

B′ *The diversity and unity of the spiritual gifts:* the application, 14:1b-36.

A′ *Conclusion:* The leaders and the gifts: the Lord, 14:37-40.

The following is an arrangement of the extremes of the preceding outline, namely, the introduction and conclusion.

And the rest I will *set in order* whensoever I come. 34b
X But concerning the *spiritual gifts,* 12:1
Brethren,
I would not have you *ignorant.*

Ye know that when ye were Gentiles, 2
ye were led away unto those dumb idols,
Wherefore *I make known* unto you, 3
Y howsoever ye might be led,
That no man in the *Spirit of God* speaking,
Saith, *Jesus is anathema,*
And no man can say, *Jesus is Lord,*
But in the Holy Spirit. (11:34b-12:3).

(The material contained in vss. 12:4-14:36 will follow later).

If any man thinketh himself to be a prophet or a spiritual, 14:37
Y′ *Let him take knowledge* of the things which I write unto you,
That they are the commandments of the *Lord.*

But if any man is *ignorant,* let him be ignorant. 38
Wherefore, my *brethren,* 39
X′ Desire earnestly to *prophesy,* and forbid not to *speak with tongues,*
But let all things be done decently and in *order.* (14:37-40). 40

The sections designated XYY′X′ are the frame-passages that inclose Paul's discussion of the spiritual gifts. The words in italics in XX′ indicate the order of the ideas is chiastic. "Prophecy" and "tongues" (X′) are the subject of these chapters; Paul commends the former while he tolerates and regulates the latter (14:39). In sections YY′, although there is less regularity of form, the contents are parallel. In Y there is much more material than in Y′, but the trend of thought is clear. The former leaders of the Gentile Corinthians led them to idols, and the present would-be prophets and *pneumatikoi* also aspired to a kind of leadership. What Paul wants to "make known" to the church these leaders should "take knowledge of." The test of the leaders was their attitude toward Jesus, as the concluding chiasmus of four lines indicates. By this same test they should be able to recognize Paul's instructions as "the commandments of the Lord." Both statements are introduced by "that" (ὅτι), and the title "Lord" occurs only here—a fact which is no mere coincidence. Although these lines are not chiastic but alternating, a definite order of the ideas is nevertheless discernible. We recall how in the similar frame-passages in chapter seven there was also a more *personal* note (cf. 7:6, 7, 17; 7:25, 35, and 40).

Division B, 12:4-30:
The Diversity and Unity of the Spiritual Gifts:
The Principle

Part I, vss. 4-11

Now there are diversities of *gifts*, 4
But the same *Spirit*.
A And there are diversities of ministrations, 5
And the same *Lord*.
And there are diversities of *workings*, 6
But the same *God*, who worketh all things in all.

But to each one is given the manifestation of the *Spirit* to profit withal. 7
For to one is given through the *Spirit* the word of wisdom, 8
And to another the word of knowledge according to the same *Spirit;*
To another faith, in the same *Spirit;* 9
B And to another *gifts of healings* in the one *Spirit;*
And to another *workings of miracles;* 10
And to another prophecy,
And to another discernings of *spirits;*
To another kinds of tongues,
And to another interpretation of tongues.

C But all these things worketh the one and the same *Spirit*, 11
Dividing to each severally as he will.

Part II, vss. 12-13

For as the *body* is one 12
And hath many members,
A And all the members of the *body*,
Being many
Are one *body*.

So also *Christ.*

For even in one Spirit we all into one body were baptized, 13
Whether Jews
A′ Or Greeks,
Whether bond
Or free;
And all one Spirit were made to drink.

Part III, vss. 14-19

For the *body* 14
A Is not one member,
But many.

If the foot shall say, 15
B Because I am not hand,
I am not of the *body;*
It is not therefore not of the *body.*

And if the ear shall say, 16
C Because I am not eye,
I am not of the *body;*
It is not therefore not of the *body.*

If the whole *body* were an eye, 17
D Where were the hearing?
If the whole *body* were hearing,
Where were the smelling?

E But now hath *God* set the members, 18
Each one of them in the *body*, even as it pleased him.

And if they were all 19
A′ One member,
Where were the *body*?

Part IV, vss. 20-27

A But now there are many members, 20
But one *body.*

And the eye cannot say to the hand, 21
B I have no need of thee;
Or again the head to the feet,
I have no need of you.

(feeble, 22
Nay, much rather, those members of the *body*, which seem to be more
C Are necessary;
And those parts of the *body*, which we think to be less honorable,
Upon these we bestow more abundant honor.

And our uncomely parts
D Have more abundant comeliness;
But our comely parts 24
Have no need.

But *God* tempered the *body* together,
C′ Giving more abundant honor to that part which lacked:
That there should be no schism in the *body*, 25
But that the members should have the same care one for another.

And whether one member suffereth, 26
B′ All the members suffer with it;
And one member is honored,
All the members rejoice with it.

A′ Now ye are the *body* of *Christ*, 27
And severally members thereof.

Part V, vss. 28-30

C And *God* hath set some in the church,

First apostles, 28
Secondly prophets,
Thirdly teachers,
A Then *miracles*,
Then *gifts of healings*,
Helps,
Governments,
Kinds of tongues.

Not all are apostles, 29
Not all prophets,
Not all teachers,
B Not all (workers of) *miracles*, (are they?)
Not all have *gifts of healings*, 30
[Not all discern spirits,]
Not all speak with tongues,
Not all interpret, (do they?)

Division B, or vss. 4-30, is made up of five distinct parts, which are closely knit both in regard to form and content. A glance will show that Parts I and V function as frame-passages, since their content and form prove that they are to be treated as counterparts. They offer some new examples of artistic arrangement; but when the nature of their artistry is once grasped, their symmetry will be found to be perfect and consistent. In Part I section A is made up of three couplets in chiastic order. If the beginning of the lines be examined, they will be found to open with *καὶ* in *both* lines in the central couplet, while the second line of the other two has δὲ. This is due to a desire to distinguish the central couplet from the other two which are parallel. These couplets carry respectively the terms "gifts" and "workings." The two terms are found also in section B, not in the extreme lines but in the central couplet. There the terms are found in their full form "gifts of healings" and "workings of miracles," or *powers* (Greek). The shift of the terms from the extremes of one section to the centre of the other is a well-established literary principle of which already we have found Old Testament patterns (cf. Ps. 30). That the two terms *must* be placed at the centre of section B will be shown by several converging lines of evidence. The terms are also found to be central in Part V, in the two sections A and B, though there we have them *in the inverted order:* "miracles" and "gifts of healings." That they are central there also and that they are inverted, is conclusive proof that Parts I and V were designed to be frame-passages. It is a common practice, when two parallel sections are far apart in the text, to show their interdependence by inversion of two or more of their terms, or ideas. The keynote of the whole Division B is sounded in the three opening couplets; the theme is unity in diversity—ideas that occur side by side in each couplet. There are *diversities* of gifts, ministrations, and workings, but the source of all these things is *the same* Spirit, Lord, and God. As we shall see presently, this train of thought reappears in each one of the following parts in various ways.

In section B there is a peculiar arrangement, which is not often found; it is this: that the *first half* of the system carries a number of details to which there are no parallels in the last half. If the ten lines that make up this system be examined, it will be found that in each of the first five there is a reference to the divine Spirit, who manifests himself in his gifts. In the last half there is no reference to the divine Spirit, for the "discerning of spirits" (vs. 10) has reference to *other* spirits. The extreme care with which the passage is written is shown even here in the use of the word πνεῦμα, which, when it occurs, is in the *central* of the last five lines. More evidence of careful composition is found in the distribution of the grammatical *cases* of "Spirit" in the first half; the first and the second lines have a genitive, the fourth and the fifth a dative, and the third (or central of the five) the only accusative case.

Such claims will surely appear far-fetched and fanciful until we have come upon other evidence which shows the same careful attention to details in the composition of the epistle. Johannes Weiss has collected much evidence in his *Beiträge zur paulinischen Rhetorik* to prove that the epistles of Paul were carefully written. One piece of such evidence is found close at hand, though its true meaning has not been discovered by the commentators. There are *eight* instances in which the pronoun "another" appears. In every case it has a strikingly prominent position at the beginning of each line. In *six* instances the Greek text has ἄλλος, but in *two* ἕτερος is substituted for no obvious reason whatsoever. These two instances are printed in italics to distinguish them from the rest. To render this substitution more conspicuous the particle δὲ, which is found in the other six cases, is also missing. Is it any wonder that the attentive reader of the Greek text at these two points feels that he is stopped by an unexpected ictus? Because the classical distinction in meaning between the two pronouns is maintained (at least to some extent) in some New Testament passages (cf. Gal. 1:6), Meyer feels himself under obligation to make use of the distinction in the interpretation of the passage and therefore bases his classification of the gifts on the substitution of the two pronouns (Commentary, *ad loco*). De Wette, on the other hand, denies that there is any such logical distinction between the two pronouns in this passage, and Alford concurs with him in his judgment. Alford, nevertheless, thinks "that at the same time there is a *sort of arrangement*, brought about, not so much designedly (!) as by the falling together of similar terms."[5] Though there is a classical distinction between the two pronouns, similar to the distinction between *alter* and *alius* in Latin, the difference between the two has faded out of many passages in the New Testament.[6] It is precarious to build exegesis on distinctions that possibly do not exist, especially when the results, as in this case, do not justify the attempt. The reader will already have discovered for himself that whenever ἕτερος appears it is *in the next to the last line.* The substitution serves the very practical and somewhat prosaic purpose of calling the reader's attention to the approach of a turning point, for the *centre* and the *end* of the system are such points. The

[5] Henry Alford, *The Greek New Testament*, Vol. II, p. 578.
[6] R. C. Trench, *Synonyms of the New Testament*, paragraph XCV.

exchange of pronouns at these points and the re-enforcing by the omission of the particle act very much upon the reader as the bell upon the operator of a modern typewriter. For the *sense* of the whole section will be found by reading its lines after chiastic fashion, and not by constructing categories of the gifts on the basis of the pronouns used.

It is already made clear why the central couplet must remain central, since the "gifts of healings" and "workings of miracles" are parallel in every instance where they occur. "Faith" and "prophecy" in the next pair of lines may also be grouped together, as they are in Rom. 12:6; in the structures in 1 Cor. 13:2, and in Eph. 4:11-13a. The first line emphasizes the *usefulness* of the gifts of the spirit—a parallel idea to *interpretation* of tongues (cf. 1 Cor. 14:5, 6, 13). To connect "knowledge" in the third line with "discerning of spirits" in the eighth should not offer insuperable difficulties. To insist that parallelism must be expressed in identical terms, and not merely in similarity of thought, is to impose stricter rules for this particular form of parallelism than is placed on the ordinary parallelisms of the psalms. Not only the actual denotations of words, but their connotations as well, should be taken into account. No one, for example, would have thought of grouping faith and prophecy together, had there not been several cases of such parallelism in other epistles of Paul. There may be instances in which the present writer is not able to make out clearly the parallelism between a pair of lines in any given system; but if the parallelism of other pairs in the system appear to be fairly clear, the presumption should be for the acceptance of the others that are less clear, even though we may not be fortunate enough to point to identical parallels elsewhere. It should also be kept in mind that in this form of literary expression, as well as in any other, form is always more or less nearly perfect, depending upon writer and conditions.

In section C we find the same truth stressed which we have seen emphasized in the first five lines of B, namely, that the separate gifts are all from "*one* and the *same* Spirit." The two adjectives which are used separately of the Spirit in B are here brought together. There is no way of working C either into the preceding or the following structures. The statement must stand apart from the rest, as in the several similar instances which we have discovered in chapter seven. In Part V, which opens with a single line (C), we are told that God has placed the various gifts in the church. The terms, "God" and the "Spirit," are parallel also in the first and third couplets of A in Part I, and their presence in the two sections C and C′, which bracket the three middle sections II, III, and IV, is the result of a desire to reiterate the same truth and to distribute the reiteration of it in accordance with a symmetrical pattern.

Part V is very much like Part I in content and in structure, yet with notable differences. The two central couplets of A and B with their characteristic inversion of terms are the most striking similarities. We observed that the first half of B in Part I carries as a special distinction five references to the divine Spirit not found in the second half. In the *last* half of B in Part V we have also a special distinction not to be found in the first: namely, that each line carries a finite verb. The bracketed words in the third line from the end indicate a critical reconstruction of the text; since there are obviously eight lines in A, we expect the same number in B. We notice further that the last two lines of B carry the "tongues" and the "interpretation of tongues," as was the case in the two lines of B in Part I. May we not therefore be reasonably sure that the missing line can be supplied by the aid of the counterpart above, adapting it to suit the conditions of the other two lines? Thus the last three lines are made to carry the same content as the corresponding three lines of Part I. The present writer is not able to prove that parallelism exists between the various lines of these two structures A and B, but he feels reasonably certain that such a parallelism might be established, if we knew more of the *functions* of the offices here enumerated. One suggestion is, however, that the "helps" and "governments" are to be included among the "ministrations" in the central couplet of A in Part I. We can find no better comment on these two sections than to print Eph. 4:11-13a for the sake of comparison. Here the five offices mentioned seem capable of being easily distributed among the functions that follow them.

And he gave

Some to be apostles,
And some *prophets*,
And some evangelists,
And some pastors,
And teachers;
For the perfecting of the saints,
Unto the work of ministering
Unto the building up of the body of Christ,
Till we all attain unto the unity of *faith*,
And of the knowledge of the Son of God.

Prophecy and faith fall into parallel lines. The absence of "some" with "teachers" does not mean that Paul intends pastors to function as teachers also. The absence of the word provides the passage with an ictus which marks the turning point, just as the absence of conjunction in the following four lines is abruptly interrupted by the presence of the conjunction "and" in the *last*. These are merely tricks of style, similar to the substitution of pronouns and the absence of particles in B of Part I. The omission of "some" and the inclusion of "and" occur in the *last* line of each half of the system. Of a similar nature and function are the two "then" (ἔπειτα) in the centre of A (12:28).

In Part II (vss. 12-13), where there are two sections (AA′) which set forth the common subject, unity in diversity, the arrangement is similar in both sections. For the idea of unity is carried by the extreme lines and the idea of diversity in the intervening lines. In A the "body" is mentioned in the two extreme and in the central lines (cf. Mt. 9:17, "wine"). Between the two sections Christ is mentioned; in other words, the head of the church is used for the church (B). Here is another instance of a line which must stand apart from the preceding and following structures, since these are complete and symmetrical without it (cf. 1 Cor. 7:34, "and is divided"). In A′ there is no doubt that the two extreme lines were written "for the *ear*" (Weiss) since they end in a similar sound and otherwise appear to be balanced.[7]

[7] There is some evidence in Tischendorf, both from early versions and the fathers, that the last line of A′ originally may have had the phrase ἓν πόμα just before the verb. The word is an un-Attic word for πῶμα and is found in 1 Cor. 10:4. The presence of the phrase originally may explain the persistent application of the line to the Lord's supper in the fathers. When the phrase had once

The general principle of unity in diversity is now presented in the following verses under the guise of a parable of the body and its members, a device for which there are classical precedents. Paul has a well-planned psychological approach in dealing with the super-sensitive *pneumatikoi* of Corinth. In the parable of the body and its members they are confronted with a general proposition which no one would be ready to dispute, since the particular application of it was as yet hidden. Only after the assembly has been taken through the lofty appeal of chapter thirteen is it confronted with the practical application of the principle enunciated in the parable of the body and its members. The figure of members which are honorable or less honorable, comely or uncomely, in Paul's discussion, is then applied to the tendency of some to place "tongues" before "prophecy." To the design of the three chapters Paul might well have applied his own words, "being crafty, I caught you with guile" (2 Cor. 12:16).

In Part III (vss. 14-19) there are two frame-passages (AA′) which inclose the intervening sections. In two of these sections (BC) objections raised by the members of the body to the functions assigned to them are stated, and in a third (D) the objections are reduced to an absurdity. Once more it is affirmed that the present arrangement is divine (E), after which the passage is concluded as it began (A′). No chiastic arrangement of the sections is evident. In Part IV (vss. 20-27) we have the same frame-passages as in the previous part, but with only two parallel lines in each (AA′); they, too, state the general principle of unity in diversity. Here we have in addition a chiastic arrangement of the sections with reference to one another. In B the unity is expressed

---

been dropped, the original ἐν ἕνι πνεύματι had to be made the object of the verb, as it now is. The preposition εἰς was then introduced, either unintelligently by someone who felt the influence of the *first* line of A′, or more intelligently by some one who, still thinking of baptism, took the verb in the sense of "were drenched." Paul, however, deduces the unity of Christians from the participation of the one loaf (1 Cor. 10:17), and it is not unlikely that he should have deduced the same truth from the one cup. If this be the history of the text in this passage, the last line of A′ originally read: καὶ πάντες ἐν ἑνί πνεύματι ἓν πόμα ἐποτίσθημεν. On the other hand, with the elimination of εἰς, the present text might well have read as it stands, though the idea of "*drinking* of the Spirit" does appear strange.

in a mutual *need* and in B′ in a mutual *feeling*. It is remarkable that there is no reference to the body in these two sections and in D. The absence of this term, which is so conspicuous in every section of Parts II, III, IV, is not accidental but the result of a literary plan.

A glance at the other sections within Part IV shows that the term "body" is symmetrically distributed, so that it is made to appear even in parallel lines (CC′). The method reminds us of the similar procedure in the distribution of the name Yahweh in some of the psalms. If the seven sections of Part IV be examined in order, it will be found that the sections which belong to the series of *odd* numbers (1, 3, 5, 7) carry a reference to the "body," whereas in the sections that belong to the *even* series (2, 4, 6) the term is missing. The reader will recall how in Psalm 29 the appearance of "the voice of Yahweh," singly or doubly, and how in Psalm 67 the terms "peoples" and "nations" were governed by the same law of symmetrical distribution. There is nothing accidental about such features. The consummate skill with which these features are introduced and the unobtrusiveness of their presence, testify to the mastery of the writer over his form. They also reveal the extent to which Paul is indebted to the Old Testament in matters of style.

Resuming our analysis of the contents, we observe that sections C and C′ are parallel. In C the first two lines present the *feeble* members and the last two the *less honorable*. Turning to C′ we discover that this order has been reversed, for the words "more abundant honor" (last line of C) are in C′ transferred to the *first* half of the system. It may be safe to assume that the words, "the same *care* one for another," imply the presence in the writer's mind of the *feeble* members mentioned in C.

No discussion of the style of these passages can do justice to them, unless an arrangement of the Greek text is before the reader. Certainly this passage was written "for the ear." The *beginning* and sometimes the *end* of the lines match one another. Prepositions, verbs, and nouns recur in symmetrical order. The rendering of such passages in the original Greek by trained readers must have been an aesthetic feast for those who were in the position to appreciate such forms. The presence of such forms in a document produced for public reading in the Christian assembly presupposes a certain cultural level, which is not always taken into account in modern discussions of the apostolic church. Impressions of this kind are deepened as we enter into chapter thirteen, in which similar forms are found. The difference between chapter thirteen and the preceding and following chapters is not that the one is a literary production and the others are not, but rather that the contents of chapter thirteen bring the reader to a higher emotional level and therefore produce upon him a deeper impression. The longer one studies the details of this marvelous chapter, the more one admires the perfect mastery which enables the apostle to write strictly in line with the practical problem before him and not once plunge from the heights into the harassing practical details of the situation. All such matters, though they were present in his mind, are deliberately set aside and reserved for treatment in chapter fourteen, a treatment which preserves all the literary beauty and logical clearness which characterize the preceding chapters.

Division C, 12:31-14:1a

The Gifts and the Graces[8]

X But desire earnestly the greater gifts, 12:31
And moreover a most excellent way show I unto you.

A If I speak with the tongues of men and of angels, 13:1
A′ *But have not love,*
I am become a sounding brass, or a clanging cymbal.

And if I have *prophecy* 2
All the mysteries,
B And know And
All the knowledge;
And if I have all the *faith*, so as to remove mountains,

Y

B′ *But have not love,*
I am nothing.

C And if I bestow all my goods to feed the poor, 3
And if I give my body to be burned,

C′ *But have not love,*
It profiteth me nothing.

[8] N. W. Lund, *Journal of Biblical Literature*, Vol. L, Part IV, "The Literary Structure of Paul's Hymn to Love," where the Greek text of this chapter is printed in full as arranged above.

Z

A
Love 4
Suffereth long;
Kind is
Love. (Love does)

B
Not envy,
Not vaunt itself,
Not *become* puffed up,
Not behave itself unseemly, 5
Not seek its own,
Not *become* provoked,
Not take account of evil,
Not rejoice in unrighteousness, 6
but does rejoice with truth. (Love)

A′
All things beareth, 7
All things *believeth*,
All things *hopeth*,
All things endureth.

Y′

A Love never faileth; but 8

B
Whether there be *prophecy*, it shall be done away,
Whether there be tongues, they shall cease,
Whether there be *knowledge*, it shall be done away.

C
For we *know* in part, 9
And we *prophecy* in part;
But when that which is perfect is come, 10
That which is in part shall be done away.

D
When I was a child, 11
I spake as a child,
I had a mind as a child,
I thought as a child.
When I am become a man, I have put away childish things.

C′
For now we *see* in a mirror, darkly, 12
But then face to face;
Now I *know* in part,
But then shall I know fully even as also I am fully known.

B′ But now abideth { Faith, Hope, Love, } these three; 13

A′ But the greatest of these is love.

Follow after love, 14:1a
X′ But desire earnestly the spiritual gifts.

General Outline

X Exhortation, 12:31.
Y Comparison of love with the gifts: love gives them value, vss. 1-3.
Z The characteristics of love: love stands the test of life, vss. 4-7.
Y′ Comparison of love with the gifts: love abides while the gifts cease, vss. 8-13.
X′ Exhortation, 14:1a.

The frame-passages XX′ are chiastic and have the verb "desire earnestly" (cf. "envy," in vs. 4, in central section). Within this frame Paul discusses the excellence of love. In Y Paul shows how even the most precious gifts of the Spirit are without value, unless they are administered in love. In a series of statements, each of which culminates with the words, "but have not love," (A′B′C′), the futility of gifts without love is shown. These words are like a recurrent refrain. They are the first example of a triplet arrangement of which we shall find several instances in the chapter. There are three main parts (YZY′). In Z there are three parts (ABA′). In Y′ which has seven parts there are three triplets (BDB′). In a closer examination of Y we make the observation that the order of its statements is climactic, for there is a distinction in *degree* between what we say, what we have, and what we do (ABC). Paul himself has stated that prophecy is higher than tongues (14:5); that he regards Christian conduct more important than either of the two we may take for granted from the emphasis he places on love in this chapter. Taking the sections in order we discover that the two kinds of tongues (of men and of angels) are balanced by the two kinds of sound (of brass and of the cymbal A).

The chiastic form of B is more striking in Greek than in our version, since the two κἂν ἔχω are parallel, and the variation καὶ εἰδῶ occurs in the centre. Prophecy and faith are found together in Rom. 12:6, but there we have "the proportion of our faith," while here we have "all the faith." That the two are not accidentally brought together in parallel position may be proved by the fact that they are found in parallel lines in the structure of 12:8-10 and Eph. 4:11-13a. While the order in the former of these passages is faith and prophecy, the order here is reversed (prophecy and faith). The mysteries and the knowledge form an antithetic parallelism with πάντα καὶ πᾶσαν between them, thus creating another chiasmus. To the words, "so as to remove mountains," there is no parallel, suggesting that they are either a minor irregularity or a scribal reminiscence of Matt. 17:20. C consists only of a couplet in which both lines open with κἂν. If the ἵνα-clause did not exist they would both end with μοῦ. Whether we accept the reading καυθήσομαι with Tischendorf or καυχήσομαι with Westcott and Hort, the clause is not easy, since the latter seems to introduce irrelevant matter into the passage (Alford), and the former is difficult because burning at the stake is unknown to us at this early date. The New Testament uses παραδίδωμι in the sense of deliver into custody (Matt. 4:12; Mk. 1:14), and in 2 Macc. 7:37 it is used for delivering one's body and soul for one's country. On the other hand, the passage may be an echo of Dan. 3:28 (95) (LXX). It is not necessary to insist on absolute perfection in the symmetry,[9] for at the close of such structures an extra flourish is sometimes added. Just as we traced a connection between section B and 12:8-10 in the recurrence of faith and prophecy in the inverted order, so we are tempted to trace a connection between the whole first part Y and 12:28-30. For in section A of the latter passage we have the three terms: "helps, government, kinds of tongues." In Y we have tongues (A), and C deals with such activities to which the term "helps" might be applied. Since we have in B such gifts as we regard as intellectual, we might in this section find the counterpart to "governments." The recurrence in inverted order of the three ideas which were designated by the three terms in the previous chapter would serve to knit the two parts together.

In the second part Z (vss. 4-7) Paul shows the excellence of Love in standing the test of life. There can be no question about the correctness of grouping the eight verbs with their striking array of negatives (B), nor of the four πάντα with their verbs (A′). There remains to be accounted for the material which has been assigned to A and the chiastic order in which it has been arranged. What love does when under provocation is described in the sections (AA′) and what it does *not*, in the central section B. It is tempting to seek to distribute these sections among the factions at Corinth. The first six verbs in B describe nothing that may not easily be duplicated among our modern πνευματικοί, and the seventh and eighth verbs may have reference to the habit of keeping count of the offences of an opponent and the unholy joy

[9] Matt. 13:13, "neither do they understand"; and 13:15, "and should turn again and I should heal them."

felt when he is discomfited. On the other hand, the positive statements concerning love in AA′ may be directed to the members of the church that shared with Paul his attitude toward the πνευματικοί. These members would be in special need of endurance under the stress of controversy. They would also need to believe and hope all things, when the ugliest side of human nature put their trust in men to the breaking point.

The artistic skill with which the three graces are worked into the pattern is at once apparent. Love is twice repeated, forming a chiasmus with the two verbs in A. Faith and Hope are represented by their verbs in the middle lines of A′. The verbs "beareth" and "endureth" express essentially the same idea. The verbs, "suffereth long" and "is kind," express the passive and active attitude under provocation and do not differ much from the other two verbs. When the two sections are compared, we find that the graces are expressed in the outer lines of A and in the middle lines of A′, while the qualities of endurance which are characteristic of love are shifted about in the reverse order.

If the eight verbs of B are examined, it will be found that two of them, the *third* and the *sixth*, are passive in form and in meaning. The two verbs express parallel ideas, for to be "puffed up" and to be "stirred up," or provoked, are emotions that usually go together. These two verbs divide the series of eight into three couplets, the central couplet of which contains the striking change to οὐκ in its first line. If these three couplets are compared, we we shall find in them a climax similar to the one in Y. The first couplet has no object, the second has one, and the third has, in addition to an object, a specially emphatic closing line which repeats in positive form what the preceding line has stated. The present writer thinks it probable that all the verbs in section B in some way are to be related to the controversy concerning the tongues. The chief interest of Paul in the three chapters is neither theological nor aesthetic but practical. He is concerned with the problem of instructing Christians of different temperaments and divergent points of view, who are nevertheless desperately in earnest, how to live together in peace and harmony. This is the practical objective Paul has in mind, and toward this objective he proceeds among a bewildering wealth of ideas.

The third part Y′ (vss. 8-13) is a chiastic arrangement of seven sections, in which the numbers three and four also play a part. Although the arrangement of the *sections* is chiastic, that of the *lines* within the sections is only partly chiastic (D) and partly alternating (CC′). The whole of this part is to be regarded as the counterpart of Y, which has this in common with Y′: they both contain a comparison between love and the gifts of the Spirit with a view of showing the excellence of love. First of all, "love never faileth" (A). This characteristic of love is contrasted with the three gifts of prophecy, tongues, knowledge and their respective verbs, which all express the temporary character of the gifts. Prophecy and its verb should be singular as in the marginal reading of Westcott and Hort, since this reading maintains the perfect parallelism between the first and the third lines. The central line, though expressing the same idea, has a different verb to express it. This gives us an inversion in B, the reason of which becomes apparent in C, in which section Paul operates only with prophecy and knowledge, the two parallel members in B, leaving out tongues.

In B′ we find as a contrast to the three gifts which are temporary the three graces which are abiding. The words τὰ τρία ταῦτα, which seem to be loosely appended to the sentence, receive their true emphasis only as they are read in contrast with those three temporary gifts enumerated in B. We observe how the principle of inversion operates—perhaps unconsciously—even in minute details. While the words τὰ τρία ταῦτα are found at the end of B′, their corresponding three εἴτε, which mark the enumeration, occur at the beginning of B. Likewise we see how the three verbs expressing the temporary nature of the gifts are found at the end of each line in B, while the verb that describes the abiding nature of the graces is put at the front in B′. The discussion is then brought around to the point where it began in A with a reference to love (A′). Again, love opens the statement in A and closes it in A′. These are examples in which the chiastic principle can hardly have been a conscious literary pattern.

Sections C and C′ give the reason why the gifts by their very nature must be temporary. They are imperfect and are therefore to be supplanted by something perfect. The two are compared in both sections, but they are distributed differently within each section. In C the imperfection of the gifts is described in the first two lines: "We know in part and we prophesy in part." The last two lines deal with the supplanting of the imperfect by the perfect. In C′, however, this order is varied, so that the idea of perfection is treated in the second and fourth lines, while the idea of imperfection is dealt with in the first and the third. These two sections are to be regarded as parallel not only because of their content but also because of their form. In C we have the verbs "we know" and "we prophesy," but in C′ the ideas are inverted and we have "we see" and "I know." The application of the verb βλέπω to prophetic vision is supported by usage in LXX. The passage is also clearly reminiscent of Num. 12:6-8 (LXX) in which the prophet is mentioned. We are therefore justified in tracing the chiasmus made of prophecy and knowledge in C and C′. We may regard it as another way of knitting together the two parts of the discourse.

But if Paul operates with knowledge and prophecy in the conduct of his argument, why has he not mentioned tongues? Except for a reference to them in vs. 1 and in the central line of B (vs. 8) they do not in any way enter into the argument of this chapter. Yet we know from the previous and the following discourse, that the tongues were the chief cause of the trouble and therefore the pivot of his argument. That the tongues had not been forgotten is indicated by the implication of the central section D, where, though he does not explicitly use the term, Paul states a general principle of all growth which is applicable to both knowledge and prophecy. We have reason to believe that he regards tongues as belonging more specifically to the state of spiritual childhood. Tongues to Paul represented an abandoned position, not in the sense that he could not speak with tongues, but in the sense that he had ceased to use them in the Christian assembly (14:18). Paul's attitude toward the tongues is clearly brought out in the following chapter. He regards them as the gift of the Spirit, which he prefers to use privately. He urges such control in their use in the assembly as will gradually tend to restrict, if not altogether eliminate, the public use of tongues in the church. The tongues to him represent a less mature state than prophecy and knowledge. If, therefore, even these more commendable gifts shall disappear, will not the end of the less important gift come surer and sooner?

Paul has dealt with prophecy and knowledge in sections C and C.′ It is therefore highly probable that he has dealt with tongues in the central section D, since this is the order in which these subjects are treated in B. Such a conclusion receives a definite support in 14:20. In this passage Paul exhorts the Christians not to be children in mind (φρενίν). The corresponding verb in the central line of D should probably be rendered "I had a mind as a child." The mind of a child would express itself in the speech and thought of a child. Instead of the noun νήπιος in D we find the verb νηπιάζετε in 14:20. These verbal parallels together with the fact that the exhortation in 14:20 follows immediately the comparison between the intellectual and the ecstatic gifts in 14:18, 19 seem to indicate that Paul is following the same trend of thought in sections CDC′. In speaking openly of the temporary quality of the gifts of knowledge and prophecy, those gifts which he himself regarded as the more desirable, and only by way of implication of the tongues which were also to cease, Paul is graciously giving his opponents in the church an opportunity to draw their own conclusions. And that is to put into practice the love that does not vaunt itself.

All these evidences of careful literary structures prove that Paul's Hymn to Love is something more than a literary rhapsody. With all its deep emotion it is nevertheless a closely knit logical argument that never loses sight of the practical objective. Link is added to link in a convincing manner. According to the chapter a Christian should be capable of intelligent, mature choice: (1) He should among all the varied gifts of the Spirit select "the greater," i.e., "the spiritual gifts" (cf. XX′), which in every situation in life would enable him not to seek his own satisfaction but show due consideration of others (cf. ζηλόω and τὰ in XX′ and in

XB). (2) He should also seek the Christian graces, Faith, Hope, and Love, which are abiding, rather than the gifts which are temporary, designed as they were for the building up of the church. It is even tempting to try to apportion the three graces among the three divisions of the chapter. Faith is at least mentioned in Y (vs. 2); Love in its practical manifestations is certainly the emphasis in Z; and Hope may fittingly describe the content of Y′. It is at least possible that we have in this famous chapter an example of how Paul himself would have worked out in detail his own triplet in 1 Thess. 1:3: "your work of faith and labor of love and patience of hope in our Lord Jesus Christ."

Division B′, 14:1b-36

The Diversity and Unity of the Spiritual Gifts:
The Application.

Part I, 14:1b-5a

But rather that ye may prophesy; 1b
For he that speaketh in a tongue, 2
A Speaketh not unto men but unto God;
For no man understandeth.
But in the Spirit he speaketh mysteries.
B But he that prophesieth speaketh unto men { edification, and exhortation, and consolation. 3
He that speaketh in a tongue 4
Edifieth himself;
A′ But he that prophesieth edifieth the church.
Now I would have you all speak with tongues, 5
But rather that ye should prophesy.

Part II, vss. 5b-13

X Greater is he that prophesieth than he that speaketh with tongues,
Except he interpret,

Y That the church
May receive edifying.

Z

A But now, brethren, if I come unto you speaking with tongues, 6
What shall I profit you

B Unless I speak to you by way
of revelation,
or of knowledge,
or of prophesying,
or of teaching?

B′ Even the things without life, giving *voice*, whether pipe or harp, 7
If they give not a distinction in the sounds,
How shall it be known what is piped or harped?

A′ For even if a trumpet give an uncertain *voice*, 8
Who shall prepare himself for war?

Z′

A So also ye by the tongue, 9
Unless ye utter speech easy to be understood,

B How shall it be known what is spoken?
For ye will be speaking into the air.
There are, it may be, so many kinds of *voices* in the world, 10
And nothing is without *voice*.
If then I know not the meaning of the *voice*, 11
I shall be to him that speaketh a barbarian,
And he that speaketh will be a barbarian unto me.

A′ So also ye, 12
Since ye are zealous of spirits,

Y′ Unto the edifying
Of the church seek that ye may abound.

X′ Wherefore let him that speaketh in a tongue pray 13
That he may interpret.

Part III, vss. 14-19

For if I pray in a tongue, 14
A My spirit prayeth,
But my understanding is unfruitful.
What is it then? 15

I will pray with my spirit,
B And I will pray with the understanding also;
I will sing with the spirit,
And I will sing with the understanding also.

Else if you bless with the spirit, 16
He that filleth the place of the unlearned,
B′ How shall he say Amen at thy giving of thanks,
Seeing that he knoweth not what thou sayest?
For thou verily givest thanks well, 17
But the other is not edified.

I thank God I speak with tongues more than you all: 18
A′ Howbeit in the church I had rather speak five words with my understanding,
That I may instruct others also, 19
Than ten thousand words in a tongue.

Part IV, vss. 20-36

X { A Brethren, be not children in mind. 20
Yet in malice be ye babes,
But in mind be men.

B In the *Law* is written, 21

Y {
A That "by men of strange tongue, and by lips of strangers,
Will I speak unto this people;
And not even thus will they hear me, saith the *Lord*."

B {
x Therefore the *tongues** not to them that believe, 22
but to the unbelieving,
y unto a sign are - - -
not to the unbelieving,
x′ But *prophesying** but to them that believe.

C If therefore the whole church be assembled together 23

B′ {
x And all speak with *tongues*
And there come in men - - - unlearned,
or unbelieving,

y Will they not say ye are mad?

x′ But if all *prophesy* unbelieving, 24
And there come in one - - - or unlearned,

He is reproved by all,
y′ He is judged by all,
The secrets of his heart are made manifest. 25

And thus he will fall down on his face and "worship" *God*,
A′ Declaring
That "God is among you indeed."

Y′

A What is it then, brethren? When ye come together, each one - - - Let all things be done unto edifying
- hath *a psalm*,
- hath a teaching, 26
- hath a revelation,
- hath a tongue,
- hath an interpretation.

B
If any man speaketh in a *tongue*, by two, or at most three, and in (turn; 27
And let one interpret.
x But if there be no interpreter, 28
Let him keep silence in the church.

But to himself
y Let him speak,
To God.

And let the *prophets* speak by two or three, 29
And let the others discern.
x′ But if a revelation be made to another sitting by, 30
Let the first keep silence.

A′ For ye can all prophesy one by one, 31
That ye may all learn and may be exhorted.

B′
And the spirits of the prophets are subject to the prophets. 32
x For God is not of confusion, but of peace. 33
As in all the churches of the saints,

y Let the women 34

In the churches keep silence.
x′ For it is not permitted unto them to speak,
But let them be in subjection,

X′

B As also saith the *Law*.

A
And if they would learn anything, 35
Let them ask their own husbands at home:
For it is shameful for a woman to speak in the church.

What? was it from you that the word of God went forth? 36
Or came it unto you alone?

With the fourteenth chapter Paul reaches the practical application of the parable contained in chapter twelve. The arrangement of the material here is partly alternating and partly chiastic, as the following presentation will reveal. There are varieties of form discoverable in this passage which have not appeared in any of the passages discussed so far. This is only a further proof of the adaptations to which the chiastic order is capable. Before going into the details of the passage it may help to keep the trend of the argument clear, if a tabular view of the main parts be given.

Part I. Comparison: Prophecy is more useful to the church than tongues, for the one who uses it addresses himself, not to God but to men, and so edifies not himself, but the church. 14:1b-5a.

Part II. Speaking with tongues, unless it is interpreted, is of no profit to the church, because it is not intelligible, has all the effect of a strange language, and therefore contributes nothing to the edification of the church. 5b-13.

Part III. Comparison: Prophecy is of a greater relative value than tongues, for the one who uses it is engaged not only "with the spirit," but also "with the understanding," hence contributing to the edification of others, and training his own intellect also. 14-19.

Part IV. Speaking with tongues, when used in a full assembly, has only a limited usefulness, for it has not reference to all, but to some. Though the same limited reference is also true of prophecy, it has the advantage of being able to convert outsiders ("unbelieving," "unlearned"). cf. Y 21b-25.

Therefore, both should be used only with proper restriction and proper observance of order, and, whether men or women are involved, with proper self-control, so that the purpose of the Christian assembly, namely, the edification and instruction of all, may be attained. cf. Y′ 26-34.

These summaries of the four parts are intended to indicate broadly the contents. For the subtle hints with which each of these parts is linked to its counterpart the reader is referred to the explanatory notes under each part.

Division B′ continues the discussion of the gifts of the Spirit without interruption. Chapter thirteen did not, as some writers hold, come out of one of Paul's portfolios. It was written as an integral part of the present discussion. The three chapters are one literary unity, and the first part of Division B′ takes up the thread of the argument at the point where the last section of Division C left off, even without the formality of beginning a new sentence. Strange as this procedure may seem to us, it was natural to a writer whose written word was a faithful reproduction of the spoken. Nothing could be more formal and symmetrical than the long and beautiful passage in Eph. 5:22-33; yet, this highly artistic passage begins without a verb, the participle of the preceding verse performing that function. Part I (vss. 1b-5a) is devoted to a comparison between the tongues and prophecy with a view of appraising their relative value in the services of the Christian church. In this comparison Paul shows that tongues may have some value to the individual, but that prophecy has value to the whole Christian community. The whole point is clearly elaborated in a series of striking contrasts which are revealed, line by line, as soon as the centre of the structure is passed. The centre itself is clearly marked by a characteristic triplet for which there are Old Testament patterns (cf. Lev. 24:13-23, et al.). The emphatic manner in which the gift of prophecy is described as a desirable attainment (cf. "but rather") in the extreme lines finds its explanation in the central line, where the social nature of the gift is explained. We have here another example of the law of distribution at the extremes and at the centre.

For the time being we shall pass over Part II and for purposes of comparison devote our attention to Part III (vss. 14-19), which is the counterpart of I. We would have suspected this relationship for purely formal reasons, since the two passages are of approximately the same length. In addition the contents are identical. In two frame-passages the individual benefits of the tongues are contrasted with the social benefits of prophecy. Line matches line (AA′) with the possible exception of the two innermost lines. These, however, may be taken as the formal introduction and conclusion to the development of the subject discussed in sections B and B′. Paul does not want to forbid the use of tongues, but merely to regulate their use in public assemblies. The emotional and intellectual phases of Christian worship are clearly present in his mind and are represented in his discourse by the terms "spirit" and "understanding," which are contrasted in B. The ideal worship is the worship which can attract *all* into participation, and in this case the apostle even looks beyond the circle of baptized members of the church to the "unlearned," who was apparently an outsider (cf. vs. 23). To make the deepest emotions of Christians articulate, and their expression in common worship *orderly,* are the two qualifications imposed by Paul on public worship. Back of both demands is the realization of the social nature of worship. The first of these qualities is discussed in Part II and the second in Part IV. When analyzed the whole chapter will be found to be a marvel of logical presentation. The situation is first analyzed into its fundamental elements, *articulation* and *order;* then each in its turn is systematically developed with penetration and vividness in a separate part of the discourse.

Part II (vss. 5b-13) is thus devoted to the necessity of articulated expression of experience in common worship, if such experience is to be profitable to all that participate. Unless the tongues are interpreted and thus are made intelligible to all they do not edify the church. This is the content of X and Y. The structure concludes with two exhortations which have for their objective the edification of the church (Y′) by the interpretation of tongues (X′). The four frame-passages are chiastic with reference to one another and so are their separate lines in YY′; in XX′, however, they alternate. In two middle panels the necessity of articulate expression is developed. Once more we have frame-passages. In Z the question is asked, "What shall I profit you?" (A), that is, by using tongues; and in A′ the same idea is figuratively presented by the trumpet whose signal is "uncertain," that is, not clear and distinct enough to become intelligible. In B a single line branches off into *four* terms, each setting forth some type of intelligible and useful speech. In B′ three long lines present the same idea figuratively under the simile of the pipe and the harp. Thus the difference between the intelligible and the unintelligible is made clear to all; in the first half (AB) without figurative language, and in the last half of the system (B′A′) with figurative language (cf. the Greek of A ἐὰν, τί with ἐαν, τίς in A′). The practical application of the foregoing is now given in Z′. The two frame-passages (AA′) are easily distinguished by the striking phrase, "so also ye," with which they open (οὕτως καὶ ὑμεῖς). There may be a touch of sarcasm in the words, "since ye are zealous of spirits" (A′). In the central section B we have once again a central triplet in the three forms of the word "voice" (φωνὴ). This triplet of lines sets forth the need of clear articulation, and in the two lines on either side of this triplet the lack of this quality is said to make communication between men impossible. It will be noticed that section B has *seven* lines, divided into a triplet with two lines on either side—a split quatrain such as is found in the psalms. It is tempting to view this numerical feature as the literary counterpart of the *four* and *three* lines which constitute the central sections of Z. The precedents in the Old Testament for such arrangements may be seen in sections AA′ in Psalm 67. From our analysis it appears that Part II from beginning to end is exclusively devoted to the task of proving the necessity of distinct articulation in public worship. If a modern teacher of elocution is in need of apostolic support in his calling, he will find it here. That which is unintelligible has no place in public worship, is Paul's dictum. Even though he mentions the possibility of *interpretation* of tongues in public (XX′, cf. 12:10), he makes very little of it. Evidently his own personal preferences are revealed in the words, "Howbeit *in the church* I had rather speak five words with my understanding, that I may instruct others also, than ten thousand words in a tongue" (14:19).

Part IV (vss. 20-36) is nearly twice as long as its counterpart, Part II; yet in content it is parallel, for it deals with the other quality of public worship, its *orderliness*. There are frame-passages here also, XX′. There are some things in these frame-passages which remind us of similar frame-passages in chapter seven. There, too, the first is directed to the *men* and the last to the *women*. (Cf. 7:1 with vs. 40.) One of the most peculiar and striking features of the whole structure, however, is the occurrence and the recurrence of the reference to the *Law* (XB and X′B). In the first of these cases the term can be used only by stretching it greatly as was customary at times (cf. John 10:34, 15:25), for the quotation is from Isaiah 28:11 ff. and not from the Torah.[10] These are the only two instances in which "the Law" (ὁ νόμος) occurs in the chapter. We recall how in chapter seven "commandment" was found in two parallel frame-passages and *in these only* (cf. ἐπιταγή in 7:6, 25). The parallelism of XX′ is rendered more striking, if we remember that the word "babe" (A) is often used of one who is undeveloped in knowledge (Matt. 11:25) and as such is a good parallel to the *learners* among the women (X′A).

Within these well-defined limits we have two structures (YY′) of which the first, but not the second, has frame-passages. In Y the frame-passages are made up of quotations from Isaiah, the

[10] C. G. Montefiore, *The Synoptic Gospels* (2d ed.), Vol. II, pp. 57, 58.

first given freely after LXX (A) and the second from the Hebrew (A′). The extent of the quotation is in either case made clear by the quotation marks in our arrangement. The word "that" (ὅτι) and the *first* divine name in A′ are added. In both cases the balanced style of the passage is the reason. The reader who is inclined to doubt the possibility of such literary mosaics is asked to suspend his judgment until he has had an opportunity to examine more striking instances of the same procedure.[11] Section Y opens with a quotation from Isaiah to show why speaking with tongues in the public assembly will have no effect, and closes with another quotation from the same prophet to show what the effect will be when Christians substitute prophesying for tongues in their public meetings. Between the two frame-passages are two sections (BB′), the first of which (B) is chiastic; the second (B′), alternating. The central line (C) informs us that it is a public assembly of the *whole church* with which we are dealing, a very important factor, indeed, for the correct understanding of Paul's presentation of his argument. We shall analyze B′ first, since that analysis may aid in solving some of the problems of B. In B′, then, the two alternatives considered are, whether all should speak with tongues (x) or whether all should prophesy (x'). The question as to whether strangers, characterized as "unlearned" or "unbelieving," should be permitted to come in is also discussed. When x and x' are compared, there seems to be a chiastic arrangement of the terms, though they come at the end of their respective lines. In y and y' the *results* are contrasted. If they all speak with tongues, strangers will say that they are mad (y); but if they all prophesy, they will be convicted of their sin (y'). Section B′ is a clear and concise alternating structure, which shows the disastrous results of tongues upon visiting strangers and the wholesome results of prophesying.

With this in mind we now approach section B. The first statement that meets us there is that "tongues are unto a sign, not to them that believe, but to the unbelieving." But, we may ask, if tongues are intended for a sign to unbelievers, why should their use lead the unbelievers to the conclusion that those who speak in

[11] Lk. 4:16-20; Mt. 13:13-18; Phil. 2:9-11, etc. See *infra*, pp. 216, 233, 236.

tongues are mad? On the other hand, we have the second statement, "But prophesying (is a sign) *not* to the *unbelieving*, but to them that believe." How then, may we ask again, shall we explain that prophesying, which was *not* intended as a sign for the unbelieving, has such a wholesome effect on just these people? As B and B′ now read in our present Greek text they flatly contradict each other, for what happens in B′ is the exact opposite to what the statements in B would lead us to expect. But the remedy for this confusion is very simple. Reverse the position of the two terms, "tongues" and "prophesying," which are marked with an asterisk in B, and the statements in B will naturally lead up to the results described in B′.

But more than this will be achieved, for the quotation from Isaiah says that the result of speaking to Israel by strange tongues will be that they will *not* hear. How, then, can anyone make Paul out to say in the same breath, that these same tongues are a sign to the unbelievers? The transposition of the two terms, as suggested, will at once clear up the passage and make it consistent, not only with the quotation from Isaiah, but with itself. Another result will be achieved, which has reference to the stylistic arrangement of the passage. We have already observed the writer's play upon the terms believe-unbelieving-unbelieving-believe in B, and the similar play upon the terms unlearned-unbelieving-unbelieving-unlearned in B′. If our suggestion as to the transposition of terms in B is correct, we shall have as the result thereof a similar symmetrical distribution of the terms as follows: prophesying-tongues-tongues-prophesy. A suggestion like this would never have been made on the basis of style alone, for it is conceivable that while the other two pairs of terms follow the chiastic pattern this pair should have followed the alternating. When the emendation appears to be desirable on other grounds, however, the argument from style may be brought in to support it.[12]

We have now analyzed the first half (Y) of Part IV, and as

[12] Meyer thinks that tongues and prophecy are signs in the sense that *they make the respective groups known* as believers or unbelievers, as the case might be. However, this is not the usual meaning in Scriptures of a sign, whose function is not to reveal the character of men but to make known the presence and power of God.—*Commentary, ad loco.*

we look toward the counterpart II, we find that its contents closely correspond to the contents of Z′ in Part II, for there also we were examining the *results* of unintelligible speech. We therefore conclude that the *last* section of Part II corresponds to the *first* of Part IV and that this is due to a deliberate design on the part of the writer.

We shall now turn our attention to the *last* half of Part IV; when we do so, it becomes quite clear that we are dealing with a counterpart to the *first* half of Part II. If we examine the section Z we shall find that it enumerates *four* types of articulated and therefore intelligible and edifying *speech* (B). This is followed by a figurative reference to *music*. When we examine Y′ in Part IV, we encounter a group of *five* terms, of which four have also to do with types of edifying *speech;* these types are preceded by one, "a psalm," which has to do with *music*. The psalm is the only item in this whole section which has reference to music, and it is just this term which is *additional* and makes five instead of four terms. The conclusion is irresistible that the feeling for balance accounts for its presence. The inversion of the two ideas is, once more, the clue to their relationship in the structure, for instead of edifying *speech* and *music*, as in Part II, Z, the order is here *music* and edifying *speech*. It would be interesting to attempt to draw some further conclusions with regard to the order of these terms in both places in which they occur, but the digest of readings by Tischendorf indicates some uncertainty as to the order. With reference to Y′A the following deductions may be safe. Of the four types of edifying speech, the last two (tongues and interpretation) come first in B (cf. *x*); and the first two (teaching and revelation) come last in B (*x*′), assuming that there is some relation between teaching and prophesying. For prophets, not teachers, are speaking in *x*′. However this may be (and the conclusion must remain uncertain), all of Y′ is an alternating structure in which we have the demands voiced, that the speech in the public assembly should be edifying (A) and of such nature that all may learn and be exhorted (A′). How this is to be achieved is set forth in the more elaborate structures BB′. Section B has alternating lines within each group, but the groups themselves are chiastic. Section B′, on the other hand, does not only have chiastic groups, but the lines themselves are chiastic. The centre of B is devoted to the *men;* the centre of B′ to the *women.*

Although the right to speak with tongues in the public assembly is not denied the men altogether, it is to be governed by two definite restrictions: (1) they must not speak unless an interpreter be present; (2) *several* must not speak at the same time but "in turn." Unless these conditions are observed, they should remain silent in the church, but speak to themselves and to God. Neither are the prophets entirely unrestrained in their liberty. The other members are to "discern"; and if another has a revelation, the prophets must yield the right of the floor to him. The structure of these sections corresponds line for line. That the prophets also are to speak only "in turn" may be seen from the words, "For ye can all prophesy *one by one.*" To do this requires self-restraint, but "the spirits of the prophets are subject to the prophets." This demand (B′) for subjection of the spirit of the prophets to the prophets (x) is balanced by another demand for subjection, that of the women to their husbands (x'). The absence of either of these forms of subjection in the apostolic churches would result in confusion in the assembly, and Paul is here discussing the means of obtaining an orderly assembly.

The editors of the Greek text have experienced some difficulties in construing the sentence beginning, "For ye can all prophesy one by one," etc. Westcott and Hort make a parenthesis of the words, "and the spirits . . . but of peace," and conclude the sentence with the words, "as in all the churches of the saints." Nestle, on the other hand, begins the sentence, "As in all the churches," etc.; this seems a better construction. Because the women are introduced rather abruptly, some writers transpose 14:34-35 to a place after 14:40, and even some manuscripts support the change of the text.[13] The mention of the women at this point may find a very natural explanation in the fact that they were probably susceptible to ecstatic influences connected with the tongues and therefore in their own way contributed to the disorders in the assembly. That they are introduced without being discussed at length is no more

[13] James Moffat, *Introduction to the Literature of the New Testament,* p. 114.

surprising than the brief references to "the unmarried" and "the widows" in 7:8, or to "the virgins" in 7:28, 34. The problem of order in the public assembly, like the sexual problem, was a complex one; and while Paul is dealing with the main issues, likewise, when it is convenient, he draws in other factors that are related to the main problem. If there is any cogency in the analysis which is based on the presence of chiastic and alternating constructions in this chapter, it becomes clear at once that vss. 34-35 are in proper place and should not be removed. If a later redaction is to be thought of at all in this passage, it must have included all of section B′, since AA′ might be regarded as frame-passages for B. However, since the first half of Y in Part IV has two middle panels, the balance of probability is in favor of two similar panels in Y′, which excludes all thought of later redaction.

Just before we reach the final frame-passage (14:37-40), which incloses all three chapters, and which has been discussed previously in connection with its counterpart (11:34b-12:3), we have two brief questions:

> What? was it from you that the word of God went forth?
> Or came it unto you alone? (14:36)

Paul had urged upon the Corinthians two authorities: namely, the word of God as revealed in the Torah, and the universal practice of the apostolic church. The two questions, which are quite pointed and not without a touch of sarcasm, remind the Corinthians that their church was neither a mother church nor were their inspired men the only divinely illuminated men in the world.

With these remarks we conclude our analysis of the three chapters which discuss the question, *Concerning Spiritual Gifts*. The logical clearness of the argument and the literary elegance of the style will make their own impression on the reader. Paul's main objective, however, was neither theological nor literary, but an exceedingly practical one. Problems like the one discussed in these chapters are deeply rooted in temperamental and cultural differences in individuals. The man who is predominantly intellectual and the man who is predominantly emotional always find it difficult to mingle in the act of worship. The two will always hold divergent views in regard to the mode of worship. In creative epochs in the history of the church, when the new is crowding out the old and men are more likely to be desperately in earnest, the reconciliation of the two divergent views is at the same time more difficult and more necessary. There must be a synthesis made between the two, and it must be found in love. For a practical rule of life, when such matters are engaging the mind of the church, none better may be found than the words of Paul:

> Desire earnestly to prophesy,
> And forbid not to speak with tongues.

CHAPTER VIII

THE EPISTLE TO THE EPHESIANS

No literary study of the epistles of Paul would be complete without some reference to his later epistles. Philippians, Colossians, and Philemon must be included, and, under whatever view of authorship one may hold, Ephesians also. The right to include Ephesians among the genuine letters of Paul has been questioned in modern time for linguistic, stylistic, and theological reasons. The material that has passed in review in these discussions of the authorship of Ephesians has been valuable for the understanding of the epistle and more or less convincing. One serious defect, however, has appeared in these arguments. If Paul did not write Ephesians, under what circumstances and for what purpose did the post-Pauline author of the epistle write? It is the merit and strength of the hypothesis presented by Doctor E. J. Goodspeed[1] that it remedies the weakness of all the attempted solutions by previous authors by supplying a plausible occasion for the writing of the epistle.

Dr. Goodspeed holds that there is no evidence of such Pauline influence in the Synoptic Gospels as may be directly traced to Paul's letters. With the publication of Luke-Acts, however, a definite change is discernible. The significance of Paul's work now becomes more widely known in the whole church, and a definite interest in his extant writings is aroused. A post-Pauline Christian of Asia Minor, who already knew Colossians well, set himself to collect and publish a corpus of the Pauline letters. The letters of Paul which before publication had been of merely local interest, and had made their appeal singly, now suddenly were given a prominence that they had not previously known. Their influence which had been only local and temporary now became widespread

[1] E. J. Goodspeed, *New Solutions of New Testament Problems*, The University of Chicago Press, 1928; *The Meaning of Ephesians*, 1933; *An Introduction to the New Testament*, 1937; *New Chapters in New Testament Study*, New York, 1937.

and permanent. The collective influence of the Pauline corpus is registered immediately in a series of epistles, like Hebrews, First Peter, and the Epistles to the Seven Churches of Asia in the Book of Revelation, in the New Testament, and First Clemens and the Ignatian Epistles among the Apostolic Fathers.

The characteristic style and thought of Ephesians find their most plausible explanation, according to Doctor Goodspeed, if we regard the letter as a general introduction to the whole corpus by which the publisher commends it to the reading Christian public. He achieves this result by extolling what Paul used to call "my gospel" very much in Paul's own words. To what extent he has done this is revealed by the fact that of 618 brief phrases into which the epistle has been broken up for comparison with the writings of Paul, not less than 550 may be recovered from the Pauline epistles.

The high percentage of parallels between Ephesians and the other letters in the corpus is not due to mere copying, or an attempt to imitate. The writer does more than imitate, he interprets the Pauline gospel to his own generation which was now harassed by the schisms and suffered from a lack of appreciation of its true Christian heritage. Doctor Goodspeed expounds the epistle at length with a view of showing how much better its phraseology suits the conditions of the tenth decade of the first century than those of earlier decades.

Finally Doctor Goodspeed accepts and gives great prominence to the earlier views of Holtzmann and Ewald that there is a certain liturgical ring in the long sentences that are so characteristic of Ephesians. This emphasis is particularly attractive to the present writer, who regards the chiastic form in the Old and the New Testament as an ancient liturgical style.

The following three selections from Ephesians are exhortations, which in the total structure of the epistle constitute a distinct unit. The first is Eph. 5:22-33.

Husbands and Wives.

A *Wives* unto your own husbands as unto the Lord. 22

For the husband is the head 23
Of the wife,

As Christ also is the head,
Of the church,
B Himself the savior of the *body;*
But as the church 24
Is subject to Christ,
So the wives also
To their husbands in everything.

C *Husbands*, love your wives, 25
even as Christ loved the church, and gave himself for it.

D *That* he might *sanctify* it, 26
having cleansed it by the washing of the water by the word.

E But *that* he might present 27
to himself a glorious *church*, not having { spot,
or wrinkle,
or any such thing;

D′ But *that* it should be *holy*
and *without blemish*

C′ Even so ought *husbands* to love their own wives, 28
as their own bodies.

He that loveth his own wife loveth himself, (vs. 29a, a gloss?)
Even as Christ also the church; 29b
Because we are members of his *body.* 30
"For this cause shall a man leave his father and mother, 31
B′ and shall cleave to his wife,
and the two shall become one flesh."
This *mystery* is great, 32
But I speak of Christ and of the church,
Nevertheless do ye also severally love each one his own wife even as himself. 33

A′ But the *wife* that she fear her husband.

The apostle begins this elaborate passage without taking the trouble to make a fresh start; the verb must be supplied from the preceding verse, "subjecting yourselves one to another in the fear of Christ," etc. Yet, in spite of the informality of the opening, the passage is carried through in rigid conformity to a chiastic pattern. The two admonitions directly addressed to the wives occur in the two extremes (AA′). There are also two admonitions in which the husbands are directly addressed, namely, the two single lines CC′. The argument supporting the admonition to the wives will be found in section B, and that supporting the admonition to the husbands in section B′. To the question, "How should husbands love their wives, or the wives their husbands?", Paul gives this answer: "As Christ loved the church." In other words, the argument is based on Christ's relation to the church—a relationship which is fully described in the three central lines, DED′.

In section B the chiasmus is simple in form and needs no further explanation. In C husbands are exhorted to love their wives as Christ loved the church, which is *his* body; and in C′ they are urged to love their wives as *their* own bodies. The parallelism is here implied in the comparison. In the central lines we have the three ἵνα and in the middle line of the three (DED′) a special triplet. The words, "any such thing," add nothing to the content, but are similar in function to our *et cetera*. They were added because of the feeling for rhythm which required a triplet at the turning point of the passage; this is true in many other cases. In DD′ "sanctify" and "having cleansed" are balanced by "holy" (cf. Greek) and "without blemish." There is a great deal of parallelism compressed in these three lines.

When we direct our attention to section B′, there appear to be some irregularities which disturb the otherwise perfect symmetry of this beautiful passage. In the first place, we have at the centre a quotation from Gen. 2:24, in which we should not expect a chiastic form, since the original passage has none. That the quotation is placed at the centre of the system, however, is in conformity to a centripetal tendency of quotations in such systems (cf. Eph. 6:1-4). In the second place, there are the words, "of his flesh and of his bones," in vs. 30b; these are found in A. V. but are left out by the revisers. Aside from the manuscript evidence against them, it is clear that their inclusion would break up the symmetry of the system. The third and most important irregularity, however, is found in vs. 29a, which is here eliminated. There are several good reasons for this removal. The passage reads like a gloss. It would be the only instance in the passage where the body would be designated as "flesh," it interrupts the sentence as it stands, and its elimination brings the sentence into conformity with other similar sentences in the passage in which the injunction is *immediately* followed by ὡς, καθὼς (cf. vss. 22, 23, 24, 28, 33). The principal reason for eliminating vs. 29a is that the presence of these words would break up the chiastic system. When its counterpart above (B) has a perfect symmetry, there is every reason for assuming that B′ also originally was a balanced composition, and that whatever destroys the balance is a later accretion to the text. The fact that there is manuscript evidence for assuming addition to the context (vs. 30b) strengthens this assumption.

Before proceeding to another passage we should observe that the word "body" as referring to the church is central in B; and, if the quotation is lifted out, this is true in B′ also, where the term "mystery" is in a parallel line. This is a well-known Pauline synonym for the church, as may be seen in Eph. 3:3-6, 9 and especially in Col. 1:26, 27. It has no reference to marriage, but as Paul says, to "Christ and his church." That the church is given a central position in the structure is not a mere coincidence but a deliberate plan, for the word "church" is found also in the line which is the pivot of the whole system (E).

The triplet in the centre is also part of a literary pattern. There are many such triplets in the epistles of Paul, and at times he seems to go out of his way to produce them. A passage which best illustrates this tendency is found in Eph. 5:8-11.

For ye were once darkness, but are now light 8
In the Lord:
Walk as children of light — { goodness,
For the fruit of the light is in all { and righteousness,
Proving what is well-pleasing 10 { and truth— 9
Unto the Lord;
And have fellowship with the unfruitful works of darkness. 11

In this system the sentence is interrupted by a central line which carries a triplet. The whole centre could be removed and the sentence would continue and conclude in the most natural manner. The procedure of the writer to introduce the triplet by means of a parenthetic remark shows even more clearly than the additional words, "any such thing," in Eph. 5:27, that the triplet was really, in some cases, deliberately planned when the sense of rhythm required it.

We shall now proceed to the second of the sections in the group of three, namely, Eph. 6:1-4.

Children, obey your parents in the *Lord:* 1
For this is right.
"Honor thy father and mother 2
(which is the first commandment with promise)
that it may be well with thee, and thou mayest live long on the earth."
And, ye *fathers*, provoke not your children to wrath: 3
But nurture them in the chastening and admonition of the *Lord.* 4

The passage carries two exhortations, one to children and the other to parents, both having a reference to the Lord. Between the two is the quotation and in the middle of the quotation is placed a parenthetic remark. Nothing could better illustrate the centripetal tendencies of quotations in such systems. This is only one of the methods used in placing quotations, for we found the quotations in the frame-passages (YAA′) in 1 Cor. 14:20-36.

The third section is of an altogether different type than any of the other two in the group. It is one of the instances in which two chiastic systems stand side by side in the text, and yet have their interdependence expressed by a definite interweaving of ideas. Eph. 6:5-9 deals with a theme which must have been one of the most common practical problems of the early church in a slave-holding society.

Servants and Masters

Servants, be obedient to them that according to the flesh are your *lords*, 5
With fear and trembling,
In singleness of your heart,
As unto Christ;
A Not in the way of eye service, 6
As men-pleasers,
But as servants of Christ,
Doing the will of God from the soul,
With good will
Doing service as unto the *Lord* and not unto men;

Knowing that each one, 8
If he hath done any good thing,
The same shall he receive again
From the *Lord*,
A′ Whether bond,
Or free.
And, ye *lords*, 9
The same thing do ye unto them,
And forbear the threatening,
Knowing that he who is both their Lord and yours is in heaven, and respect of persons is not with him.

The two sections have ten lines each and illustrate in their own way certain important principles of chiasmus. In A the system opens with an exhortation to servants. When the centre is reached, the positive exhortation changes to a negative one. After the centre is passed, the positive exhortation is resumed. This is the law of the shift at the centre of which several instances already have come to our notice.[2] In A′ the first half of the system is devoted to the servants and the last half to the masters. Of such an arrangement several examples have also appeared.[3] In the first and last lines of A there is a contrast between the lords (masters) and the Lord, the first having the phrase, "according to the flesh," and the last line the words, "not unto men." In A′ the two are again presented, not in the extreme lines, but in the lines nearest the centre; and not in the order in A, but in the inverted order, Lord, lords. In other words, the two terms have been taken and turned over, as it were, and removed from the extremes of one system to the centre of the corresponding system. We have already discovered evidence of such procedure elsewhere (cf. Ps. 30). There are many such shifts from extremes of one system to the centre of another—a shift not only of ideas but, as in the psalms, of whole strophes.[4]

There seems to be a still closer relationship between the two systems, for "with fear and trembling" in the second line of A is parallel to "and forbear the threatening" in the ninth line of A′. Likewise "with good will" in the ninth line of A is parallel to "if he hath done any good thing" in the second line of A′. The two sections have been shaped with reference to one another. They resemble two ornaments at the end of a frieze which are made to face each other in order to produce balance in the decorations. It would not be surprising if exhortations of this kind formed an important part of the instruction given by the early church to converts. In such cases the artistic form would be conducive to pedagogy, since it would help to fix such passages in memory. Such results, however, would be merely by-products; for the motive that led to the production of such passages, since they are merely part of a far-flung artistic scheme extending over the whole epistle, must have been liturgical.

[2] Cf. Gen. 12:16; Isa. 60:1-3; 28:15-18.

[3] Cf. Amos 5:4b-6a; Num. 15:35-36; Gen. 4:17-11:8; Lk. 4:16-21a.

[4] "Chiasmus in the Psalms," *AJSL* (July, 1933), pp. 298, 299. Psalms 42, 43 illustrate such a shift in the refrain.

In Eph. 6:10-17 we have a well-known passage dealing with the spiritual struggle and the Christian's armor.

The Warfare and Armor of Christians

A Finally, be strong in the Lord and in the strength of his might. 10
Put on the whole armor of God, that ye may be able to stand. 11

Against the wiles of the devil; for our wrestling is not 12
Against blood and flesh, but
X B Against the principalities,
Against the powers,
Against the worldrulers in this darkness,
Against the spiritual (hosts) of wickedness in the heavenly (places).

A′ Wherefore, take up the whole armor of God, that ye may be able to with-
In the evil day, and, having done all, to stand. (stand. 13

Stand therefore, having girded your loins with truth, 14
And having put on the breastplate of righteousness, (peace;
X′ And having shod your feet with the preparation of the gospel of 15
Withal taking up the shield of faith,[5] 16
And take the helmet of salvation, 17
And the sword of the Spirit, which is the word of God.

These two sections have much in common. In X we have a sixfold description of the enemies introduced by six prepositions πρὸς (cf. B). The first and the last lines of B are synonymous, presenting the devil and his hosts, and "our wrestling" as being staged "in the heavenly (places)," that is to say, in the sphere in which Christians have been made to sit with Christ (cf. Eph. 2:6). The next two lines are antithetic, for "blood and flesh" has reference to human beings, while "the worldrulers in this darkness" possibly means spiritual powers, not earthly rulers (cf. 1 Cor. 2:8; 2 Cor. 4:4, where other terms are used). Yet, the term may apply to earthly rulers as well. They are represented in the New Testament as bringing about the crucifixion of Jesus (cf. Acts 4:27, 28), and this is nowhere stated of the devil. The two central terms occur together in other central sections (cf. Eph. 3:10; Col. 1:16). This tendency of certain terms to gravitate toward the centre of their respective systems we have observed with reference to the "body" as a synonym for the church. It also holds good for

[5] The following words, "wherewith we shall be able," etc., are probably a gloss. If the words are retained they would be the *only* instance of the six in which the *use* is stated.

"bond or free" (cf. Eph. 6:8; 1 Cor. 12:13). It may be compared to the tendency of some terms to occur in company in parallel lines of a system, like "faith" and "prophecy" (cf. Rom. 12:6; 1 Cor. 12:8-11; 13:2, 9, 11; Eph. 4:11-13a). In AA′ the lines nearest the middle section B have the closest parallels, but the other lines also have a certain similarity, since in the first we are asked to become strong in the Lord, while the last refers to "having done all."

In X′ we have a description of "the whole armor of God." "Truth" in the first line and "the word of God" in the last line are parallel. The girdle, or belt, directs our attention to the place from which the sword is suspended. In the next two lines, the breastplate and the helmet are means of protecting the upper part of the body. The two central lines direct our attention to the feet, and, in the phrase, "taking up the shield of faith," by implication to the hand also. Though this is not explicitly stated, it may be assumed with a certain degree of certainty, for hands and feet have a tendency elsewhere in such systems to occupy parallel positions, like the examples given below (cf. Rev. 1:14-16). The words, "wherewith we shall be able to quench all the fiery darts of the evil one," have been eliminated from the passage, since they look like a gloss. They would, if included, break up the otherwise perfect symmetry of the passage. It is also remarkable that these words are the *only* instance in which a description of the *purpose* of any part of the armor has been given. Thus the six enemies and the six parts of the armor of God, or panoply, are made to match one another. That the number six should occur in a description of the struggle against evil does not surprise us in view of the similar use of the number in Rev. 13:18. This is but another detail, among many others, which convinces us that we are not dealing with more or less striking coincidences but with a definite literary method which followed rigid rules of composition (cf. 1 Thess. 5:8).

Finally, the passage is largely made up from allusions which may be recovered from the O. T. The metaphor in the *first* line of vss. 14-16 is found in Isa. 11:5, and that in the *last* line in Isa. 11:4; the second and fifth lines are both from Isa. 59:17; the third is from Isa. 52:7; the fourth has no O. T. source. It is significant that this line alone carries an explanation of the purpose of the shield, probably from a glossator, who recognized the need of some explanation. If the literary process which is here postulated should appear too mechanical to be accepted, we should remind ourselves that it is precisely by this kind of procedure that the very elaborate and symmetrical passage in Luke 4:16-21a has assumed its present form, for in this passage one line that is found in the quotation from Isa. 61:1, 2a is removed from the gospel passage, and another line which is not found is brought in from Isa. 58:6, which procedure, together with some minor modifications, results in a very artistic structure (cf. *infra*, p. 236).

CHAPTER IX

THE EPISTLE TO THE COLOSSIANS

In the epistle to the Colossians there are many structures which both in content and form are similar to those already described. Together with a discussion of the formal aspects of the first chapter we shall attempt to compare some of these forms with those occurring in the epistle to the Ephesians. In Col. 1:3-9a the thanksgiving of the apostle contains some interesting forms.[1]

The Apostle and the Church

A We give thanks to God the Father of our Lord Jesus Christ, praying always for you; 3

Having heard of 4
Your *faith* in Jesus Christ,
B And of the *love* which ye have toward all the saints,
Because of the *hope* which is laid up for you in the heavens, 5
Whereof ye heard before.

In the word of the truth of the gospel, 6
Which is come unto you;
Even as it is in all the world
C Bearing fruit and increasing,
As in you also,
Since the day ye heard
And knew the grace of God in truth;

Even as ye learned of Epaphras 7
Our *beloved* fellow-servant,
B′ Who is a *faithful* minister of Christ on your behalf,
Who also declared unto us your *love* in the Spirit; 8
For this cause we also from the day we heard 9

A′ Do not cease to pray and make request for you, . . .

Only a few comments are needed on this passage. In AA′ there are references to prayer. In BB′ there are regular triplets at the centre. Other instances occur in which "faith" and "hope" are parallel in a system (cf. Eph. 4:4-6; Col. 1:23). In C the phrase "bearing fruit and increasing" is central, a fact which is not

[1] Martin Dibelius, *Handkommentar zum Neuen Testament: An die Colosser* (Tübingen: 1927), p. 3, has some observations on the form of this passage.

without significance; this will be apparent when we come to the next section. There cannot have been in the author's mind any clear idea of division between the two sections. The chiastic pattern begun in A is rounded out in A′ by a reference to prayer, which at the same time begins a new line of thought. This is developed in a new literary pattern in Col. 1:9b-13. Examples of this kind, and the similar informality with which Eph. 5:22-33 begins, tend to show that the chiastic form is, in many instances, carried out in obedience to laws of rhythm not always consciously present in the author's mind. There can be no contradiction between this assumption and the insistence upon rigid rhetorical rules, for the rules become an unconscious equipment in the degree that they have been mastered. The passage, then, continues:

Christian Life and Conduct

That ye may be filled 9b

With the knowledge of his will,
A In all wisdom
And spiritual understanding,

To walk worthily of the Lord 10

Unto all pleasing,
In every good work,
B Bearing fruit and increasing by the knowledge of God;
In all power made powerful according to the might of his glory, 11
Unto all patience and longsuffering;

With joy giving thanks to the Father, 12

Who made us meet to be partakers of the inheritance of the saints in the light,
A′ Who delivered us out of the power of darkness, 13
And translated us into the kingdom of the Son of his Love.

The lines in italics appear to be the leading parts of the sentence. Section A describes the apprehension of spiritual truth by the believer and A′, the new status which is the result thereof. Thus AA′ deal with the inner life, while B sets forth the results of this inner life in conduct among men. Yet, even here, there is an allusion in the central line to the source of the good life, namely, "the knowledge of God." The central section is remarkable for its symmetrical array of prepositions (cf. εἰς, ἐν), and for the repetition of the phrase, "bearing fruit and increasing," in a central position. In this instance the order of the prepositions enables us to check our decision that the phrase is really central in the scheme of the author and is not due to our own more or less subjective arrangement. The phrase is another example of the tendency of certain phrases and terms to gravitate toward the centre in a system.

Again the passage proceeds without any grammatical break and develops an extensive literary pattern in Col. 1:14-22a.

Christ Is Supreme in Creation and Salvation

In whom we have our redemption, the forgiveness of our sins; 14
Who is the image of the invisible God, 15

X
A The firstborn of all creation;
For in him were created 16
All things,

B In the *heavens*,
And upon the *earth*,
Things visible,
And things invisible,

B′ Whether thrones,
Or dominions,
Or principalities,
Or powers,

A′ All things
Have been created through him and unto him
And he is before all things. 17

Y And in him all things consist,
And he is the head 18
Of the body, the church,
Who is the beginning, the firstborn from the dead;
That in all things he might have the preeminence,
For it was the good pleasure that in him should all the fulness dwell, 19

X′
A And through him to reconcile all things unto himself, 20
Having made peace,
Through the blood of his cross,
Through him,

B Whether things upon the *earth*,
Or things in the *heavens*,

A′ And you, being in the past time alienated, 21
And enemies in your mind in your evil works,
Yet now hath he reconciled in the body of his flesh, 22
Through death;

This passage is the first part of a longer structure which extends to and includes 2:1. The introductory words, though in form unrelated to the context, nevertheless introduce the central ideas of the following structure. In X the supremacy of Christ in creation (AA′) and the scope of this supremacy are discussed (BB′). The chiasmus in B is evident, but it is also clear that the four εἴτε in B′ do not introduce a chiasmus. "Principalities and powers" go together in Paul (cf. Eph. 3:10; 6:12; Col. 2:10, 15).

In regard to BB′ it is not sufficient to consider merely the immediate context, for in the later counterpart to this whole division of the epistle there is another central panel in which a similar arrangement of eight terms occurs. In Col. 3:11 Paul is describing the *new* creation in Christ. This is the new humanity, "the new man, that is being renewed unto knowledge after the image of him that created him" (vs. 10)—an idea that is further elaborated in the following literary pattern: "where there cannot be

Greek
  And Jew;
  Circumcision
And uncircumcision;

Barbarian,
Scythian;
Bond,
Free."

In section Y Christ is described as the supreme head of the church. Again we find the church, the body, in a central position, since these terms are found not only in the central section of the three (Y), but also in the central lines of the section. Once more we notice an amazing sense of balance: since the term, "the body," has been qualified by the term, "the church," the next line follows the same form by explaining "the beginning" as "the firstborn from the dead."

In section X′ the redemption wrought by Christ is described, the extent of which is said to be identical with the scope of Christ's creative activity, including earth and heaven (cf. Eph. 1:10, also central). The inversion of the two terms in such structures in this passage is a common device by which the relationship of a later section to a former parallel section is indicated (cf. 1 Cor. 12:9, 10 with vs. 28, 30). In AA′ the lines are alternating, the first two of A describing the reconciliation and the first two of A′, the hostility which made reconciliation necessary. The last two lines of each section are synonymous and closely parallel. The passage then runs on without interruption into a passage of more practical content, Col. 1: 22b-23, in which triplets are prominent.

The End and Means of Christian Life

To present you 22b
Holy,
A And without blemish,
And unreprovable
Before him,

If so be that ye continue in the *faith*, 23
Grounded,
B And steadfast,
And not moved away
From the *hope* of the gospel,

Which ye heard,
C Which was preached { in all creation
under heaven,
Of which I Paul was made minister.

The end of Christian life is perfection before God in the day of judgment. The means of achieving this end is, on the objective side, the preaching of Paul's gospel, and, on the subjective, an unswerving faith in its content. The manner in which the triplets are obtained in this passage shows clearly an aesthetic rather than a logical interest. In A the last two terms are merely the negative side of the first, and in B the last of the three expresses the negative side of the first two. In C one feels that the *ear* has determined the structure of the triplet (cf. οὗ, τοῦ, οὗ). That which is true of the beginning of the lines in C is also true of the endings in A and B.

The whole passage serves as a transition between the preceding passage and the one which follows. In C the universality of the preaching "in all creation under heaven" reminds us of the terms "creation" and "heaven" in 1:14-22a. Likewise we shall find that the aspirations for the perfection of the church which are expressed in A have close parallels in the following passage, Col. 1:24-2:1 (cf. X'A, which follows)—another cross-stitch, as it were.

Christ Is Supreme in God's Revelation and in Paul's Preaching

Now I rejoice in my sufferings for you, 24
And fill up on my part that which is lacking in the afflictions of Christ
In my flesh
X For his body's sake,
Which is the church;
Whereof I was made minister, 25
According to the dispensation of God
Which was given me towards you,

To fulfil the word of God, 26
The mystery,
Which hath been hid from the ages and from the generations,
But now hath it been manifested
Y To his saints,
To whom God was pleased 27
To make known
What is the riches of his glory
Of this mystery among the Gentiles,
Which is Christ in you, the hope of glory:

X′
A Whom we proclaim { admonishing every man,
and teaching every man in all wisdom,
that we may present every man as perfect in Christ. 28

Whereunto I labor also, 29
B Striving according to his power,
Which worketh in me in power.

A′ For I would have you know how greatly I strive { for you,
and for them that are in Laodicea,
and for as many as have not seen my face in the (flesh. 2:1

The tendency of the term "body" in the sense of church to appear at the centre is once more evident in the two central lines in X. In Y we have "the saints" in a similar position. In X′, however, the two triplets, AA′, relate to the church. The law of the shift from centre to the extremes of parallel sections has been in operation in the construction of this passage, for in X the first three and the last three lines deal chiefly with Paul and his ministry in the church (cf. the two "for you" and "towards you," in the first and last lines), while the two central lines deal with the church itself. In X′ this order is completely reversed; B pertains to Paul's ministry and AA′ to its objective, the church. While AA′ are centered in the church, the introductory words refer to Paul's work. The three laws concerning leprosy in Lev. 14 are evidence of the practice of placing triplets in positions other than the centre of chiastic structures.

The structure of Y is regular were it not for the phrase,

"among the Gentiles," which would fit better in the line above; there it would be parallel to "the generations." As the text now reads, none of these phrases has a parallel in the structure. To lift the phrase "among the Gentiles" to the line above would involve a transposition of two lines in a manuscript like Sinaiticus. The phrase would either follow the word "glory" or be placed between the word "mystery" and the definite article that precedes. Though such speculations may seem attractive, it is not necessary to insist on absolute perfection in form. There are some cases where several lines in a system are perfectly matched, whereas others are less convincing. Even when some systems are not perfect in form there may be present in them features that enable us to check the arrangement. Thus the references to Christ and God in parallel lines in X and in Y are hardly a mere coincidence. That God is mentioned also in the centre of Y indicates the law of distribution of similar terms at the centre and the extremes. Since the structure in Eph. 3:2-5 offers some striking resemblances to section Y, it may be worth while to give an arrangement of the passage. The interrupted sentence from vs. 1 proceeds:

> If so be that ye have heard of that grace of God which was given me to you-ward;
> How by revelation
> Was made known to me
> The mystery,
> As I wrote before in few words,
> Whereby when ye read, ye can perceive my understanding
> In the mystery of Christ; which in other generations
> Was not made known unto the sons of men,
> As it hath now been revealed
> Unto his holy apostles and prophets in Spirit.

In this passage the parallelism of the lines is rather striking, except in the lines which contain references to mankind: "the generations" and "the sons of men." The first of these two is precisely the term which was found without parallel in section Y in Col. 1:24-2:1. The second, however, may be treated as a parallel to the phrase, "to me," in the third line.

A still more interesting passage is Eph. 4:4-6a, which excites our interest because of a single irregularity among its many regularities.

One body
And one Spirit, even as also ye were called
In one *hope* of your calling,
One Lord,
One *faith*,
One baptism,
One God and Father of all.

In this passage "hope" and "faith" keep company, as they do in several other passages to which we have already called attention.[2] The "spirit" and "baptism" in parallel lines require no defense in view of the usage in passages like Acts 2:38; 8:12 and 16. Only in the first and last lines of the system do we fail to discover any parallelism. If we were permitted to transpose the central line and the first line, the two names would offer a common parallel. Such a transposition, however, would effect more startling results. We would then have the term, "one body" (referring to the church) in the centre—a feature which we have found in both Ephesians and Colossians.[3] In addition, we would have also a symmetrical distribution of the numerical adjectives (cf. εἷς, ἓν μιᾷ, ἕν, μία, ἕν, εἷς); as the text now reads, this is interrupted. We have already discovered a similar arrangement of the prepositions in Col. 1:10-11. Though the variations of this passage quoted from the church fathers by Tischendorf fail to disclose any reading that includes the transposition here suggested, the results thereby obtained would appear to justify the alteration, especially since it is easily explained why the "body" should have come to head the list. This might easily have happened by its attraction to the next term in the list, due to such natural combinations as "body and spirit" (cf. 1 Cor. 7:34), which would be sufficiently familiar to suggest the present combination to a scribe. If the copyist had no knowledge of the chiastic form, the mistake would pass unnoticed because the sense of the passage was in no way changed.

The passages we have now discussed do not exhaust the chiastic forms in Ephesians and Colossians. Indeed, it is possible to show that the scheme of each epistle is chiastic to the extent that whole major divisions are arranged with reference to one another

[2] Cf. Col. 1:4, 5; 2:23.
[3] Cf. 1 Cor. 12:12; Eph. 5:23, 24; vss. 30-33; Col. 1:18; vs. 24.

with parallel ideas and terms common to both. A discussion of the whole problem would make it necessary to print a complete analysis of both epistles, and this is not within the scope of our present task. There is no doubt that a thorough comparative study of the two epistles, together with other materials from admittedly Pauline epistles, would yield some new details in regard to the authorship of Ephesians. At any rate, such a study would provide us with a new approach to an old problem. More recently the liturgical quality of Ephesians has been demonstrated by exhibiting its sonorous phraseology and fulness of statement.[4] A similar conclusion will be reached by fully setting forth the chiastic form of the various sections and of the epistle as a whole. At what stage in the history of the church such writings began, or could begin, to appear, depends very largely upon the view that is held about the development of the primitive church itself. If the eschatology of the primitive church is made out to be so thorough and consistent as to preclude all interest in and all planning for a more remote future, then we cannot expect an interest in such things as liturgical writings until comparatively late, when the early interests had either entirely faded out, or had become materially modified by other interests.[5] If, on the other hand, the primitive church started, not with empty hands in matters religious, but with a rich heritage of worship and with a keen appreciation of didactic processes and writings, which it had taken over from Judaism,[6] then the age of liturgical writings need not be deferred, but could well have come with the first and second generation of Christians. In fact, there is something liturgical even in such an epistle as First Corinthians which was intended to serve more permanently and in circles far beyond its immediate destination (cf. 1 Cor. 1:2).

[4] Edgar J. Goodspeed, *The Meaning of Ephesians*, Chicago, 1933.

[5] Donald W. Riddle, *Early Christian Life* (Chicago: 1936), pp. 91, 112 ff.

[6] S. J. Case, *The Evolution of Early Christianity* (Chicago: 1914), pp. 118-122. Johannes Weiss, *Das Urchristentum*, Bk. I, chap. 3.

CHAPTER X

THE EPISTLES TO THE PHILIPPIANS, PHILEMON, AND ROMANS

The epistle to the Philippians shows a great deal of similarity in form to the other epistles of Paul. The following passage from Phil. 2:1-11 may serve as illustration:

If there is therefore any exhortation in Christ, 1
If any consolation of love,
If any fellowship of the Spirit,
If any tender mercies and compassion, make full my joy, 2

A
That ye be of the same mind,
Having the same love, being of one accord,
Of the same mind;

Nothing through faction or through vainglory, 3
But in lowliness of mind each counting other better than himself,
Not looking each of you to his own things, 4
but each of you also to the things of others.
Have this mind in you which was also in Christ Jesus: 5

Who, existing in the form of God, 6
Counted not the being of an equality with God a thing to be grasped,
But himself 7
He emptied,

B
The form of a servant taking,
In the likeness of men becoming;
And in fashion being found as a man, 8

He humbled
Himself,
Becoming obedient unto death,
The death of the cross.

C
Wherefore also God highly exalted him, 9

And gave unto him { the name
which is above every name,
that in the name of Jesus 10

"Every knee should bow,"
Of those in heaven,
And of those in earth,
And of those under the earth,
"And every tongue should confess" 11

That { Lord
Jesus
Christ (is)

Unto the glory "of God" the Father.

The passage begins with a solemn exhortation, each line of which is introduced by "if" (A). Just before the centre is reached the structure of the sentence changes with the words, "make full my joy." There is a central triplet[1] as in Eph. 4:4-6. The marginal reading of Westcott and Hort (vs. 2) seems preferable in view of the symmetry of the triplet. Yet, "one mind," which is the alternate reading, would also be parallel to "the same mind." The pair of lines which are nearest the centre are antithetic, each carrying two contrasted terms. The next pair of lines mentions and describes "fellowship." The next line mentions "love," and its counterpart in a couplet describes the nature of love in a manner which recalls to our mind the Pauline description in 1 Cor. 13:5, "love seeketh not its own." Finally, the system winds up, as it began, with a reference to the Master himself.

The introduction of the name of Christ the second time (vs. 5) opens a new line of thought, which is artistically developed in a new literary pattern (B) almost identical in form with the preceding. In the first line the highest possible exaltation of Christ is described in that he had "the form of God"; and in the last line the lowest possible degradation with the abrupt qualifying phrase, "death of cross," in which even the article is wanting. The second line contrasts the absence of aspirations to equality with God on the part of Christ with his obedience unto death. In the next two lines there is a similarity in sound in Greek which is quite striking (cf. ἑαυτὸν ἐκένωσεν and ἐταπείνωσεν ἑαυτὸν). The centre again is a triplet in which the nature of Christ's humanity is emphasized (cf. "form," "likeness," "fashion," and "servant," "men," "man").

The third section (C) sets forth the exaltation of Christ. The first and the last lines carry the references to God, and the next two lines carry triplet statements about Christ's name. We have already observed in the case of the three leprosy laws in Lev. 14 and in the law of retaliation in Lev. 24 how triplets may be introduced in positions other than the centre of a system. Just as the central triplet in B described the nature of Christ's humiliation, so the central triplet in C describes the extent of his exaltation in terms that remind us of Eph. 1:22. Again we find a scripture

[1] Cf. αὐτὸ, αὐτὴν, αὐτὸ.

quotation in the centre of the system (cf. Eph. 5:31) and once more is the quotation split in two by a qualifying remark (cf. Eph. 6:2). Although the whole description of Christ's humiliation and exaltation is introduced casually and with an ethical rather than a doctrinal interest (as the context in vss. 1-5 proves) it is impossible to treat a passage of such a nature as merely incidental. Passages like these, whether they are found in the epistles or in the gospels, are liturgical.[2] They were meant to be read in the Christian assembly, to be read often, and to be used in Christian instruction and memorized by members of the church. There can be no doubt that their peculiar form also made them particularly effective for such use.

The teachings of Paul are often expressed in great contrasts. We have already examined two parallel systems describing the humiliation and exaltation of Christ. The following passage from Phil. 3:7-10a is a bit of spiritual autobiography, dealing with Paul's loss and gain.

Howbeit *what things* were to me gains, these have I *counted* 7
For Christ
A loss.
A Yea verily, and I *count all things* 8
To be a loss
For the excellency of the knowledge of Christ Jesus my Lord:
For whom I suffered the loss of *all things*, and do *count* them but refuse,

That I may gain *Christ*, and be found in him, 9
Not having my own
Righteousness,
That which is of the law,
B But that which is through faith in *Christ*,
That which is of God
Righteousness
Upon the faith
That I may know *him* and the power of his resurrection.

To exhibit the order of the Greek sentence it is necessary in this case to violate the order of the English. The most significant feature in these two sections is that one is devoted to what Paul had lost (A) and the other to what he had gained (B). In either

[2] Cf. Ernst Lohmeyer, *Kyrios Jesus: eine Untersuchung zu Phil. 2:5-11* (Heidelberg: 1928), has concluded that it is "a Jewish Christian Psalm" (p. 9), but has evidently missed that chiastic form which supports his view.

case the dominant ideas in the respective sections are distributed according to that law which places similar ideas at the extremes and at the centre of the system. Thus the terms that refer to Paul's loss ("things") and the verb "count" are in such position in A, while those which describe his gain, namely, Christ and the fellowship with him, are placed in a similar position in B.

The Epistle to Philemon[3]

The epistle to Philemon is built up in accordance with chiastic principles. Its general contents may be summed up in the following brief outline.

A Salutation, vss. 1-3.

B Philemon's conduct toward all the saints.
He is the object of Paul's prayer, vss. 4-6.

C Paul had experienced much joy in the past, because his brother had refreshed the hearts of the saints, vs. 7.

D Paul refrains from pressing his claims on Philemon and prefers to ask a favor of him: The name Paul, vss. 8-11.

E Paul and Onesimus: He is beloved by Paul, vss. 12-15.

E′ Paul and Onesimus: Philemon should love him also, vss. 16-17.

D′ Paul offers to reimburse Philemon, though he might have pressed his claims on him: The name Paul, vss. 18-19.

C′ Paul expects much joy in the future in that his own heart will be refreshed through his brother, vs. 20.

B′ Philemon's conduct toward Paul, who is an object of the prayers of the saints, vss. 21-22.

A′ Salutation, vss. 23-25.[4]

The two central sections of this outline will be discussed with a view of displaying a new type of arrangement which has not as yet received any attention. We have discussed a number of chiastic structures in which words and lines have been parallel. The two passages here given show a definite arrangement of *couplets* in chiastic patterns (Philemon vss. 12-17).

[3] John Knox, *Philemon among the Letters of Paul*, Chicago, 1935.

[4] Thomas Boys, *Tactica Sacra* (London: 1824), has an analysis of this epistle, which is given in John Forbes, *The Symmetrical Structure of Scripture* (Edinburgh: 1854), p. 40. The disagreement in detail with his outline is due to what seems to be a definite strophic arrangement of the material of the letter, of which two samples are given here. These forms provide definite limits to the separate sections in which the letter is written, and Boys's outline seems to cut across some of these sections.

Whom I have sent back to thee in person, 12
That is my very heart;
Whom I would have fain kept with me, 13
That in thy behalf he might minister unto me in the bonds of the gospel;
A But without thy mind 14
I would do nothing;
That thy goodness should not be of necessity,
But of free will.
For perhaps he was therefore parted for a season, 15
That thou shouldest have him forever;

No longer a servant, 16
But more than a servant,
A brother,
A beloved,
B Specially to me,
But how much rather to thee,
Both in the flesh,
And in the Lord;
If then thou countest me a partner, 17
Receive him as myself.

In these two structures (AB) we may observe how in the central lines Paul and Philemon are brought into a striking contrast. The rest of the two sections is devoted to their mutual relations with Onesimus, the slave. There seems to be a parallelism between the first couplet of A and last of B, between "I have sent back" and "receive him," between "my very heart" and "myself." This feature reminds us of Eph. 6:5-9.

The arrangement of *couplets* into chiastic systems is not a very common feature in the epistles of Paul. There is nothing like it in Colossians, which was contemporary with Philemon. In Philippians, on the other hand, there are some passages in which the same type of arrangement may be found.

In Phil. 2:12-18 we have a passage which somewhat at length illustrates the literary mannerisms of Philemon.

So then, my beloved, even as ye have always obeyed, 12

Not in my presence only,
But now much more in my absence,
With fear
And trembling
Your own salvation
Work out;
A For God is he 13
Who worketh
In you
Both to will
And to work for his good pleasure;
All things do without murmurings 14
And questionings;

That ye may become blameless 15
And harmless,
Children of God
Without blemish
B In the midst of a generation
Crooked
And perverse,
Among whom ye shine as lights in the world,
The word of life holding forth; 16

Unto my glorying
Unto the day of Christ,
That not in vain did I run,
Neither in vain did I labor.
A′ Yea, and if I am poured out as a drink-offering 17
Upon the sacrifice
And service of your faith,
I joy, and rejoice with you all;
And in the same manner do ye also joy, and rejoice with me. 18

In A the statements come in pairs. The first and the last couplets deal with obedience to Paul. The next pair of couplets present two different frames of mind. The central five lines, although they have no couplets, are plainly chiastic. The whole section is a statement of Paul's interest in the character and work of the church. A similar trend of thought is discernible in section A′. The last couplet carries a *double* statement in each line, the repetition acting as a check upon the reader and serving as a signal that this particular section of the epistle is at an end. The parallelism between "glorying" in the first couplet and "rejoicing" in the last is obvious; so, too, with "labor" and "service" in the next pair of couplets. Sections AA′ are parallel in this respect: they both deal with Paul's personal interest in the church, and they deal with the character of the church. The character of the church is also set forth in section B, but with special reference to the wicked world. The character of the church is described negatively in the first and positively in the last couplet. Christians are contrasted with the men of the world in the next two couplets.

Although our main interest in giving an arrangement of this passage has been the peculiarities of style as manifested in the chiastic arrangement of couplets, the passage has affinities not only to Philemon but also to Ephesians. The whole section B moves in the same sphere as Eph. 5:7-13. The term, "without blemish," is found also in Eph. 5:27; "fear and trembling" in Eph. 6:5; "his good pleasure" in Eph. 1:9. It is not only the fact that these terms recur in Philippians that is significant, but the fact that at least "fear and trembling" (which in Eph. 6:5-9 is balanced by "good will," vs. 7) is here balanced by "good pleasure." In the Greek there is a similarity in the sound of the two words—a fact which certainly in other instances in Paul has played some part in the selection of terms in parallel position (cf. εὐδοκία, εὔνοια). The evidential value such details may have in determining the question of authorship would depend on the fact that they are undesigned similarities.

As a closing passage in this study of form in the Pauline epistles we give the following arrangement of Rom. 11:33-36:

> O the depth of the *riches*,
> And of the *wisdom*,
> And of the *knowledge* of *God!*
> How unsearchable his judgments,
> And past tracing out his ways!
> For who *hath known* the mind of the *Lord?*
> Or who hath been his *counsellor?*
> Or who hath first *given* to him,
> And it shall be recompensed unto him again?
> For of him, and through him, and unto him, are all things.
> To him be the glory for ever. Amen.

The structure of this passage helps us to determine the question of construction and punctuation of the first three lines. All three are coördinated; they are not to be rendered, "O the depth of the riches, both of the wisdom and the knowledge of God." The margin of the American Revised Version seems to be the correct rendering, for after the central exclamation in regard to "his judgments" and "his ways," the structure concludes with three statements in the inverted order, which evidently are parallel to the three that open the passage: (1) "For who hath known the mind of the Lord," i.e., in whom is such a depth of knowledge? (2) "Or who hath been his counsellor," i.e., in whom is such a depth of wisdom? (3) "Or who hath first given to him," i.e., in whom is such a depth of riches? It is no mere coincidence that the name God should occur in the last line of the first group of three, and that the name Lord should be found in the first line of the second group of three, and that both should be placed at the end of their respective lines.[5] Such things do not happen by themselves, but are the results of a careful literary training in accordance with definite models. Even in the variation of the names we have Old Testament patterns, for in many of the psalms Elohim and Yahweh alternate in a regular order. The liturgical nature of the passage and its Old Testament pattern are unmistakable. It forms a very fitting close to the section in Romans in which Paul has discussed the hope of Israel. We must remain in uncertainty with reference to the closing ascription of glory, for it is possible that the three prepositions are to be related more definitely to the preceding. On the other hand, the triplet form may be merely a general liturgical form whose details have no direct connection with the three preceding statements.

The evidence presented of chiastic forms in the epistles of Paul is by no means exhausted. All of the epistles to the Ephesians, Colossians, Philippians, Philemon, and First Corinthians are constructed after these patterns. There are clear traces of such structures also in First and Second Thessalonians, Second Corinthians, and Romans. The implications of this evidence are far-reaching. In the light of these forms one must admit that the Pauline epistles belong to a type of literature. They may no longer be regarded as artless compositions, penned after the rush

[5] Cf. Matt. 9:15, 23:30-32.

of the day's work and without regard for the art of literary composition. Such estimates of Paul as a writer are based on a complete misunderstanding of what his epistles really are. They are possible only as long as we insist upon a one-sided classical approach. That Paul is indebted to Hellenism we may take for granted, but that he also took his Semitic heritage seriously, and that this heritage included, not only religious ideas but also their form of expression, appears to be a legitimate deduction.

Not only were the Pauline epistles literary productions; they were also liturgical documents. This precludes the idea that they were written merely to take care of local and temporary problems. Even an epistle like First Corinthians, which undoubtedly was written in response to definite questions, gives evidence of permanency. Its problems were, no doubt, more or less the problems of every church. A remarkable quality in the epistle is the light hand with which the writer touches the *local* situation. Local conditions create the problem and provide the writer with the point of departure, but the discussion soon disengages itself from the local situation and becomes general in tone. The outlook is not local but universal. There are explicit statements to the effect that the rules prescribed are universal regulations governing the whole church (cf. 1 Cor. 7:17; 14:33). Since these letters were written to be read publicly and to be read repeatedly, they were written in a form that made it possible to read them outside the local church to which they were first sent. Their character as public liturgical writings is accentuated by the fact that they were cast in the well-known Old Testament liturgical forms.

One of the most important implications is that these epistles by their form gave the early church a model for subsequent liturgical productions. The early church in Palestine was influenced directly by the Old Testament. The Gentile church outside of Palestine through a large Jewish constituency felt indirectly the influence of the Synagogue and its liturgical forms. It is impossible to estimate the influence of Paul's epistles upon the Gentile churches, but the fact that these epistles carried over liturgical forms of the Synagogue into Greek must have been of great importance in the liturgical development of the early church. Nor need we hold that this influence could make itself felt only after the Pauline writings had been collected in a corpus. If Paul found this form a natural mode of expression, others, no doubt, wrote more or less skilfully after the same fashion. The creation of this "middle-type" of literature, as von Wilamovitz-Moellendorff has called it, would not be the work of one man, but the natural outcome of the mingling of Greek and Semitic culture, which had been on its way for three hundred years before Paul's time. We may be certain, however, that the personal influence of Paul was no small factor in the subsequent literary development of the church—a factor with which we must reckon when we come to account for the form of the gospels.

THE GOSPELS

CHAPTER XI

THE UNITS IN THE GOSPELS

In our historical survey of the study of form we made mention of the most recent tendency in gospel criticism as expressed by Martin Albertz, namely, to discontinue all attempts to find for the gospels a place in literature. "Literary" investigations, according to this critic, should be replaced by "form-history." Modern criticism of the gospels, in so far as it has been influenced by this method, is on its way back to a study of the Christian tradition in its pre-literary stage. It is concerned with the units that make up our gospels, their form and their history. Whether we are thinking of the doings or of the sayings of Jesus we may accept without hesitation the conclusion that these units have circulated widely in oral form as part of the preaching and teaching of the early church. They were "paradigms," or teaching-models—illustrative material used by the early teachers to bring out certain points which were important in their teaching about Jesus. Often we find upon closer examination that narrative units are stripped of all superfluous details and that the story is made to converge at a given point, which is sharpened by a striking saying embodied in the story. The study of form-history has brought this fact into clearer perspective and given to it a greater emphasis than it had ever before received.

Does it follow, however, that when these results are accepted as facts, such forms must be treated as pre-literary? The position of the form-historians is that literary interest and literary procedure has had nothing whatsoever to do with the shaping of the material. These stories and sayings have assumed their present form, not by the influence of any one individual, but by the influence of the whole Christian community. They are not even the work of any one generation, but of several generations. To prove this contention, analogies are drawn from the general laws that seem to be governing the formation of folklore in all nations and ages. Having discovered that the form of the gospels does not correspond to any known literary forms in Greek or Latin, critics have naturally concluded that they are non-literary. Even though a writer like Justin Martyr calls the gospels "memoirs," it must be conceded that the writings so described do not look like anything that goes by that name in antiquity. Since, therefore, it does not seem possible to make room for the gospels in any known ancient literary category, they must be treated as non-literary. They belong in the category of folklore, and the history of their formation must be sought along the lines of the folklore of all nations. This position is clearly stated by Dibelius.[1] The conclusion appears to be irresistible, once the premises are accepted.

But are the gospels as we have them non-literary documents? Are the various units that compose them devoid of literary form? It is granted that both these questions must be answered in the affirmative, if Greek rhetorical forms alone deserve to be considered. But when we begin to take seriously the fact that the early church was Jewish from its inception and that in some localities for decades during its formative period it had a large Jewish constituency among its membership; that it took over the Jewish canon and made use of it in its services and that the books of the Old Testament were the literary monuments of an ancient Hebrew culture, then we begin to recognize the presence of an influence other than the Greek—a literary influence of no small proportion. If it can be shown further that not only separate units of the gospels, but the whole structure of a gospel may be accounted for by a more or less conscious imitation of extant Hebrew literary forms, would we then have to accept the rigid alternative of the form-historians which insists on a literary or non-literary classification? The alternative would rather be between Greek or Hebrew literary models.

But the writings of the Old Testament were not only literary; they were also liturgical, brought together for the purpose of serving in public worship in the Jewish community. Many of the problems of these writings solve themselves, when we bear in

[1] Martin Dibelius, *From Tradition to Gospel* (Eng. trans. Bertram Lee Woolf. London: 1934), pp. 1-8.

mind that they were edited for liturgical use. We have already presented evidence from the Old Testament which shows that not only brief passages but also larger groups of passages were arranged in accordance with chiastic and alternating patterns or combinations of both. We have also shown how these combinations recur in the epistles of Paul. If it can be shown, likewise, that the same forms prevail in the gospels, there should be no reason for refusing the conclusion that the gospels are literary writings and that their peculiar form is due to the fact that they are liturgical documents. They have assumed their present form largely because of the direct influence of the earliest liturgical documents read in the church. Since the composition of our gospels historically followed that of the epistles of Paul which already embodied Hebrew literary patterns, the present form of the gospels would be due, not only to Old Testament influence, but to the example of the Pauline epistles as well.

In the following discussion we shall have frequent occasion to refer to Q, by which is meant neither a gospel nor a written document containing merely sayings, but only the non-Marcan material common to Matthew and Luke. At several points there will be good reasons for assuming that this common material has been derived from a "common source," but the distinction between the Q material and the Common Source from which most of it has been derived will always be maintained.[2]

It will be assumed throughout our investigation that the original form of the Common Source is best preserved in the Q ma-

[2] Kirsopp Lake, *Landmarks in the History of Early Christianity* (New York: 1922), has some pertinent remarks on the subject of Q on pp. 28, 29. Q, after all, is the name, not of an existing document, but of the critical judgment that there is a documentary source behind material common to Matthew and Luke but absent in Mark. This critical judgment is accepted by theologians as well as critics; but theologians with a distrust of criticism not wholly unjustified, prefer a mechanical to a rational application of this discovery, and dignify their preference by calling it objective, though it is difficult to see why a process should be regarded as objective, in any valuable sense of the word, because it automatically accepts as derived from Q everything common to Matthew and Luke, and leaves out all the rest. It is merely a method of canonizing the subjectivity of Matthew when it agrees with that of Luke, or of Luke when it agrees with that of Matthew, and damning both of them when they happen to disagree. Why the subjectivity of the editors of the gospels becomes objective when it is accepted by modern writers is a little difficult to see.

terial as it is found in Matthew. This conclusion is based on the observation that the chiastic forms are best preserved in Matthew, whereas they more often break down in Luke. We shall not accept as a working hypothesis the proposition that the form of the Q material in Luke is the more primitive, because in many instances it is less explicit and more fragmentary. For in judging the case we are not dealing with ordinary prose, but with a definite form of prose, as definite as some of our own forms of poetry. A passage, therefore, which shows the presence of chiastic forms perfectly preserved must be assumed to be more nearly original than a similar parallel passage which is imperfect in form. The basic assumption is that a writer who is at all interested in such forms may be supposed to use them uniformly. A critic who is called upon to decide between two stanzas from Shakespeare, one of which is deficient a line or two or perhaps a foot here and there, would not hesitate to accept the perfect stanza as the original form.

For an appreciation of the chiastic and alternating structures it matters little what literary history we postulate for the Common Source. These structures are what they are in Matthew, and they speak for themselves. Since, however, they are bound to have a bearing on the Synoptic Problem, some theory of literary relationship must be postulated at the outset, if only tentatively and with much hesitation, in order to give consistency in the treatment of the material. The presence of extensive chiastic structures in the Greek Matthew renders it probable that the gospel originated in a Christian community in which the Hebrew cultural heritage was still appreciated. The tradition preserved by Papias (H. E. III, 39) of a gospel written by Matthew for Palestinian Christians in their own language would sufficiently answer the requirements for a historical situation. An Aramaic gospel, written for use in the Palestinian community, is the kind of document which is most likely to have first incorporated the chiastic forms.[3]

Our Synoptic Gospels, however, are not directly dependent

[3] This idea of Papias is alluded to by Augustine, *Harmony of the Gospels*, Bk. I, chap. ii, 4, who also calls Mark "lackey and abridger of Matthew." These words, however, have reference to *Hebrew Matthew*. One may abridge by *elimination* of material as well as by *condensation*.

upon an Aramaic source. Their literary peculiarities are better explained by postulating an early Greek translation of the Aramaic source.[4] It should be clearly understood, however, that for our hypothesis an *Aramaic* original is not indispensable. The only assumption that need be made is an early Jewish-Christian community in which there still prevailed an acquaintance with and a taste for the literary heritage of the Old Testament. These forms could be and were produced in the epistles of Paul, which were certainly composed in Greek, and they might just as well have been incorporated in original Greek gospels. We may not, however, abandon altogether the Jewish influence in our theory of origin, for such literary structure was unknown to Greeks and must have been uncongenial to them. A comparative study of the Common Source, as it is represented in parallel sections of Matthew and Luke, shows clearly that chiastic forms which are found perfect in Matthew, in brief panels and in longer sections, in many instances are broken up in Luke in conformity to his Greek literary taste.

We shall now present (1) brief passages that show a conscious imitation of Old Testament models; (2) longer discourses in which blocks of material are arranged in chiastic structures; (3) a comparison between discourse material in Matthew and Luke with a view of establishing priority and literary dependency; (4) some narrative sections to show that these are also built up after the pattern of the discourses.

Teaching in Parables

A Therefore speak I to them in *parables;* 13

  B Because seeing
  They *see* not;

    C And hearing
    They *hear* not; neither do they understand.

      D And unto them is fulfilled the *prophecy* of Isaiah, 14
      Which *saith,*

        E "By hearing ye shall *hear,*
        And shall in no wise understand;

[4] Bernhard Weiss, *Manual of Introduction to the New Testament,* Vol. II, pp. 235 ff.

F And seeing ye shall *see*,
And shall in no wise perceive:

For this people's *heart* is waxed gross, 15
And their *ears* are dull of hearing,
G And their *eyes* they have closed;
Lest haply they should perceive with their *eyes*,
And hear with their *ears*,
And understand with their *heart*, and should turn again, and
I should heal them."

F′ But blessed are your eyes, 16
For they *see;*

E′ And your ears,
For they *hear.*

D′ For verily I *say* unto you 17
That many *prophets* and righteous men desired

B′ To see the things which ye *see*,
And saw them not;

C′ And hear the things which ye *hear*,
And heard them not.

A′ Hear ye then the *parable* of the sower. (Matt. 13:13-18). 18

The parallel terms in this passage are set forth by means of italics. The central section (G) has long been known as a chiastic structure and is so printed in Westcott and Hort's Greek text. Of the more extensive symmetry of this passage there is no mention made among writers on the gospels. Yet this symmetry is no less definite than that of the central section. The whole structure is a series of chiastic couplets, which are interrupted by two alternating couplets in B′C′. These two couplets are parallel to BC, as is shown by the verbs of seeing and hearing. These verbs in the *present tense* occur in the *second* lines of BC but in the *first* lines of B′C′. Nor is this the only instance of such care in the balance of the verbs, for in the other pair of couplets the two verbs occur in the first lines (EF), while they are found in the second lines in the two parallel couplets (F′E′). The verbs "understand" and "perceive" have no counterparts in F′E′, but they recur in the *second* half of G. Likewise the nouns "eyes" and "ears" have no counterparts in EF, though they are found twice in G. The words, "neither do they understand" (C), "and should turn again, and I should heal them" (G), have no parallels in the structure. They are, in either case, merely a concluding flourish, as it were, of which there are other examples (cf. Eph. 6:9).

There is nothing in this passage which does not conform to the types already found in the Old Testament. In one respect only is this passage extraordinary. It will be observed that the quotation from Isaiah 6:9, 10 begins at E and ends at the conclusion of G. The structure, however, begins long before the quotation commences and is continued after the quotation is concluded. It creates the same impression as if one should discover older stones surrounded by newer material in order to complete an arch. Since the present writer is convinced that chiastic forms are achieved by a conscious imitation of accepted literary models, and are not merely the result of an unconscious feeling for rhythm and balance in the sentence, he is particularly interested in the value of this passage as evidence of a conscious effort on the part of its author. The passage contains a statement the purpose of which is to explain the use of parables in the teachings of Jesus. It is injected between the Parable of the Sower and its interpretation. One suspects that the passage is the central panel in a group of parables, setting forth the purpose of such a method of teaching, though it may not be possible to say definitely what the number and arrangement of the parables originally were.

The following passage is a piece of narrative, which is constructed according to patterns similar to the one just discussed.

Jesus among His Own People

A And coming to *his own country*, 54
He taught in their *synagogue*,

B Insomuch that they were *astonished* and *said*,
Whence hath this man this *wisdom* and these *mighty powers?*

Is not this the *carpenter's son?* 55
C Is not his *mother* called Mary?
And his *brethren*, James, and Joseph, and Simon, and Judas?
And his *sisters*, are they not all with us? 56

B′ *Whence* hath this man *all these things?*
And they were *offended* in him. But Jesus *said* unto them, 57

A′ A prophet is not without honor, save in *his own country*,
And in his own *house*. (Matt. 13:54-57).

In AA′ the lines alternate. In view of the parallelism we may raise the question as to whether "his own house" in A′ has reference to his family and not to "the synagogue" (A). In B the first favorable reactions of the audience are set forth and in B′ the later hostility. "All these things" (B′) refers to the "wisdom" and the "mighty powers" (B), and both lines open with "Whence." The lines in BB′ are chiastic. In C, as in AA′, the lines alternate, for the male members of the family are introduced in lines 1 and 3, while the female members are mentioned in lines 2 and 4. We notice the striking array of questions (not less than six) when the centre of the structure is reached (cf. Ps. 30:9).

When Israel had definitely rejected the Messiah and subsequent historical developments had made it clear that the gospel concerning the Messiah would also to a very large extent be rejected by the Jewish community, the teachers of the church would often emphatically impress upon the members the hostile attitude of the chosen people. Passages like the one above would find their place in the liturgical writings of the church and would be read publicly. That such passages existed in more than one form is plainly the implication of the following passage. With all the difference in form, however, the lesson they conveyed was the same.

Jesus in the Synagogue

And he came to Nazareth, where he had been brought up, 16
And entered as his custom was on the sabbath day into the *synagogue*,
A And *stood up* to read.
And there *was delivered* unto him the book of the prophet Isaiah, 17
And *he opened* the book and found the place where it was written,

"The Spirit of *the Lord* is upon me, because he anointed me 18
To preach good tidings to the poor:
*He hath sent me** to proclaim to the captives *release*,
B And to the blind recovering of sight,
To send the crushed into *release*,**
*To proclaim**** 19
The acceptable year of *the Lord*."****

And *he closed* the book, 20
And *gave it back* to the attendant,
A′ And *sat down*,
And the eyes of all in the *synagogue* were fastened on him, 21
And he began to say unto them, etc. (Lk. 4:16-21a).

Although the form of this passage differs considerably from that of the preceding, its function in the service of the church was practically the same. It consists of three distinct parts: The first describes the actions of Jesus before his reading of the Scriptures (A), and the third enumerates his actions after he had completed the reading. The terms are found to be antithetic and in the inverted order (A′), when compared with their parallel terms in A. The central section (B) contains a quotation from Isaiah 61:1, 2a. That the quotation is central in such a structure is not unusual, but in this instance the quotation is fitted into its central position only after it has been subjected to the four significant modifications indicated by the asterisks. A closer study of the nature of these modifications of the original passage shows clearly that they were undertaken in the interest of a perfect chiastic form.

In the first instance (*) the LXX adds, "to heal the broken-hearted." This phrase is eliminated, obviously because it finds no parallel in the corresponding line. In the second place (**) a whole line, which does not exist at all in Isaiah 60:1 ff., is brought in from Isaiah 58:6, with merely a slight change from imperative to infinitive to adapt the verb to the context in Luke. This being done, a most remarkable parallelism is achieved in the two lines. Both now *begin* with the verb, "to send," and *end* with the noun "release"—a most striking feature indeed. Thirdly, the verb "to call" in the LXX text is changed into "proclaim," again in the interest of parallelism (***). The corresponding line above opens with εὐαγγελίσασθαι; to this verb κηρύξαι offers a closer parallel than καλέσαι. In the New Testament the verb "to call" means to call anybody to anything, while the verb "proclaim" usually means to proclaim the truths of the gospel, i.e., "to preach the good tidings." Finally, the words in Isaiah read (LXX), as follows:

> "To call the acceptable year of the Lord, (****)
> And a day of recompense."

The Hebrew completes the parallelism of the couplet with "day of vengeance *from our God*," but the LXX is incomplete. Commentators of the "dispensational" persuasion have seen in the elimination of the second line of the couplet in Luke's quotation a distinction between "the acceptable year of the Lord," which was then present, and "the day of vengeance," which was yet to come. The elimination of the second line, however, is best explained on the same ground as the three preceding changes in the passage. Its inclusion would introduce material to which there would be no parallels in the first line of the quotation.

Our study of the passage shows that all four changes in Luke's version of the LXX text of Isaiah 60:1 ff. are made in the interest of a more perfect chiasmus in the centre. The adaptations are skilfully made. We may be sure that Luke himself did not make these adaptations but found them in the source he used which, no doubt, was the Common Source from which the Q material is derived by Matthew and Luke. Very frequently in other passages the chiastic forms are broken up in Luke by minor editorial adjustments in the interest of a more compact Greek sentence. His reason for retaining this splendid structure without modification is probably due to the fact that the scene is laid in *the synagogue*. Luke, with true artistic feeling for the scene he describes, permits the quotation to retain the form he knew was prevalent in the synagogue, even though he must have considerably shortened the discourse. He refers to "the words of grace which proceeded out of his mouth" (Lk. 5:22), but quotes nothing from this part of the discourse, while the words of judgment are given more fully (vss. 23-29). In Luke's account the question, "Is not this Joseph's son?" is found (vs. 22 together with vs. 24), probably the only reminder of the structure in Matt. 13:54-57; the name Joseph is substituted for "the carpenter."

Having examined the three passages we may now draw certain conclusions from them. The passage explaining the use of parables and the one describing Jesus' reading the book of Isaiah in the synagogue are of such nature, that their form may be explained only as the result of a conscious effort on the part of the author. And this effort is made with definite literary patterns in mind—patterns which have been derived from the Old Testament. We are not here to think of the unconscious gropings of a community made up of many individuals and extending through several generations, as in the case of folklore. The contention of the students of form-history that such passages were constructed with a didactic purpose as for propaganda may readily be granted. But that they are non-literary and therefore must belong to a pre-literary stage does not necessarily follow. We would come closer to the truth by assuming that they are both didactic and *liturgical.* They were deliberately designed for the purpose of repeated public reading or recital. While there is nothing to prevent us from holding that some of these brief passages assumed their present form already in the oral tradition that no doubt preceded the written gospels, they were even in the oral stage conditioned by the Old Testament forms; their occurrence in larger structures, or groups, moreover, indicates that some of them, at least, were at an early date put into this form to satisfy an emergent liturgical need of the community.

CHAPTER XII

THE SERMON ON THE MOUNT

The interest in chiastic forms is expressed by the gospel writers not only in brief passages, but in longer structures as well. Our next step, therefore, is to give a complete analysis of five of the longer discourses in "The Gospel according to Matthew" in which there are traces of the chiastic forms not only in brief paragraphs but in the total structure of the discourse. These discourses are:

1. The Sermon on the Mount, 4:25-8:1
2. The Missionary Discourse, 10:5-11:1
3. Concerning the Authority of Jesus, 12:22-45
4. Concerning Eating with Unwashed Hands, 15:1-20
5. The Discourse against the Pharisees, 23:1-39

Since the purpose of the following remarks is to point out the total structure of these discourses, we shall omit detailed observations on the separate paragraphs except in such cases where something of unusual interest occurs. By indenting the margin and by printing in italics parallel terms and groups of terms that show a numerical interest on the part of the author, we hope to give the reader the drift of the argument without detailed comment.

There are in the Gospel according to Matthew many passages that show the author's interest in numerical combinations. The numbers two, three, four, five, seven, and nine frequently enter into the scheme of his arrangement of the material. In several instances the Q material in Matthew preserves only two terms whereas Luke has three. In some cases, we have reason to believe, this is due to a process of condensation to which much of the material has been subjected in Matthew. This process is most clearly seen in the narrative sections, dealing with the doings of Jesus, but it may also at times be seen in some eliminations among the sayings. In rare instances, as we shall see, the probability is that Luke has preserved the full account of the Common Source. It is, of course, impossible to determine whether these instances of elimination of one member out of three are to be traced to the original draft of our Greek Matthew or are to be accounted for by a later editorial revision for the purpose of making room for other material. Both possibilities should be kept in mind in the survey of the following discourses.

The Sermon on the Mount

Matthew 4:25-8:1

X *Introduction:* multitudes, mountain, teaching, 4:25-5:2.

Y *General Observation on the Nature and Function of the Church,* 5:2-19.

A The Beatitudes: the qualities of the members of the church, 5:3-9.

B The True Prophets: their persecution and reward, 5:10:12.

C Unfaithful and faithful Disciples: salt and light, 5:13-16.

D Obedience or disobedience: "break" or "do," 5:19 (vss. 17, 18 to *follow* vs. 19).

Z *The Higher Quality of Christian Righteousness.* 5:17-7:12.

"The Law and the Prophets" are fulfilled in this manner, cf. 5:17, 7:12.

ZA *It is Higher than that of Jew or Gentile:* the old order, 5:20-47.

A Higher than that of Scribes and Pharisees, 5:20.

B A new definition of *killing:* three sections, 5:21-26.

C A new definition of *adultery:* three examples (Mt. 18:8, 9), 5:27-32.

D A new rule about *oaths:* four examples, "Swear not at all," 5:33-37.

C′ A new rule about *retaliation:* three examples, 5:38-42.

B′ A new rule concerning *love* of neighbors: three (Lk. 6:27, 28, 35), 5:43-45.

A′ Higher than that of publicans and gentiles, 5:46, 47.

ZB *It is Perfection according to the Golden Rule;* the new order, 5:48-7:12.

A The highest possible ideal: perfection, 5:48.

B A new way of performing religious duties: three, 6:1-18. Alms (vss. 2-4), prayer (vss. 5-15), fasting (vss. 16-18).

C A new way of performing daily duties, 6:19-7:6.

B′ A new attitude in regard to prayer: a religious duty, 7:7-11. Delayed answer (Lk. 11:5-8), invitation (vss. 7-8), disappointing answers to prayer (vss. 9-11) cf. triplet in Lk. 11:12.

A′ The highest possible ideal realized: the golden rule, 7:12a. "For this is the Law and the Prophets" (vs. 12b), together with 5:17, brackets the whole division Z, dealing with the *new* righteousness.

Y′ *General Observations on the Nature and Function of the Church,* 7:13-27.

A The Two Ways: those outside and those inside the church, 7:13-14.

B The False Prophets: their test and their punishment, 7:15-20.

C Unfaithful and Faithful Disciples: the will of God, 7:21-23.

D Obedience or Disobedience: "doeth them," "doeth them [not,"7:24-27. Observe the inversion of these ideas in YD, 5:19.

X′ *Conclusion:* teaching, mountain, multitudes (cf. inversion in X), 7:28-8:1.

The Sermon on the Mount

And there *followed him great multitudes*, 4:25
From Galilee and Decapolis and Jerusalem and Judaea and beyond the Jordan.
And seeing the multitudes, *he went up into the mountain:* 5:1
X And when he had sat down, his disciples came unto him.
And he opened his mouth *and taught them*, saying, 2

A
Blessed are the poor in spirit, 3
For theirs is the kingdom of heaven.
Blessed are they that mourn, 4
For they shall be comforted.
Blessed are the meek, 5
For they shall inherit the earth.

Blessed are they that hunger and thirst after righteousness, 6
For they shall be filled.

Blessed are the merciful, 7
For they shall obtain mercy.
Blessed are the pure in heart, 8
For they shall see God.
Blessed are the peacemakers, 9
For they shall be called sons of God.

Y

B
Blessed are they that have been *persecuted* for righteousness' sake, 10
For theirs is the kingdom of *heaven.*
Blessed are ye, 11
When they shall *reproach* you,
And *persecute,*
And shall *say* all manner of evil against you falsely for my sake.
Rejoice and be exceeding glad, 12
For great is your reward in *heaven.*
For thus *persecuted* they the prophets that were before you.

C
Ye are the *salt* of the earth: 13
But if the salt have lost its savor,
Wherewith shall it be salted?
Unto nothing is it good henceforth,
But to be cast out and trodden under the foot of men.

Ye are the *light* of the world: 14
A city set on a hill cannot be hid.
Neither do they light a lamp and put it under a bushel, but on a stand: 15
And it shineth to all that are in the house.
Even so let your light shine before men, 16
That they may see your good works,
And glorify your father who is in heaven. (omit vss. 17, 18).

D
Whosoever therefore *shall break* one of these least commandments,
And shall teach men so, 19
Shall be called least in the kingdom of heaven.

But whosoever *shall do,*
And shall teach them,
Shall be called great in the kingdom of heaven.

Think not that I came to destroy THE LAW AND THE PROPHETS, 17
I came not to destroy, but to fulfill (vs. 18 a gloss?) cf. 7:12b.

ZA

For I say unto you, 20
A That except your righteousness shall exceed that of the scribes and Pharisees,
Ye shall in no wise enter into the kingdom of heaven.

Ye have heard that it was said to them of old time, 21
Thou shalt not *kill;*
And whosoever shall kill shall be in danger of the judgment;
But I say unto you, 22
That everyone who is angry with his brother,
x Shall be in danger of *the judgment;*
And whosoever shall say to his brother, Raca,
Shall be in danger of *the council;*
And whosoever shall say, Thou fool,
Shall be in danger of *the Gehenna of fire.*

B If therefore thou art *offering thy gift* upon the altar, 23
And rememberest that *thy brother* hath aught against thee,
y Leave there *thy gift* before the altar, 24
And go thy way, first be reconciled to *thy brother,*
And then come and *offer thy gift.*

Agree with thine adversary quickly, 25
While thou art with him in the way.
Lest haply the adversary deliver thee to *the judge,*
x′ And the judge deliver thee to *the officer,*
And thou be cast into *prison.*
Thou shalt by no means come out thence, 26
Till thou hast paid the last farthing.

Ye have heard that it was said, 27
Thou shalt not commit *adultery:*
But I say unto you, 28
x That everyone that looketh on a woman to lust after her,
Hath committed adultery with her already in his heart.

And if thy right *eye* causeth thee to stumble, 29
y Pluck it out, and cast it from thee:
For it is profitable to thee that one of thy members should perish,
And not thy whole body go into Gehenna.

C

And if thy right *hand* causeth thee to stumble, 30
y′ Cut it off, and cast it from thee;
For it is profitable to thee that one of thy members should perish,
And not thy whole body go into Gehenna (foot? cf. Mk. 9:43-47. Mt. 18:8,9).

It was said also, 31
Whosoever shall put away his wife,
Let him give her a writing of divorcement;
But I say unto you, 32
x′ That everyone that putteth away his wife, saving for the cause of fornication,
Maketh her an adulteress:
And whosoever shall marry her, when she is put away,
Committeth *adultery.*

D

Again, ye have heard that it was said to them of old time, 33
Thou shalt not *forswear* thyself,
But shall perform unto the Lord thine oaths;
But I say unto you, 34
Swear not at all;
Neither by the *heavens*,
For it is the throne of God;
Nor by the *earth*, 35
For it is the footstool of his feet;
Nor by *Jerusalem*,
For it is the city of thy great King.
Neither shalt thou swear by thy *head*, 36
For thou canst not make one hair white or black.
But let your speech be, Yea, yea; Nay, nay; 37
And whatsoever is more than these is of the evil one.

C′

Ye have heard that it was said, 38
An eye for an *eye*,
And a tooth for a *tooth;*
But I say unto you, 39
Resist not him that is evil:
But whosoever *smiteth* thee on thy right cheek,
Turn to him the other also.
And if a man would go to law with thee and *take away* thy coat, 40
Let him have thy cloak also.
And whosoever shall *compel* thee to go one mile, 41
Go with him two.
Give him that asketh thee, 42
And from him that would borrow of thee, turn not away.

B′

Ye have heard that it was said, 43
Thou shalt *love* thy neighbor,
And *hate* thine enemy.
But I say unto you, 44
Love your enemies,
And *pray* for them that persecute you; (triplet? cf. Lk. 6:27, 28, 35)
That ye may be sons of your Father who is in heaven, 45
For he maketh his sun to rise on the evil and the good,
And sendeth rain on the just and the unjust.

A′

For if ye love them that love you, 46
What reward have ye?
Do not the publicans do the same?
And if ye salute your brethren only, 47
What do ye more (than others)?
Do not even the Gentiles the same?

A Ye therefore shall be perfect, 48
As your heavenly Father is perfect.

(6:1
Take heed that ye do not your righteousness before men, to be seen of them:
Else ye have no reward with your Father who is in heaven.

When therefore thou doest *alms*, 2
Sound not the trumpet before thee, as the hypocrites do,
In the synagogues and in the streets,
That they may have glory of men.
Verily I say unto you, They have received their reward.

x

But when thou doest alms, 3
Let not thy left hand know
What the right hand doeth,
That thine alms be in secret: 4
And thy Father who seeth in secret shall recompense thee.

And when ye *pray*, 5
Ye shall not be as the hypocrites,
For they love to stand and pray in the synagogues,
And in the corners of the streets,
That they may be seen of men.
a Verily I say unto you, They have received their reward.

But thou, when thou prayest, 6
Enter into thine inner chamber,
And having shut thy door,
Pray to thy Father who is in secret,
And thy Father who seeth in secret shall recompense thee.

And in praying use not vain repetitions, as the Gentiles do, 7
For they think that by their much speaking
They shall be heard.
B y *b* Be not therefore like unto them. 8
For your heavenly Father knoweth what things ye have need of,
Before ye ask him.
After this manner therefore pray ye: 9

Our Father who art in heaven,

Hallowed be thy name.
Thy kingdom come. 10
Thy will be done,

As in heaven, so on earth.

a′ Give us this day our daily bread. 11

And forgive us our debts, as we also have forgiven our debtors. 12
And bring us not into temptation, 13
But deliver us from the evil one.

For if ye forgive men their trespasses, 14
Your heavenly Father will also forgive you;
But if ye forgive not men their trespasses, 15
Neither will your heavenly Father forgive your trespasses.

Moreover, when ye *fast*, 16
Be not, as the hypocrites, of a sad countenance,
For they disfigure their faces,
That they may be seen of men to fast.
Verily I say unto you, They have received their reward.

x′

But thou, when thou fastest, 17
Anoint thy head,
And wash thy face,
That thou be not seen of men to fast, 18
But of thy Father who is in secret:
And thy Father who seeth in secret shall recompense thee.

Cx
Lay not up for yourself *treasures* upon the earth, 19
Where moth and rust consume,
And where thieves break through and steal;

But lay up for yourself *treasures* in heaven, 20
Where neither moth nor rust doth consume,
And where thieves do not break through, nor steal;

For where thy treasure is, 21
There will thy heart be also.

Cy
The lamp of the body is *the eye.* 22

If therefore thine eye be single,
Thy whole body shall be full of light;
But if thine eye be evil, 23
Thy whole body shall be full of darkness.

If therefore the light that is in thee be darkness,
How great is the darkness.

No man can serve two masters, 24
For either will he hate the one,
a And love the other;
Or else will he hold to one,
And despise the other.
Ye cannot serve God and Mammon.

Therefore say I unto you, *Be not anxious* for your life, 25
b What ye shall eat, or
What ye shall drink, nor yet for your body,
What ye shall put on.

Is not life
c More than food,
And the body,
Than the raiment?

Behold the birds of the heavens, 26
d That they sow not,
Neither do they reap,
Nor gather into barns;

e And your heavenly Father *feedeth* them.
Are ye not of much more value than they?

And which of you by being *anxious* 27
f Is able to add one cubit unto the measure of his *stature?*
And concerning *raiment*
Why are ye *anxious?* 28

Cz

Consider the lilies of the field
d′ How they grow;
They toil not,
Neither do they spin:

e′ Yet I say unto you, that even Solomon in all his glory 29
Was not *arrayed* like one of these.

But if the grass of the field, which today is, 30
c′ And tomorrow is cast into the oven,
God doth so clothe,
Shall he not much more clothe you, O ye of little faith?

Be not therefore anxious, saying, 31
b′ What shall we eat? or,
What shall we drink? or,
Wherewithal shall we be clothed?

For after *all these things*, 32
Do the Gentiles seek;
a′ For your heavenly Father knoweth that ye have need of *all these things.*
But seek ye first his kingdom and his righteousness, 33
And *all these things* shall be added unto you.

Be not therefore *anxious* 34
For the morrow,
For the morrow
Will be *anxious* for itself.

Sufficient unto the day is the evil thereof.

Judge not, 7:1
That ye be not judged:
For with what judgment ye judge, 2
a Shall ye be judged;
And with whatever measure ye mete,
Shall it be measured unto you.

And why beholdest thou 3
The mote
That is in the eye
b Of thy brother;
But in thine own
Eye
The beam
Thou considerest not?

Cy′ Or how wilt thou say 4

To thy brother,
Let me *cast out* the mote
Out of thine eye;
And behold,
The beam is
In thine own eye?
c Thou hypocrite, *cast out* first 5
Out of thine own eye
The beam;
And then shalt thou see clearly
Out of the eye
To *cast out* the mote
Of thy brother.

Cx′ Give not that which is holy to the *dogs*, 6
Nor cast your pearls before the *swine*,
Lest haply they *trample* them under their feet,
And turn and *rend* you.

x (Lk. 11:5-8. The Importunate Friend, no doubt, was in the common [source.)

Ask, and it shall be given you, 7
Seek, and ye shall find,
y Knock, and it shall be opened unto you:
For every one that asketh receiveth, 8
And he that seeketh findeth,
And to him that knocketh it shall be opened.

B′

Or what man is there of you, 9
Who, if his son shall ask him for a *loaf*,
x′ Will give him a stone;
Or if he shall ask him for a *fish*, 10
Will give him a serpent? (triplet? cf. Lk. 11:12, "egg".)

If ye then, being evil, 11
Know how to give good gifts unto your children,
How much more shall your Father who is in heaven
Give good things to them that ask him?

A′ All things therefore whatsoever ye would that men should do unto you, 12
Even so do ye also unto them.

For this is THE LAW AND THE PROPHETS. cf. 5:17.

A

Enter into the narrow gate: 13
For wide is the gate,
And broad is the way,
That leadeth to destruction,
And many are they that enter thereby.

For narrow is the gate, 14
And straitened the way,
That leadeth unto life,
And few are they that find it.

B

Beware of the *false prophets*, 15
Who come to you in sheep's clothing,
But inwardly are ravening wolves.

By their fruits ye shall know them. 16
Do they gather grapes of thorns,
Or figs of thistles?

Even so every *good* tree bringeth forth *good* fruit; 17
But the *corrupt* tree bringeth forth *evil* fruit.
A *good* tree cannot bring forth *evil* fruit, 18
Neither can a *corrupt* tree bring forth *good* fruit.

Every tree that bringeth not forth good fruit is hewn down, 19
And cast into the fire.
Therefore by their fruits ye shall know them. 20

Y'

C

Not everyone that saith unto me, Lord, Lord, shall enter into the (kingdom of heaven, 21
But he that doeth the will of my Father who is in heaven.

Many shall say unto me in that day, Lord, Lord, 22
Did not we by thy name prophesy,
And by thy name cast out demons,
And by thy name do many mighty powers?
And then will I profess unto them, I never knew you: 23

Depart from me,
Ye that work iniquity.

D

Every one therefore that heareth these words of mine, 24
And doeth them,
Shall be likened unto a wise man,
Who built his house upon the rock:
And the rains descended, 25
And the floods came,
And the winds blew,
And beat upon that house;
And it fell not:
For it was founded upon the rock.

And every one that heareth these words of mine, 26
And doeth them not,
Shall be likened unto a foolish man,
Who built his house upon the sand:
And the rains descended, 27
And the floods came,
And the winds blew,
And smote upon that house,
And it fell,
And great was the fall thereof.

X′ { And it came to pass, when Jesus had finished these words, 28
The multitudes were astonished at *his teaching:*
For he taught them as one having authority, and not as their scribes.
And when *he was come down from the mountain,* 8:1
Great multitudes followed him. }

The Sermon on the Mount opens with a passage giving the setting of the sermon: Jesus was followed by great multitudes, he went up into the mountain, and he taught them (X). These items of information are repeated in the inverted order at the conclusion of the sermon (X′). It is not a mere coincidence that these three items should recur in the second of the frame-passages that encase the sermon; it is a part of a general plan in the gospel or of the Common Source from which this discourse, together with several others, is derived. Within the two frame-passages the material making up the sermon is arranged in three great divisions. The first and the third (YY′) contain four sections each (ABCD), the contents of which show that they have been arranged in an alternating order. Between these extremes we find the central division (Z), which is the longest of the three and made up of two subdivisions (ZA and ZB). The general content of this long division of the sermon is an exposition of the Christian righteousness, or the real meaning of the Law and the Prophets, as it is expounded for the Christian community in conscious opposition to both Jew and Gentile.

It will add to the clearness of our discussion of YY′ if we compare the parallel sections of each division as we go along. This procedure will also eliminate needless repetition and tedious cross-references. The sermon opens with the Seven Beatitudes (YA). Whether the Beatitudes are seven, eight, or nine, has been discussed since the days of Augustine.[1] The literary analysis of vss. 3-9, on the one hand, and of vss. 10-12, on the other, shows that only seven Beatitudes have been in the author's mind. The arrangement of the series of seven into two groups of three with a fourth Beatitude in the center is determined by the structure of the Lord's Prayer (6:9-13), with which the Beatitudes show a close literary relationship. A comparison of the seven petitions reveals striking parallels both of thought and language. The hunger

[1] *The Sermon on the Mount*, chap. 3, end.

(5:6) and the daily bread are closely related (6:11), and more so if we accept Luke's version as the original (6:21). To be merciful and to obtain mercy (5:7) means the same as to forgive and be forgiven (6:12). Purity of heart (5:8) is closely related to not being led into temptation (6:13). It is more difficult to see the parallel between the peacemakers (5:9) and deliverance from the evil one (6:13b), unless we are to think of the deliverance in comparison with the reference to the sons of God (cf. Col. 1:13). In the first group of three Beatitudes we have the words heaven (cf. 5:3, 6:9) and earth (5:5, 6:10). And the comfort spoken of (5:4) may without much difficulty be regarded as the comfort experienced in such progress of the truth in the world as signalized the coming of the kingdom (6:10). To be meek (5:5) is to submit without complaint to the will of God (6:10). The kingdom of God is prominent in both groups.

But why should the *first* and the *third* members of each group of three be regarded as parallel, especially since there is no sign of any such parallelism in the seven petitions of the Lord's Prayer? The answer to this question must be sought in the thought of each Beatitude. "The poor" is a term which in the Old Testament has religious connotations.[2] That the word "meek" has similar connotations is seen in several passages, such as Isa. 11:4, 29:19, where it occurs with "poor" as a parallel term in the couplet. Likewise, to be "merciful" and to be "peacemakers" are related terms, for they indicate a similar frame of mind. The three terms which, under this arrangement, have a central position in the scheme are descriptive of a similar experience (5:4, 6, 8). There is satisfaction in beholding the face of the Lord (Ps. 17:15). The arrangement, therefore, of a series of seven into two groups of three with a central fourth Beatitude may be defended, in this case, by the parallel contents. That this arrangement is found not only here but also in other passages may be seen in the series of Seven Epistles in the Book of Revelation.

From this analysis of the form of the Beatitudes we now turn to the parallel section in Y'A, describing the Two Ways. This

[2] Isa. 66:2; Zeph. 3:12, 13; Zech. 11:11, and G. F. Moore, *Judaism*, Vol. II, p. 156.

manner of contrasting two ways of living is known from Ps. 1:6, and evidently was taken over from Judaism into the church.[3] Since the qualities set forth in the Beatitudes are required of Christians, entrance into Christian fellowship must be characterized as a narrow gate. The Two Ways urge upon men the necessity of making their choice of the life set forth in the Beatitudes. It will be found that every section in Y′ follows the first (A) in sounding a solemn note of warning and that this note becomes perfectly clear when read in connection with the parallel sections in Y.

In YB Christians are complimented on their suffering for Christ's sake—a suffering which is said to be the mark of the true prophetic succession. This idea runs through the New Testament like a red thread (cf. 1 Pet. 4:12-16; Acts 5:45; 1 Thess. 1:6, etc.). The section is a perfect specimen of the chiastic arrangement, the parallel terms being indicated by italics. The verb "persecute" is found in the center and in the two extremes. There are three verbs, forming a central triplet which describe the suffering of Christians. Their comfort is that in enduring such things they are proved to be in the true prophetic succession.

By way of contrast the *false* prophets are described in Y′B. The passage opens and closes with the general statement that prophets are known by their fruit (vss. 16a, 20). In two parallel couplets the corrupt nature of the false prophets is likened to thorns and thistles (vs. 16b), and their destruction is described (vs. 19). The close parallelism that really exists between these couplets may be seen in passages like Isa. 33:12; Ps. 58:9. The popularity of such an application of the figure for spiritual teaching in the church is implied in Heb. 6:8. The central quatrain (vss. 17, 18) develops the proposition that each tree bears fruit according to its own nature. Each of the four lines is made up of two halves, the first dealing with the nature of the tree and the last with the quality of the fruit. The first half of the quatrain is alternating in form, while the last half is chiastic, as a glance at the terms in italics will show. This arrangement is unique in that it is the only instance of its kind, as far as the knowledge of the present writer goes. That the allocation of the terms "corrupt"

[3] *The Didache*, chap. I, and *The Epistle of Barnabas*, chaps. XVIII-XX.

and "evil" was not made accidentally may be assumed in view of Matt. 12:33-35. There is also a hint given of the ultimate fate of each of the two classes of prophets; the one is assured of a reward in heaven (5:12), while the other will be "cast into the fire" (7:19).

The next section characterizes Christians as the salt of the earth and the light of the world (YC). A closer examination, however, will show that the former of the two phrases is used to describe Christians that have failed in their calling, for they are a salt that has lost its savor, while the latter phrase is used to describe the faithful. The fate of the former is to be "cast out," while the latter glorify their Father "who is in heaven" (5:16, 7:21). The corresponding section (Y′C) deals with the same classes of people. On the one hand, those who address Jesus familiarly as, "Lord, Lord," expecting to enter the kingdom of heaven, are told to depart from him; on the other hand, those who do the will of the Father are permitted to enter. All others are workers of iniquity (7:21, 23b). They speak as if they knew him (vs. 22a), but he speaks and disowns them (vs. 23a). The central triplet describes what they claim to have done in his name. The salt that has lost its savor finds its interpretation in these people who are always calling Jesus "Lord," but do not practice the will of the Father in heaven.

In 5:17, 18 an exegetical problem claims our attention. It is of importance to observe that the problem is centered not in vs. 17 but in vs. 18, which seems to maintain the eternal validity of the whole Mosaic Law. In view of the treatment of the Mosaic prescriptions about the law of retaliation and of divorce, it is difficult to accept vs. 18 as part of the original text, for certainly these two laws have "passed away" in the hands of Jesus. This verse may be regarded as a gloss added by some Judaizing Christian, who felt the honor of the Law to be endangered (cf. Matt. 23:3; Lk. 16:17). In vs. 17, although it is possible to interpret "fulfill" in the sense of bringing to full realization the original purpose of the law, there is here a literary problem to be solved. In Y, sections C and D are complete without vs. 17 and vs. 18. To keep these verses in their present position, or even to preserve only vs. 17, would make "these least commandments" (5:19) refer to minutiae of the Mosaic Law, observance of which Jesus would then be represented as enjoining upon all Christians. With vss. 17, 18 removed from the context, "these least commandments" would refer to those words of Jesus which give *his own* interpretation of the Law (cf. Matt. 24:35).

There is a literary basis for regarding vs. 17 as part of the original text, if the verse may be removed to a position between vss. 19 and 20. Here the verse will serve as an introduction to the whole section Z; its counterpart would then be the conclusion in 7:12b. These are the only two instances in which there is a reference to "the law and the prophets" in the sermon. When the reader recalls a similar reference to the Law in 1 Cor. 14:21, 34 which has significance as part of the structure of that chapter, he will be inclined to treat this as an analogous case. Just as ZA opens and concludes with a similar summary statement (cf. 5:20 with 5:46, 47) and just as ZB follows a similar arrangement (cf. 5:48 with 7:12a), so too the whole division (Z) of the sermon properly opens and closes with a statement declaring the Christian righteousness to be but an expression of the spirit and purpose of the law and the prophets (cf. Rom. 3:21). The treatment of vs. 18 as a later gloss and the transposition of vs. 17 would at once remove an exegetical difficulty and restore the literary balance of the passage.[4]

We are now prepared to consider YD and its counterpart, Y'D. Both sections describe two attitudes of those that heard Jesus. "These least commandments" (5:19) are matched by "these words of mine" (7:24, 26). Those who reject and those who accept the words of Jesus are mentioned in this order (5:19) with the accompanying threat or promise. This order is inverted in Y'D, for those who *do* are mentioned first and they that *do not*, last. The promise and the threat are not wanting. They recur and are elaborated with great solemnity in the figure of the two houses built upon the rock or upon the sand. Since there is absolutely nothing in 7:24-27 to match 5:17, 18 and since 5:19, though brief and simple in construction, makes a perfect counterpart both

[4] C. G. Montefiore's *The Synoptic Gospels* (3d ed.), Vol. II, pp. 46-55.

in regard to its alternating *lines*, and the inverted order of its *sections*, we conclude that our literary analysis may be regarded as expressing the original state of the Greek text of the sermon as it occurred in the Common Source. In XX′, then, we have the introduction and conclusion and in YY′ four sections which are parallel and have an alternating order. Within this somewhat elaborate frame the central portion of the sermon, expounding the spiritual meaning of the law and the prophets, is placed. We shall now take up the analysis of this central portion (Z).

Of the introductory and closing statements to the central division (cf. 5:17 and 7:12b) nothing need be said in addition to the remarks already made. All the material that intervenes between these two verses may be regarded as an exposition of the manner in which Jesus came to "fulfill" the law and the prophets. This material is adapted to distinguish Christian righteousness from that of the Pharisees (5:20), on the one hand, and from that of the Gentiles (5:46, 47), on the other. In these references we become conscious once more of the two battle-fronts of the early church, one facing Judaism and the other the Gentile world. The material in ZA is arranged in five distinct blocks, the general contents of which deal with human relations along the lines indicated in the *last* five of the Ten Commandments (cf. Ex. 20:13-17). The commandments against killing (B) and adultery (C) are represented in separate sections. The commandment against stealing may be hinted at in C′ (cf. 5:40). Although the word "neighbor" is mentioned in B′ (cf. 5:43 with Ex. 20:17), the reference is probably too slight to connect this block with the tenth commandment. The impulse to connect D with the ninth commandment (Ex. 20:16), since both deal with swearing, is checked when we consider that the commandment refers to swearing in court, while section D has reference to the making of vows. While the effort to connect the five sections with each of the five commandments in some instances is questionable, it must be admitted that ZA, taken as a whole, corresponds to the last five of the commandments in a general way, since both deal with human relations. Section D is an exception; it discusses relations with the deity (5:33-37). Nor is it easy to find detailed parallelisms in BB′ and CC′. The anger described in B (5:22) may be regarded as an antithesis to the behavior contemplated in B′. Likewise to commit adultery (C) may be a way of coveting the neighbor's wife (Ex. 20:17), and hence with some justification may be grouped with the taking away of the cloak in C′, though it must be admitted that the parallelism is neither detailed nor striking.

In regard to the numerical arrangement of these sections the correspondence is more striking. In B three degrees of anger and their punishment are enumerated (cf. x); these find their counterpart in the admonition to agree with the adversary (cf. x′); this also carries a triplet. The references to offering upon the altar which interrupt this sequence (y) are cast in a perfect chiastic structure, with "thy gift" occurring in the extremes and at the centre. Turning now to B′ we find a close parallel to this reference to "thy brother," in the words, "that ye may be sons" (5:45). The triplet is missing in B′, yet its presence in Lk. 6:27, 28, 35 makes it probable that it was found in the Common Source. It was probably eliminated because of the need of condensation, when the edifying application in vs. 45 was to be introduced together with its counterpart in 5:23, 24.

A similar problem arises in the present text of C. We look for a regular triplet here also, to match that of C′. According to Mk. 9:43-47 the saying in 5:29, 30 did exist in triplet form. That this triplet was even made use of in a condensed form by our Matthew may be seen in Matt. 18:8, 9. The Marcan order (hand, foot, and eye) is here changed, since the context required that the eye be introduced *first* (cf. 5:28). The section about divorce (vss. 31, 32) bears the mark of a later hand. Its introductory formula differs from the rest (vs. 31), and its substance recurs in Matt. 19:7, 9. At the time of its introduction here, possibly the third member of the triplet was dropped because the need of condensing the passage was felt. Considerations of space must always be present to an editor, but they become more urgent when the editor is concerned with a number of already balanced sections, the symmetry of which may not be too violently disturbed. In all these sections the number *three* is so prominent that one suspects that the Common Source contained a definite numerical grouping of passages. The fact that the central section (D) should have the number *four* is part of the law of the shift at the centre, the four forms of swearing being in striking contrast to the threefold arrangement in the other sections. ZA makes a total of seven sections in all.

The second subdivision of Z differs in some respects from the one just analyzed (cf. ZB). It is much longer, and its order is the exact inversion of that found in ZA, in the central section of which God was the chief topic, whereas in ZB man is centralized. This apportionment is not surprising, since ZA clearly moved in the realm covered by the five last commandments. In ZB, however, we are traversing the field of religious duties, that phase of man's life which is turned toward God. We find, accordingly, that sections BB′ are given over to considerations of religious duties, while the central section C, which here is most elaborate, deals with human relations. It would be impossible to distribute the contents of these sections in such a way as to establish exact relations between them and the first five commandments; and yet these sections cover the same general field as the first five commandments in that they focus attention on man's religious duties.

Sections AA′ are, as we have already observed, the introduction and conclusion to ZB, giving perfection as the goal of Christian life and the golden rule as the method by which it is to be practiced in human life. Section B sounds the keynote, a warning against ostentation (6:1). This general injunction is now developed in *three* sections with reference to alms (6:2-4), prayer (vss. 5, 6), and fasting (vss. 16, 18). These sections, it will be observed, are exactly alike. Each has two parts, of which the first states the wrong and the second the correct practice; each has two concluding formulae exactly alike, namely, (1) "Verily I say unto you, They have received their reward," and (2) "And thy father who seeth in secret shall recompense thee"; each is directed against "the hypocrites," who in these verses are the Pharisees. In connection with the central section on prayer, however, some matter is introduced which may be regarded as a specific form of ostentation. In vss. 7-8 a warning is given against "vain repetitions"; the corrective is the Lord's Prayer (vss. 9-13), which is concluded with what looks like an amplification of the fifth petition (cf. vss. 12 with 14, 15). The presumption is in favor of regarding vss. 7-15 as having been brought into the context from some other location in the Common Source. The central section in vss. 7-9a contains references to the Gentiles and has the phrase, "For your heavenly Father knoweth," etc. It therefore has affinities to the brief section in 6:32, 33—a section which seems to have been brought in to balance the chiastic pattern in 6:24. It is quite possible that the Common Source contained, among other things, a section devoted to warning against repetitious praying, just as it contained more than one section about swearing (cf. 5:33-37 with 23:16-22). In such a section the Lord's Prayer may well have stood as the model prayer.

The fact remains that the material devoted to prayer in Lk. 11:1-13 opens with the Lord's Prayer, here in a shorter form (vss. 1-4). Then follow three sections on prayer, the central one of which contains a threefold invitation to ask, seek, and knock, together with a threefold assurance of results (vss. 9-10). On either side of this section is a parable, beginning with the words, "Which of you. . . ?" The first presents what ought to be the Christian attitude when the answer to prayer is delayed. This is the Parable of the Importunate Friend (vss. 5-8). The second is the illustration of a father, which undoubtedly meant to encourage faith in God, even though the answers to prayer appear to be contrary to expectation. Observe the striking threefold contrast between a loaf, a fish, and an egg, on the one hand, and a stone, a serpent, and a scorpion, on the other (vss. 11-13). There is a fine climax in the triplet, for the postulated gifts become worse with each new item. To this triplet there is a parallelism, however slight, in the preceding parable of the Importunate Friend, for the needy man asks for three loaves (vs. 5). The two parables on either side of the threefold invitation to prayer, each beginning with the the same introductory formula, indicate that we here are doubtless dealing with the Common Source. In Matthew this source is partly condensed by eliminating the Parable of the Importunate Friend and partly by eliminating the third item, the egg (cf. 7:10 with Lk. 11:12).

From a structural point of view, however, the most interesting feature of the passage is the fact that, though the Lord's Prayer has been separated from the rest of the passage dealing with prayer, it has been put in a *parallel* section (BB′). For section C has been injected between the two. In the Common Source, then, the three simple sections dealing with alms, prayer, and fasting (without Matt. 6:7-15) would form a fine counterpart to the three sections preserved fully in Lk. 11:5-12, and partially in Matt. 7:7-11 (B′). Looking back to 5:23-24, we notice a passage in which a conciliatory attitude toward brethren is made the condition for rendering the sacrifice acceptable. In 6:14, 15 another passage is found in which a forgiving attitude is made the condition for obtaining forgiveness. Although none of these passages appear to be needed in their context, they are nevertheless introduced. Their structural significance is discovered in that they are located in the B-sections of ZA and ZB. That ZB maintains connection with ZA in a similar way is seen in the allusions to the Gentiles, the references to whom are placed in parallel position to Jews in ZA (cf. 5:20 and 5:46, 47). This is not done in ZB, but we are not permitted to forget the Gentiles, even though most of the attention is given to "the hypocrites," the Pharisees. The Gentiles are alluded to in 6:7 and in 6:32. By such means a balance of ideas is maintained in the two halves of Z.

Section C (6:19-7:6), made up of five parts, constitutes the central section of ZB and is, from a literary point of view, one of the most remarkable in the Sermon on the Mount. In Cx the real treasures of a Christian are contrasted with the treasures of this world, while in Cx′ a warning is given not to waste these treasures ("the holy") on the unappreciative people of the world. Then follows the rather enigmatic section on "the single eye" in Cy. Nothing within this section and nothing in the immediate context sheds light as to the meaning of this saying. For all we know, it informs the reader merely of the physical fact that light comes through a healthy eye and darkness results from an unhealthy eye. But in the parallel section Cy′, which also deals with "the eye," the solution of the enigma is given. Here in three separate statements (*abc*) the Christian duty of rendering a candid and unbiased judgment, never obtainable without a consciousness of one's own shortcomings, is emphasized. Although there is a great deal of difference as to form, the content is closely parallel. The fine chiastic structure in 7:4, 5 runs smoothly and without flaw till we reach the words, "And then shalt thou see clearly *to cast out the mote* out of the eye of thy brother." The words in italics have been removed from their present position in the Greek text and transposed from the third to the second line from the end. With this slight change—only a single line in a manuscript like Sinaiticus and easily dislocated in copying—a most perfect chiasmus is obtained. In the Greek the *endings* of the first three, central three, and last three lines of the system are rather striking. In each of these groups of three lines some form of the verb "cast out" is found in the *central* line. That a chiastic structure of thirteen lines, with the word of address in the centre, can be constructed with so much spontaneity as to leave the impression of being unstudied in spite of such detailed symmetry, certainly is a testimony to the author's mastery of literary form. The passage also shows the necessity of considering, not only the nearer, but also the remoter context of a passage like Cy in order to obtain a correct exegesis of some of the apparently detached sayings of Jesus.

The central section Cz is the longest and most intricately constructed of them all. It is impossible to appreciate the literary beauty and perfect symmetry of this long passage unless it is read in Greek.[5] Briefly, the order of the various parts of this section is as follows: In *a* the necessity of choosing between the two masters, God and Mammon, is presented, and in *a'* the two kinds of life resulting from this choice, the Christian and the pagan, are described. In *bb'* the cause for anxiety is described as threefold: food, drink, and clothing. It is obvious that the second question, "Or what ye shall drink" (vs. 25), which is missing in some manuscripts, was a part of the original text (cf. vs. 31). In *c* the argument proceeds from the greater to the lesser: You receive life and body as a gift from God, can you not, then, trust him for food

[5] *Anglican Theological Review,* Vol. XIII, No. 1 (January, 1931), pp. 38-39.

and raiment? In *c'* this procedure is reversed, for here the argument is from the lesser to the greater: Since God takes care of the ephemeral grass, shall he not much more take care of his children? This lesson from reason is now enforced with two lessons from nature (*dd'*). The two chief causes for anxiety are food (in which here drink is included) and clothing. The first is disposed of in *d* by the example of the birds of the heavens, clinching the argument in *e*. The second is treated in *d'* by a reference to the lilies of the field and finished in *e'*. The central section *f* is a simple chiasmus of four members, in which the anxiety is mentioned in the extremes and the two causes of anxiety in the central lines. The verb "to be anxious" is symmetrically distributed in the structure, for it occurs in *bb'* and *f*, and in the concluding strophe vs. 34. The analysis of the passage shows that the logic of the argument is closely united with the symmetry of form. In the Greek text the euphony of words is prominent, especially in the endings of all the verbs and of the whole first lines of sections *dd'*.

These passages offer some splendid illustrations of the basic proposition of this treatise, namely, that in this form of writing neither length nor number of lines are essential; the order of the ideas is the only necessary consideration. Some sections have many lines and some few; some lines are long and others short; some are chiastic and some alternating. There is a great deal of flexibility in all these respects, but amidst all these variations the parallelism of ideas is maintained.[6]

[6] The criticism that may be passed on the analysis of the Sermon on the Mount by John Forbes, *The Symmetrical Structure of Scripture*, pp. 158 ff., is that he does not make proper allowances for this flexibility of form, though his work, which is based on previous observations by Bishop Jebb, offers many useful hints. I am indebted to Forbes for directing my attention to the Sermon on the Mount and its characteristic form, and for occasional hints, among which may be mentioned the relations between the Seven Beatitudes and the Seven Petitions in the Lord's Prayer. In the analysis, however, I have more often departed from than followed the analysis of Forbes, as a comparison of the results will show.

CHAPTER XIII

THE MISSIONARY DISCOURSE

The Missionary Discourse (Matt. 10:5-11:1) is unique in that it is located in the midst of a frame-passage in the gospel. Its position may best be brought to the attention of the reader by a simple outline of Matt. 4:12-11:6.[1]

Jesus heard of John's arrest (4:12).
 The territory and the message: Israel, the kingdom of heaven (13-17).
  Four disciples chosen (18-22).
   General summary: Jesus' work consists of teaching, preaching, healing. His cures include disease, sickness, demons (23-24).
    The *Sayings* of Jesus: The Sermon on the Mount (4:25-8:1).
     Three miracles of healing illustrating the summaries in 4:23, 24 and 9:35-10:1 (8:2-17).
    The *Doings* of Jesus: a series of miracles (8:18-9:34).
   General Summary: Jesus' work consists of teaching, preaching, healing. His cures include disease, sickness, demons (9:35-10:1).
  Twelve disciples chosen (10:2-4).
 The territory (vss. 5, 6) and the message (vs. 7): Israel, the kingdom (5-11:1).
 The Missionary Discourse (10:8-11:1).
John in prison heard of Jesus' work (11:2-6).

In these two frame-passages which enclose a larger block of the text in the gospel there are four separate items of information which are arranged in chiastic form. In this arrangement 10:5-7 present the *territory* which was to be covered by the new missionary enterprise and the *message* that was to be preached. This is parallel to 4:13-17 above. But in 10:8-11:1 we have the discourse which does not fit into the frame-passage but which is in itself nevertheless a perfect chiastic structure, the several parts being balanced in content and form after the fashion of the Sermon on the Mount. The discourse is concluded by the same formula which occurs five times in the gospel (cf. 7:28; 11:1; 13:53; 19:1; 26:1), namely, "And it came to pass when Jesus had fin-

[1] "The Influence of Chiasmus upon the Structure of the Gospel According to Matthew," *Anglican Theological Review*, Vol. XIII, No. 4 (Oct. 1931), pp. 415, 416.

ished," etc. The formula in 11:1, however, receives a significant addition, "finished *commanding his twelve disciples*"; these words turn the reader's attention back to 10:5. The words "*preach* in *their cities*," also have their parallels in 10:6 (cf. "the house of Israel").

The Missionary Discourse

Matt. 10:5-11:1

A
These twelve Jesus sent forth and charged them, saying, 10:5
Go not into a way of the Gentiles,
And enter not into a city of Samaritans;
But go rather to the lost sheep of *the house of Israel*, 6
And as ye go, *preach*, saying, The kingdom of heaven is at hand. 7

B
Heal the sick, 8
Raise the dead,
Cleanse the lepers,
Cast out demons:
Freely ye *received*,
Freely give.

Get you no gold, 9
Nor silver,
Nor brass
In your purses,
No wallet for a journey; 10

Neither two coats,
Nor shoes,
Nor staff:
For the laborer is worthy of his *food*.

C
And into whatsoever city or village ye shall enter, 11
Search out who in it is worthy,
And there abide till ye go forth.
And as ye enter into a house, 12
Salute it.

And if the house be *worthy*, 13
Let your *peace* come upon it;
But if it be not *worthy*,
Let your *peace* return to you.

And whosoever shall not receive you, 14
Nor hear your words,
As ye go forth out of that house or that city,
Shake off the dust of your feet.
Verily I say unto you, It shall be more tolerable for the land of Sodom
and Gomorrah in the day of judgment, than for that city. 15

Behold, I send you forth as sheep in the midst of wolves: 16
Be ye therefore wise as serpents and harmless as doves.

But beware of men! 17
For they will deliver you
a Up to councils,
And in their synagogues
They will scourge you.
And before governors and kings 18

b Shall ye be brought *for my sake*,
For a testimony to them and to the Gentiles.

But when they deliver you up, *be not anxious* 19
how or what ye shall speak:
D c For it shall be given you in that hour what ye shall speak.
For it is not ye that speak, 20
But the Spirit of your Father that speaketh in you.

And brother shall deliver up brother to death, 21
And the father
a′ His child;
And children shall rise up
Against parents,
And cause them to be put to death.

b′ And ye shall be hated of all men *for my name's sake;* 22
But he that endureth to the end the same shall be saved.

But when they persecute you in this city, 23
c′ Flee into the next: for verily I say unto you,
Ye shall not have gone through the cities of Israel,
Till the Son of man be come.

A disciple is not above his teacher, 24
Nor a servant above his lord.
It is enough for the disciple that he be as his teacher, 25
E And the servant as his lord.
If they have called the master of the house Beelzebub,
How much more them of his household.
Fear them not therefore. 26

For there is nothing covered,
a That shall not be revealed;
Nor hid,
That shall not be known.

What I tell you in the darkness, 27
b Speak ye in the light;
And what ye hear in the ear,
Proclaim upon the house-tops.

And *be not afraid* of them that kill the body, 28
c But are not able to kill the soul;
But rather fear him who is able
To destroy both soul and body in Gehenna.

D′

Are not two sparrows sold for a penny? 29
c′ And not one of them shall fall to the ground without your
But the hairs of your head are numbered. 30 (Father:
Fear not therefore: ye are of more value than many spar-
(rows. 31

Every one therefore who shall confess me 32
b′ Before men,
Him shall I also confess
Before my Father who is in heaven.

But whosoever shall deny me 33
a′ Before men,
Him shall I also deny
Before my Father who is in heaven.

Think not 34
a That I came to send *peace* on the earth;
I came not to send *peace*,
But a sword.

For I came to set at variance a man against his father, 35
b And the daughter against her mother,
And the daughter in law against her mother in law:
And a man's foes shall be they of his own household. 36

He that loveth father and mother more than me 37
C′ Is not *worthy* of me;
b′ And he that loveth son and daughter more than me
Is not *worthy* of me;
And he that doth not take his cross and follow after me 38
Is not *worthy* of me.

He that findeth 39
His life
a′ Shall lose it;
And he that loseth
His life for my sake
Shall find it.

B′

a
He that *receiveth* you 40
Receiveth me,
And he that receiveth me
Receiveth him that sent me.

b
He that receiveth *a prophet* 41
In the name of a prophet
Shall receive a prophet's reward.

c
And he that receiveth *a righteous man*
In the name of a righteous man
Shall receive a righteous man's reward.

d
And whosoever shall give *to drink* unto one of these *little ones* 42
a cup of cold water only
In the name of a disciple,
Verily, I say unto you, he shall in no wise lose his reward.

A′
And it came to pass when Jesus had finished commanding his *twelve disciples*, 11:1
He departed thence to teach and *preach* in *their cities*.

Outline

A Jesus and the Twelve: the scope of the mission: "the house of Israel," vs. 6.
B Instructions to the disciples: "receive," "food," vss. 8, 10.
C Testimony under persecution: from strangers: "not worthy," vs. 13.
D Comfort under persecution: "be not anxious," vs. 19.
E The Master's own example is recalled: "fear them not," vs. 26.
D′ Comfort under persecution: "be not afraid," vss. 28, 31.
C′ Testimony under persecution: "from their own household," "not worthy," (vss. 37, 38.
B′ Instructions to the churches: "receive," "to drink," vss. 40, 42.
A′ Jesus and the Twelve: the scope of the mission: "their cities," 11:1.

When it is observed that all the intervening material between sections A and A′ of the Missionary Discourse constitutes a literary unit as it stands in the gospel and that this unit is now located in the frame-passage, where it obviously could not have been placed from the beginning, the presumption is very strongly in favor of regarding this whole discourse as derived from another document, from which it had been brought into the gospel. Since the concluding formula is very nearly identical in the other instances where it occurs, one may raise the question whether these discourses also may not have been derived from the same document, that document being the Common Source, which no doubt was a very inclusive collection of the sayings and doings of Jesus.

The general features of the Missionary Discourse have already been briefly set forth in the outline. In BB′ we have Jesus' instructions. These are, in both sections, addressed to The Twelve. In B their task (vs. 8) and their equipment (vss. 9, 10) are briefly summarized. It will be noticed that a literal obedience of the orders contemplates a certain generous attitude among those with whom they are to work. In the parallel section (B′) this attitude is described. Although formally addressed to The Twelve these commands obviously concern chiefly the Christian community. The general statement that Jesus identifies himself with those who come with his authority (vs. 40) is made more specific in the following three sections (vss. 41-42), which are of a similar structure and which evidently deal with three classes of Christians: a prophet, a righteous man, and "one of these little ones." The first two occur together also in Matt. 13:17. A comparison will show that the principle, "Freely ye received, freely give," (vs. 8) is applicable not only to The Twelve but also to the church (B′). The references to food and drink are found in these sections only (vss. 10, 42).

In section C the two extreme parts are chiastic and the central part is alternating. In vss. 11, 12 the entrance in the city is described and in vss. 14, 15 the exit. The nature of the arrangement is quite similar to that of Lk. 4:16-21a. The two terms, "peace" and "worthy," which are conspicuous by their repetition and by their central position, recur in the parallel section (C′). The two parts of this section which are central (*bb′*) deal with the relations of parents and children. In *b* the male members of the household are dealt with in the extreme lines and the female members in the central lines. This arrangement according to sex was also found in the alternating lines of Matt. 13:54-57. These sections recall vividly the strife in ancient society as the result of the gospel.[2] The threefold repetition, "He is not worthy of me," is impressive and recalls the term "worthy" in C. The term "peace" is found twice in vs. 34. The paradox of this verse is matched by another paradox in vs. 39. The substance of CC′ seems to be:

[2] Origen, *Against Celsus*, BK. III, chaps. lv, lvi.

"From the very beginning and throughout your life as Christians you are to face opposition, from strangers as well as from those of your own family, and you must prove yourself worthy of me by making your choice." It should be observed that the terms, "peace" and "worthy," are found in CC′ only. The chiastic structure of vs. 39 would be perfect, were it not for the phrase "for my sake," which probably represents an editorial addition (cf. vss. 18, 22). The phrase is absent in Lk. 17:33 but is found in Matt. 16:25; Lk. 9:24; Mk. 8:35. In the last passage it has another addition, "and for the gospel's." Such accretions show later attempts to make the original paradoxes more precise and to guard them against possible misunderstandings of them.

Sections DD′ continue the subject of testimony before the world, but with a special emphasis on comfort for those who suffer affliction because of their faithfulness. The sections in D are alternating; those in D′ are chiastic. Their parallel features may be expressed as follows: Section D opens with a general introductory statement, setting forth the difficulties of the mission and the requirements needed to meet them (vs. 16). Persecution from strangers is treated in vs. 17; from those in the family in vs. 21. All this is "for my sake" (vs. 18) or "for my name's sake" (vs. 22). The following two sections open with the same construction, "But when . . .;" and contain comfort. On the one hand, they may rely on the guidance of the Spirit (vss. 19, 20) and, on the other, they may flee from city to city; after all, the time will be very short (vs. 23). The words, "and to the Gentiles," (vs. 18) are not in harmony with the limitations imposed upon the mission by the words in vs. 5; these words are, as we have already seen, part of the original frame-passage into which the discourse has been fitted, beginning in vs. 8. In these persecutions of Christians, not only scourgings (vs. 17) but also death is anticipated (vs. 21).

When we turn to section D′, we find the possibility of death strongly emphasized, in fact taken for granted (vs. 28), while the comfort is offered that even this is within their Father's will (vss. 29-31). The twofold exhortation, "be not afraid" and "fear not therefore," (vss. 28, 31) has its parallel in D in the words, "be not anxious" (vs. 19). While in D′ the afflictions and comfort of the witnesses are treated in *cc′*, their testimony is treated in *ab* and *b′a′*. In vs. 26 the reference is not to hidden deeds of darkness that are to be revealed (cf. Rom. 2:16), but to the fact that the gospel, which in the beginning of Jesus' ministry was confined to a few, shall cast off its temporary limitations and spread. So understood, vs. 26 finds its explanation in vs. 27, the latter verse saying in plain words what the former verse said in figures. There are in this gospel several intimations of this secretive, or restricted, use of the gospel, which is encouraged by Jesus' own words and example (cf. Matt. 13:13-18; 9:30, 31). In *ab* we have a clear announcement that whatever restrictions there might have been imposed upon the gospel message by Jesus himself, they are not to be regarded as permanent restrictions. To these sections *b′a′* offer close parallels, for one emphasizes public confession and the other denial of Jesus.

The central section (E) sets forth the example of the Master himself. The followers of Jesus cannot expect any better treatment by the men of the world than that accorded Jesus himself. How the contemplation of Jesus' example as a suffering witness may be invoked for the purpose of comforting and strengthening Christians in times of persecution may be seen in 1 Tim. 6:11-13. The concluding exhortation, "Fear them not therefore" (vs. 26), belongs to the central section, as the structure of the following sections clearly indicates. The discourse thus has the climax in the centre, namely, the supreme example, the Master himself. The whole is symmetrically arranged. The duties of both the missionaries and the church are given in BB′; the opposition they may expect from strangers and from their own household and what they are expected to endure as the result thereof, in CC′; then, the comfort they may draw from the presence of the Holy Spirit, from the nearness of the return of Jesus, and from the providential care of God, in DD′; lastly in E, the example of Jesus who endured a similar treatment but became victorious.

There are two major problems in the discourse, namely, the scope of the missionary enterprise outlined in it and the type and date of the persecutions that are referred to. The phrase, "and to the Gentiles," (vs. 18) need not be brought into conformity to vs. 5 for reasons already stated. The scope outlined in this phrase is strictly in line with other similar allusions in the Q sections (cf. 8:11; 13:31-33; and possibly 13:38). Many scholars are of the opinion that persecutions of such severe nature as those contemplated here could not have occurred at such early date, but must be due to the reflection of later times by which historically late situations have been read back into earlier times.[3] These references to persecutions are, no doubt, historical and may not be waved aside as merely "apocalyptic references to persecution" (Abrahams). If the discourse is derived from the Common Source, either as a whole or in part, it is earlier than any of the gospels. It must be historically wrong to assume that the generation that crucified Jesus was anything but hostile to Christian propagandists. A situation within a family, like that reflected in vs. 21 or in vss. 35-38, is easily conceived, when a dissenting religious minority is confronted by resolute and fanatical members of an established religious order. Where the charge involves blasphemy, as in the case of Jew against Christian (cf. Acts 6:11-14), and where the Law is taken seriously (Lev. 24:13-16), as it is not among members of modern Reformed Judaism, occurrences like those described in vss. 17-23 and vs. 28 could easily have occurred.

Besides, we have very definite historical references to persecutions by early Palestinian Jews against their Christian fellow-citizens. Paul refers to definite situations when he says, "For ye, brethren, became imitators of the churches of God which are in Judaea in Christ Jesus: for ye also suffered the same things of your own countrymen, *even as they did of the Jews;* who both killed the Lord Jesus and the prophets, and drove us out" (cf. 1 Thess. 2:14, 15). These words have reference to events that must have transpired before the year 50 A.D. The matter-of-fact tone of the passage indicates that Paul takes for granted the things he describes in regard to *the churches of Judaea.* He reinforces the evidence of these churches by experiences of his own. One

[3] Montefiore, *The Synoptic Gospels*, Vol. II, pp. 149-151.

clear-cut and definite statement like that ought to count more than anything that the Talmud does *not* say, when the historian is making up his mind as to the temper of the Jews of Palestine in the first half of the first century.[4]

[4] Montefiore, *op. cit.*, Vol. I, p. cvii, and also pp. ciii, civ.

CHAPTER XIV

DISCOURSES ON AUTHORITY AND THE LAW

The following two discourses are of a controversial nature. In the first of these (Matt. 12:22-45) Jesus is in conflict with the religious leaders of Israel regarding his power to cast out the demons. The second discourse deals with transgressing the traditions of the elders by eating with unwashed hands (Matt. 15:1-20). The first of the two discourses is a fairly regular disposition of the argument in the usual chiastic forms, but the second is more unconventional, one might say, irregular, especially in the latter half (15:10-19); there the alternating arrangement of the sections prevails. The curious recurrence of the adjectives "good," "corrupt," and "good," "evil" (12:33, 35) in a parallel position, which though of a different arrangement than in the central section of 7:16-20, yet is strongly reminiscent of the former passage, is hard to explain, unless by assuming a common origin. The epithet "blind guides" (15:14) serves to connect the discourse in which it occurs with the great invective against the religious leaders in 23:1-32, in which it recurs (vss. 16, 23). There are some grounds for the assumption that all three of these discourses against the religious leaders of Israel belong together and that they were originally found in the Common Source, perhaps with more material of a similar content.

It is, of course, impossible to venture an opinion both in regard to the extent of this material and its original arrangement in the Common Source. Yet there are certain qualities in the two discourses with which we are immediately concerned which would make it probable that they were intended to balance each other in a larger structure.

Concerning the Authority of Jesus

Matt. 12:22-45

There was brought to him one possessed with a demon, 22
Blind
A And dumb:
And he healed him
So that the dumb man spake
And saw.

And all the multitude were amazed, and said, 23
Can this be the Son of David?
But when the Pharisees heard it, they said, 24
This man does not cast out demons,
But by Beelzebub, the prince of the demons.
And knowing their thoughts he said unto them, 25
Every kingdom divided against itself is brought to desolation,
And every city and house divided against itself
Shall not stand:
And if Satan 26
Casteth out Satan,
He is divided against himself;
B How then shall stand
His kingdom?
And if I by Beelzebub 27
Cast out demons
By whom do your sons cast them out?
Therefore they shall be your judges.
But if I by the Spirit of God cast out demons, 28
Then the kingdom of God is come unto you.

Or how can one enter the house of the strong man, 29
And spoil his goods,
Except he first bind the strong man?
And then will he spoil his house.

He that is not with me is against me; 30
And he that gather not with me scattereth.

Therefore I say unto you,
Every sin and blasphemy shall be forgiven unto men; 31
But blasphemy against the Spirit shall not be forgiven.
And whosoever shall *speak* a word against the Son of man, 32
a It shall not be forgiven him,
Neither in this world,
Nor in that which is to come.

Either make the tree *good*, 33
b And its fruit *good;*
Or make the tree *corrupt*,
And its fruit *corrupt.*

C

For out of the fruit the tree is known.
Ye offspring of vipers, 34
c How can ye *speak* good things,
Being evil.
For out of the abundance of the heart the mouth speaketh.

For the good man out of his *good* treasure 35
b′ Bringeth forth *good* things;
And the evil man out of his *evil* treasure
Bringeth forth *evil* things.

And *I say unto you*, that every idle word that man *speak*, 36
a′ They shall give account thereof in the day of judgment.
For by thy words thou shalt be justified, 37
And by thy words thou shalt be condemned.

B′
a
Then certain of the scribes and the Pharisees answered him, saying, 38
Teacher, we would see a sign from thee.
But he answered and said unto them, 39

b
An evil and adulterous generation seeketh after a sign,
And there shall be no sign given to it but the sign of Jonah the prophet:
For as Jonah was three days and three nights in the belly of the whale, 40
So shall the Son of man be three days and three nights in the heart of the (earth.

c
The men of Nineveh shall stand up in *the judgment* of this generation, 41
And shall condemn it:
For they repented at the preaching of Jonah;
And behold, a greater than Jonah is here.

d
The queen of the south shall rise up in *the judgment* of this generation, 42
And shall condemn it:
For she came from the ends of the earth to hear the wisdom of Solomon;
And behold, a greater than Solomon is here.

A′
But when the unclean spirit is gone out of man, he passeth through waterless 43
places, seeking rest, and findeth it not. Then he saith,
Into my dwelling 44
I will return
Whence I came out;
And having come
He findeth it { empty, and swept, and garnished.
Then goeth he 45
And taketh with him seven other spirits more evil than himself,
And having entered in
They dwell there.
And the last state of that man becometh worse than his first.
Even so shall it be also unto this evil generation.

Outline

A *The demon cast out.*

B *The Pharisees reject the divine authority of the signs of Jesus:*
Their sons shall be their *judges*, vs. 27.
Jesus enters "the house of the strong man," vs. 29.

C *The Pharisees sin in words against Jesus:*
Their sins of *speech* are mentioned in *aca′*.
The *tree* in *b* and the *treasure* in *b′* are parallel.

B′ *The scribes and the Pharisees demand new signs from Jesus:*
The Gentiles shall be their *judges* (*cd*), for they accepted less evidence.
Jesus enters "the heart of the earth" (vs. 40), cf. Heb. 2:14, 15.

A′ *The demon returns:* central triplet.

The general features of the discourse have already been indicated in the outline. The casting out of the demon is told, because this incident provides the starting point for the objection against Jesus' authority (A). Before the discourse closes, the reader is once more reminded of its beginning by the parallel chiastic structure dealing with the returning demon (A′). Although this section is more elaborate, there can be no doubt as to its chiastic structure and its function in the structure as a parallel to section A. The first half deals with the return, and the second half with the entrance of the demon. The triplet marks the turning point of the system (cf. Lk. 4:16-21a; Matt. 10:11-15).

In sections BB′ the attitude of the Pharisees toward Jesus with reference to signs is discussed. The first two lines raise the question of Jesus' Messiahship (vs. 23), and the two concluding lines answer the question (vs. 28). The next three lines give the objection of the Pharisees (vs. 24), and the corresponding three lines Jesus' answer to their objection (vs. 27). The intervening lines give the basis of the argument, namely, the general observation that division in a kingdom usually means disintegration. Although the first half of this structure is somewhat fuller in detail than the last half, the order of the ideas is nevertheless scrupulously maintained, making a perfect chiastic system. There is only one serious break in the scheme, the words, "Therefore they shall be your judges" (vs. 27); but even the presence of this reference to judgment, which has no counterpart in the first half of B, finds a sufficient justification in two references to judgment in the corresponding section (B′). In view of the casting out of the demon, Jesus' independence and supremacy over Beelzebub is affirmed. He has "entered the house of the strong man" and taken spoil (vs. 29). Even for this apparently detached saying there is a parallel (vs. 40) in section B′.

Section B′ has no chiastic structure. The Pharisees are introduced a second time, now together with the scribes, and the demand for a sign is made (vs. 38). The only sign they will receive is the resurrection (vss. 39, 40). It is significant that the reference to "the heart of the earth" should be introduced *first,* for it is a parallel idea to "enter the house of the strong man," which comes last in B (cf. Heb. 2:14, 15). The following two sections are very formal and impressive. Representative Gentiles who were satisfied with much less evidence will arise in judgment and condemn

Israel. This idea of judgment finds its only parallel in those words in B which had no counterpart in that system (vs. 27b). Details like these prove that the writer (or editor) of the discourse considered not merely the immediate but often the more remote context as well. A climax may be observed in the contents of the latter half of the discourse. The content of A′, as well as the form, is certainly more impressive than that of A. That the Pharisees are to be judged by their own disciples (sons) is bad enough (B), but that they are ultimately to be judged and condemned by Gentiles is still worse (B′).

The central section (C) is one of fine symmetry and is devoted to an exposition of the sins of speech. In vs. 30 a general introductory statement is given, showing how impossible it is to be neutral in regard to Jesus. The references to speech are distributed in the two extreme sections and in the centre (*aca′*). The sins of speech are either blasphemy (vs. 31), such as the Pharisees had been guilty of when they ascribed a miracle of Jesus to the power of Beelzebub, or "idle words" (vs. 36), such as any man may use carelessly. Here also the thought of judgment is introduced in "the world to come" (vs. 32) and in "the day of judgment" (vs. 36). Again, there is a parallelism in "forgiven" (vs. 32) and "justified" (vs. 37) as well as in their opposites, "not forgiven" and "condemned." In *bb′* we have two well-balanced sections dealing with the trees and their fruit and the treasures and the things that issue from them. There is a definite arrangement of the adjectives, "good" and "corrupt" in *b*, and "good" and "evil" in *b′*. A similar grouping of these adjectives occurs in the central section of 7:16-20; it is hardly possible that such terms could recur in company unless there was a certain degree of literary effort to produce such results. In *c* the first and last lines open with "For out of"; this should be compared to the first words in the two sections (*cc′*) in 10:19, 23, "But when. . . ." This section contains a statement about the *source* of speech, namely, the human heart. The words of address, "Ye offspring of vipers," are found in this central section, which, once more, is in conformity to examples found elsewhere (cf. 7:4, 5, "thou hypocrite" with 15:7).

The analysis shows that the discourse is a well-balanced literary unity, compared to which the material preserved by Luke looks like a ruin (Lk. 11:14, 15, 17-23). In an even higher degree this appraisal applies to Mk. 3:22-30, with its dislocations, gaps, and general state of incompleteness. The presence of a symmetrical literary structure in the discourses naturally raises the question of whether, after all, the Common Source, wherever it is used, has not been substantially preserved by Matthew. The other two accounts, then, represent editorial mutilations of that source. Rejecting this solution, we have the alternative of regarding the discourse as a conflation of Mk. with Q. Of course, with such conspicuous examples as Matt. 13:13-18 and Lk. 4:16-21a of what may be achieved by literary workmanship, conflation does not seem an impossible hypothesis. Ordinarily, however, ruins are derived from buildings, though, at times, by a process of restoration the reverse may be true. The problem may only be raised. The solution can come only after a careful study of *all* the material. For such a fresh study the chiasmus may provide a new approach.

Concerning the Ceremonial Law

Matt. 15:1-20

Then there come to Jesus from Jerusalem Pharisees and scribes, saying, 1

A Why do thy disciples transgress the traditions of the elders? 2
For they *wash* not their *hands* when they *eat* bread.

B {
And he answered and said unto them, Why do ye also transgress *the commandment of God* because of *your tradition?* 3
For *God said, Honor* thy father and thy mother, and, 4
He that *speaketh evil* of father and mother,
Let him die the death.
But *ye say*, Whosoever *shall say* to his father and mother, 5
That wherewith thou mightest have been profited by me is given to God;
He shall not *honor* his father or his mother. 6
And ye make void *the law of God* because of *your tradition.*

C {
Ye hypocrites, Well did Isaiah prophesy of you, saying, 7
"This people honoreth me with their *lips*, 8
But their *heart* is far from me,
But in vain do they *worship* me, 9
Teaching as their doctrines the precepts of men."

B′

a And he called unto him the multitude, and said *unto them*, 10
Hear and *understand*.

Not that which *entereth into the mouth* 11
b *Defileth the man;*
But that which *proceedeth out of the mouth*,
This *defileth the man.*

Then came his disciples and said unto him, 12
Knowest thou that the *Pharisees* were caused to *stumble*, when they
heard this saying?
c But he answered and said, Every *plant*, 13
Which my heavenly Father *planteth* not, shall be rooted up.
Let them alone; they are *blind guides;* 14
And if the blind guide the blind, both *shall fall* into the pit.

a′ And Peter answered and said unto him, Declare *unto us* this parable. 15
And he said, Are ye also even yet without *understanding?* 16

b′

Perceive ye not, that whatsoever *goeth into the mouth* 17
Passeth into the belly and is cast out in the draught?
But the things which *proceed out of the mouth* 18
Come forth out of the heart.
And these *defile the man;*
For out of the heart come forth – – – – – evil thoughts, murders, adulteries, fornications, thefts, false witness, blasphemies. 19
These are the things that *defile the man.*

A′ But to *eat* with *unwashen hands* defileth no man.

There are many strands in this discourse that unite it with the preceding in 12:22-45. There are Pharisees and scribes, who are arguing with Jesus. The words of address occur, once more, in the central section (cf. 12:34; 15:7), and in the same context we find the emphasis on the words and the heart. With all these parallels in mind, it is hard not to conclude that there is a conscious parallelism intended by the author in the arrangement of the seven sins that come forth from the heart (15:19) and the seven other spirits that enter into the heart (12:45), especially since in Mk. 7:21 the list includes thirteen items! The general contrast between man's inner life and his outward conduct pervades both discourses, strikingly expressed in the tree and its fruit and also in the plant which is to be rooted up (12:33; 15:13). These discourses offer so many striking parallels in both content and form that they may well have been balanced sections in a larger structure of such controversial material, very much after the pattern of the sections observed in the Sermon on the Mount.

Since the Common Source probably was Palestinian in origin, we are not surprised to find in these discourses a content which was relevant only under Palestinian conditions and when addressed to Jews.

Turning our attention to their discourse we observe that the disciples of Jesus had been charged with infractions of the ceremonial law (A). In characteristic fashion the charge—eating without first washing the hands—is mentioned in the first line and never again until we reach the concluding line (A′). This line is conspicuous because it does not appear in the Marcan account (Mk. 7:23). Jesus answers the charge by a counter-charge, which is the substance of section B. This section corresponds to section B of the previous discourse, because both contain the direct argument with the Pharisees. How the chiastic structure works out in detail is indicated by the lines in italics. If we accept the reading of Nestle in vs. 6 ("word of God"), it will still be parallel to "the commandment of God" (vs. 3). Into the question whether these words reflect a historical situation, or are merely an invective against the synagogue, we need not enter here. Section C contains a quotation from Isa. 29:13. This is one more instance in which we have observed the tendency of quotations to gravitate toward the centre in a system (cf. Matt. 13:13-18; Lk. 4:16-21a). In striking contrast "the lips" stand for externalism (cf. Matt. 23:23, 24a, below), while the "heart" stands for the religion of the spirit.

Section B′ is made up of Jesus' explanation why eating with unwashed hands is not defiling. The material is arranged in alternating sections (*ab* and *a′b′*), and the words in italics call attention to the order of the ideas. In *b* that which goes in and that which goes out of the mouth alternate with the idea of defilement in four lines. Not so in *b′* which is more lengthy and provides the *reason* for the statements in *b*. The idea of defilement, however, recurs twice in *b′* also though elaborated into a special section in which the number seven is central. Between the two alternating sections we find *c* which is devoted to a denunciation of the Pharisees. Their doctrine is to be uprooted, and they and their disciples shall fall into the pit. This is in the same vein as the judgment is described in B′ (12:41, 42). Finally, it may be worth observing, as a final strand that ties the two discourses together, that whereas the Pharisees appear singly in the first part of the former discourse and in company with the scribes in the latter part (12:24, 38), the order is exactly reversed in this discourse (15:1, 12); so is the statement that the Pharisees "heard" about Jesus (15:12, 12:24). If, as has already been suggested, these two discourses once have stood balanced against one another in a larger chiastic structure in the Common Source, such inversions as these would have structural significance. The assumption that such a longer arrangement of discourses against the scribes and the Pharisees actually did exist gives new interest to the fact that they are called "blind guides" in *c*, a central section of B′ (15:14), for the term recurs in another central section D (23:23-24a) under identical conditions, that is to say, toward the end of the section and as a parallel to Pharisees in the beginning of the section. There is, of course, some difficulty in gathering such elusive hints, scattered widely apart as they are, and in marshalling the evidence in a comprehensive manner. For the task includes the parallel material in Mark and Luke also which must be brought together and tested from this point of view. If and when this is achieved, we may, nevertheless, have on hand evidence of an altogether new type, which may in some measure aid us in determining what has usually been called "the extent of Q."

A comparison with Mark at this point is of great interest. Mk. 7:3-4 is clearly a parenthetic note. The quotation from Isa. 29:13 appears much earlier in the passage (vss. 6-7). There are several additions, not found in Matthew: namely, vss. 13b, 17a, 19c, six additional sins in the list in vss. 21, 22; the words, "corban" and "defiled hands," with the explanation of the former (vss. 5, 11). There is also an important elimination, namely, Matt. 15:12-14, which is the more remarkable since it is *central* in B′, and is the section containing the striking parallelism to Matt. 12:33-35. If Mark did not have this section, it is strange that he should have a reference to "the parable" (Mk. 7:17). There is nothing parabolic in the statement in the preceding verses 14-15, and not even metaphorical as in the use of the term in Mk. 3:25 of Satan and his kingdom. If, on the other hand, he is referring to the material in Matt. 15:12-14, the term is intelligible. The final reference to eating with unwashed hands (Matt. 15:19) is also eliminated. Mark's account looks like a ruin of the symmetric structure preserved by Matthew. The difficulty of finding "the parable" in our present Marcan text renders it highly probable that the reference to "the plant" and to "the blind guiding the blind" was in Mark's source.

CHAPTER XV

THE DISCOURSE AGAINST THE PHARISEES

Among the controversial discourses in the gospel the one in Matt. 23:1-39 is not only the longest, but the most vigorous, and, in some respects, the most interesting. There are many features that recall the Sermon on the Mount. As far as these features relate to terminology and structure they will be discussed as the analysis proceeds. The strong antithesis between the religious leaders, on the one hand (vss. 4-7), and the disciples of Jesus, on the other (vss. 8-12), remind us of the similar antithetic arrangement of the new gospel against the old law in the Sermon on the Mount.

Our first task will be an analysis of the whole discourse (vss. 1-32) with a view of establishing the structure of the whole and its separate units. This will include an appraisal of the contents of the material in vss. 16-22 and the relationship of this material to the reading that is now vs. 14 in the Authorized Version and a marginal reading in the American Revised Version. Finally, we shall include a comparative study of the discourse in Matthew and of its sayings as they are found in the account of Lk. 11:42-52. This part of our study is done by the aid of the comparative outlines that follow immediately after the text and by the later comments on these outlines. The figures in the right margin of the outlines indicate the order of the sayings in Luke and in Matthew. A study of this material will give a fairly good idea of Luke's method of handling his material, his aversion to chiastic forms as well as his freedom in re-distributing the sayings. Luke's treatment of chiastic forms is seen also in a comparison between vss. 33-39 and its parallels in the gospel of Luke, where the chiastic forms are consistently broken down by slight changes in the structures.

On several occasions we have called attention to the value of these forms for purposes of textual criticism. There is in the present text of the gospel signs of a certain type of legalistic emphasis (cf. Matt. 5:18; 23:3) which is also revealed by the additional words in vs. 23b. Best is the application of form to textual criticism seen in vss. 16-22.

The Discourse Against the Pharisees

Matt. 23:1-39

Then spake Jesus to the multitudes and to this disciples, saying, 1
Upon the seat of Moses the *scribes* and the *Pharisees* sat down: 2
All things therefore whatsoever they bid you, do and observe, 3
But after their works do not; for they say and do not.

Now, they bind heavy burdens, 4
A And lay them on the shoulders of men,
But they themselves with their own fingers
Are not willing to move them.

B But all their works they do to be seen of men: 5

C For they make broad their phylacteries,
And enlarge the tassels.

D And they love the chief places at the feasts, 6
And the chief seats in the synagogues.

E And the greetings in the marketplaces, 7
And to be called of men, Rabbi.

E′ But you, be not called Rabbi, 8
For *one* is your Teacher, and ye are all brethren.

D′ And your father call no one upon the earth, 9
For *one* is your Father, he who is in heaven.

C′ Neither be ye called leaders, 10
For your Leader is *one*, the Christ.

B′ But the greater of you shall be your minister. 11

And whosoever shall exalt 12
Himself
A′ Shall be humbled;
And whosoever shall humble
Himself
Shall be exalted.

Outline

Introduction, vss. 1-3.

A Description of the Jewish leaders: aloofness, vs. 4.
B General statement of their motive: "to be seen of men," vs. 5a.
C Ostentation in dress, vs. 5b.
D Ostentation in regard to places of honor, vs. 6.
E Ostentation in regard to salutations, vs. 7.
E′ One only is Teacher, vs. 8.
D′ One only is Father, vs. 9.
C′ One only is Leader, vs. 10.
B′ General statement of the Christian ideal: service, vs. 11.
A′ Description of the Christian leaders: humility, vs. 12.

But woe unto you, scribes and Pharisees, hypocrites! 13
A For ye shut the kingdom of heaven against men:
For ye enter not in yourselves,
Neither suffer ye them that are entering in to enter.

Woe unto you, scribes and Pharisees, hypocrites!
B For ye compass sea and land to make one proselyte;
And when he has become so, 15
Ye make him twofold more a son of Gehenna than yourselves.

Woe unto you, scribes and Pharisees, hypocrites! 14
C For ye devour widows' houses,
Even while for a pretense ye make long prayers:
Therefore ye shall receive the greater condemnation.

Woe unto you, scribes and Pharisees, hypocrites! 23
D For ye tithe *mint* and *anise* and *cummin*,
And have left undone the weightier matters of the law,
Justice and *mercy* and *faith:*[1]
Ye blind guides, that strain out the gnat, but the camel swallow. 24

Woe unto you, scribes and Pharisees, hypocrites! 25
For ye cleanse the outside of the cup and the platter,
C′ But within they are full of extortion and excess.
Thou blind Pharisee, 26
Cleanse first the inside of the cup and the platter,
That the outside thereof may become clean also.

Woe unto you, scribes and Pharisees, hypocrites! 27
For ye are like unto whited sepulchres, which outwardly appear beautiful,
But inwardly are full of dead men's bones and of all uncleanness.
B′ Even so ye also: 28
Outwardly ye appear righteous unto men,
But inwardly ye are full of hypocrisy and iniquity.

[1] In vs. 23 the words, "but these . . . undone," appear to be extraneous to the form. In Lk. 11:42 these words are missing from MS D. The words appear to have been added for the purpose of saving ritual practices under the Law from the implied condemnation (cf. Matt. 23:3; 5:18).

Woe unto you, scribes and Pharisees, hypocrites! 29
For ye build the sepulchres of the prophets,
And garnish the tombs of the righteous, and say,
A′ If we had been in the days of our *fathers*, 30
We would not have been partakers with them in the blood of the *prophets*,
Wherefore ye witness to yourselves that ye are sons of them that slew the
Fill ye up also the measure of your *fathers*. 32 (*prophets*. 31

Woe unto you, blind guides that say, 16

[Whosoever shall swear by *heaven*, it is nothing;
But whosoever shall swear by the (throne) of heaven, he is a debtor.
A Ye fools and blind:
For which is greater, the (throne),
Or the heaven that sanctified the (throne)?]

[And] whosoever shall swear by the *temple*, it is nothing; 16b
But whosoever shall swear by the gold of the temple, he is a debtor.
B Ye fools and blind: 17
For which is greater, the gold,
Or the temple that sanctifieth the gold?

And whosoever shall swear by the *altar*, it is nothing; 18
But whosoever shall swear by the gift that is upon it, he is a debtor.
C Ye [fools and] blind: 19
For which is greater, the gift,
Or the altar that sanctifieth the gift?

C′ He therefore that sweareth by the *altar*, 20
Sweareth by it, and by all things thereon.

B′ And he that sweareth by the *temple*, 21
Sweareth by it, and by him that dwelleth therein.

A′ And he that sweareth by *heaven*, 22
Sweareth by the throne of God, and by him that sitteth thereon.

Comparative Outlines of Matt. 23:1-32 and Lk. 11:42-52

Introduction, vss. 1-3.
A Description of the Jewish leaders: aloofness, vs. 4. 4
B General statement of their motive: "to be seen of men," vs. 5a.
C Ostentation in regard to dress, vs. 5b.[2]
D Ostentation in regard to places of honor, vs. 6[3] 2
E Ostentation in regard to salutations, vs. 7[3]
E′ One only is Teacher, vs. 8.
D′ One only is Father, vs. 9.
C′ One only is Leader, vs. 10.
B′ General statement of the Christian ideal: service, vs. 11.
A′ Description of the Christian leaders: humility, vs. 12.

[2] Not used in the Woes, but in Lk. 20:46, and derived from Mk. 12:38, 39.
[3] DE are combined by Lk. Cf. ἐν ταῖς συναγωγαῖς and ἐν ταῖς ἀγοραῖς.

A Their violence: preventing by force entrance to the kingdom of heaven, vs. 13. 6
B Their evil influence: making converts "twofold more a son of Gehenna," vs. 15.
C Their greed: "devouring widow's houses," vs. 14 (cf. "extortion" in C′), vs. 14.
D Externalism *versus* spirituality: two central triplets, vss. 23, 24. 1
C′ Ostentation: the outside; *and* greed: "extortion," vss. 25, 26.[4]
B′ Ostentation: the outside; *and* evil: "dead men's bones" (cf. Gehenna, B), vss. 27, 28 3
A′ Ostentation: garnished tombs; *and* violence: "filling up the measure," vss. 29-32. 5

Lk. 11:42-52

A Externalism *versus* spirituality, vs. 42. 1
B Ostentation in regard to places of honor *and* salutations, vs. 43. 2
C Hidden tombs, vs. 44. 3
D Interlude: the lawyers and Jesus, cf. Matt. 23:2.
A′ Their aloofness, vs. 46. 4
B′ Building the tombs of the prophets, vss. 47, 48 (and vss. 49-51). 5
C′ Preventing men by force from entering the kingdom of heaven, vs. 52. 6

The Discourse against the Pharisees opens with a few introductory remarks (vss. 1-3) after which the discourse proper follows in three distinct parts. The first part extends through vss. 4-12, the second through vss. 13-32, and the third through vss. 33-39. We shall first discuss the structure of these parts, then examine some textual problems revealed by the examination of the whole discourse and the corresponding material in Luke, with a view of showing that the priority of composition must be ascribed to Matthew and that there exists a literary dependency of Luke upon Matthew.

In the first part (vss. 4-12) we discover a chiastic structure of not less than ten members. The first section (A), describing the aloofness of the spiritual leaders of Israel, is chiastic, since references to the shoulders and fingers are in the two central lines, and the verbs setting forth two contrasts of behavior occur in the extremes. This description of the Jewish leaders is paralleled by another section (A′), which by way of contrast describes the humility of the Christian leaders. The chiastic form is very striking, and its rhythmic quality is such that it easily serves as a signal that the reader is concluding the first part and is about to pass over to the second.

The single line (B) introduces the principle of ostentation,

[4] Not used in the Woes, but in Lk. 11:39, 40. Observe how *both* eliminations (vs. 5b and vss. 25, 26) are *first* in a series of three sections on ostentation.

which is said to dominate the conduct of the Jewish leaders. This line is the text of which the following three couplets are the exposition. These couplets deal with ostentation in dress (C), in places of honor (D), and in titles (E). These couplets are so regular in structure that they remind one of hundreds of similar couplets in the poetic books of the Old Testament. We have now reached the centre of the structure. The following three couplets are evidently intended as contrasting statements of what the Christian leaders should observe. There is a threefold repetition of the word "one" in the second line of each couplet; this is very emphatic. The point made by these statements is that the disciples should give attention, not to themselves, but to Christ, who alone is worthy of the titles. Teacher is parallel to Rabbi (EE′). Father was a common title of distinction among the Jews (cf. Pirke Aboth, "Sayings of the Fathers"). There may be a contrast also between their vain aspirations to places of honor (D) and the highest place held by God (D′). We may hold that the unusual size of the tassels and the phylacteries (C) in some way was supposed to indicate their religious leadership, and that they therefore are in contrast to the Christian ascription of leadership to Christ alone (C′). The single line (B′) may not be assimilated by either C′ or A′, for these are perfect structures which may not be disrupted. The single line is evidently a summary of what ought to be the Christian attitude. Instead of useless ostentation they should substitute real service. Instead of claims to distinction in dress, places of honor, and titles they should forego all distinction and seek the humbler position of a servant. One can hardly imagine a briefer and more pointed contrast than the one drawn in this chiastic structure. The turning point is, as always, in the centre.

The second part of the discourse (vss. 13-32) consists of the Seven Woes. Why they are regarded as seven and not eight and why the reading in vs. 14 is accepted as the original third woe rather than the present third woe (vss. 16-22) will be explained presently, when the whole structure has been discussed. Accepting provisionally the text as it is here given, we observe that the first three woes are of equal length and of similar structure. The first line gives the regular formula of address; the second, introduced by ὅτι, gives the reason for denouncing the leaders. This is then elaborated in the next two lines. These sections accuse the leaders of preventing men from entering the kingdom (A), of making proselytes twice worse than themselves (B), and of devouring widows' houses while pretending to hold long prayers (C). All three sections deal with the relations of the leaders to their fellows. There are no chiastic forms in these sections.

When the fourth, or central section, is reached, a great change occurs in the structure. The introductory formula is identical with the others, but in addition this section concludes with another formula of address, "Ye blind guides." This is the only instance in the series, and it is significant that it should be found in the central section of the seven. We have frequently observed how the centre of structures is adorned with triplets. In this case "mint, anise, and cummin" are balanced by "justice, mercy, and faith." The following words, "These ye ought to have done, and the others not have left undone," (vs. 23), introduce a disturbing element into the otherwise perfect chiasmus. We observe that in Luke 11:42 the triplets are destroyed, but these words are kept except in MS D, where vs. 42b is missing. Their presence in some MSS of Lk. 11:42 Harnack regards as due to interpolation from Mattt. 23:23b. The form of that passage, however, indicates that they are probably extraneous even there.

Probably MS D has preserved the original text of the Common Source. Matt. 23:23b, then, is an editorial gloss, which is strictly in line with 23:3; 5:18 and other additions, the purpose of which is to guard the sanctity of the law. This "tendency of Matthew,"[5] then, should not be ascribed to the original draft. It seems to be the result of editorial activity. Harnack's suggestion that "the weightier matters of the law," which are in conflict with vs. 4, are *therefore* eliminated by Luke carries less weight, for here the *truly* weighty matters, justice, mercy, and faith, are mentioned; this is not the case in vs. 4. It should be said that, though the elimination of vs. 23b seems justified both on textual and literary grounds, the presence of these words would not

[5] Harnack, *The Sayings of Jesus*, pp. 96, 101.

seriously disturb the form of the section. This section again presents in striking contrast two ideals in religion in triplet form. This is merely a repetition of the procedure already observed in the six couplets in vss. 4-12. The section concludes with a chiastic turn to the last line, namely, "strain out/the gnat,/but the camel/swallow," which in this verse, as in vs. 12, gives the signal that we are to pass from one part to another. When compared to the first three, the following three sections show a considerable change both in form and content.

The three sections C′B′A′ have the same introductory formula in the first line as the preceding sections have; the second line, introduced by ὅτι, carries the condemnation of the leaders. The development of this thought, however, results in a series of three *alternating* lines (C′B′) and in a concluding chiastic structure in A′ (cf. vss. 12, 24). In a very emphatic manner the difference between the inside and the outside is set forth, i.e., between the externalism of the old religious order and the spirituality of the new. This means that the keynote sounded by the two triplets in D is still the subject of the three following sections. When we compare the second part (vss. 13-32) with the first (vss. 4-12), we observe that the subject of *ostentation* is dwelt on in the *first* three couplets (CDE) in vss. 4-12 and in the *last* three sections (C′B′A′) in vss. 13-32. In other words, these two parts are written as one literary unit, in which the inverted order prevails also with reference to the contents of its separate sections. Those leaders who do all their works "to be seen of men" (vs. 5) are the same who are merely concerned about "the outside." Whether we are dealing with "the cup and the platter" (C′) or "the whited sepulchres" (B′) or "the garnished tombs" (A′), the theme is the same throughout all the different variations. We find, then, that a fine sense of literary balance is maintained in the first and second half of the discourse, partly by the two triplets at the centre, and partly by the manner in which the sections dealing with ostentation have been distributed. We shall see later how this sense of balance was appreciated by Luke and taken into account in his use of the material in the Common Source.

As yet we have made no attempt to justify our arrangement of the Seven Woes in a chiastic structure, but a glance at their content, as they now stand in our arrangement, will disclose parallelisms. Beginning at the centre and working toward both ends we first find that the third woe deals with the greed of the leaders in "devouring widow's houses" (C), while the fifth accuses them of "extortion and excess" (C′). The former of these two terms indicates unrighteous acquisition of property (cf. Heb. 10:34). In the next woe the leaders are accused of making a proselyte "twofold more a son of Gehenna" than themselves (B), and in the parallel woe they are said to be "full of hypocrisy and iniquity" (B′). There is also a parallelism of related ideas in the term Gehenna, on the one hand, and "the whited sepulchres" and the "dead men's bones," on the other. Finally, we may regard the action of preventing men from entering the kingdom of heaven (A) as involving the use of force against them (cf. 1 Thess. 2:14-16). Thus we would have a close parallel to the use of violence mentioned in the seventh woe (A′).

There is, then, a parallelism of ideas in these Seven Woes which justifies their present chiastic arrangement. As we pass over the centre of the structure we also become conscious of a climactic emphasis. We pass from greed to hypocrisy and iniquity, and from these to actual deeds of violence; we also become aware of the gradual *lengthening* of the woes until we reach the seventh, which contains more material than any of the preceding. The whole series winds up with a chiastic structure of four lines (vss. 30-32) in which the references to the "fathers" are placed in the extreme lines and the "prophets" are referred to in the two central lines. In all four instances the terms are found at the *end* of the lines. That such chiastic embellishments occur only at strategic points in the system cannot be accidental (cf. vss. 12, 24, 30-32). By these forms the writer introduces a perceptible change in the rhythm of the sentence which may serve as guidance for reader and audience alike that they are now to pass from one line of thought to another. The nearest example of this procedure in English literature would be the rhymed couplets that conclude some of the scenes in the dramas of Shakespeare. If these discourses in Matthew owe their present form to the fact that they were intended for liturgical use in the church, both the climax and the rhythm become intelligible.

We are now to consider the textual problem of vs. 14, which the Authorized Version places in the text and the Revised Version relegates to the margin. *Textus Receptus* places vs. 14 after vs. 13, but the verse is deleted from the text by most modern editors and regarded as an interpolation from Mk. 12:40 and Lk. 20:47 into the Greek text of Matthew. Some editors place the verse *before* our vs. 13, but in most cases it follows vs. 13. This woe has been included in our arrangement because the present third woe (vss. 16-22) cannot possibly have been the original third woe in the series. In vs. 14, on the other hand, we have a woe, which exactly corresponds in length and in structure to the other two (AB). For structural reasons, therefore, it must be regarded as part of the series. Its *position* in the series is fixed after rather than before vs. 15 because of its *content*, which is manifestly parallel to that of the fifth woe (C′). The original woe (vs. 14) was displaced by the present third woe in vss. 16-22, probably because this woe was regarded as a stronger expression of judgment against the greed of the Jewish leaders. The original woe, having been displaced, nevertheless, was not forgotten, but is found in the MSS, however uncertain its location in the text might have been. The presence of this woe in the text of Mk. 12:40 and Lk. 20:47 would prove, if our hypothesis is accepted, that the woe was present in the text of the Common Source.

There are three objections against accepting vss. 16-22 as the original third woe of the series. It has a remarkable variation in its introductory formula, "Woe unto you, blind guides," whereas in the other six instances the formula reads, "Woe unto you, scribes and Pharisees, hypocrites." This feature alone is sufficient to arouse suspicion in regard to its claim to a place in the series. The suspicion is confirmed, when we observe that this woe has four times as much material as any of the first two woes. It is the *structure* of the woe, however, which makes it necessary to exclude it from the series. The designation of the Pharisees as "blind guides" occurs in 15:14; 23:24. There is, however, a much stronger connection between this woe and another section dealing with swearing in 5:34-37. That passage begins and ends with a general statement about swearing; between these statements occur four couplets which list things by which men are in the habit of swearing. The climax is a descending one: heaven, earth, Jerusalem, and the head. A similar climax, but of the ascending order, may be discovered in the threefold statement of 23:20-22, namely, altar, temple, and heaven. In view of the fact that these verses sum up *three* things by which men are in the habit of taking oaths and since the last-mentioned, heaven, is the most important of the three, one naturally looks for its counterpart at the beginning of the passage. Though the words are missing in the present text, the stereotyped form of the other two passages dealing with the altar and the temple makes plausible an approximate reconstruction of the missing counterpart to the term *heaven*. In the text as printed in the reconstruction above, the added material is found within brackets.

The scheme of each section is uniform. The leaders are represented as teaching that swearing by the whole is futile, but that swearing by a part is more effectively binding the person who takes the oath. The first half of each system carries the statement of the case and the last half its refutation. It is assumed that the central formula of address, "Ye fools and blind" (vs. 17), was uniform both for vs. 19 and for the reconstructed section (A) as well. For the tendency of such terms to gravitate toward the centre of a system several examples are at hand (cf. 7:5; 15:7; 15:14, which occur at the centre of systems or in central sections). This is, of course, due to the habit of writers to make a fresh start at the centre of the system and to devote the latter half to another phase of the question. Accepting the reconstruction, we would then have a structure of six parts, of which the first three would be brief chiastic structures of uniform pattern and the last three parts, uniform couplets. The principle which makes the writer use the first half of each chiastic structure to the statement of the proposition and the last half for its refutation, is also applied to the whole passage; for the three couplets fulfill this function. They demonstrate how illogical such casuistry really is.

Such is the structure of vss. 16-22. If we accept in general the hypothesis that the Seven Woes originally were a series designed to be a well-balanced statement in accordance with certain literary and liturgical patterns then in vogue among Jewish Christians in Palestine, a glance at vss. 16-22 will show that this material does not fit the pattern, whereas vs. 14 makes a very excellent section, both in regard to content and form. But if the present third woe has been substituted for the original third woe (vs. 14) we must find a reason for such a procedure. Fortunately, the reason is not difficult to find. The original woe denounced the greed of those who "devoured widow's houses" on the pretense of making long prayers. Now, vss. 16-22 evidently deal with the same subject, though in a more effective way. The fine-spun casuistry in regard to oaths has for its purpose to make men more securely "debtors," i.e., bind them in their pledges. The substitution therefore may be explained on the ground that these verses were felt to be more elaborate and effective in exhibiting the foolishness and blindness of the Jewish leaders in their efforts to make men feel responsibility for the revenues of the sanctuary. The first section (A) was left out, partly because of brevity and partly because it was felt to be only remotely connected with the end in view, while the sections dealing with the altar and the temple were retained as being more to the point. It is obviously very difficult, if not altogether impossible, to bring into line an editorial adjustment which has for its purpose to sharpen the already violent attack upon the Pharisees with other editorial remarks, such as 5:18, 23:3, 23b, which seem to look after the interests of the Law. The textual history of the gospel, however, has undoubtedly subjected it to more than one influence of which there may be traces in its present text. In search of such traces observance of chiastic and alternating structures and of the frequent numerical arrangements may provide us with a new approach to the problem.

The two parts of the discourse which we have now analyzed are more intimately connected with one another by literary structure and content than is the third part (vss. 33-39). We shall therefore defer our treatment of this part to a later stage and immediately proceed with a comparative study of Matt. 23:1-32 and Lk. 11:42-52. The first impression given by these two accounts of the woes is that there can be no literary connection between them. The first impression, however, will have to be revised after we have carefully considered *the manner in which Luke diverges* from Matthew's account of the discourse. It will be shown that his divergencies may be reduced to a definite method, which, in its turn, may be explained only on the basis of some sort of literary relationship between Luke and Matthew or between both and the Common Source.

Before attempting the analysis of the two accounts we observe that some material which is found in Matthew is eliminated in the Lucan account of the woes. Matt. 23:5 which describes the phylacteries and the tassels does not appear among the woes of Luke. In a modified form ("long robes") we find a reference to the passage in Lk. 20:46, and the context clearly shows that it is derived from Mk. 12:38, 39. The fact that this material is used elsewhere in Luke would not in itself be a sufficient reason for eliminating it from Luke's version of the woes, for the references to salutations and places of honor are made use of by Luke in two places (cf. Lk. 11:43; 20:46). It is obviously the Jewish character of the phylacteries and the tassels that prompts him to change them into "long robes."

The next passage that has been eliminated from the Lucan account of the woes is Matt. 23:25, 26, "the outside of the cup and the platter." The reason is that this material has been used already in the account of the dinner in the Pharisee's house which immediately precedes (Lk. 11:39, 40). The mere fact that these two passages have been eliminated from the Lucan account of the woes is well known and is of comparatively little interest to us. But if the reader will make a comparison, he will find that 23:5 is found in the *first* couplet (C) dealing with ostentation, and that 23:25-26 is taken from the *first* woe dealing with ostentation (C′). Although these facts, considered alone, appear to have little significance, in the light of other facts of a similar nature, that which at first sight might be taken as a mere coincidence is proven to be a part of a definite editorial method.

The two comparative outlines given above (pp. 285-6) will facilitate a study of the two discourses. The figures in the right margin of the outlines indicate the order of the woes in Luke's version. A comparison of these figures reveals at a glance Luke's editorial method. He has had before him an account of the discourse substantially the same *in structure* to the one already analyzed in Matthew. His method may be reduced to two definite laws. In the first place he begins by selecting from the second part of the discourse (vss. 13-32), then moves to the first part (vss. 4-12), and keeps moving back and forth until he has exhausted his material. For want of a better name we may call this procedure the *pendulum method* of selection. While we thus follow the selections made by this method, we become aware of another method as definite as the first. Luke selects for his first woe the central woe (D). A glance at the figures at the right margin shows that while he moves between the two parts of the discourse, he also moves in a definite order *from the centre* of each chiastic structure *toward the extremes*. We may designate this his *centrifugal method* of selection. With the selection of his fifth woe he has reached the limits of the structure in vss. 13-32, but, still maintaining the pendulum method, he moves clear across the whole structure to the beginning and selects Matthew's first woe for his sixth. We may ask the question: Why is it that Luke makes no selection from 23:8-12 and from vss. 13-15, i.e., until he has exhausted his material and is compelled to do so for his *last* woe? The answer to this question is quite clear. Luke has observed and appreciated both the content and the literary structure of the discourse. He lays his finger on the crux of the matter, the contrast between externalism and spirituality, as expressed in the two central triplets (Matt. 23:23). From this starting point he goes to those couplets of the first part and to those woes of the second which deal with the ostentation of the leaders. Had he not eliminated the couplets dealing with the phylacteries and the tassels (C) and the title of Rabbi (E) because they were too Jewish, he would never have had any occasion to depart from his two methods of selection. As it now is, the selection for his *fourth* and *sixth* woes carries him beyond the material which in the structure is devoted to ostentation. In regard to the sixth woe only does he depart from the centrifugal method.

Not only Luke's selection, but his rejection of material as well, indicates a definite and ascertainable method. Could we obtain such results as these unless the theory of Luke's dependency on a document in structure similar to our Matthew is correct? This document is none other than the Common Source from which most of the Q material is derived.

For our purpose it is not necessary to insist upon a source in the Aramaic language from which the Common Source is a translation. We only postulate an origin of the Common Source in a community in which the Hebrew cultural heritage and the literary models of the Old Testament were still appreciated, whether in Jerusalem, in Galilee, or in Antioch.[6] When the Aramaic specialists have determined what constitutes Aramaisms and have determined to what extent these exist in the gospels, we shall know whether or not there was an underlying Aramaic gospel. That there was a Common Source in Greek the Q material indicates; and that this source was produced in a community where Hebrew cultural influences prevailed the chiastic structures in the discourses of Matthew show clearly.

If, however, Luke was acquainted with these structures, why does he not preserve them? The answer is, that they were Hebrew and not Greek. However such structures might have appealed to a Jew, to a Greek they must have looked like unnecessary repetition. It is easily seen when we compare smaller sections of Matthew (where these forms are perfect) with parallel sections in Luke (where the forms break down) that some such motive of taste underlies the modifications. The failure to repeat a word, the recasting of the order of the sentence, the elimination of a term or two, or the substitution of one for another—all these things are done by Luke with a Greek interest in style, but they result in destruction of much of that which is characteristic in Matthew's style. A comparison of the third part of the discourse against the Pharisees (vss. 33-39) with the Lucan version of it will serve as an illustration of many other such modifications as are found in Luke.

[6] Carl H. Kraeling, "The Jewish Community at Antioch," *Journal of Biblical Literature,* Vol. LI, Pt. II, pp. 130-160.

A Ye serpents, ye offspring of vipers, 33
How shall ye escape the judgment of Gehenna?

Therefore, behold, I send unto you prophets, 34
And wise men,
B And scribes:
Some of them shall ye kill and crucify,
And some of them shall ye scourge in your synagogues,
And ye shall persecute from city to city.

That upon you may come all the righteous blood shed on the earth, 35
B′ From the blood of Abel the righteous
Unto the blood of Zechariah son of Barachiah,
Whom ye slew between the sanctuary and the altar.

A′ Verily I say unto you, 36
All these things shall come upon this generation.

A O Jerusalem, Jerusalem, that killeth the prophets, 37
And stoneth them that are sent unto her—

How often would I
Have gathered together thy children,
B Even as a hen
Gathereth her chickens under her wings,
And ye would not.

Behold, your house is left unto you desolate; for I say unto you, 38
A′ Ye shall not see me henceforth, till ye shall say, 39
Blessed is he that cometh in the name of the Lord.

The conclusion to the discourse contains two distinct parts, one of which (vss. 33-36) sets forth Israel's treatment of divine messengers sent to her (BB) and the resulting judgment (AA′); and the other (vss. 37-39) describes her attitude toward the same messengers (AA′) whose coming were an expression of divine compassion (B). A comparison with Lk. 11:49-51, shows that vs. 33, then, is removed, yet in substance occurs in Lk. 3:7b; that vs. 34 is a quotation from "The Wisdom of God," which phrase is missing in Matthew; that the three classes of messengers are reduced to "prophets and apostles" (Lk. 11:49); that the three types of sufferings allotted symmetrically in the alternating lines are also reduced to two; that the well-balanced chiastic vs. 35 is disrupted in various ways; that, finally, the balance of vs. 36 with vs. 33 in the words "offspring" and "generation" also disappears.

Comparing vss. 37-39 to Lk. 13:34, 35 we are particularly interested in section B which in Matthew is a fine chiastic structure.

The perfect balance of the words in lines 1 and 5, with their striking contrast between the Lord's will and the will of the Jews, and the identical word order of lines 2 and 4 disappear in Luke. The failure to repeat the verb "gathereth," when it occurs the second time and the placing of the pronoun "her" between the article and the noun, are slight changes indeed, but they are disastrous to the form. Here, as in other such instances, our conclusion is that Matthew has preserved the original form, which is broken down in Luke for purely stylistic reasons.[7]

This treatment of chiastic style is typical in Luke. We may take almost any passage like Matt. 5:10-12; 6:32, 33; 7:15-20 and find that forms which are perfect in Matthew break down in Luke. Of the long structure in Matt. 6:25-31 Luke has preserved almost all, but how it has changed in form! The triplets in 6:25, 31 and the euphonious endings of the lines in vss. 26, 28 (we may almost call it rhyme), have all disappeared in Lk. 12:22-31. Yet, these stylistic features must have been in his source, for he gives the passage about the two masters in perfect chiastic form (Lk. 16:13). The reason for retaining the form of this passage lies probably in the rapid contrasts between the two masters, which were acceptable even to a Greek sense of style.

The saying about finding and losing one's life offers an interesting study of what happens to a chiastic form in the different versions of it. The paradox occurs in its original form in Matt. 10:39, a chiastic structure of six members.[8] The phrase "for my sake" is probably added in the interest of clarity. This perfect symmetry breaks down to some extent in Lk. 17:32. The saying also occurs in a less balanced form in Matt. 16:25 and Lk. 9:24, but this form again breaks down by the additional phrase, "and the gospel's" sake, in Mk. 8:35. The criterion by which the originality is to be determined must be, in either case, the regularity of the form. This would at all events be true of paradoxes in general, but especially if they are chiastic.

In Matt. 11:25-30 a well-known passage, whose "Johannine" character has caused a good deal of discussion, offers an interesting

[7] Harnack, *op. cit.*, pp. 29, 30 and 103, 104.
[8] Cf. Structure in *Missionary Discourse*, Matt. 10:39.

example of what may happen to chiastic structures in the hands of Luke.

At that season Jesus answered and said, 25
I thank thee, Father, Lord of heaven and earth,
A That thou didst hide these things from the wise and understanding,
And didst reveal them unto babes:
Yea, Father, for so it was well-pleasing in thy sight. 26

All things have been delivered unto me of my Father, 27
And no one knoweth the Son,
B Save the Father;
Neither the Father
Doth any one know, save the Son,
And he to whom the Son willeth to reveal him.

Come unto to me, all ye that labor and are heavy laden, 28
And I will give you rest.
C Take my yoke upon you and learn of me; 29
For I am meek and lowly in heart:
And ye shall find rest unto your souls.
For my yoke is easy, and my burden is light. 30

There is a progressive thought developed in these three sections. In A Jesus speaks of his Father (lines 1, 4), his sovereignty and his will, and the revelation, hidden to one class and revealed to another (lines 2, 3). What "these things" are (i.e., the object of his revelation) we learn in B. It is a revelation mediated by the Son, to whom it has been "delivered," and who therefore may reveal it to "whom he willeth" (lines 1, 6). The substance of it is a true knowledge of the Father. The occurrence of the principal terms at the *end* of each line renders the parallelism particularly striking (cf. Matt. 23:30-32). Section C presents the conclusion of the preceding development. If Jesus does reveal the true knowledge of the Father, then all men ought to come to him and learn, and, in learning the true knowledge about the Father, find rest to their souls. The symmetry of this section is exceedingly striking, two items in lines 1, 6, and two in lines 3, 4. The word "rest" is common to lines 2, 5, and in Greek "heavy laden" and "burden" are related words. It would seem that the symmetry of the three sections is perfect and that there is little difficulty in tracing the development of thought in them. They are evidently a unity, the separate parts of which should not be divided, or apportioned among several sources.

Turning now to Luke 10:21-22 what can we discover? Luke gives section A precisely in the words of Matthew with a slight change of the introductory formula. Section B is reproduced in content, but its form is broken up by eliminating the prefix of the verb, by failure to repeat it the second time, and by introducing the explanatory "who is." It would seem, once more, that the paradoxical brevity of Matthew is the more original form of the saying. Luke's elimination of the verb, when it recurs the second time, is really the only detail which destroys the symmetry, here as in Luke 13:34, while it is clear that the elimination makes for a more compact sentence. Section C is left out by Luke altogether. If there is any cogency in the attempt to show a unity of thought in the three sections, the conclusion must be that C also was found in the Common Source but was eliminated by Luke. This section, the content of which must have commended it to a writer with the social sympathies of Luke, was probably felt to be too Jewish because of the words, "Take my yoke upon you, and learn of me."

By assuming the unity of the three sections and their presence in the Common Source, we are committed to an early date (before 50 A.D.) and to a Palestinian locality. This would seem impossible in view of the "Johannine" character of B. We know very little, however, about the trends of thought that were current in Palestine during the first half of the first century among Jewish Christians. May it not be possible that ideas which we find fully developed in the Gospel of John half a century later were even in this early age current in some circles? The preference of John for "eternal life" instead of the Synoptic concept "the kingdom" is well known, yet the Synoptic gospels are not altogether without evidence that the two were identified even at an earlier date (cf. Matt. 19:16, 17, 23 together with Mk. 9:43, 45, 47). Although it may be impossible to fix the exact date, it would seem that the identification of "eternal life" with "the kingdom" was made earlier than the Gospel of John. Other Johannine ideas, no doubt, had had a long history before they were reduced to literary form in the gospel, and some of them may have been reduced to writing at a much earlier date. If so, our section B might well have been a part of the Common Source, as the presence of it in the first and third gospels indicates, and need not be regarded as an interpolation at a later date.[9]

Nor is it necessary to relate the "knowledge" of which it speaks to a purely Hellenistic Gnosis. If, as Montefiore has pointed out (p. 176), there are rather close parallels to this whole passage in Sirach 51:1, 10, 26; Jer. 6:16, may it not be possible that his own decision (p. 184) that it is of Hellenistic and not Hebrew origin, should be reversed? Its presence in the Q material favors an early Palestinian date for vs. 27, and for the rest of the passage as well. This is, it would seem, a question entirely apart from the question of whether or not we have in vs. 27 an authentic saying of Jesus. The former decision should rest on historical and literary grounds and not be mixed up with the latter question, into which dogmatic presuppositions concerning the self-consciousness of Jesus of necessity will enter. It should also be recalled, that the connection between Matt. 11:25-30 and Sirach 51:1-30 is not merely one depending on a few phrases, but on the structure of the whole chapter. Sirach 51:1-12 deals with thanksgiving (vs. 1) and praise (vss. 11, 12), which is close to our section A. In the next part (51:13-22) the search for wisdom is described, which corresponds to the content of section B. Finally, 51:23-30 contains the invitation to share in the wisdom found, which certainly is closely parallel in sentiment and in *terms* to section C.

[9] Harnack, *op. cit.*, pp. 17-20, 135, 272-310; and for criticism, Montefiore, *op. cit.*, pp. 168-187; Norden, *Agnostos Theos*, pp. 302, 303.

CHAPTER XVI

THE DOINGS OF JESUS

In the preceding chapters we have discussed chiefly the sayings of Jesus, but in this chapter we shall deal with the doings of Jesus. To one who has become accustomed to the more elaborate classification of gospel materials used by the writers on "Formgeschichte" the two categories "sayings" and "doings" may seem too simple. For our present purpose, however, they are sufficient; they represent the classification that was in the mind of the gospel writers themselves (cf. Mk. 6:30; Lk. 24:19; Acts 1:1), and while employing them we are not imposing upon the materials that make up the content of our gospels factitious classifications that would have been disowned by the writers themselves.

In the following pages we shall endeavor to show how larger divisions in the gospels containing the doings of Jesus, or narrative material, have been constructed with the chiasmus as the organizing principle. A number of separate narrative units have been assembled by the gospel writer, forming a well-defined group, and the various members of this group are arranged so as to be parallel to one another. These stories that recited the doings of Jesus are obviously not told merely to convey so many items of information about Jesus, but in order to bring out some definite point relating to the person of Jesus. When all these members that constitute such a group are brought together and a comparative study of the parallel units in the group is made, they are found to contain a well-rounded presentation of some definite topic. Usually there is some phrase, question, proverb, example, or some other detail which shows that one unit is balanced by its corresponding unit in the same group. These features of the narrative units are so characteristic that they cannot fail to attract the reader's attention. The fact that they are the residue that lingers in the average Bible reader's mind merely proves how effectively the gospel writers have done their work in impressing the special point upon the mind of their public. In the early church when the gospels were heard in the assembly rather than read by the individual, these particular features of the gospel units must have impressed themselves more forcefully upon the constituency. When such details are specially indicated in the following outlines, it is done for the purpose of calling attention to some parallel feature in the corresponding member of the structure.

In Mk. 2:13-3:8 a group of passages such as described above is found, dealing with the Christian's attitude toward the Law.

By the seaside: "all the multitude."	2:13
Scribes and Pharisees: Why eat with sinners? Justifying example: A proverb about the physician.	14-17
Jesus' disciples and the Pharisees: Why not fast? Justifying example: A proverb about the sons of the bridechamber.	18-20
The guiding principle: The new patch on the old garment.	21
The guiding principle: The new wine in the old skins.	22
Jesus' disciples and the Pharisees: Why do it on the sabbath? Justifying example: David and the priests.	23-28
Pharisees and Herodians: Is it lawful on the sabbath day? Justifying example: the sheep in the pit (Matt. 12:11).	3:1-6
By the seaside: "a great multitude," with other details.	7-8

The function of this section of the gospel is evidently to set forth what the Christian position is in controversies about the Jewish law. The principle which should guide Christians in such conflicts is stated in the centre; how Jesus himself asserted this principle in controversy with the Jewish leaders is developed in four examples on either side of the centre. There is much uniformity in these four examples: there are antagonistic leaders present; they ask questions that bring out the point of the controversy; the answer is very similar in form, either a proverbial, easily remembered expression, or an example from sacred history or from life. In Mk. 3:1-6 the example of the sheep in the pit is lacking, but it seems probable that it was found in the Common Source, since the Q material used in Matt. 12:11 and Lk. 14:5 has preserved the allusion. For a local setting the seaside is given. Recalling the structure of Lev. 24:13-23 we are impressed by the similarity of the arrangement to the passage in the gospel. There the central principle—the law of retaliation—is surrounded by three specific applications of the law, which are also placed on either side of the centre, all of which has for its local setting the place of execution "without the camp." Such similarities suggest that the new Christian community in formulating its own rules was guided very largely by patterns already made familiar by the liturgical use of the Old Testament in the Synagogue.

We shall now turn to the gospel of Matthew in order to ascertain what disposition of the material in the group of Mark (2:13-3:8) has been made by the first evangelist. In order to obtain the proper perspective it will be necessary to introduce two outlines of the central portions of the gospel of Matthew, which may be designated E (4:12-11:6), "The Sayings and Doings of Jesus"; and E′ (11:7-14:12), "The Doings and Sayings of Jesus."[1]

Part E: The Sayings and Doings of Jesus, 4:12-11:6.

Jesus heard of John's arrest, cf. 4:12-24 with 9:35-11:6 (4:12).

The territory and the message: Israel, the kingdom of heaven (13-17).

Four disciples chosen (18-22).

General summary: Jesus' work is teaching, preaching, and healing.
His cures include disease, sickness, demons (23-24).

The Sayings of Jesus.

Great multitudes follow, go up into the mountain, and are taught (4:25-5:2).

The Sermon on the Mount, cf. detailed analysis in chapter XII (5:3-7:27).

Great multitudes follow, go down from the mountain, having been taught (7:28-8:1).

A general summary: (8:2-17)
Variety of diseases: leprosy, palsy, fever.
Variety of places: mountain (vs. 2), city (vs. 5), home (vs. 14).
Variety of method: touch and word (vss. 3, 4), word without touch (vs. 13), touch without word (vs. 15).
Jesus heals all sorts of diseases, in all sorts of places, and by all sorts of methods. This triplet form should be compared with the triplet form of the general summaries in 4:23-24 and 9:35-10:1.

[1] N. W. Lund, "The Influence of Chiasmus upon the Structure of the Gospel according to Matthew," *Anglican Theological Review*, Vol. XIII, No. 4, pp. 405-433, contains a full outline of the gospel.

The Doings of Jesus.

A believing scribe and another disciple: friendly to Jesus (8:19-22).

The tempest: they marvelled, "What manner of man is this"? (18, 23-27).

Two possessed men: cried, "Son of God" (publicity avoided, Mk. 5:19, 20) (28-34).

The paralytic: the faith of others; "Son, be of good cheer," blasphemy (9:1-8).

Pharisees: Why eat with sinners? A proverb: the physician (9-13).

Pharisees: Why not fast? A proverb: the sons of the bridechamber. The garment and the wine skins, vss. 16, 17 (14-17).

Jairus' daughter: (the faith of others, Mk. 5:36); the woman with an issue of blood: "Daughter, be of good cheer," ridicule (18-26).

Two blind men: cried, "Son of David," publicity avoided (27-31).

The dumb man: they marvelled, "It was never so seen in Israel" (32-33).

Unbelieving Pharisees (MSS D a and k omit vs. 34): hostile to Jesus (34).

General summary: Jesus' work is teaching, preaching, and healing. His cures include disease, sickness, demons (9:35-10:1).

Twelve disciples chosen (10:2-4).

The territory and the message: Israel (vss. 5, 6), the kingdom of heaven (vs. 7), to which is added the Missionary Discourse, setting forth the method (5-11:1).

John in prison heard of Jesus' work (cf. 9:35-11:6 with 4:12-24) (2-6).

The preceding outline shows that Part E (Matt. 4:12-11:6) has two frame-passages which enclose the whole. Beginning with 4:12 there are four sections which set forth in turn the following items: Jesus and John, the territory and the message, the choosing of disciples, and a concluding general summary of Jesus' work in which two triple statements occur. Comparing this frame-passage with the one beginning in 9:35 we find precisely the same trend of thought, with the exception that the order is here inverted. The only serious objection to this statement is the inclusion of Matt. 10:8-11:1, but this passage contains the Missionary Discourse which must be regarded as extraneous material which has been inserted, thus disturbing the balance of the original structure. The discourse, as we have already seen, is a literary unit by itself.

Within the two frame-passages we find one group of the sayings of Jesus, the Sermon on the Mount, with whose characteristics we have already been made familiar. The other group is made up of the doings of Jesus (8:19-9:34), and to set forth the characteristics of this group will be our immediate task in the following pages. Between these two well-defined groups there occurs a cluster of three miracles which may not under any circumstances be classified either with the preceding or following groups. The significance of Matt. 8:2-17 in the structural scheme of the gospel appears as soon as we observe the nature of the general summaries in the frame-passages, each describing the activities of Jesus in two triple statements. The three miracles at the centre of the structure, we conclude, are designed to teach more fully the scope of Jesus' activity, which the frame-passages treat only summarily. By slight touches of description we are informed of the variety of diseases Jesus cured, the variety of places in which he healed, and the variety of methods that he employed. These touches are all faithfully preserved in the gospel of Matthew.

In the group of narrative units designated as the doings of Jesus in the outline each unit is balanced by another in which the same point is set forth. Together they may be thought of as a series of mural panels in a long hall, painted in pairs on opposite walls. Thus 8:19-22 describe how a friendly scribe and another person were impressed by Jesus and wanted to follow him; in 9:34, on the other hand, unbelieving Pharisees dispute the authority of Jesus and ascribe his power to heal the afflicted to the prince of demons. The latter incident is textually uncertain for it is lacking in MSS D a and k which omit vs. 34. If we examine 8:18, we find that this verse is the introduction to the story of the tempest and has become separated from its original context by the insertion between vss. 18 and 23 of vss. 19-22. In several instances of our analysis of the discourses of Matthew we have had occasion to ask whether passages that break up or otherwise disturb the uniformity of the structure represent later editorial revisions of the gospel or modifications of the Common Source made by the original writer of the gospel. The same question must be raised with reference to the passage we are now considering; the former of the two alternatives seems the more probable.

The next unit contains the story of the tempest (8:18, 23-27). The power of Jesus over nature draws from the marvelling disciples the exclamation, "What manner of man is this?" In the parallel unit describing the healing of the dumb man (9:32-33) the multitudes also marvelled, saying, "It was never so seen in Israel." The story of the Gadarene demoniacs is in Matthew a *double* miracle (8:28-34), contrary to Mark's version. The two men cried out the confession that Jesus is "the son of God." In the story of the blind men we have another double miracle (9:27-31); the men cried out, "Thou son of David." These confessions contain the two Messianic titles of Jesus. The arrangement of parallel panels containing the titles of Jesus is a regular feature in the gospel of Matthew. In view of the many instances of symmetrical distribution of the divine names Yahweh and Elohim in parallel strophes in the psalms there is nothing surprising in this feature in Matthew. Once the liturgical nature of the gospel is acknowledged and then taken seriously the full significance of such phrases in parallel panels becomes clear.

In the healing of the two blind men Jesus places emphasis (9:30, 31) on their maintaining secrecy. This feature is missing in the story of the demoniacs as given by Matthew; but if we may lean on Mark 5:14, 15, 20 for further details we can there discover a similar reason for not permitting the man to follow Jesus. He is told to go home (vs. 19) but instead wanders all over Decapolis (vs. 20). In the habitual condensation of narrative material so characteristic of Matthew it sometimes happens that some such detail is left out, but in many instances it may be recovered from Mark, who in those instances doubtless has preserved the significant detail from the Common Source. The need of secrecy is one of the major interests of the gospel of Matthew and is taken care of in various ways, either by placing expressions of it in parallel positions or by placing them in the centre of structures (cf. the following outline of Part E′). The fact that two double miracles which are peculiar to Matthew should be found in parallel position in one of his structures is a strong confirmation of our hypothesis of chiastic structures. The natural conclusion seems to be that the Common Source contained the story of more than one blind man, for the summary in 11:5 reads, "the blind" (plural) "receive their sight." When this statement is repeated in Lk. 7:22

it is accompanied by an explanatory remark in vs. 21, for Luke has not up to this point recorded any healings of blind men.

The story of the paralytic (9:1-8) is matched by the story of the raising of Jairus' daughter (9:18-26). In the latter story, however, has been included a recital of what happened while Jesus was on his way (vss. 20-22). Wernle has observed what he calls Mark's habit of "uniting incidents by enveloping one within the other." He explains this feature as part of what he calls "the connective machinery of Mark."[2] Be this as it may, on the hypothesis adopted of parallel panels which have for their function to present similar points relating to the person of Jesus, the inclusion of the section about the woman with an issue of blood in the story of the raising of Jairus' daughter receives a natural explanation. Jesus is represented in the one story as saying to the paralytic, "Son, be of good cheer," and in the other as saying to the woman, "Daughter, be of good cheer." The press of the crowd is featured in Mark's account (cf. 2:1-4; 5:25), though left to the imagination in the more condensed account of Matthew. Jesus' cheerful words to the two persons who sought him under such adverse circumstances reveal how accessible the Master was. That Jesus heals because of the faith of others is explicitly stated in the case of the paralytic (9:2), but merely implied in the case of Jairus' daughter (9:18). If we may, once more, lean on Mk. 5:36, this feature was also clearly expressed in the Common Source, for Jesus says to the father, "Fear not, only believe." Finally we have a dramatic presentation of the two reactions of men toward Jesus. On the one hand we have the unbelieving mass that "laughs him to scorn" (9:24), and scribes that say within themselves, "This man blasphemeth" (9:3); but on the other we have also those who "were afraid and glorified God" (vs. 8) together with the statement that "this fame went forth in all the land" (vs. 26). When we observe that the words of Jesus, "Son (daughter), be of good cheer" are peculiar to Matthew, and that they occur only in the two panels in the structure that are parallel, we begin to appreciate the degree of careful planning that is evinced by such structures. Taken together with the parallel position of the two double mir-

[2] Paul Wernle, *Sources of Our Knowledge of the Life of Jesus*, pp. 119 f.

acles in the same structure they constitute the strongest proof of the contention that such topical groups in Matthew are both chiastic and liturgical.

The two central units of the group are of about equal length, and they deal with the same topic, namely, the controversy between the old established order and the one newly initiated by Jesus. The parallel features of the two units are rather striking. In one (9:9-13) the Pharisees ask, "Why eateth your teacher with the publicans and the sinners?" In the other the disciples of John ask the question, but even here the Pharisees are in the picture, for the question is, "Why do we, *and the Pharisees*, fast often, but thy disciples fast not?" Evidently these two units are intended to illustrate the two aspects of the conflict with legalism in the early church, one fronting the Pharisees and the other the followers of John the Baptist, who, we have reason to believe, persisted as a separate movement even after the death of Jesus. The answers given to these questions are interesting, not only in content, but also in form. The answer to the one question is given in the form of a proverb (vs. 12), and the whole matter is clinched by a quotation from Hosea 6:6.

> "Mercy I desire,
> And *not* sacrifice."
> For I came not to call the righteous (who sacrifice),
> But sinners (who need mercy).

The chiasmus is here formed by adding comments to the quotation and this method of completing the structure in such fashion is illustrated more extensively by Matt. 13:13-18.

The answer to the second question reads as follows:

> Can the sons of the bridechamber *mourn*,
> As long as with them is the *bridegroom?*
> But come will the days when shall be taken away from them the *bridegroom*,
> And then will they *fast*.

This passage is purposely translated so as to maintain the Greek order of the sentence. When this is done the four main terms come at the end of the lines, thus giving a special emphasis to them. The association of mourning with fasting is made clear in Matt. 6:16. We have thus seen that these two units are similar in the manner in which the problem is put and the answer is given as well as in the technique employed in clinching the whole argument by a saying which is chiastic in form. This method of winding up a unit may be illustrated by Matt. 23:12, 24, and especially 30-32, for in the latter passage we have another instance where the four important terms in the chiasmus occur at the end of the lines. Assuming the Common Source to have been an early liturgical document used in the Palestinian community, it is natural to ascribe these mannerisms to that document from which it was taken over by Matthew. In Lk. 5:32, 34 and Mk. 2:17, 19, 20 all this symmetry breaks down, the third evangelist being dependent on the second at this point, and the second in his version of the words of Jesus probably showing what happens to the wording of a liturgical document when used freely in preaching and teaching.

Since, then, these two central units are complete in themselves and even have that formal clincher which we have discovered in other instances, why should vss. 16, 17 have been added, or rather retained in this position when they are structurally out of place? The answer is that Matthew found them in the Common Source in central position as indicated in Mk. 2:13-3:8. Recognizing them as expressing the fundamental Christian principle, he retained them, especially since adding vss. 16, 17 to the unit in vss. 14-15 would make this unit more equal in length to the other parallel unit in Matt. 9:9-13. That the compiler of the gospel of Matthew really has been concerned with the *length* of his units is shown first by his severe condensation of narrative material, and secondly, in those instances where he leaves out parts of triplets even when we know that they were in his sources (cf. Matt. 5:27-32). These two brief passages which convey the Christian principle of allowing new life to express itself in new forms are true chiastic structures, the second a little more ornate than the first.

No one puts a piece of undressed cloth
Upon an old garment;
For taketh the filling (patch) of it,
From the garment,
And worse the rent becomes. Matt. 9:16.

Neither do they put new *wine* into old skins,
Else burst
The skins
And the *wine* is spilled,
And the skins
Are destroyed;
But they put new *wine* in new wine-skins, and
both are preserved. Matt. 9:17.

The central portion of the gospel of Matthew comprises two longer parts, of which Part E has been given in outline above, and its corresponding Part E′ (11:7-14:12) is to follow. Matthew's plan calls for Part E, containing the Sayings and Doings of Jesus, and Part E′, containing the Doings and Sayings of Jesus. The following outline will serve to give orientation, although we may not discuss all its details. Some of its most striking sections have already come before us in the previous chapters.

Part E′: The Doings and Sayings of Jesus, 11:7-14:12.

John the Baptist: prophet, multitude, king's houses, a messenger only (11:7-19).

A critical generation: aloofness, wisdom, mighty works, Capernaum (20-24).

A receptive group: "these things" are revealed; may be learned from Jesus (25-30).

The Doings of Jesus.

Pharisees: "Why do it on the sabbath"? (12:1-8).
Justifying example: David and the priests.

Pharisees: "Is it lawful on the sabbath day"? (9-14).
Justifying example: The sheep in the pit.

The principle of secrecy: Isa. 42:1 ff. (15-21).

A demon cast out (22).

The Pharisees reject the signs of Jesus: (23-29).
Their sons shall be their judges.

Their sins of speech; the tree and the treasure (30-37).

The scribes and the Pharisees demand new signs from Jesus (38-42).
The Gentiles shall be their judges.

A demon returns with seven other demons (43-45).

A receptive group: Who belongs to the family of God? (46-50).

The Sayings of Jesus.

The Sower: a parable (13:1-9).
The principle of secrecy, Isa. 6:9 ff. (10-18).
The Sower: an interpretation (19-23).

The Tares: a parable of mixture (24-30).
The Mustard Seed: a parable of extensive growth (31-32).
The Leaven: a parable of intensive growth (33).
The principle of secrecy, Ps. 78:2. (34-35).
The Tares: an interpretation of the parable of mixture (36-43).

The Treasure: a parable (44).
The Pearl: a parable (45-46).
The Dragnet: a parable of mixture, with interpretation (cf. The Tares) (47-50).

A receptive group: "these things"; a disciple of the kingdom (51-52).

A critical generation: aloofness, wisdom, mighty works, "his own country" (53-58).

John the Baptist: prophet, multitude, the king's court, John's death (14:1-12).

Examining more closely Matt. 11:7-30 we find that it is another frame-passage setting forth in order the position of John the Baptist in regard to the new order of things in the church, the resistance of the present generation of Jews toward the influences of the gospel and the works of Jesus, and finally the presence of a receptive group who had received the revealed truth. The other frame-passage (13:51-14:12) contains the same topics but with their order inverted. There is a fine sense of balance preserved in the presentation of Jesus as the revealer of God, inviting men to take his yoke upon themselves (11:27, 29) and the description of the scribe who has understood all these things spoken by Jesus and who therefore is made a disciple of the kingdom (13:51, 52). A similar balance is maintained in the sections that give Jesus' words against Capernaum and the other Galilean cities (11:20-24) and describe his cool reception "in his own country" (13:53-58). Although John the Baptist is said to be greater than any man born of woman, he is nevertheless not as great as a member of the kingdom of God (11:11). That such a statement should be needed in a gospel read in the church is full of significance. Whatever competition there existed between the disciples of John and the Christians should have ceased in view of these words and the death of John as set forth in 14:1-12. There are several allusions that are common to both of these sections.

Between the frame-passages are installed the material dealing with the doings of Jesus, followed by a group of sayings, which is the exact reversal of the order in Part E. Among the doings we find the two passages dealing with the sabbath question (12:1-8 and vss. 9-14), which have been detached from their original structure as that has been preserved for us in Mk. 2:13-3:8. To these two units must be added vss. 22-45, for although they contain a great deal of discourse material they belong properly to the doings of Jesus. Although the discourse wanders far afield, it returns nevertheless to the miracle that gave occasion for the discourse (vss. 43, 45). There are three instances in which the secrecy of the gospel is emphasized (cf. 12:15-21; 13:10-18, and vss. 34, 35), and in every instance there is a quotation from the Old Testament. Whatever the function of these passages may have been in the scheme of the gospel, both by the quotations and by their position are they made prominent. A most conspicuous position is given to the passage in 12:46-50 by placing it in the centre. This passage introduces deftly a suggestion of opposition, or at least misunderstanding, from members of Jesus' own family, and concludes with introducing the larger family of all the children of God, which is merely another name for the kingdom of God (12:46-50). We thus find in the centre a suggestion of the two groups, critical and receptive, which are more fully described in the frame-passages. We are here reminded of the similar arrangement in the extremes and centre of Part E in the matter of general summaries.

It is not within our purpose to discuss at length the parables under the sayings of Jesus. Recalling, however, the grouping of parallel sections which we found so frequently in the Sermon on the Mount, it is difficult to escape the conclusion that these parables come from a larger collection which contained some kind of topical arrangement. The Mustard Seed and the Leaven, the

Treasure and the Pearl, the Tares and the Dragnet, expressing the ideas of the spread of the gospel, the value of salvation, and the far-from-ideal state of the Christian community of which the New Testament otherwise abundantly testifies, may well be conceived of as having occupied parallel positions in an early liturgical writing designed to be read in the church. Since the first part of E contained sayings of Jesus that set forth the life and conduct of Christians as it had been defined with reference to the Jew, on the one hand, and the Gentile, on the other, it was appropriate that the last part of E′ should also carry discourse material, dwelling on the broader aspects of Christianity in its relation to the world as a whole. Likewise the doings of Jesus in the last part of E, which led to controversies with the old established religious order of his day, are properly balanced by similar material in the first part of E′. In this controversy Jesus is accused of working his miracles by the aid of Beelzebub (12:24-28), which accusation, as we have already seen, had its parallel in the textually uncertain verse in 9:34. This verse and its counterpart in the structure by virtue of its position between 9:18 and vs. 23 create the suspicion of later editing. May we, perhaps, in the feeling for balance find the urge which led to the introduction of this material in the structure devoted to the doings of Jesus in Part E?

What view of Jesus would a section like the one outlined in Matt. 8:19-34, with its balanced panels and selected characteristic sayings, bring before the primitive Christian community assembled for worship? Going down our imaginary hall and looking at the parallel portraits of Jesus, what features of his person would we find represented by this early artist? Beginning at the extremes of the structure and working our way toward the centre we would in turn meet with the following descriptive touches, all centering in the personality of Jesus: that he was accepted by some friendly scribes and violently opposed by unbelieving Pharisees; that his miraculous powers extended, not only to men, but over the powers of nature as well, exciting the unbounded admiration, not only of his disciples, but of all men; that demon-possessed men knew him as Son of God and blind men as Son of David, but that these testimonies to his Messiahship compelled him, at least for a time, to veil himself in obscurity; that he at times healed people and resuscitated the dead, and that in doing it he acted because of the faith of others, and was exceedingly gracious, even when persons approached him under unfavorable circumstances; that all these activities led him into conflict with the reputed religious leaders of the established order, but that he defended himself by showing how the new spiritual life that he was bringing into the world must of necessity create new forms. These touches are deftly introduced by the evangelist into his portrait of Jesus, yet as soon as his technique is discovered there can be little doubt as to where he places the emphasis. If we look for the origin of his technique, we need not wander far afield in the Hellenistic world to discover the masters under which he has studied or the models that he has reproduced, for they are all found in the Old Testament, whether the original Hebrew or the Septuagint version.

During the analysis of the preceding units we have encountered many of those characteristics which Dibelius[3] ascribes to the *paradigm*. These units contain a minimum of detail; they all emphasize some definite point, expressed by a brief saying by Jesus, or some other person, or by a collective statement of the by-standers. That the use of such illustrative stories about Jesus in missionary preaching should result in a stereotyped form seems probable. We need not assume, however, that missionary propaganda is the *only* cause that would produce such an effect. For it would seem that all these influences that the proponents of "Formgeschichte" postulate to explain the present stereotyped form of the narrative material in the gospels would be in operation, and even to a greater extent, in the compilation of a liturgical document like our Matthew. There would be, first of all, a great need of economizing with space in order to make the document as rich in content as possible within the given limits; the need of religious and didactic content in liturgical writings is evident; to sharpen the point which the narrative was intended to convey would be even more necessary in reading than in preaching, since explana-

[3] Martin Dibelius, *From Tradition to Gospel* (English translation by Bertram Lee Woolf, London: 1934), pp. 44 ff.

tory remarks or gestures would be out of order. If the idea was to convey to a Christian audience the position that the Master himself took in regard to the problems that agitated the early church, nothing could be more appropriate than to quote his own words at the end of the illustrative anecdote. There is probably nothing new in the suggestion that the gospel of Matthew is liturgical, but this idea must be taken seriously when we try to understand the gospel. If this is done we will find that most, if not all, of those factors that may be conceived of as shaping material used in missionary preaching may also, and even in a higher degree, be influential in shaping the units of a liturgical document.

The historical situation in which the gospel units take shape, however, would be an entirely different one. Instead of the unconscious gropings of the Christian community, shaping the material by oral use and through several generations of preachers, we would have a definite and highly skilled literary art, employed by qualified persons, and brought to bear upon definite practical problems at a definite occasion. The historical situation would not differ materially whether we are considering the origin of our Greek Matthew or the Common Source, whose existence in a Greek translation is postulated. Whenever the Christian community felt the need of instruction in specific Christian truths, which time probably arrived long before the Gentile mission was in full swing, efforts would be made to assemble all the available material of the sayings and doings of Jesus. There was no need of making an entirely new excursion into an unknown field of literature. The statements made by modern writers to the effect that our gospels represent an entirely new type of literature are true only in so far as they have Greek and Roman literature in mind. The practice of looking to these ancient literatures for standards by which the gospels may be appraised is very old, but nevertheless misleading.[4] The true models of the gospel writers are found in the Old Testament, and not in the memoirs of contemporary writers. In the Septuagint version the sacred writings of the Synagogue were known all over the Mediterranean world, and were read in the Pauline churches. The language of this version had

[4] Justin Martyr, *Apology*, I, 66.

deeply tinged the religious vocabulary of the early church, and moulded its religious conceptions. To this influence of the Old Testament upon the early church we must add a definite stylistic and literary influence, which we have tried to trace in the preceding chapters. For it would appear to be inconsistent to grant such forms a literary status when they appear in the Psalms and to deny them literary character when they appear in the epistles of Paul or in the gospels. Nor is it possible to seek refuge in the proposition that while the units were shaped by some sort of social process after the manner of folklore it is first in the assembling of them into a gospel that we detect some faint trace of literary activity.[5] Can anyone for a moment contemplate passages like Matt. 13:13-18; 13:54-57; Lk. 4:16-21a, and many others which have come before us in the preceding pages and refuse to grant these units the status of literature, produced by the conscious artistic effort of men? Such passages are certainly far removed from both folklore and the so-called popular literature (*Kleinliteratur*).

The implications of these facts that we have reviewed are far-reaching. It is no longer possible to treat either the epistles of Paul or the Synoptic Gospels as non-literary products of an early Christian community. The fact that they were written in the Greek language has too long obscured the fact that these writings rest on a very old Semitic literary tradition which formed the common Jewish heritage of the primitive church in Palestine and in the whole Mediterranean world. Instead of regarding the literary approach of the gospels as "a flirtation with aesthetic standards" and a retrogression[6] the literary study of the gospels should be pursued with new vigor, but with the proper Semitic orientation. The observation made by von Wilamovitz-Moellendorff with reference to the epistles of Paul that they constitute "a middle-type" may be extended to the gospels as well. While not neglecting the Greek angle of the question—and we need have no fear of that—the Semitic strand of the cultural background of the early church must be more carefully investigated. The investigation of the Semitic literary tradition should in no way be confounded with

[5] Martin Dibelius, *op. cit.*, pp. 1-4. [6] *Ibid.*, pp. 5-8.

the present discussion about the gospels as translations from the Aramaic, which is a linguistic problem, and has nothing to do with the literary patterns we have been discussing.

The forms discussed in the preceding chapters should also have some bearing on the Synoptic Problem. Much of the gospel material commonly assigned to Q contains the chiastic structures, and it seems reasonable to assume that the Common Source from which this material was derived by Matthew and Luke, and probably also Mark, was a Palestinian Source in a Greek translation. Palestine would be the first place where the Jewish literary heritage most likely would remain intact and its traditions cherished; but a larger Jewish community outside of Palestine, like Antioch, could also be the home of a document like the Common Source, or the Gospel of Matthew. The fact that the chiastic forms are more often found intact in Matthew's excerpts from the Common Source than in Luke's is interpreted to mean that we are in Matthew closer to the original form of such passages than we are in Luke. This is, of course, an important reversal of the judgment of many great New Testament scholars of today, but with the entrance of such a rigid form as the chiasmus into the problem the implication seems natural. Streeter, in speaking of the Sermon on the Mount and the Missionary Discourse, says,

> These discourses are elaborately arranged so as to form compendia of maxims on related topics. It seems quite intelligible that an author should wish to bring together all the most characteristic of our Lord's teachings on general Christian Ethics as in Mt. v-vii, or Missionary work as in Mt. x, and for this purpose should bring together what he found scattered in his source. It is not intelligible that finding them in his source arranged as they are in Matthew, he should scatter them up and down, on no conceivable plan, as they appear in Luke.[7]

The purpose here ascribed to Matthew we have already assumed in an earlier compiler, the author of the Common Source. It is quite conceivable, however, that Luke's purpose might not have been served sufficiently by that earlier collection, and that he therefore felt the impulse to make a fresh collection in accordance with a plan all of his own. This is also the view of Wernle.[8]

[7] B. H. Streeter, *Oxford Studies in the Synoptic Problem*, p. 147.

[8] Paul Wernle, *op. cit.*, p. 145.

Knowing that the doings and sayings of Jesus already in his source had no historical but only a literary and liturgical connection necessitated by the purpose for which they were to be used, Luke would feel no compunction whatsoever in rearranging the same material to suit his own practical needs. Neither can it be said that this rearrangement was made "on no conceivable plan." A comparative study of the Q material as it has been preserved in Matthew and Luke reveals that Luke more often breaks up the chiastic patterns than he preserves them, and the explanation nearest at hand is, that these forms were to him and his prospective readers un-Greek and un-literary judged by Greek standards. Neither can it be said that he follows no plan in the handling of his source. If there is any cogency in our argument presented in the comparative study of Matthew's and Luke's version of the Discourse against the Pharisees, it is plain that Luke has a very definite technique in handling his source, which for want of a better terminology we have designated his "pendulum" and "centrifugal" method of selection. Similar objectives and methods may possibly be discovered in a fresh comparative study of the other discourses, and—although it may impose an almost intolerable burden on one's imagination—of Luke's plan as a whole. Efforts directed along these lines are likely to yield some very interesting results.

THE BOOK OF REVELATION

CHAPTER XVII

THE GENERAL OUTLINE

The Book of Revelation has passed through several stages in the history of interpretation. From ancient times up to our own age men have sought to discover in the book the trend of history by devising ingenious methods of extracting men and events from its symbols. Emperor Frederic II, Napoleon, and Mussolini have in turn been candidates for apocalyptic office, and the end is not yet. Such methods of interpretation have doubtless served to popularize the book in the church, but this apparent gain has been considerably reduced by the false impressions which have been spread as to the purpose of the book and by the general distrust created in the minds of disillusioned followers of these systems of interpretation.

In the eighth decade of the last century the era of source criticism began. Not having satisfactorily solved the riddle of the book by treating it as a unity, writers now began to apply the same methods of source criticism which already had become popular in the field of Old Testament criticism.[1] Whatever may be said in detail of each of these attempts, two factors stand out clearly: (1) the book was studied with much of learning, industry, and critical acumen, and (2) these studies have made the real problems of the book stand out in clear perspective.[2] In the next decade, chiefly through the researches of Gunkel, the scope of these investigations was extended to include, not merely the field of Jewish Apocalyptic literature[3] which had earlier begun to attract the attention of scholars, but Oriental mythology as well. Each of these various fields of research has yielded a valuable set of important and illuminating facts.

[1] Daniel Völter, *Die Entstehung der Apokalypse*, 2te Aufl., 1885.

[2] Eberhard Vischer, *Die Offenbarung Johannes eine jüdische Apokalypse*, 1886.

[3] Hermann Gunkel, *Schöpfung und Chaos*, 1895.

It was natural, however, that the methods of the source-critics should lead to excesses. Johannes Weiss has pointed out that in this form of research the psychological and artistic uniqueness of the book had often been overlooked and that the results obtained by this method seemed to lack any connection with contemporary life.[4] Weiss indicates at least two prerequisites for a sound interpretation of the book: (1) to find for the book a place in the history of the first century, and (2) to start with the assumption that it is to be treated as a unity which does not, to be sure, insist that the book had been produced in every part by one mind, but which holds that one mind is responsible for its present main features and that these are the expression of a definite purpose on the part of the author.

In the present analysis of the book we shall assume (1) that it was written to comfort the church which was suffering from persecution from two quarters, namely, from Judaism and from Roman imperialism; (2) that the unity infused into its materials by the writer is still discernible, if only the original method of arranging these materials can be discovered; (3) that in addition to its marked originality, there is considerable literary dependency, illustrated in the writer's use of the Old Testment.[5]

There is no reason to suppose that the author treated whatever extra-biblical materials he made use of in any other manner than that discernible in his use of the Old Testament. These materials have not the appearance of being loosely assembled and pasted together more or less mechanically. They had previously entered the writer's mind as a religious and cultural heritage and had become fused in his own religious experience before they became the symbolic vehicles for his message of warning and comfort. That such is the case with reference to the Old Testament may be definitely ascertained by studying the quotations.[6] The probability is strong that other apocalyptic materials have been assimilated and made use of in a similar manner.

The new element in the present analysis of the book is a con-

[4] *Die Offenbarung des Johannes* (Göttingen: 1904), pp. 1-6.

[5] Cf. Rev. 13:2 with Dan. 7:4-6; Rev. 11:4 with Zech. 4:1-5, 11-13.

[6] H. B. Sweet, *The Apocalypse of St. John* (2nd ed., London: 1907), pp. cxxxix-clvii.

sistent application of the chiasmus. Previous studies have too often taken for granted the existence of logical sequence, or have found fault with the absence of sequence. Even scholars who have clearly understood the symbolic nature of the scenes have often failed to carry out consistently the implications of the exegetical principles which they themselves have accepted. A complete study of the structure of the book reveals one factor which may be regarded as basic in the interpretation of all its scenes, namely, that *sequence in the visions does not indicate chronology of fulfilment.* The full meaning of this observation will become clearer as soon as some of the following series of seven visions have been analyzed.

The General Outline of the book indicates the main divisions and their relationship to one another. In the preparation of the outline two separate interests have been kept in view: (1) to indicate briefly the content of each division; (2) to show the structure of each division in its relation to its counterpart. In order to achieve the purpose of the first an element of interpretation has entered into the summaries of the divisions. It is hoped, however, that the interpretation of the sections will seem fair, when all the facts have been considered. In order to achieve the second purpose it has been necessary to consider the scenes of the book, not only in their nearer, but also in their more remote context. To trace these far-flung symmetries of the book may seem tedious, and, at times, imposes a strain on the reader's imagination. The results of these efforts, however, will be a truer conception of the greatness of the Book of Revelation.

General Outline of the Book of Revelation

John and the Angel, 1:1-3.
A *Prologue:* John and the Coming Jesus, 1:4-8.
John's Commission to the Church, 1:9-20.

Three
B *Seven Epistles:* One The Church and the World, 2:1-3:22.
Three

Heaven: two scenes: salvation, 4:1-5:14.
Three
C *Seven Seals, etc.* One The Seals: judgment, 6:1-17; 8:1, 3-5.
Three
Heaven: two scenes: salvation, 7:1-17.*

Four, 8:2**, 6-12, judgment.
D *Seven Trumpets:* The eagle, 8:13, interrupting the series.
Three, 9:1-21; 11:14-18, judgment.
The Sanctuary, 11:19.

E The Church's *Testimony* in the *Roman Empire*, 10:1-11.*
Angel arrayed in symbols of Christ's power (vs. 1).
Authority extending over *sea* and *earth* (vss. 2, 5, 8).
The *Seven Thunders*, thrice referred to (vss. 3, 4), but not described.

F The Church's *Testimony* in *Judaism*, 11:1-13.
The "court" not measured (vs. 2).
The "city where also their Lord was crucified" (vs. 11).

F′ The Church *Persecuted* officially by *Judaism*, 12:1-17.
The birth of the man child (vs. 5), an earlier stage.
The woman's flight (vss. 6, 14, cf. "wilderness," 17:3), a later stage.

E′ The Church *Persecuted* officially by the *Roman Empire*, 13:1-18.
The first beast out of the *sea* (vs. 1), the civil power, cf. E.
The second beast out of the *earth* (vs. 11), the cult, cf. E.

The Sanctuary, 15:1**, 5-8, cf. 11:19.
D′ *Seven Bowls:* Three, 16:1-4.
Angel and Altar, 5-7, interrupting the series.
Four, 16:8-21.

Heaven: one scene: salvation, 14:1-5 (cf. 7:1-17)*.
Three
C′ *Seven Angels, etc.* One The Angels: judgment, 14:6-20.
Three
Heaven: one scene: salvation, 15:2-4 (cf. 4:1-5:14).

Three
B′ *Seven Angels:* One The Church and the World, 17:1-22:5.
Three

John and the Angel, 22:6-9.
A′ *Epilogue:* John and the Coming Jesus, 22:10-15.
John's Commission to the Church, 22:16-21.

*Indicate the longer projections (7:1-17; 10:1-11:13; 14:1-15:4).
**Indicate the shorter projections (8:2; 15:1).

Only a few brief remarks relating to the most important features of the general outline need be made. The minute intricate symmetries which may be found in almost any passage in this book can be made clear only by a systematic arrangement of the whole text. Before proceeding, a word of explanation is necessary in regard to certain sections designated as *projections*. They are of two kinds; the longer are marked with one asterisk (7:1-17; 10:1-11:13; and 14:1-15:4), and the shorter are marked with two (8:2 and 15:1). If the various sections of this outline are regarded as so many blocks laid out in order on the table, and if we attach the three longer projections to one lever, this lever may be raised and moved forward one step and the three blocks would be dropped into the position they now occupy in our extant Greek text. If we examine 8:2, we shall find that it connects with 8:6, and that 15:1 in a similar fashion has been detached from 15:5. In either case we have material which has been projected from the rear toward the front of the book. The longer projections were made first; *after* they had been made, the shorter projections, thus leaving the Greek text in its present form.

If we reverse this process and move 8:2 and 15:1 back to their original position, introducing 8:6 and 15:5 respectively, we have taken the first step toward restoring the original literary pattern of the book. When we have repeated this procedure in the same direction with the three longer projections, we shall have the structure as the author conceived it, or as it is here represented by the General Outline. Two misconceptions, equally common, are to be guarded against: (1) These five passages are not accidental dislocations made by careless scribes; (2) the *content* of two of them has nothing to do with their placement within the Seal or Trumpet series rather than after them, where they clearly belong. They are not dislocations but are deliberate projections, made either by the author himself in order to indicate to the reader the proper sequence of the book, or by some later editor.[7] In a book that follows such a literary pattern as this, in which the series of seven, and the passages in which they are framed, match one another like the stones in an arch, it is absolutely essential that the reader coming upon 7:1-17 should somehow be made to look forward for its immediate counterpart in chapters 4 and 5 rather than backward to its more remote companion (14:1-5), cf. General Outline.

[7] If made by an editor, he may have been prompted by the desire to obtain *Episodes*, after the fashion of the Greek drama.

Likewise, in reading the Trumpet series it is essential that he be made to direct his attention toward the latter half of the book for the companion series of the Bowls. This purpose has been achieved by projecting 10:1-11:13 between the sixth and seventh trumpet. Finally, in 14:1-15:4 there would be a danger of connecting the series of seven angels in 14:6-20 with the series of seven angels in 17:1-22:5, and so the more remote connection with the Seven Seals be lost sight of (cf. CC′). The projection of this material to its present place *before* the Bowl series (D′) makes the reader look toward the beginning of the book for its counterpart; this is material with which he is already acquainted through the reading of section C. The fact that in *all* five instances the material has been moved *from the rear toward the front* of the book is too striking a fact to be treated as accidental and is strong proof of a deliberate literary method either on the part of the original author or some editor. The fact that a simple movement backward of this material effects a striking chiastic symmetry in the total structure and establishes parallelisms, both in the immediate context and in the more remote sections (cf. CC′), confirms our hypothesis that we are dealing with a definite literary method.

An apparently fatal objection to our hypothesis with reference to the purpose of the projections is the one which might urge that if the author had such an end in view, he certainly was successful in defeating his own purpose. There is, however, a good reason why the original purpose of the projections should have been lost sight of in the history of the interpretation of the book. Already in the Lucan modifications of the Q material, which may be checked by the Matthaean parallels, we detect the parting of the ways with the older literary tradition and its Old Testament models. This tendency must have made itself felt more strongly as the church became transplanted in the Hellenistic world. A cultural heritage which must be traced to the Semitic world would easily survive in Jewish Christian communities, but could only appear increasingly strange to Greeks and Romans of a later age. Since it was no longer cultivated, this particular literary form was soon lost. The purpose of the projections, therefore (sufficiently clear to one who was conversant with the chiastic structure of the book), would soon be lost to men of Hellenistic background, and the presence of the projections would add more confusion to a book which was already difficult to understand.

When the projections have been restored to their respective contexts in the manner already indicated, the symmetry of the book is made clear. In its major divisions as well as in minor details the writer's interest in numerical symbolism is evident. The book is divided into *twelve* sections, which are easily grouped in *three* parts. The *first* part has a Prologue and three series of seven (ABCD); the *second* part, which is the heart of the book, develops in four symbolic scenes the struggle of the church along two separate battle-fronts, the Jewish (FF′) and the Roman (EE′). From the former struggle the church was already emerging victorious at the time the book was written. Most of its hardships already lay in the past, and could be used for encouragement and instruction. The struggle with the Roman empire, on the other hand, was impending, and the chief purpose of the book is to impart to the church the hopefulness and courage it needed to win that great struggle also. The *third* part has also three series of seven and an Epilogue (D′C′B′A′). In the divisions of the book designated C′ and B′ it is of particular interest to observe that we are there also dealing with two series of *seven.* Strictly speaking there are only six angels,[8] for the fourth (or central) angel is missing in the two series, the Lord of the church occupying the central position. To observe the nature of these central panels is essential, for this habit of marking off the centre in a series is part of the author's technique and may be observed in the counterparts B and C as well. Failure to observe such details has resulted in an inadequate treatment, especially of the series of seven in 14:6-20, and in the seeking of the climax at the end rather than in the centre of both series B′C′.

Only a brief reference to the Prologue and Epilogue is necessary; its main parts are designated in the outline. There are many common phrases in the latter that remind the reader of the former, and even in the disposition of the material itself there are parallels. In 1:5b-7 we find a presentation of the two main groups

[8] *The Shepherd of Hermas* (Lake's Ed.), Simil. IX, 6:2, 12:8.

in the book, the church and the world. The former is referred to as those whom Christ has loved and loosed from their sins and made into a kingdom (vss. 5b, 6); the latter do not share at all in his redemptive work (vs. 7b), but are hostile to Christ. Both groups are described with reference to Christ's coming, the grand climax of the whole book; the church is praising him and the world is mourning over him. These two groups come before us again in 22:10-15, and their actions are there also appraised with reference to Christ's coming. The two groups are before us in vs. 11 and vss. 14-15, and the coming Lord is characterized in the intervening vss. 12, 13.

CHAPTER XVIII

THE SEVEN EPISTLES AND THE LAST SEVEN ANGELS

The existence of Seven Epistles in an apocalyptic book is in itself a problem. Apocalypses, as well as epistles, were well known in the early church, but epistles combined with an apocalypse are not found. Writers on the Book of Revelation have therefore at times assumed either that the Seven Epistles represent the work of a redactor or that they were written earlier by the author and incorporated in the apocalypse when it was finished. Opinions also differ as to whether the letters are single units that were sent to their respective churches or a unified series which is addressed to the church universal. All these questions are legitimate. Every investigation of such problems, however, should begin by ascertaining the literary structure of each epistle and the mutual relationship of all the epistles in the series. We shall find that each epistle has a definite structure and that all are arranged in definite groups in accordance with the laws of parallelism.

Even a casual reading of the whole series shows that there are certain phrases which, like the refrain of a song, recur throughout. A closer study, however, reveals (1) that these phrases do not occur in *all* epistles, but have been eliminated in some; (2) that the various parts of the epistles do not follow the same order in each member of the series; (3) that there exists one definite literary relationship between the epistles that make up the *odd* numbers (1, 3, 5, 7) and another between those that make up the *even* numbers (2, 4, 6) in the series. The main facts may conveniently be presented in graphic form by means of the following outlines, which will receive fuller consideration later.

Outline I

I. Address: "To the angel of the church in ——— write," etc.
II. Introduction of the speaker: "These things saith he that," etc.
III. Estimate of the church: "I know," etc.

IV. Commendation or Condemnation of the church: "but," and "if," etc.
V. Call to repentance: "Repent," etc.
VI. Exhortation: "He that hath an ear," etc.
VII. Promise: "He," or, "to him that overcometh," etc.

These seven parts are not found in all the epistles. When there are *eliminations* or *rearrangements* of this order these occur in accordance with definite patterns as follows:

The *Call to Repentance* is eliminated in the epistles to Smyrna, Thyatira, and Philadelphia, i. e., the *even* numbers in the series (2, 4, 6).

The *Exhortation* and the *Promise* occur in this order in the *first* three epistles and have order *reversed* in the *last* four.

The *Commendation* or *Condemnation* precede the *Call to Repentance* in the Epistles to Ephesus and Pergamum and this order is *reversed* in the epistles to Sardis and Laodicea after the following scheme:

Outline II

I. Ephesus: Condemnation, 2:4; Call, 2:5.
II. *Smyrna:* Commendation, 2:10; *No Call.*
III. Pergamum: Condemnation, 2:14, 15; Call, 2:16.
IV. *Thyatira:* Condemnation (2:20) *and* Commendation (2:24). There is *no Call* to repentance, for 2:21 shows that repentance is no longer possible.
V. Sardis: Call, 3:3; Condemnation, 3:4 ("few names" only remain).
VI. *Philadelphia:* Commendation, 3:10; *No Call.*
VII. Laodicea: Call, 3:19; Condemnation, 3:20 ("if any hear," but doubtful).

In the running series of seven, there is one series of *even* (2, 4, 6) and another of *odd* numbers (1, 3, 5, 7). In each epistle of the former series there is no Call to Repentance, but each of the latter series contains this Call. Two epistles of the *even* series (2, 6) contain the term "synagogue of Satan," while those of the *odd* series have no such name. In 4 we read about "the deep things of Satan" (2:24).

Any analysis of the epistles which is based on the arrangement of the seven parts of each epistle or on the elimination of some of these parts yields two groups with three epistles in each group, the fourth (or central epistle) standing alone. The most obvious feature of the central epistle to Thyatira is its greater length. In Westcott and Hort's edition this epistle has 27 lines of Greek text.

Further comparison shows that epistles 1 and 3, which we regard as parallel, have each 17 lines of text, while epistle 2 has only 12 lines. In the last group of three epistles we find that epistle 6 has 23 and epistle 7 has 22, while epistle 5 has only 17. Since epistles 5 and 7 (in accordance with the scheme adopted) should balance each other, this seems to be a serious flaw. If, however, we adopt the suggestion of R. H. Charles[1] and others, that Rev. 16:15, which is obviously misplaced in its present context, originally stood in the midst of 3:3, we would have at least 20 lines in this epistle instead of 17. Thus the length of the epistles in the last group would be approximately the same.

In the arrangement of the Seven Epistles we have adopted the hypothesis that within the two groups of three epistles there is a parallelism of *content*. There are certain ideas and occasionally certain terms which balance one another like the parallelisms in the psalms; like these they are either synonymous or antithetic. We are therefore to make a detailed comparison of the ideas and terms in the two epistles to Ephesus and Pergamum, which are parallel members of the first group; then of Sardis and Laodicea in the second group; and finally of Smyrna and Philadelphia, which are central in their respective groups. The following outline will make clear their most striking resemblances.

THE CONTENTS OF THE SEVEN EPISTLES

False apostles, 2:2
1. Ephesus: Nicolaitans, 2:6.
The tree of life, 2:7

The blasphemy of them
2. *Smyrna:* They *say* they are Jews, and they are not.
But are a synagogue of Satan, 2:9

My witness, my faithful one, 2:13
3. Pergamum: Nicolaitans, 2:15
Hidden manna, 2:18

The Son of God, 2:18
The Woman Jezebel, who *calleth* herself a prophetess (2:20
4. *Thyatira:* *All* the churches shall know, 2:23
The deep things of Satan, 2:24
And he that keepeth my works, 2:26
The Morning Star, 2:28, cf. 22:16

[1] R. H. Charles, *A Critical and Exegetical Commentary on the Revelation of St. John* (2 vols., New York: 1920), *ad loco.*

"That thou hast," etc. 3:1
5. Sardis: White garments, 3:5
Before my Father, 3:5

The Synagogue of Satan, of them
6. *Philadelphia:* That *say* they are Jews, and they are not
But they lie, 3:9

"That thou art," etc. 3:16
7. Laodicea: White garments, 3:18
With my Father, 3:21

In that section of the epistles to *Ephesus* and *Pergamum* which contains the Lord's estimate of the church, introduced by the words, "I know" etc., we find approval of their faithfulness expressed, the one church being told, "Thou didst bear for my name's sake" (2:3) and the other, "Thou holdest fast my name" (2:13); one church hates "the works of the Nicolaitans" (2:6) and the other has "some that hold the teachings of the Nicolaitans" (2:15); one has discovered false apostles (2:2) and the other has had a shining example of faithfulness in Antipas, who is called "my witness, my faithful one" (2:13). Finally the reward is promised in similes which are somewhat related, for the victorious members are promised in one epistle that they will eat of "the tree of life" (2:7) and in the other that they will eat of "the hidden manna" (2:17). It should also be observed that the formula which introduces the promise in these two epistles alone, has the form, "To him that overcometh. . . ." In all other epistles we have: "He that overcometh" (cf. τῷ νικῶντι with ὁ νικῶν).

In the two epistles just mentioned the good seems to predominate and the bad is the exception. When we turn to the epistles to *Sardis* and *Laodicea,* on the other hand, the general condition of the churches is bad and the good is an exception. Of one church it is said, "Thou hast a name that thou livest, and thou art dead" (3:1), and of the other, "Thou art neither cold nor hot" (3:15); both statements denote the same spiritual condition. That section of the two epistles which contains the estimate of the church has for its introductory formula the words, "I know thy words, *that,*" etc. Only in these two instances is this formula followed *immediately* by ὅτι, for in 2:8 other material intervenes between these words and ὅτι. This variation should be compared with the variation in the formulae introducing the promise in the first and third epistles. These variations of stereotyped formulae are slight, but we have reason to believe that they are part of a deliberate literary pattern. The terms describing the reward of those who overcome are similar in the two epistles, for in one the Lord promises to confess their name before the Father (3:5) and in the other they are to occupy the throne with the Lord and with the Father (3:21). In the verses immediately preceding, the "few" in Sardis who have not defiled their garments are promised, "they shall walk with me in white" (3:4) and the self-satisfied members of the church of Laodicea are advised, "buy of me . . . white garments" (3:18). If we insert 16:15 in the midst of 3:3, as has previously been suggested, in order to balance the length of the two epistles, we shall find that the words, "lest he walk naked, and they see his shame" (16:15) are balanced by the words, that "the shame of thy nakedness be not made manifest" (3:18).

Such correspondences in thought and in terms are too many and too striking to occur by chance. They must be the result of deliberate planning on the part of the author. The fact that many of these terms are found only in the places where they are parallel strengthens the argument. In only one instance, namely, where the *name* of the Lord is referred to in epistles 1 and 3, do we find references to his name in epistle 6 also (cf. 2:3, 13 with 3:6, 12). But there are other examples in this book in which the terms that occur in the *extreme* members of one system are found in the *centre* of the corresponding system. Such arrangements, which temporarily seem to break up the immediate symmetry, will often be found to be a part of a more extensive symmetry. Another example of this kind is close at hand. In epistle 7 we have the boast, "I am rich" (3:17). To this there is no parallel in epistle 5, as we would expect, but we recall the fact that 16:15 is a part of the text and that it deals with the "thief." It is not beyond the range of possibility that the original text also carried a reference to "riches." We recall how even by adding 16:15 we obtained only 20 lines, though epistle 7 has 22 lines. However this may be, in epistle 2, which is the *central* epistle of the first group, we find the words, "but thou art rich" (2:9). They are in the centre of a continuous construction, and are plainly parenthetic. Our decision in regard to a reference to "riches" in epistle 5 will of necessity be uncertain, but in epistles 7 and 2 we have references to riches. Other examples of a similar nature cannot be discussed in this connection (cf. Ps. 101 strophes BB′).

According to our hypothesis the epistles to *Smyrna* and *Philadelphia* should be parallel. Some evidence for this may have been observed already from the fact that these two churches receive unmixed praise, while in all other epistles the praise is counteracted by censure. There is, therefore, no call to repentance in the two epistles. These are the only instances in which any of the regular seven parts of the epistles has been eliminated. We shall soon see how this absence of one part in epistles 2 and 6 is balanced by the *additional* material in the central member of the even series, the epistle to Thyatira. The epistles to Smyrna and Philadelphia are central in each group of three. If there is any intention on the part of the author to indicate that the two *groups* are in some fashion related to one another, we should look for it in the two central epistles. In this expectation we are not disappointed, for the inverted order of the ideas they have in common, definitely ties the two together. The *blasphemy*, the *Jews*, and *the synagogue of Satan* (2:9) recur again in 3:9, but with their order inverted, "*The synagogue of Satan*," *the Jews*, and "*they lie*." There is also in 2:10 a reference to *trial* with the additional statement that the duration of the tribulation will be *ten days;* this is doubtless a symbolical designation. This reference is matched by another in 3:10 which mentions the duration first and the trial last in the words, "the *hour* of *trial*." The inversion of similar ideas that recur in parallel position is one of the characteristics of the chiastic form; their occurrence we may accept as evidence of interrelation (cf. 1 Cor. 12:9, 10 and vs. 28; Col. 1:16 and vs. 20b).

Although these two epistles are parallel, one is by no means to be regarded merely as an echo of the other. In the epistle to Smyrna the church is encouraged to prepare to endure persecution from the Synagogue, and the possibility of death is held before its members (2:10), but in the epistle to Philadelphia the Synagogue is described as prostrated before the church (3:9). In one epistle they are urged to be faithful and thus obtain "the crown of life" (2:10) and in the other they are asked to hold fast what they have, "that no one take thy crown" (3:11). The epistle to Philadelphia is longer than the epistle to Smyrna, this being chiefly due to the exuberant richness of the section containing the promise (3:12). Epistles 2 and 6, then, introduce the reader to one of the major enemies of the church, the Synagogue. The second major enemy is Roman imperialism, which appears in the book in two forms, as a political and as a religious power. It is in the character of a seductive religious influence that we meet it in the Seven Epistles in the symbolic woman Jezebel, "who calleth herself a prophetess," described in the epistle to Thyatira.

The epistle to *Thyatira* is the centre of the series. The chief danger is some peculiar form of idolatry which had already crept into the church. We observe with interest that the references to idolatry are distributed equally in *all* epistles except 2 and 6, the only two which mention the Synagogue (cf. 2:6 with 2:14, 15; and 3:4 with 3:18). The church is described as defiled by the practices of an idolatrous community. It is significant that the strongest representation of idolatry, namely, by the woman Jezebel, and the ultimate doom of that perversion of worship, namely, when the bed of pleasure will become a bed of pain (3:22), should be found in the central epistle of the seven.

There are several *additions* found in this epistle to the stereotyped formulae all of which are significant. In every epistle we have the same exhortation without variation: "He that hath an ear, let him hear what the Spirit saith to the *churches*." The plural form would have been sufficient to indicate to the reader that he is not to think of the individual church whose name heads the epistle but of the church universal. To make this doubly certain we find now the statement, "*All* the churches shall know" (3:23). The formula "He that overcometh" introduces the promise immediately in all the other epistles, but is here followed by the additional qualification, "and he that keepeth my works unto the end" (3:26). In no other epistle is the person who was presented in the vision in 1:14-16 identified and *named*. All the other epistles introduce the Speaker by a uniform formula, "These things saith he that," etc., but here the formula has a significant addition, "These things saith *the Son of God*, who hath," etc. (3:18). To later generations of Christians, who had become acquainted with the figure of their heavenly Lord through the creeds and the hymnology of the church, such an identification would hardly have been necessary, but to an audience not already familiar with the symbolism by which the Lord was usually represented an identification was very much needed. In six other epistles the identification could have been introduced, but the author chose the fourth epistle, because it was the pivot in his scheme.

There can be no difference of opinion concerning the meaning of the phrases which introduce the speaker. In regard to the similes which are used to describe the *promises* to the faithful and victorious members of the church, however, there is a great variety of opinion among commentators both as to their origin and meaning. There is only one of them which is identified with Christ, in the book, namely, the Morning Star (2:28). Toward the end of the book we read, "I am the root and the offspring of David, the bright, *the morning star*" (22:16). Since the phrases introducing the speaker all refer to the Son of God and since this identification is made in the central epistle only, may we not assume that this lone identification of the simile describing the promise and occurring in the central epistle is likewise to be distributed among the similes whose meaning is as yet unknown? The result would be that the Lord of the church is represented under various symbols as giving himself to his faithful ones and that the substance of these promises is a communion with Christ, which can only be established by faith and maintained by faithfulness.

The *naming* of the Son of God in the central epistle is not a mere coincidence, but part of a deliberate plan. This becomes evident at once, when we turn our attention to other series of seven in the book which have a similar arrangement. Thus in Seven Seals we find that Death and Hades are named in the *fourth* Seal (6:8, cf. C). In the parallel series of Seven Angels (C′) we find that there are first three angels who are distinctly enumerated (14:6, 8, 9), and later three more angels (14:15, 17, 18), but the fourth, or central angel, does not appear in the series. In his place we have "one like a Son of Man, having on his head a golden crown" (14:14). It is clear that the actions of the Son of Man are to be distributed over other members of the series (cf. vss. 15, 18), but his *naming* is found in the central panel only. A similar arrangement is found in the last series of Seven Angels (B′), which concludes the book. There are first three angels, the *first* of which is identified with one of the preceding angels that have poured out the Bowls (17:1; 18:1, 21) and later three more angels (19:17; 20:1; 21:9) the *last* of which is again identified with one of the Bowl angels (21:9). But instead of the fourth angel we have in the central panel a long description in which the Lord of the church is named, "The Word of God," and "King of Kings and Lord of Lords." We have, then, in those four series of seven, which in the structure of the book balance one another, as a regular feature the naming of the chief character in the central panel. This custom of the author is first introduced in the epistle to Thyatira. Only in the Trumpet and Bowl series (DD′) is this feature wanting, but they follow another pattern in their arrangement. They are the only two series in the book in which the climax comes at the *end*.

One more line of investigation must be followed before our study is completed. We must undertake a comparative study of all those phrases which are used in the Seven Epistles to introduce the Speaker. One of these phrases, "the beginning of the creation of God" (3:14), does not come from the first chapter but is possibly an echo of Col. 1:15, 18. The reference to the reading of the Epistle to the Colossians in the church in Laodicea (Col. 4:16) lends probability to this suggestion. This phrase, however, since it is not found in the first chapter, cannot enter into the scheme designed by the author. Judging from the following words, the "key of David" (3:7) is a quotation from Isa. 22:22, but it doubtless points to Rev. 1:18, the only passage in the first chapter where "the key" is mentioned (20:1). Its position in the following outline makes this suggestion a certainty. The study of all those phrases used to introduce the Speaker in the Seven Epistles indicates that they are chosen in pairs in accordance with the scheme already described. A simple outline will make this clear:

"the seven spirits"	1:4	Sardis	5	1 Ephesus
"the faithful witness"	1:5	Laodicea	7	2 *Smyrna*
				3 Pergamum
"the Son of God" (2:18)				
"eyes like a flame of fire"	1:14	*Thyatira*	4	4 *Thyatira*
"feet like burnished brass"	1:14			
				5 Sardis
"the seven stars"	1:16	Ephesus	1	6 *Philadelphia*
"a sharp two-edged sword"	1:16	Pergamum	3	7 Laodicea
"the first and the last"	1:17	*Smyrna*	2	
"the keys"	1:18	*Philadelphia*	6	

The column on the right indicates what is supposed to be the author's own arrangement of the Seven Epistles. After he had written the epistles, introducing similar ideas and terms in those which were to be parallel in the two groups of three, he set himself to connect each epistle in a definite fashion with the vision of the Lord in the first chapter. The introductory phrases were picked so that the phrases which occur in parallel epistles were taken from the *same context* in the first chapter. A comparison of the three columns of the outline will demonstrate very clearly that such was his procedure. That the habit of chiastic arrangement was thoroughly absorbed by the writer may be seen from the fact that the phrases in epistles 1 and 3, which belong to the first group, come *after* 1:14, while those of epistles 5 and 7, which belong to the last group, are found *before* 1:14. The most convincing single fact in this involved scheme is the occurrence side by side of the phrases in epistles 2 and 6. These two epistles are central in their respective groups of three, and they are connected by a chiastic arrangement of the ideas and terms common to both. The selection of the phrases from the same context in the first chapter definitely shows that they lay side by side in the author's mind.

One more detail, which at first appears somewhat disturbing to this otherwise perfect scheme, should not be overlooked. The epistles to Ephesus and Sardis have each *two* phrases to introduce the Speaker. The *first* of the two in each epistle has already been located in the preceding outline, but the *second* phrase still remains to be accounted for. The following outline will show the location of all the four phrases in the two epistles and their relations to the total scheme:

"seven spirits," 1:4 — Sardis
  "seven golden candlesticks," 1:12 — Ephesus
    "the Son of God" (having "eyes" and "feet") 1:14 — *Thyatira*
  "seven stars," 1:16 — Ephesus
"seven stars," 1:20 — Sardis

From this outline we discover that the four phrases adorning the epistles to Ephesus and Sardis contain the number *seven.* This number occurs in no other introductory phrase in the Seven Epistles. We also find that they are chosen with reference to the centre (1:14) in such a fashion that the two phrases in the epistle to Ephesus are made to encase *the centre* and the two from that of Sardis to encase *the whole.* But why of all the epistles should these two be distinguished in this fashion? The reason probably is that each epistle opens the group and that its leading position is thus indicated. Such a designation is also found in the *first* and *fifth* angel in the series of Seven Angels in 14:6-20, for *the hour* of judgment is mentioned only in vss. 7, 15.

Several converging lines of evidence, which we have tried to bring together in our study, prove that the seven epistles were from the beginning a literary unity. The literary patterns which are employed to unite the members of the series are too many and too intricate to be accounted for by any theory of later editing. The strands that link the epistles with the rest of the book are also too many and far-flung and enter too deeply into the fundamental structure of the book to be accounted for by any source hypothesis. Sources there are, no doubt, for the writer obtains the pigments for his canvasses from the Old Testament, from Jewish Apocalypses, and, as Ramsay[2] has shown, from local customs also. They are so freely combined in the visions, however, that one must assume that they had been fused in the writer's own mind

[2] W. M. Ramsay, *The Letters to the Seven Churches of Asia*, 1904. From the Jewish Apocalypses the influence is general rather than specific, i.e., grotesque symbolism, serial arrangement, and the gloating over the enemy's destruction. The influence of the Old Testament is much more direct, showing that the author was steeped in its language as he evidently was not in the language of the Apocalypses.

and religious experience through long years of practice in expressing himself through the medium of symbolism. The message from the Lord of the church is poured into the mould provided by his own art, and the details are distributed among the members of the series in accordance with the rules governing chiastic structures. These forms were familiar to the writer and his readers in the first century. We possess nothing like it in our own literature. It may be compared to a design in architecture or to a theme in a musical composition. An idea is expressed in a musical phrasing which may recur in a bewildering variety of combinations without losing itself until the genius of the artist has fully expressed the idea in his mind.

We are now ready to take up the analysis of the last series of Seven Angels (17:1-22:5) which in the General Outline is designated the literary counterpart (B′) of the Seven Epistles (B). For this decision there are good reasons. Many early intimations of the literary relationship of the two series in the form of parallel terms and phrases have already appeared to the attentive reader. The promises made in the Seven Epistles find here their explanation and fulfilment.

In the following outline an attempt is made to summarize and to put into graphic form the points in which the various panels of the series of Seven Angels are parallel to one another. The full force of the argument cannot be conveyed to the reader without a detailed arrangement of the whole text, for each of the seven panels is constructed with intricate designs all of which are interrelated to one another.

THE LAST SERIES OF SEVEN ANGELS, 17:1-22:5

A *The Harlot: Babylon the Great*, 17:1-18.
An angel of the Seven Bowls: come hither: wilderness.
She has the glory of the world (vs. 4).
Rules nations and the kings of the earth (vss. 1, 15, 17, 18).
Persecutes the church (vs. 6, 14).
Admired by all whose names are not in the book of life (vs. 8).

B *Babylon's Idolatry and Its Commerce*, 18:1-20.
An angel from heaven: great authority: "fallen, fallen" (cf. 14:8).
Separation: "come forth, my people" (vs. 4).
Her reign: "I sit a queen" (vs. 7).
Her doom: "She shall be utterly burned" (vs. 8).

C *Babylon's Impending Desolation*, 18:21-24.
A strong angel: the sea.
She shall utterly vanish (vs. 21).
No music, no production, no light, no weddings (vss. 22-23a), and no luxuries (vs. 18:14-23b).

A Heavenly Scene, "I heard," 19:1-10, cf. 21:1-8.
A Rejoicing, corruption of the Harlot ended, 1-5.
B Rejoicing over the Marriage of the Lamb, 6-8.
C The Seer and the Angel, 9-10.
"Write": message of comfort: "fellow servant" (cf. son, 21:7).

D *The Coming of the Lord with the Church to Judgment*, 19:11-16.
No Angel mentioned (cf. 14:14).
The Lord is *named* three times: Faithful and True; The Word of God; King of Kings and Lord of Lords (vss. 11,13,16). "The armies of heaven" are the saints (cf. vs. 14 with vs. 8). Compare vss. 12-15a with 1:14-16 for description.

A Heavenly Scene: "I saw," 21:1-8 (transposed*).
B′ The Bride adorned for her Husband, 1-5a.
C′ The Seer and the Lord, 5b-7.
"Write": message of comfort: "my son" (cf. 19:10; Heb. 3:5,6).
A′ Destruction of all corruption of paganism, vs. 8.

C′ *Destruction of the Beast and the False Prophet*, 19:17-21.
An angel in the sun: midheaven.
The Great Supper of God (mockery) vs. 17: the *mighty* are eaten.
This is the feast that replaces those in C.
The Beast and the False Prophet, i.e. Rome-Babylon under the political and religious aspects (cf. vs. 20 with 13:13, 14) are now finally destroyed.

B′ *Destruction of the Dragon, Death and Hades*, 20:1-15.
An angel from heaven: authority (key, cf. 1:18).
Separation: "those who worshipped not the beast" (vs. 4).
Their reign: "They lived and reigned a thousand years" (vs. 4).
The rest were doomed: "burned in the lake of fire" (vs. 15).

A′ *The Bride: New Jerusalem*, 21:9-22:5.
An angel of the Seven Bowls: come hither: a mountain.
She has the glory of God (vs. 11).
Nations and kings of the earth own her sway (21:24, 26).
Those in the Lamb's book of life (21:27) shall reign forever (22:5).

*21:1-8 originally followed 19:16. Thus the second death is defined (21:8) *before* 20:6, and the *city* is on *earth* before 20:9.

The last series of Seven Angels is a great chiastic structure of seven sections. Strictly speaking there are only six angels, for the central angel of the series is missing. His place is taken by the Lord himself. We may think of the series as the panels of a mural decoration in an octagonal room. Upon entering the door, one would see the fourth panel, which described the coming of the

Lord with the armies of heaven, directly opposite the entrance. On either side of the door would be the first and the seventh panels; on the left, the scene depicting the Harlot, Babylon the Great; and on the right, the Bride, New Jerusalem. Both are introduced by the angels of the Bowl Series, and both cry, "Hither!"[3] There are no more references to the angels of the Bowl Series in the following sections. The purpose of the two panels is evidently to depict state-supported idolatry in its splendor, on the one hand, and a pure church in which the glory of God resides, on the other. The inherent character and the ultimate fate of both are strikingly presented. In some of the details a literary interest is manifested. Since the book was produced for liturgical use in the church, its purpose is to persuade the hearers to make their choice between Babylon and New Jerusalem, and thus to fortify themselves against the impending ordeal of persecution.

The next two panels (BB′) on the walls of our imaginary octagonal room are introduced by angels that come down from heaven (18:1, 20:1). One of them has "great power" and the other a key to the bottomless pit and a "great chain." In one panel there is a striking contrast between the nations that have submitted to Babylon's rule, and the people of God who are separated (18:3, 4); in the other a similar sharp distinction is maintained between the deceived nations and the camp of the saints (20:8, 9). In one the Harlot is boasting that she sits as queen over the world (18:7); in the other the saints occupy thrones with Christ (20:4). The ultimate fate of the two cities is never left in doubt. In the end the wicked are to be burned (18:8; 20:15).

The contrast between the godly and the wicked has been more fully expressed in the sixth panel (20:1-15), in which is found the much-discussed passage dealing with the binding and loosing of Satan. Much of the trouble that the exegete experiences with this passage is due to his insistence on sequence. But the four scenes depicted come in pairs, members of which must be synchronized (AA′ and BB′).

A *A vision:* "I saw"; Satan bound, 20:1-3.

  B *A vision:* "I saw"; thrones, the saints in judgment, vss. 4-6.

[3] δεῦρω is found in 17:1 and 21:9 only.

A′ No vision: a longer note, introduced by ὅταν (cf. 4:9 for a similar note). Satan's activities during the "little time" (vs. 3) are described, but they are *not seen* (cf. "I saw," is missing in vs. 7), vss. 7-10.

B′ *A vision:* "I saw"; the white throne, the judgment scene of vs. 4 is here continued and concluded, vss. 11-15.

We are not here concerned with similar passages in other apocalypses and their meaning. Granting that there is a conventional way of presenting such ideas as these, we are chiefly concerned with our author's technique in presenting them. We may obtain some guidance from 4:9-11. This passage is no part of the scene described in chapter four. The tense of all the verbs (give, fall down, worship, cast down) is the *future*, and the force of ὅταν is frequentative.[4] The reader is told that whenever the conditions described in vs. 9 exist, the action described in vss. 10, 11 will take place. The first instance in which the elders fall down *and worship* occurs in 5:14. Other occasions are described in 11:16; 19:4. The significance of these passages is that the description of the action once given is *not repeated;* a passing reference to it is considered sufficient, and the reader is expected to call to mind at any given point the action more fully described in 4:9-11.

In 20:7-10 we have a similar note introduced by ὅταν. We have already been told in vs. 3 that Satan shall be loosed "for a little time," and in vss. 7-10 we are told what Satan does during that time. These activities, however, are not depicted in a vision but in a *note*. The conception of a "little time" is well known in this book[5] and the author need not further define it. He expects his readers to remember the previous passages and to synchronize the period of Satan's activity referred to in 20:3 with the period of activity already alluded to in 12:12. The "little time," then, is not a brief period of time at the end of this age; it is *this present age*. And there is no need of depicting again Satan's activities in a new vision. The visions of the book have been very largely devoted to this subject, and the subject may therefore finally be disposed of in a note. Is it not in this age that "the deceiver of the whole world" (12:9) is engaged in deceiving the nations?[6] And

[4] H. B. Swete, *The Apocalypse of John, ad loco.*

[5] Cf. 6:11; 10:6; 12:12.

[6] Cf. 13:14; 19:20; 20:3, 8, 10.

"the war" (20:7) has also been fully described in the book.[7] The outcome of that war is here described. The purpose of the note is to recall briefly the activities of Satan before he is finally disposed of in the lake of fire (20:10).

In a similar manner, the action of the two throne-scenes must be synchronized. They are both scenes of judgment (vss. 4, 12). The time element being already disposed of by the phrase, "for a little time," the thousand years (vss. 3, 4, 5, 6) cannot be taken to refer to any specific time, long or short. It is conceivable that just as the idea of perfection, or fulness, in this book has been expressed by the cube applied to *space* (21:16) it should also have been expressed by the same symbol applied to *time*. For a thousand is the cube of ten. It is to be observed that this terminology applies equally to the extent of Satan's imprisonment and the rule of the saints with Christ. In fact, the former is conditioned by the latter. Thus the binding and loosing of Satan must in some sense be regarded as a *present* reality. This is certainly in accordance with the teaching of other passages in the New Testament.[8] It is only with reference to those who are not members of Christ's kingdom that Satan may still be regarded as being loose.[9] Neither the two descriptions of Satan (AA′) nor the two descriptions of the reign of the saints with Christ and their judgment activities (BB′), should be entirely removed from this present age. The saints are already a kingdom (1:6; 5:10), and their reign is a present reality which has been symbolically depicted by the twenty-four elders with crowns, sitting upon thrones. Even in this respect the two sections (BB′) bring out merely what has already been stated in earlier sections of the book. In the *visions* there must necessarily be a sequence, for each vision can only deal with one phase of the situation that is to be depicted. This does not imply, however, that data which merely indicate the sequence in the visions should be interpreted to mean a chronology of fulfilment. They are merely stage directions. Two symbolic murals of George Washington as statesman and military officer, or a description of

[7] Cf. 11:7; 16:14; 17:4; 19:19.
[8] Cf. Mk. 3:27; Lk. 11:21, 22, 23; 10:18; I John 5:18.
[9] Cf. Col. 1:13; Acts 26:18; I Pet. 5:8, 9.

them in two succeeding paragraphs, would not be applied to successive periods in his life but to contemporaneous functions.

Advancing toward the centre in the General Outline we come upon two sections (CC′). The first of these panels, although brief, is rich in details which set forth the desolation of Babylon. There will be no music at her feasts, no production in her mills, no light in her windows, no weddings, no luxuries of her commerce. The refrain, "no more at all," rings out again and again like the knell of doom (C). With the cessation of her feasts and luxuries fresh in our minds we turn to the counterpart (C′) to hear an imposing invitation to the birds of midheaven to join in The Great Supper of God. Here Babylon's great men are not the hosts, but the food! The cruel mockery of this gruesome scene is evident. She that was "drunken with the blood of the saints and with the blood of the witnesses of Jesus" (17:6) is now herself to be eaten (cf. 19:21b with 17:16). Rome, the great enemy of the church, is now finally ushered out to destruction, when its two symbols, the Beast and the False Prophet, are cast into the lake of fire (19:20).

Section C, announcing the fall of Babylon and her utter destruction (18:21-24), is followed by a heavenly scene in which there is great rejoicing over this achievement (19:1-10). After this scene follows the central panel D in the last series of Seven Angels (19:11-16), where the coming of the Lord to destroy his enemies and to save his church is portrayed very impressively. After this scene we have ventured to introduce a paragraph (21:1-8), which seems out of place where it is now found; inserted after 19:16 it would form a perfect counterpart to the heavenly scene in 19:1-10. Since all the other angels in the series introduce the descriptive panel of which they are a part[10], it is not likely that the last of the seven should constitute a conspicuous exception to the general rule by having descriptive material in 21:1-8 *precede* the angel in 21:9.

The analysis of this passage given in the outline of *The Last Series of Seven Angels* shows how much there is in common between it and the passage in 19:1-10. When the knowledge of the

[10] Cf. 17:1; 18:1, 21; 19:17; 20:1.

chiastic structure of the book was lost among the Greek scribes, it is easy to see why 21:1-8 because of its content should have been joined to 21:9. Placed in its correct position, where it serves its original purpose in the structure of the book, it not only forms a perfect counterpart to 19:1-10, but several other details then find their natural explanation. The meaning of the second death is then made clear to the reader *before* formal reference is made to it in 20:6. We shall also find that, with the acceptance of the transposition, the New Jerusalem, which is to be identified with "the beloved city," is now placed upon the earth *before* it is besieged in 20:9. The latter passage seems to take for granted some previous knowledge of the besieged city, and this knowledge is easily provided the reader in its proper place by the transposition. The city is none other than the Christian Church, the tabernacle of God among men (cf. 21:3 with 13:6), and *the* war (20:8) can only mean the aforementioned war (cf. 17:14; 19:19). This war is the great conflict between pagan Rome and the Christian Church about the emperor cult, the outcome of which was as yet uncertain to the church. To this conflict and its issues the book returns again and again. The central theme is never lost sight of in the midst of most intricate and colorful literary patterns.

The grand climax in the drama is presented in the fourth, or central, panel of the series D (19:11-16). We have in that panel no angel of judgment, but the Lord himself depicted as coming to battle with the armies of heaven. A similar substitution of the Lord for an angel in the central panel is found in the series of Seven Angels in 14:6-20 (vs. 14). We should recall how in the corresponding series of Seven Epistles the speaker to the churches was not named the Son of God until we reached the central epistle to Thyatira (2:18). We shall also find that the elaborate system of cross-references, by which the speaker to the Seven Churches was shown to be the Son of Man in 1:13-17a, is repeated in this passage. A comparison will also show that the literary pattern employed in the introduction to the book to describe the Son of Man is here used once more to describe the Lord from heaven. For comparison we first print 1:13-17a.

And in the midst of the candlesticks one like unto a *Son of Man*, 13
Clothed with a garment down to the *foot*,
And girt about the breast with a golden girdle.

And his *head* and his *hair* were as white *as wool, as snow;* 14
And his *eyes* were as *a flame of fire;*
And his *feet* like unto burnished brass, (as if it had been refined in a furnace;[11])
And his VOICE like the voice of many waters; (15
And he had in his right *hand* seven stars;
And out of his *mouth* proceeded *a sharp two-edged sword;*
And his *countenance* was *as the sun shineth* in his strength.

And when I saw *him*, 17
I fell at his *feet* as one dead,
And he laid his hand on me saying, etc.

This passage is one of the central panels in a longer section dealing with John's Commission to the Church, 1:19-20 (cf. General Outline, A). In vss. 13, 17 we have the formal introduction and conclusion to the description of the Lord of the church; but in vss. 14-16 is the description itself in so far as it relates to his person. In vss. 13, 17 we have an alternating arrangement, but in the central section itself a chiastic. There are *seven* prominent features in the description of the Lord. The head and the hair in the first line are glistening white, and they are balanced in the last line by the countenance shining like the sun. The piercing eyes are likened to a flame of fire in the second line, and this line is balanced by the sixth, describing the sharp two-edged sword which proceeds out of his mouth. The feet and the hand, both extremities, are most fittingly grouped together in the third and fifth lines. It should be observed that all these features represent *vision*. In the central line alone are we dealing with *audition*, for there we hear the voice of the Lord, that voice which we are to hear again and again in the book, introducing the various judgments.

This exquisite literary mosaic, however, is not pedantically assembled from various collected parts, but is the expression of something really seen and deeply felt. The idea of a vision is not merely a literary convention; it must be taken seriously. When one reads vs. 13 with its reference to "the breast with a golden

[11] Possibly a gloss derived from 10:1.

girdle" and finds in vs. 17 only the slight reference to the laying of the Lord's hand upon the head of the prophet (certainly not the close parallelism that characterized the two preceding lines!), one is first inclined to doubt whether any parallelism is intended. Yet, the laying on of the hand certainly implies the movement of the whole arm from the shoulder down. A detail like this, insignificant as it may appear to be, shows that the idea of a vision is to be taken seriously. And the ease with which symmetry and unity of description are achieved prove that we are dealing with a writer who has perfectly mastered his technique.

We shall now give our attention to the central section D (19:11-16), in the last series of Seven Angels, in order to discover its relations to the panel just discussed and to the other six panels of its own series.

And I saw the heavens opened, and, behold, a white horse, and he that sat thereon, 11
called Faithful and True; (19:19; 21:5) V
And in righteousness he doth *judge,* (20:4, 12, 13)
And *make war.* (20:8) VI

And his *eyes* are *a flame of fire* 12
And upon his head are many *diadems;* (of the kings, 21:24,26; 12:3; 13:1) VII
And he hath *a name written* which *no one knoweth* but he himself;
And he is arrayed in a garment *sprinkled with blood;* 13
And his *name is called* the *Word of God;*
And the armies which are in heaven followed him upon white horses, clothed in
fine linen, white pure; (19:8). III 14
And out of his *mouth* proceeded *a sharp sword.* 15

And he shall *rule* them with a rod of iron, (18:3, 6) II
And he *treadeth the winepress* of the fierceness of the wrath of God the Almighty;
And he hath on his garment and on his thigh *a name written,* 16
King of kings and *Lord of lords.* (cf. inversion of terms in 17:14) I

This panel is constructed on a plan somewhat similar to that of 1:13:17a. The rider on the white horse is the Lord. He is called Faithful and True (vs. 11), and on his garment and on his thigh another name is written, King of kings and Lord of lords (vs. 16). There are double designations in either case. That the name is written on such an unusual place as the thigh is explained by the fact that the rider sat on a horse, which would make the thigh a conspicuous part of the body. The double statement of his activity (that he judges and makes war (vs. 11b)) is balanced by the rule (which to a Hebrew is but another name for judging) and the treading of the winepress (cf. 14:19, 20).

In the central section a more detailed description of the Lord is given. The central line describes his garment which is sprinkled with blood as the result of the judgment he has executed against the enemies. The name *written* occurs in the line *before* the centre is reached, and it recurs in vs. 16. The name *called* occurs *after* the centre is passed, and it is also found in vs. 11. This method of cross-stitching with terms was employed also in allocating the phrases introducing the speaker in the Seven Epistles.[12] One of these names is the mystic name, which only the Lord himself knows, and the other is the Word of God, revealed to all the world.

It seems difficult to establish the parallelism between the many diadems upon his head and the armies of heaven which followed him; yet both indicate authority, power. Only in two other passages in the book are diadems mentioned, and they are in the possession of the great enemies of the church (12:3; 13:1); the numbers *seven* and *ten* are prominent. These numbers are again prominent in the description of the kings that are hostile to the church, whose activities are described in 17:1-18, in the *first* of the last seven panels in the book.[13] When we read that these kings as yet have no kingdom but receive authority as kings with the beast for one hour (17:12), and when we recall that the first beast had ten diadems (13:1) and that the red dragon had seven (12:3) and that the same dragon gave the Beast his power, his throne, his great authority (13:2), the conclusion seems natural that the outward symbolic manifestation of such a transfer of authority would be the conferring of the diadems to the kings and the Beast. At any rate, there is none other than the enemies that possesses diadems in this book; but finally the Lord himself will wear these diadems (19:12). The kings which had authority for a brief hour in the first panel (17:12) will ultimately, as depicted in the last panel, bring their glory and the glory of the nations into New Jerusalem (21:24, 26). The means by which the victory of the nations is achieved is "righteousness" (cf. 19:11 with 12:11),

[12] Cf. Outline IV, p. 340.

[13] Cf. 17:2, 7, 9, 10, 12.

symbolically represented in the white linen of the armies of heaven (19:8).

There is another example of cross-stitching with terms in this panel. The white horse of the Lord is to be connected with the white horses of the armies of heaven (cf. vss. 11a and 14). Likewise the diadems on the Lord's head are those that formerly adorned the Dragon, the Beast, and their rulers in this world, those lords and kings whose master Christ is soon to be (vs. 16). In 1:14-16 we found the eyes like a flame of fire and the mouth from which proceeded the sharp sword in the second line from the beginning and the second line from the end of the structure. These ideas occur in 19:12-15 in the first and last lines of the system but still in parallel position. This fact is exceedingly interesting, for it shows that the writer, who has previously cast the figure of the Lord in a certain literary mould, will once more avail himself of the same mould when he has occasion again to present the figure of the Lord.

It was shown by several outlines how the Seven Epistles were related to the description of the Lord given in the first chapter of the book. In a similar manner the portrait of the Lord in 19:11-16 is related to the other six panels in the system. There are a number of identical phrases and parallel ideas that occur in these six panels, and they recur in a certain order in the fourth, or central, panel. There are two remarkable facts that stand out in this arrangement. We have, first, another example of cross-stitching, for panels V, VI, VII, which belong to the last half of the series, are represented in the first half of the central panel. Likewise panels I, II, III, which belong to the first half of the series, are represented in the last half of the central panel. We have, secondly, the ascending order of the numbers of the panels as we approach the centre. In the last series of Seven Angels panels I and VII are parallel; they are made parallel in the central panel also by connecting the diadems with the kings and the Lords. Likewise panels III and V are made parallel, by connecting the white horse and the white horses.[14]

[14] Cf. Ps. 90 vss. 5 and 13 and vss. 7 and 16 for a similar cross-stitching of terms. Ps. 88 is another example. See *supra*, pp. 122, 125.

Both in the General Outline and in the subsequent analysis it has been assumed that the Seven Epistles and the last series of Seven Angels (BB′) are counterparts in the structure of the book. The most obvious reason for this assumption is the fact that many of the statements made in the promises that are appended to the Seven Epistles do not find any adequate explanation in the book until we reach the last series of Seven Angels. Those similes which have always seemed so puzzling are at last explained. Not only is there a connection in meaning but an analysis of the literary structure again reveals that the two series were constructed with reference to one another. In the following outline of the similes used in the promises we have placed the references to the Seven Epistles on the left and those to the Seven Angels at the right.

I	2:7	The tree of life.	22:2	VII
II	2:11	The second death.	21:8	V
III	2:17	A new name written which no one knoweth.	19:12	IV
IV	2:27	Rule them with a rod of iron,	19:15	IV
		The morning star.	22:16	VII
V	3:5	The white garments.	19:14	IV
VI	3:12	New Jerusalem which cometh down out of heaven.	21:2	V
VII	3:21	The throne of Christ and of the Father.	22:1	VII

In the Seven Epistles there are, of course, several similes used in the promises that do not enter this scheme. There are such as "the hidden manna," "the white stone" (2:17), a pillar in the temple of my God" (3:12); but since these do not recur in the last series of Seven Angels, they cannot enter into the scheme. The promise, "I will in no wise blot his name out of the book of life," (3:5) has not been used for an argument, since it is merely a negative promise, while the promise of the white garments preceding it is positive. In the allocation of "the white garments" there could be a choice between 19:8 and 19:14. Since 19:14 in the central panel refers to 19:8 it has seemed better to connect 3:5 with 19:14. What strikes us as remarkable is the frequency with which the *central* panel (19:11-16) turns up in the margin to the right. But the fourth panel, we recall, represents the coming of the Lord with the armies of heaven to conquer all enemies. From this theme the martyr church, no doubt, could draw more comfort than from any other theme in this book. Lastly, it should be recalled that the allocation of the phrases in the last two outlines assumes that 21:1-8 is in its original place when inserted between 19:16 and vs. 17. Although there may be some difference of opinion as to whether 19:1-10 should be regarded as the conclusion of panel III and 21:1-8 as the introduction to panel V, or both should be thought of as frame-passages to panel IV, the decision would not change the *order* of the references.

Why the meaning of the promises to those who overcome should be explained in the last series of Seven Angels is understood best, if we consider the content of these panels and more specifically those in the last half of the series. For those panels are devoted to the dramatic destruction of all the enemies of the church. They have been marching in upon the scene of action, doubly or singly, in an orderly progression, each more formidable than the previous one, with great pomp and power. When the hour of their destruction is come, however, they are summarily removed from the scene in swift succession in exactly the *reverse order of their arrival*, as the following outline shows:

Death and Hades, 6:8.
 The Dragon, 12:3.
  The First Beast and the Second Beast, 13:1, 11.
   Babylon the Great, 17:5.
   Babylon's final destruction, 19:17, 18.
  The First Beast and the False Prophet destroyed, 19:20, cf. 13:14.
 The Dragon destroyed, 20:2.
Death and Hades destroyed, 20:14.

Again and again we meet with announcements of the impending fall of Babylon in the preceding chapters,[15] but even as late as 18:21 its fall is still impending. When, at last, the fourth, or central, panel is past (19:11-16), the one which depicts the coming of the Lord with the armies of heaven, the action of the drama is speeded up and the judgments upon the enemies follow swiftly one upon the other. The tremendous climax expressed in these few verses (19:17-20:15), is hardly realized until we observe the order of the appearance and removal of the enemies and the rela-

[15] Cf. 16:19; 14:8; 18:2, 10, 16, 21.

tive space devoted to each of those acts in the book. It is difficult to see how this quality of the book could have been made effective upon an audience except by the rendering of the book *in toto* at one occasion.[16]

[16] N. W. Lund, *Outline Studies in the Book of Revelation* (Chicago: 1935), pp. 106, 127-129 contains some of the sections of the Last Series of Seven Angels printed in full so as to display the literary form. Among these are 18:10b-17a, the list of commodities in which Babylon traded, with a most remarkable literary form, and, finally, 21:11-22:5, the description of the Holy City and its citizens.

CHAPTER XIX

THE SEVEN SEALS AND THE SEVEN ANGELS

In the General Outline it has already been indicated that the next two main divisions of the book are of a more complex structure (CC′). The first of these divisions (C) opens with the fourth and fifth chapters, which are two scenes laid in heaven; it also closes with two scenes (7:1-8 and 7:9-17). The two latter scenes constitute one of the projections, which has been placed between the sixth and seventh seals. When chapter seven is removed from this position and placed after the seventh seal, it becomes clear that its contents and much of its phraseology makes it a fitting counterpart to chapters four and five. Between these frame-passages with contents of a comforting nature are placed the Seven Seals, which express the divine judgment over the world, a judgment which is finally to terminate the martyrdom of the persecuted church of Christ in the world. This method of distributing passages of a comforting and condemnatory content in well-balanced proportions is part of the technique of the writer. It may best be explained, if we assume that the book was written to serve a liturgical purpose.

The other main division (C′) is neither as long nor as imposing as its counterpart (C) but its general features are strikingly parallel to it. The frame-passages are not double scenes, but single scenes. The first of these (14:1-5) by introducing the 144,000 makes it clear that it is the counterpart of chapter seven. The second frame-passage (15:2-4) by its song of praise indicates that it is related to chapters four and five. Between these two scenes of a comforting nature a series of Seven Angels (14:6-20) is presented, and the judgments symbolized by these angels are judgments upon the world with a view of terminating its tyranny over the church. Both the nature of the frame-passages and the contents of the Seven Seals and the Seven Angels indicate that we are to think of them as counterparts in a far-flung literary pattern. A more detailed analysis will confirm this general statement.

C *Seven Seals and Two Heavenly Scenes*, 4:1-8:5

First Double Scene: Creation and Salvation, 4:1-5:14

The Church and Creation, 4:1-11

After these things 1
I saw, and behold, a door opened
In the heavens;
And the first *voice* that I heard,
As of a trumpet, speaking with me, saying,
Come up hither,
And I will show thee the things which must come to pass
After these things.

A
Straightway I became in the Spirit: 2
And behold, a throne was set in heaven;

And one sitting *upon the throne*,
And he that sat was - - - - - - - -
like a jasper stone and a sardius to look upon,
and there was a rainbow *around the throne*,
like an emerald to look upon. 3

And *around the throne*, four and twenty thrones, 4
And *upon the thrones*, four and twenty elders sitting,
Arrayed in white garments,
And on their heads crowns of gold.

And *out of the throne* proceed - - - - - - - -
lightning,
and *voices*, 5
and thunders.

B
And seven lamps of fire burning
Before the throne,
Which are the seven spirits of God, 6
And *before the throne*
As a glassy sea like unto crystal.

A′
And *in the midst of the throne*,
And *round about the throne*,

Four living creatures,
Full of eyes, *before* and *behind*.

And the first creature was like a lion, 7
And the second creature like a calf,
And the third creature had the face of a man,
And the fourth creature was like a flying eagle.

And the *four* living creatures, having each of them *six* wings, 8
Around and *within* are full of eyes.

And they have no rest day and night, saying,
Holy,
Holy,
Holy,

Lord,
The God,
The Almighty,

Who was,
And who is,
And who cometh

A And whensoever the living creatures shall give { glory
and honor, 9
and thanks }

B To him that sitteth on the throne,
To him that liveth for ever and ever,

(*the throne,* 10
The four and twenty elders shall fall down before him that sitteth on
C And shall worship him that liveth for ever and ever,
And shall cast their crowns before *the throne,*

B′ Saying, worthy art thou, 11
Our Lord and our God,

A′ To receive { the glory,
and the honor,
and the power, }

C′ For thou { *didst create* all things,
and because of thy will they were,
and *were created.* }

After a brief introduction (vs. 1), in which the prophet is summoned by the Lord of the church (cf. 1:10, 12, 15), we are introduced to the throne scene in heaven. This is the first part of the double scene; the second part follows in chapter five. A glance at the many references to it will prove that the throne of God is central in the scene. All the details in the scene are built around the throne, or related to it by the several prepositions and adverbs that are used. In A the threefold description of the glory of God (jasper, sardius, emerald) is balanced by the threefold activities that emanate out of the throne (vs. 5a). There is a chaste restraint in the scene, for the features of the deity are not described (cf. Ps. 104:2; 1 Tim. 6:16). In the central section (vs. 4) four and twenty elders and their thrones are described. The white garments and the crowns of gold indicate a victorious church (cf. 2:10; 3:5, 11); the thrones indicate that they are sharing in the rule of their divine Lord (cf. 1:6; 3:21; 5:10; 20:4). The number twenty-four has been derived by some writers from 1 Chron. 24:1-19; but whatever the origin of the symbolic number may be, it is used here to indicate the church of Christ as ruling with him, possibly with a view of indicating the unity of the saints of the Old Testament with those of the New (cf. 21:12, 14).

In section A′ the four living creatures, or Zoa, symbolize creation. There are *four* creatures, each having *six* wings (vs. 8) thus giving us another symbolic number, twenty-four. Their exceedingly numerous eyes (vss. 6b, 8a) indicate watchfulness. Their likeness is more fully described in the central portion of A′, just as the description of the elders occurred in the central section of A. Their continuous praise may be divided into three triplets (vs. 8b). Between these two sections dealing with creation and the church, i. e., "the new creation" (cf. Col. 3:10), the symbolic representation of the divine Spirit that animates both is introduced in the form of the seven lamps of fire burning before the throne (B). Here the glassy sea is first mentioned, to appear again at a later stage (15:2); in both places there is probably a conscious antithesis to another sea (13:1).

The concluding verses (4:9-11) are not a part of the vision, but constitute a longer note. The force of ὅταν is frequentative, "whensoever," indicating repeated action.[1] The writer's meaning seems to be that as often as the condition described in vs. 9 exists, the action described in vss. 10, 11 will take place. The *future tense* of the verbs in vss. 9, 10 indicates this. Why this long note should be injected at this point does not become clear until we reach the close of the second part of this double scene (cf. 5:14), when the writer makes a closing reference to it. The addition of the words, "and were created," in C′, which has caused so much of textual emendation and comment seems to be nothing more than an attempt to obtain a chiastic triplet to match C above (cf. "the throne" in the extreme lines, cf. C, vs. 10).

[1] H. B. Swete, *The Apocalypse of John, ad loco.*

The Church and Salvation, 5:1-14

And I saw in the right hand of him that sat on the throne 1
A book written within and on the back, close sealed with *seven seals*,
And I saw a strong angel proclaiming with a strong voice: 2

A

Who is *worthy* to open the book,
And to loose the seals thereof?

And no one was able { in the heaven, / or on the earth, / or under the earth 3

To open the book,
Or to look thereon.

And I *wept* much, because no one was found *worthy* 4

To open the book, 5
Or to look thereon.

And one of the elders saith unto me, *Weep* not!

Behold, he hath overcome, { the Lion, / who is of the tribe of Judah, / the Root of David

To open the book,
And the seven seals thereof.

B *And I saw* { in the midst of the throne, / and of the four living creatures, / and in the midst of the elders 6

C

A Lamb standing, as though it had been *slain*,
Having seven horns,
And seven eyes,
Which are the seven Spirits of *God*,
Sent forth into all *the earth.*

D

And he came, and he taketh it out of the right hand of him that sat (upon the throne; 7
And when he had taken *the book*, 8

The four living creatures,
And the four and twenty elders
Fell down before the Lamb;

Having each one a harp,
And golden bowls full of incense which are the prayers of the saints;
And they sing a new song, saying, 9

Worthy art thou to take *the book*,
And to open the seals thereof:

C′
For thou wast *slain*,
And didst purchase us unto *God* with thy blood,
  Of every tribe,
  And tongue,
  And people,
  And nation,
And madest them unto *God* a kingdom and priests, 10
And they reign upon *the earth.*

B′ *And I saw*
And I heard a *voice*
Of many angels
round about the throne,
and the living creatures, 11
and the elders;
And the number of them was ten thousand times ten thousand,
Saying with a great *voice:* 12 (and thousands of thousands,

A′ *Worthy* is the Lamb that hath been slain to receive
and power,
and riches,
and wisdom,
and might,
and honor,
and glory,
and blessing.

And *every created thing* 13
  Which is in the heaven,
  And on the earth,
  And under the earth,
  And on the sea,
And *all things* that are in them hear I saying,

  Unto him that sitteth on the throne,
  And unto the Lamb be

The blessing,
And the honor,
And the glory,
And the dominion for ever and ever.

  And the four living creatures said, Amen. 14
  And the elders fell down and worshipped.

The second part of the double scene (5:1-14) deals with the Church and Salvation. After a few introductory lines (vss. 1, 2a) in which the book with the seven seals is introduced, the scene is developed after a pattern similar to that of chapter four. The scene opens with much weeping because in all creation no one is found that can open the book or look therein (cf. triplet in vs. 3a). The prophet now is told by one of the elders not to weep, because one has overcome and is therefore able to open the book and its seven seals, namely, Christ (cf. triplet in vs. 5b). Why he is worthy does not yet appear, but the answer is given as the action of the scene continues. Section A, which shows a remarkable symmetry of two chiastic parts enveloping two alternating, is balanced by section A′, which again affirms the worthiness, not of the Lion of Judah, however, but of the Lamb that hath been slain (cf. vss. 5, 12). So the scene which opens with weeping ends in jubilant praise.

Section B is introduced by the phrase, "And I saw," and has a triplet: the throne, the Zoa, and the elders. These three also form the core of the more elaborate section B′; but around this central core has been built a more elaborate structure that describes the innumerable angels of heaven singing the redeemer's praise. In 4:1 the term "voice" is used in the centre of the structure, but in B′ the same term occurs in the two extreme lines. A similar shift from extremes to centre, also involving the same term, is found in chapter 1:10, 12 and vs. 15. The rather awkward expression[2] "and I saw, and I heard a voice of many angels," becomes at least intelligible when we treat the first verb as introduction to the whole section B′ and as a conscious parallel to that of B above.

Section C introduces the Lamb standing "in the midst of the throne." Evidently the Lamb is none other than the Lion of Judah; since both symbols are conventional they are used without explanation. Likewise in 4:5b "the seven Spirits of God" are represented symbolically by "the seven lamps of fire," while in 5:6b they are represented by the "seven eyes." The terms, "slain," "God," and "the earth" occur in CC′. That the slain Lamb has significance for "all the earth" (C) becomes clearer as we read C′, where the universal significance of his redemptive work is expressed in the central group of *four* terms. As a striking illustration of the writer's care in the use of terms, we may call attention to the fact that the purchasing of the saints by the blood of the

[2] Philo has given expression to the same idea which occurs in Rev. 1:12; 5:11 when he describes the giving of the Law at Sinai: "A voice sounded forth from out of the midst of the fire, which had flowed from heaven, a most marvellous and awful voice, the flame being endowed with articulate speech in a language familiar to the hearers, which expressed words with such clearness and distinctness that the people seemed rather *to be seeing than hearing it.*"—*De decalogo*, 11.

Lamb and their transformation into a kingdom and priests (paralleled in C′) are found side by side in the same sentence in 1:5, 6. The fact that the saints reign upon the earth (5:10) has already been expressed more elaborately by the twenty-four elders on their thrones in chapter four.

It is significant that the climax of the whole scene, when the Lamb takes the book from him who sat on the throne, should be described, not at the end of the chapter but in the central section D. Again we observe the shift of a term from centre to the extremes, for the book is found in the *central* line of vss. 1, 2 but in the *extremes* of D (vss. 8, 9). It will also be recalled that the elders, representing the church, and the Zoa, representing creation, were described in sections AA′ of chapter four; they are now brought together in the central section D of chapter five, where they are described in two groups of three lines each. In 4:6 "the glassy sea" was mentioned, and in 5:9 "the new song," both in central sections. These two expressions recur once more later in the book, in the two heavenly scenes that encase the Seven Angels in 14:6-20.[3] They are found nowhere else in the whole book.

Just as the previous scene was brought to a close by a long note in 4:9-11, calling attention to the homage of the elders (i. e. the church), when the proper conditions called for it, so the scene in chapter five ends with the homage of creation to God and the Lamb (vs. 13). This homage, however, is not expressed in a note, but is an integral part of the scene itself. In vs. 8 we are told that the Zoa and the elders "fell down." The full act of homage, described in 4:10 by the verbs, "to worship" and "to cast down" their crowns before the throne, has not yet been performed. This is merely the beginning of the song (vss. 9, 10). The myriads of angels join in next (vss. 11, 12), and finally "every created thing" swells the mighty chorus (vs. 13). We thus obtain a mighty crescendo that staggers our imagination. Only a Handel could grapple adequately with such vast proportions; he has beautifully expressed the crescendo in "The Messiah."

After this crescendo vs. 14 seems somewhat out of place. This brief note, however, recalls the action of 4:9-11. The conditions of

[3] Cf. General Outline, C′ and 14:3; 15:2.

4:9 are now fulfilled, and the action described in 4:10, 11 therefore takes place. This note is not merely economy in writing, but it also indicates exceedingly good taste. Without interrupting in any way the crescendo of praise, the final acts of homage (the prostration and the casting of the crowns before the throne) are introduced. It should be recalled, finally, that the church praises God as Creator (4:11), and thus is seen joining in praise with Nature itself (5:13). This twofold division into Nature and the Church is no factitious scheme which has arbitrarily been forced upon these two scenes.[4] We shall soon discover the same distinction in the Seven Seals and in the Seven Angels in 14:6-20.

But before we enter upon discussion of the Seven Seals, we shall examine the double vision in chapter seven, which is the counterpart to the chapters just concluded. This chapter is treated as one of the major projections of the book and not as an episode between the sixth and seventh seals. The reason for this procedure is found in the parallelism of terms and of ideas which it is the purpose of our analysis to set forth.

[4] Cf. *The Liturgy of St. Mark*, quoted by H. B. Swete, *op. cit.*, p. 73.

Second Double Scene: Creation and Salvation, 7:1-17
The Church and Creation, 7:1-8

A

After this I saw *four* angels, 1
Standing at the *four* corners of the earth,
Holding the *four* winds of the earth,

That no wind should blow
on the *earth*,
or on the *sea*,
or upon any *tree*.

And I saw another angel ascending from the sunrising, 2
Having the *seal* of the living *God*.

And he cried with a great voice to the *four* angels,
To whom it was given to hurt the *earth* and the *sea*, saying,

Hurt not
the *earth*,
neither the *sea*, 3
nor the *trees*,

Till we have *sealed* the servants of our *God*,
Upon their foreheads.

B

And I heard the number of them that were *sealed*, 4
A hundred and forty and four thousand,
Sealed out of every tribe of the children of Israel:

Of the tribe of Judah twelve thousand *sealed*; 5
Of the tribe of Reuben twelve thousand;
Of the tribe of Gad twelve thousand;
Of the tribe of Asher twelve thousand; 6
Of the tribe of Naphtali twelve thousand;
Of the tribe of Manasseh twelve thousand;
Of the tribe of Simeon twelve thousand; 7
Of the tribe of Levi twelve thousand;
Of the tribe of Issachar twelve thousand;
Of the tribe of Zebulun twelve thousand; 8
Of the tribe of Joseph twelve thousand;
Of the tribe of Benjamin twelve thousand *sealed*.

The Church and Salvation, 7:9-17

After these things *I saw*, and behold, a great multitude,
Which no man could number, out of every - - - - - - - - -
{ nation, 9
and of tribes,
and of peoples,
and of tongues,

Standing before the *throne*,
And before the Lamb,
Arrayed in white robes,
And palms in their hands.

And they cry with a great voice, *saying*, 10
Salvation to our *God*, who sitteth on the *throne*,
And to the Lamb.

A′ And all the angels were *standing* round about
{ the *throne*,
and the elders, 11
and the four living creatures.

And they fell before the *throne* on their faces,
And worshipped *God*, *saying*,

Amen. 12
Blessing,
And glory,
And wisdom,
And thanksgiving,
And honor,
And power,
And might unto God for ever and ever.
Amen.

And one of the elders answered, saying unto me, 13
These that are arrayed in the white robes, who are they,
And whence *came* they?
And I said unto him, 14
My Lord, thou knowest
And he said to me,
These are they that *come* out of the great tribulation,
And they washed their robes,
And made them white in the blood of the Lamb.

B′ Therefore are they before the *throne* of *God*, 15
And they serve him day and night in his sanctuary,
And he that sitteth on the *throne* shall tabernacle over them.

They shall hunger no more, 16
Neither thirst any more,
Neither shall the sun strike upon them,
Nor any heat:

(herd, 17
For the Lamb that is in the midst of the *throne* shall be their shep-
And shall guide them unto fountains of waters of life;
And *God* shall wipe away every tear from their eyes.

There can be no doubt that the symbolism of these two visions is parallel to the two visions in chapters four and five. In the first vision (7:1-8) the symbolic number *four*, thrice repeated in vs. 1, recalls the four Zoa of chapter four. The triplets (earth, sea, tree) recall a number of similar triplets in the previous vision (4:3, 5, 8, 9, 11). The number 144,000, like the number twenty-four, is a multiple of *twelve.* Nature, which in the previous scenes has rendered its praise to God, is here seen as restrained temporarily from the execution of judgment over the earth until the church is sealed and made safe. Section A deals largely with nature, and section B with the sealing of the church. The former of these sections is an alternating structure, whereas the latter shows some inversion.[5] The prophet saw the four angels and the angel who was to seal the church (vs. 2); the act of sealing he did not see. The result of the sealing is heard (vs. 4). The twelve tribes of Israel are neither the Jewish people (cf. 2:9; 3:9), nor believing Jews who have joined the church, but the whole Israel of God, the church itself. This interpretation is assured by the phrase, "the servants of our God" (vs. 3), which in this book means believers in general.[6] The point in vs. 4 is that the tale of the martyr church is told first, and this part of the proceedings, which is only heard, should probably be connected with the remark made in 6:11b. If, as we assume, chapter seven should not precede but follow the seventh seal, then the "silence in heaven about the space of half an hour" (8:1) may have something to do with the hearing of their number. The scene of 7:1-8 is laid on earth, but the *seer* is in heaven (7:14); if he is to hear the call of the roll of the twelve tribes, this must have happened during the period of silence that preceded 8:5 and the activities there described.

The second vision (7:9-17) is like the first in one respect: the first part of it is *seen* (vs. 9) and the latter part is a conversation between the seer and the elder which is heard (vss. 13-17). For the identification of the "great multitude" with the 144,000 it should be remembered that they are arrayed in white, and that they have come victorious out of "the great tribulation" (cf. 3:5;

[5] Cf. the use of the word "sealed" in vss. 4, 5, 8.
[6] 1:1; 2:20; 10:7; 11:18; 19:2, 5.

1:9). The double mode of representation by audition and vision is found in other passages in the book (cf. 9:16, 17; 22:8). A comparison of chapter seven with chapter five will reveal many striking parallelisms. The four terms in 7:9 occurred also in 5:9b in a somewhat different order. Both groups ascribe their salvation to the blood of the Lamb (5:13; 7:10). The triplet (throne, elders, Zoa) is common to both scenes (5:6, 11; 7:11); this is also true of the sevenfold ascription (5:12; 7:12). Although there can be no question as to the identity of location, activities, and actors in these two scenes, the latter scene is no mere repetition of the first. While in the former scene myriads of angels are singing around the throne (5:12) and the Zoa say, "Amen," the elders fell down and worshipped (5:14). The writer has still this great scene in mind, when he writes: "And all the angels, were *standing* round about the throne, and the elders and the four living creatures, and *they fell before the throne on their faces*" (7:11). Thus we have the final act of homage from the angels in addition to that of the Zoa and the elders (4:9, 10; 5:14) to complete the great praise of the redemption wrought by the Lamb.

The second half of the vision (vss. 13-17) describes the bliss of the redeemed (vss. 13, 14, 16) and the source of their bliss (vss. 15, 17). The two questions, "Who are they"? and, "Whence came they"? are answered in the inverted order. This vision is intimately associated with 14:1-5, but of this we shall have something to say presently.

We shall now turn our attention to the Seven Seals, which intervene between the two frame-passages: the one in chapters four and five and the other in chapter seven.

Judgments upon the World to Save the Martyr Church
The Seven Seals, 6:1-17; 8:1, 3-5

X

And when the Lamb opened one of the seven seals, 1
I heard one of the living creatures saying as with a *voice* of thunder, Come.
And I saw, and behold, a white horse, 2
And he that sat thereon *had* a bow,
And there was given unto him a crown:
And he came forth conquering and to conquer.

And when he opened the second seal, 3
I heard the second living creature saying, Come.
And another came forth, a red horse: 4
And to him that sat thereon was given to take the peace from the earth
And that they should slay one another,
And there was given unto him a *great* sword.

And when he opened the third seal, 5
I heard the third living creature saying, Come.
And I saw, and behold, a black horse,
And he that sat thereon *had* a balance in his hand.
And I heard as it were a *voice* in the midst of the four living creatures, 6
Saying, A measure of wheat for a shilling,
And three measures of barley for a shilling,
And the oil and the wine hurt not.

Y

And when he opened the fourth seal, 7
I heard the voice of the fourth living creature saying, Come.
And I saw, and behold, a pale horse: 8
And he that sat upon him, his name was Death;
And Hades followed with him.
And there was given to them authority over the fourth part of the earth,

To kill with sword,
And with famine,
And with death,
And with the wild beasts of the earth.

And when he opened the fifth seal, 9
I saw underneath the altar the souls of them that had been slain
For the word of God,
And for the testimony which they had held.
And they cried with a great *voice*, saying, 10
How long, O Master, the holy and true,
Dost thou not judge and avenge our blood
On them that dwell on the earth?
And there was given to each a white robe, 11
And it was said unto them, that they should rest a little time,
Until also their fellow-servants should be fulfilled,
And their brethren, who would be killed even as they.

And I saw when he opened the sixth seal, 12
And there was a *great* earthquake.

And the sun became black as sackcloth of hair,
And the whole moon became as blood,
And the stars of the heaven fell unto the earth, 13
as a fig tree casteth her unripe figs,
when she is shaken by a strong wind;
And the heaven was removed as a scroll when it is rolled up. 14

And every mountain
And island were removed out of their places.
And the kings of the earth, 15
And the princes,
X′ A And the chief captains,
And the rich,
And the strong,
And every bondman,
And freeman hid themselves in the caves
And in the rocks of the mountains;
And they say to the mountains and to the rocks, 16

Fall upon us,
And hide us,
From the face of him that sitteth on the throne,
And from the wrath of the Lamb;

For the *great* day of their wrath is come, 17
And who is able to stand?

And when he opened the seventh seal, 8:1
There followed a silence in heaven about the space of half an hour
And another angel came and stood over the altar, having a golden censer: 3
And there was given to him much incense,
That he should add it to the prayers of the saints,
Upon the golden altar which was before the throne;
And the smoke of the incense, with the prayers of the saints, 4
Went up before God out of the angel's hand.
And the angel taketh the censer, 5
And filled it with the fire from the altar;
And he cast it into the earth,
And there followed thunders, and *voices*, and lightnings, and an earthquake.

Even a casual glance at the Seven Seals is sufficient to show that we have a subdivision of the seven into one group of four and another of three seals. The first of these groups deals with judgments upon the world by means of war and famine, and the reference in the third seal to Nature is clear. The famine is announced by a special voice that is heard "in the midst of the four living creatures" (vs. 6). The second group, on the other hand, deals with the martyr church, whose members pray for a termination of their troubles (vs. 10) and finally, after some waiting, receive an answer to their prayers (cf. 8:3, 4). We shall see presently how much there is in favor of a similar trend of thought in the series of Seven Angels in 14:6-20, which is the series parallel to the Seven Seals.

A closer examination reveals that the seals contain certain definite elements, some of which occur in the first and others in the last group: (1) an introductory formula: "When he (the Lamb) opened"; (2) the announcements by the Zoa: "Come"; (3) the actors: the riders on the horse; (4) the insignia given the riders: bow, sword, balance; (5) the commissions given the riders. When the recurrence of these standard parts of the seals is studied more closely, it will be seen that there are some variations which consist of additions and transpositions of the order in which they occur. In the first and the third seals the formula reads: "I heard" and "I saw"; but in the second seal occurs only "I heard." In the first and third seals the insignia of the riders are introduced before their commission is given, but in the second seal this order is reversed. We evidently confront here a method of procedure with which we have already become acquainted in the Seven Epistles. The first three seals are by this arrangement placed in a group by themselves. When we arrive at the fourth seal, we discover that the actor is *named*: Death riding forth with Hades as a groom. This procedure also reminds us of 2:18, where the one speaking to the Seven Churches of Asia is named "the Son of God," in the central epistle to Thyatira. We shall also find a similar procedure in 14:14. The fourth seal is in the nature of a summary, for it looks back upon the warfare and famine of the two preceding seals (cf. vs. 8 with vss. 4, 6). The fourth seal is significant as the first instance in which the great enemies of the church are introduced in this book, but their authority is restricted to "the fourth part of the earth." The remark in vs. 6, "And the oil and wine hurt not," is of similar import. This restricted authority should be kept in mind until we reach the parallel series in 14:6-20, where the final harvest has come at last and all things have ripened to judgment.

It is difficult to visualize the action of the first four seals. The great scroll is taken out of the hand of him that sat on the throne, and its seals are broken by the Lamb. As each seal is broken, one of the Zoa cries out, "Come," and the rider rides forth, presumably out of the scroll itself. The breaking of each seal evidently reveals a part of the scroll. This can be achieved only by assuming a series of cords passing between the coils of the scroll and gathering into sections a number of these coils, with the seals hanging loosely outside, and at the end of the scroll.

The second group of three seals introduces the martyr church. It is difficult to understand how commentators could have missed the striking parallelism between the *fifth* and the *seventh* seals. The persons involved are the same in both, namely, the saints. In both the locality is identical: before the altar. This altar, which is only casually mentioned in 7:9, is more fully identified in 8:3. In both the prayers of the saints are described; but while they bring no immediate action in the fifth seal, they are begun to be fulfilled in the seventh seal (cf. 7:10 with 8:3, 4). There is mention made of "an earthquake" in 8:5, and this earthquake is no other than the "great earthquake" which occurs when the sixth seal is opened (7:12). The fifth and seventh seals are to be regarded as two symbolic panels which match each other, and the action that the saints are waiting for is vividly depicted in the central panel of the three (vss. 12-17). By every apocalyptic color made familiar by convention the judgment is described in the sixth seal; to clinch the matter beyond doubt the terrified enemies of the church cry out, "For the great day of their wrath *is come*, and who is able to stand" (vs. 17). By these indications as well as by the greater literary art with which the sixth seal is wrought, it is made clear that it is the climax of the series.

The literary art displayed in this central panel is quite detailed. There are *seven* terms employed to enumerate the terror-stricken enemies. By logical division these fall into two couplets with a triplet between them. The Greek *endings* of these terms show that the writer has imagined these terms read in the assembly as he wrote. There are not less than twenty conjunctions (καὶ) that open the lines—a factor which must have added not a little to the impressive effect of reading the passage. The only apparent irregularity is vs. 13b, which looks like a gloss. The adjective, "great," occurs in the second seal once (vs. 4), and it recurs here twice (vss. 12, 17). The noun, "voice," (φωνὴ) occurs four times (cf. vss. 1, 6, 10, and 8:5), that is to say, in first, third, fifth, and seventh seals, or in the odd members of the series of seven, while the same noun is not found in the even members, the second and the sixth. In the fourth member it is found (vs. 7), but the fourth member in a series of seven stands in a class by itself. We shall see presently how this mannerism of the writer turns up once more in the odd members of the series in 14:6-20. The judgment with which the writer of the book is immediately concerned is the judgment of Rome. We shall see how the enemies enumerated in 6:15 appear again under similar circumstances (cf. 19:18). The certainty that the sixth seal presents to us the final catastrophe is further assured by observing how many of the terms describing the catastrophe recur in the climactic seventh panel of the Trumpet and Bowl series (cf. 11:14-18 and, especially, 16:17-21).

When the double vision of chapter seven (placed in our text between the sixth and the seventh seals) is treated as an episode, the purpose of which is to impart comfort before the final fury of the judgments breaks forth, the climax of the series must be sought either in the seventh seal or in the whole series of Seven Trumpets. But the seventh seal is in no sense climactic; and to regard the Seven Trumpets as a series that is to be extracted from the seventh seal will disrupt the whole balance of the book. If our analysis has any cogency, it must be sufficiently clear that the heavenly vision of chapter seven is parallel to the similar double vision of chapters four and five and that the seventh seal is a very close parallel to the fifth. Only when we forget that sequence in the visions does not imply chronology of fulfilment will we feel any difficulty in placing the climax in the sixth seal.

It is possible that the need of an episode was first felt among the Greeks, when the true structure of the book had been lost sight of. After the seventh chapter had been placed in its present position, however, it was felt that the seventh seal lacked all the elements of a true climax. By inserting 8:2, which introduces the seven trumpet angels prematurely, the idea was then conveyed that the climax was to come in the Trumpet Series. But 8:2 belongs properly to a position immediately before 8:6, both verses forming the introduction to the Trumpet Series. By reversing this process of projecting the passages we restore the original structure of the book. Nevertheless, the theory of a later editorial adjustment is somewhat shaken, when we arrive at 15:1—a verse which again somewhat prematurely introduces the seven angels of the Bowl series. This verse certainly belongs to 15:5, both verses being the formal introduction to the Bowl series. It is, of course, quite possible that the same considerations that prompted a later Greek editor to displace chapter seven could also have been guiding him in making the longer projection (14:1-15:4), for the two frame-passages of this section (14:1-5 and 15:2-4) are decidedly of a comforting content; they may properly be treated as another episode before the climactic fury of the Bowl series. When, however, due consideration has been given to the theory of a later editing by one who was ignorant of the original chiastic structure of the book, it seems, nevertheless, more natural to assume that the projections are the work of the author himself. Their true nature could not possibly have been mistaken in the Seals and the Trumpets; and even in the case of the third projection (14:1-15:4) there could have been little cause for making a mistake by those who by heritage and training were familiar with the chiastic structure of the book. Even if one should finally determine not to accept 14:1-15:4 as a true projection, together with 7:1-17 and 10:1-11:13, the consequences of such a decision would be very light for our total conception of the book. Such a decision would merely lead us to treat four of the main divisions of the book as alternating (CD and C'D') rather than as chiastic (CD and D'C'). The latter of these alternatives have been accepted in the General Outline for two reasons: (1) it gives a uniform chiastic arrangement of all the sections of the book; (2) it explains some details that otherwise, at least in appearance, are puzzling: The shout of triumph over the fall of Babylon in 14:8 would seem to be better placed after the event itself rather than before it (cf. 16:19). But whether we treat division C' in the book as a projection or not, it will always remain the great counterpart of division C.

We shall now proceed to an analysis of division C' (14:1-15:4), beginning with the two frame-passages, 14:1-5 and 15:2-4. Although these two panels are much briefer and simpler than the elaborate frame-passages in C, they are, nevertheless, strongly reminiscent of their more elaborate counterparts. A detailed comparison of the two panels is exceedingly interesting for the purpose of determining the author's technique. In 14:2 we *hear* a voice of "harpers harping upon their harps," and in 15:2 we *see* those responsible for the music standing upon the glassy sea. By way of identification we are informed that they are "these that were not defiled with women" (14:4); by this is meant, not an order of celibates but such as have escaped the contamination of the woman Jezebel and the Harlot (cf. 2:20; 17:1 ff.). They are identical with "them that come off victorious from the beast" (15:2). They are standing on Mount Zion (14:1), by which is not meant any earthly mount, for Mount Zion had become the antithesis to Mount Sinai and is now used as the new spiritual relationship in which the saints stood to Christ (cf. Hebr. 12:22-24). The symbolic use of Mount Zion in vs. 1 explains how the sound of their song can come from heaven (vs. 2) without the necessity of complex hypotheses of source criticism to account for the shift of locality between the first and the second verse. This symbolic Mount Zion is in heaven. Those that sing the "new song" (14:3) are those that stand on the glassy sea (15:3). In the former passage we are merely informed that they sing, but in the latter the nature of their song is given. It is "the song of Moses, the servant of God, and the song of the Lamb" (15:3). These two had formerly been sung apart by religious communities that had at times been hostile to one another, but had now become "one new man" (Eph. 2:15; Col. 3:10, 11). There are thus many strands that bind 14:1-5 and 15:2-4 together, for the latter passage is largely supplementary to the former.

These two passages, however, are just as clearly related to the frame-passages of C. The 144,000 of 14:1 are those of 7:4-8. They have the name of the Father on their foreheads (14:1) because they were sealed with that name (7:3). They are before the throne, the Zoa, and the elders (14:3), the same locality in which the former scene is laid (7:11 ff.). The fact that they have been purchased out of the earth (14:3) refers to the same people and the same situation as that described in 7:14. They follow the Lamb "whithersoever he goeth" (cf. 14:4 with 7:17).

We arrive at similar results by comparing 15:2-4 with chapters four and five. The sea of glass and the harps are common to both (15:2; 5:8, 9). If there is any hesitancy on the part of the interpreter to accept the twenty-four elders as the standard symbol of the new creation, the church of Christ, it must disappear in view of the supplementary scenes in C′. We are told "that no man could learn the song, save the hundred and forty and four thousand that had been purchased out of the earth" (14:3), and yet the twenty-four elders sing the song (5:9). The fact that the new song is given in 15:3-4 also serves to connect this section with that of chapters four and five, where some of the finest choral parts in the book are to be found.

There are two terms used in these earlier scenes, which recur in the two frame-passages of C′. They both appear in *central* sections of their respective structures, and they are never found in the whole book except in these passages. "The glassy sea" in 4:6 recurs in 15:2; the "new song" in 5:9 recurs in 14:3. That the writer has selected just these references from central positions in their own structures for the later description (which, though brief, is strongly reminiscent of the earlier and more elaborate scenes) is a certain proof of his intention to bring these scenes together in the reader's mind. Such details are laid into place and attain their full significance only when the interpretation of the book operates with the chiastic principle. We shall see how this principle again affects the interpretation of the following series of Seven Angels in 14:6-20, a section of the book that has either received very little attention or has been the experimental ground for much fruitless source criticism.[7]

In the analysis of the Seven Seals there was one fact that stood out more clearly than any other, namely, that the first four seals differed in form and content from the last three. The first four moved in the realm of Nature with war and famine; the last three brought the reader to the throne and altar of God, where the souls of the martyrs were praying for the termination of the martyrdom of the church and finally received assurance that judgment would fall upon their persecutors. The series of Seven Angels in 14:6-20 offers a very interesting parallel to this arrangement. The first three panels are, to be sure, strikingly different from the last four, and the division of *three* and *four* is made perfectly clear. For immediately after the third panel the series is brought to a halt by an interrupting voice from heaven, saying, "Write, blessed are the dead who die in the Lord from henceforth; yea, saith the Spirit, that they may rest from their labors; for their works follow them" (14:13). If we now examine the first three panels, we shall find that they are devoted to the struggle between the true and the false worship, which was the cause of the martyrdom of the church.

The first angel calls upon men to offer true worship to God (vs. 7), for the judgment is impending; the third angel warns men against the false worship directed toward the Beast and the pollutions incurred by such idolatrous practices (vs. 9); again the impending judgment is in the background. This reference to the struggle of the church with the Beast is singularly appropriate, if the first three angels in 14:6-20 are to be treated as parallel to the last three seals. The second angel announces, "Fallen, fallen is Babylon the great" (vs. 8). By being made to carry this announcement the second panel in this series becomes parallel to the

[7] For a brief summary cf. I. T. Beckwith, *The Apocalypse of John* (1922), pp. 653-654, 666-668; *Encyclopedia Biblica*, Col. 205, section 32; C. A. Briggs, *The Messiah of the Apostles*, pp. 293, 384-386.

sixth seal, which in a great scene has already depicted the terrifying aspects of the day of judgment. Thus we find that the two panels that are *central* in their respective groups of three are devoted to the same subject matter. Under the fifth seal the saints are told to "rest yet for a little time" (6:11); this rest is now assured them by the voice from heaven in 14:13. The rest spoken of is evidently intended to be in contrast to the state of the wicked, who, we are assured, "have no rest" (vs. 11). There is even a suspicion that a further contrast between the state of the wicked and that of the saints is expressed in the description of the worship, "the smoke of the incense, with the prayers of the saints, went up before God" (8:4); and in torment, "the smoke of their torment goeth up forever and ever" (14:11). For it is really the ascent of the former that brings about the latter. From these remarks it will be seen how closely the first group of three angels in 14:6-20, with the interlude, correspond in their subject matter to the last group of three seals.

When we arrive at the fourth panel (vs. 14), we find that it contains no reference to an angel but describes the Son of Man sitting upon the cloud, "having on his head a golden crown, and in his hand a sharp sickle." There are angels in all the other panels (cf. vss. 6, 8, 9, 15, 17, 18), but for the fourth, or central, angel the Son of Man is substituted (vs. 14). We found a similar procedure followed in the last series of Seven Angels (17:1-22:5, cf. 19-11).[8] He is the only agent in the series that is *named*, which is merely a repetition of the procedure in the fourth seal, where Death and Hades were named (6:8). Commentators have sometimes without any real cause wondered at the strange inactivity of this central figure. Just as the central seal in a way sums up the activity of the three preceding seals (war, famine, cf. 6:8), so the figure of the central panel in 14:14 extends his activity over the following three panels. The sickle is the symbolic emblem of the Lord's judgment, and this reappears in each of the following panels. We recall how prominent were the insignia of the riders in the first four seals. Instead of such insignia these four panels

[8] The idea of the Lord and *six* angels recurs in *The Shepherd of Hermas* (Lake's ed.), Simil. IX, 6:2 and 12:8.

contain only one emblem, thus indicating that the Lord's will is to be discovered in all the judgments.

With the third panel and the interlude we part with the struggles of the church and enter the realm of Nature. The fifth angel announces that the harvest of the earth is ripe (vs. 15). The nature of the harvest is not disclosed, but may easily be inferred from the verb, which means "to become dry" (ξηραίνω). It is the harvest of grain. The seventh angel announces that the grapes "are fully ripe" (vs. 18). There are two facts that attract our attention in these announcements: the first is that the evident restraint imposed on the judgments under the four first seals (cf. 6:7; "the oil and the wine hurt not"; 6:8, "one fourth") is here withdrawn, the situation being ripe for judgment and the harvest time come; the second is that both judgments involve the means of sustenance, grain and wine, i. e. they relate to Nature.

Both the second and the sixth panels are conspicuous for their *brevity*. In this respect they are exactly like the second and sixth epistles. The second angel announces the fall of Babylon the great (vs. 8), but the sixth is strangely inactive in his respective panel (vs. 17). It is significant, however, that whatever activity is found is related to "the sanctuary which is in heaven," the same sanctuary in which the prayers of the saints go up with the incense from the altar before the throne and from which the judgments finally emanate (cf. 8:2-5). In fact the last three angels are all related to the sanctuary (vss. 15, 17, 18). The fifth comes out of the sanctuary and the seventh from the altar. We are assuming in our treatment of the series of Seven Angels that they are constructed in two series of three around a central fourth panel, just as the Seven Seals and the Seven Epistles were.

Although the second angel is a good parallel to the sixth seal, there seems to be no such good parallelism between the sixth angel and the second seal. This is due to the strange inactivity of the sixth angel in his particular panel. This panel, however, does not, for some unknown reason, tell the whole story of the angel's activity. For when we arrive at the seventh angel, he does not himself perform the act of reaping the grape harvest but calls upon the sixth angel to act for him (vss. 19-20). The activity described in these verses is precisely of the kind we are taught elsewhere to associate with the judgment of Babylon the great (cf. the city and the winepress in 16:19; 19:15). This great massacre, were its description only confined to the sixth panel, would certainly make this panel parallel to the second seal, whose rider was given the great sword with the commission "that they should slay one another" (6:3).

The extent of the massacre is conveyed in the statement that the blood came out of the winepress "even unto the bridles of the horses" (vs. 20). But what horses? The article indicates some definite horses that the writer has in mind. There is hostile cavalry appearing in the sixth trumpet (9:16 ff.), and, if the Bowl series preceded the section we are now dealing with, the reference may be to the carnage referred to in the sixth Bowl (16:16). None of these references, however, seem very attractive. We conclude therefore that unless "*the* horses" are purely conventional and hence not to be further identified, the nearest identification would be the four horses of the Seven Seals. The symbolic number *four*, which in the seals was used to indicate restraint in the judgments (6:8), would here then be turned to its opposite use, namely, to describe the full extent of the massacre. For 1600 furlongs would be 4 x 400. To use the same symbol for two opposite ideas is not an uncommon practice of this writer.

One more feature of the series requires our attention. Four times we are told that an angel spoke with "a great voice" (cf. vss. 7, 9, 15, 18), i.e. in the first, third, fifth, and seventh panels. The reference to a voice is altogether wanting in the second and sixth panels. We have already seen how these pairs of panels which carry the reference to "the voice" in other respects are parallel, and why the two in which they are wanting should also be so regarded. The presence of the voice in the *odd* members in the series of seven, and its absence in the *even*, is also a feature in the Seven Seals. Even the exception in the occurrence of the voice which was observed in the *fourth seal* (6:7) may be matched by the voice from heaven in the interlude (14:13). The *first* and the *fifth* angels, i.e. the two that open the group of three on either side of the central panel, contain a reference to "the hour" of judgment (vss. 7, 15). The significance of this fact becomes clear as we recall that the *first* and the *fifth* members in the series of Seven Epistles also carried additional phrases to indicate that they opened their respective groups of three.

Among the many features that serve to bind together the two series we should not neglect to mention "the crown" (vs. 6; 6:2). It has often been inferred that the rider on the white horse is Christ, a statement which seems to be supported by 19:11. In 6:2, however, it would probably be more correct to hold, as in 10:1, that the person referred to, though displaying the symbols usually assigned to the Lord, is not strictly to be identified with him but is rather to be regarded as the symbolic person who takes the part of Christ in the action of the visions. There can be no doubt that the phrase, "conquering and to conquer" (6:2), has a reference not only to the first rider but to the others as well. Such an overlapping of the action of one panel into the others is clearly assumed in the fourth seal, which contains a summary of the two preceding (vs. 8b). We have also seen in a comparison of the central panel (14:14) with the following three how the sickle of the Son of Man is active in all of them, whether wielded by himself or by the angels. The significant fact is, however, that the crown adorning one of the participants should be found in both of these series. That the Lord, contrary to expectation, does not appear as the fourth rider is probably to be explained by the necessity to present Death and Hades, the two great enemies of the church, in a *central* position and their conqueror, the Son of Man, as a striking antithesis in the same position in the parallel series in 14:6-20. That the Son of Man is the conqueror of Death and Hades is already brought before the reader of the book in the Prologue (cf. 1:18). It is the purpose of the two series we have been comparing to show dramatically how Death and Hades are to be overcome by the power of the Son of Man.

The general topic presented in the series of Seven Seals and of the Seven Angels, together with the heavenly scenes of their frame-passages, appears to be the salvation of the persecuted church by means of divine judgments upon its persecutors. Their subdivision into two groups of four-three or three-four, in which *four* refers to the realm of Nature and *three* to the Church, is consistently carried out in the two series. The idea that Nature itself is at the service of God is an Old Testament idea. In the Christian view of the world this idea is included. But Nature is now in bondage and is groaning and travailing in pain. The Church also groans while it awaits the adoption, the redemption of the body. If ever these truths engaged the minds of early apocalyptists and found a symbolic expression in their writings, no better expression could have been found than that of the Seven Seals. The first four seals present the riders as riding forth in response to the call of the Zoa, which in the symbolism of the scene represent Nature; the last three seals present to us in no uncertain terms the groaning of the Church, in response to which the ultimate judgments are brought upon the world (cf. Rom. 8:22, 23). These ideas had found expression in the Pauline epistles four decades before the Book of Revelation was written, and it is reasonable to suppose that the ideas of theology sooner or later will press on toward a liturgical expression in the public worship of the church.

CHAPTER XX

THE SEVEN TRUMPETS AND THE SEVEN BOWLS

The next great divisions of the book are the Trumpet series and the Bowl series (DD′). That 8:2 is injected prematurely into the text of the seventh seal is no indication that the Seven Trumpets are to be developed out of the seventh seal or out of the whole series of Seven Seals. The two series of Trumpets and Bowls are unique in the book, for they are consecutive, each carrying on the idea of the preceding, until finally the climax is reached in the *seventh* panel. Step by step the two series move together over the same spheres of activity, with a great similarity of action and with the same type of symbolism. Of the Trumpet series it is true that the first four panels deal with *things*, while the last three deal with *men*. This is only approximately correct of the Bowl series. Instead of the division into Nature and the Church to which attention was called above, we have now Nature and the World. With the exception of some slight references to the church the two series are almost exclusively devoted to the destruction of the enemies of the church. Both series close with a note of finality.

The symbolism is strongly reminiscent of the historic deliverance of Israel from Egypt. The accounts of the Exodus given in the Old Testament had for centuries been read in the synagogue for edification. The attention given to this topic in the Jewish community must have been considerable and the lessons drawn from it many. Even in the religious poetry of the Hebrews the Exodus was celebrated (cf. Pss. 114, 81). When therefore the Christian church had begun to think of itself as "the Israel of God" in contrast to "Israel after the flesh," what could be more natural than to take over the symbolism developed in the Old Testament church. When now the apocalyptist is about to describe the release of the church from the bondage of Rome, the visions assume the form of Israel's release from the bondage of Egypt.

Events that are in themselves impressive assume symbolic significance and become applicable to analogous situations.

It will not be necessary to print the whole text of the two series. Aside from several clusters of terms in which symbolic numbers are discernible, and certain minor sections which are chiastic the series offer nothing of special literary interest. The description of the horses, however, in 9:17, 18 is interesting.

And out of their mouth
  Proceedeth
    Fire,
    And smoke,
    And brimstone.
      By these *three* plagues
      Was the *third* part of men killed,
    By the fire,
    And the smoke,
    And the brimstone,
  Which proceedeth
Out of their mouth.

The following outline will tabulate the most significant similarities and differences in the Trumpets and the Bowls.

Comparative Outline of the Trumpet and Bowl Series

The Seven Trumpets 8:2,6–9:21; 11:14–19		*The Seven Bowls* 15:1, 5-8; 16:1-21	
Introduction, 8:2,6.		*A Heavenly Scene*, 15:1, 5-8; 16:1.	
		The opened sanctuary; violent action.	
First Trumpet, 8:7.		*First Bowl*, 16:2.	
Agents:	hail, fire, blood.		
Sphere:	earth.	Sphere:	earth.
Results:	burning of earth, trees, grass.	Results:	a sore upon idolaters.
Numbers:	three.		
Second Trumpet, 8:8–9.		*Second Bowl*, 16:3.	
Agents:	a great mountain.		
Sphere:	sea.	Sphere:	sea.
Results:	sea becomes blood; a third dies.	Results:	blood of a dead man; all die.
Numbers:	three.		
Third Trumpet, 8:10–11.		*Third Bowl*, 16:4.	
Agents:	a burning star.		
Sphere:	rivers, fountains of water.	Sphere:	rivers, fountains of water.
Results:	waters made bitter; men die.	Results:	they become blood.
Numbers:	three.		

		Interlude, 16:5-7.	
		The Angel and the Altar.	
Fourth Trumpet, 8:12.		*Fourth Bowl*, 16:8-9.	
Agents:	none.		
Sphere:	sun, moon, stars.	Sphere:	sun.
Results:	they were darkened.	Results:	men scorched with great heat, no repentance.
Numbers:	three.		
Interlude, 8:13.			
An eagle: three woes.			
Fifth Trumpet, 9:1-11.		*Fifth Bowl*, 16:10-11.	
Agents:	a star.		
Sphere:	the pit of the abyss.	Sphere:	the throne of the Beast.
Results:	darkness, locusts, *pain*.	Results:	darkness, great *pain*, no repentance.
Numbers:	three (vs. 4), five (vs. 5).		
Sixth Trumpet, 9:12-21.		*Sixth Bowl*, 16:12-16.	
Agents:	four angels.		
Sphere:	the river Euphrates.	Sphere:	the river Euphrates.
Results:	armies of horsemen.	Results:	army, demons of idolatry.
Numbers:	five, three (vs. 20), four (vs. 21).	Numbers:	three (vs. 13).
Seventh Trumpet, 11:14-18.		*Seventh Bowl*, 16:17-21.	
Agents:	none.		
Sphere:	the kingdom of the world.	Sphere:	Babylon the great.
Results:	rewards and punishments.	Results:	punishments through Nature.
Numbers:	twenty-four (vs. 16); three, two (vs. 17.	Numbers:	three (vss. 18, 19).
Finality:	the kingdom is the Lord's, voices in heaven. (vs. 15).	Finality:	"It is done," vs. 17. voice out of the temple.
A Heavenly Scene, 11:19.			
The opened sanctuary: violent action.			

In 8:2 we are introduced to "the seven angels that stand before God," who may either be identical with the seven archangels (cf. Tob. 12:15), or may be a more explicit presentation of the seven Spirits (cf. 1:4; 4:5). The seven angels of the Bowls "came out of the sanctuary" (15:6), their garb being strongly reminiscent of their Lord's (1:13). Aside from their function in the Bowl Series they appear twice elsewhere (cf. 17:1; 21:9). The emphasis that is given to their coming from the presence of God may be a way of conveying to the reader the particular significance attached to their actions.

In accordance with the suggestion made in the General Outline, the two series are placed closest to the central main part of the book, which contains the divisions EFF′E′. In these the great enemies of the church, the dragon and the two beasts, are introduced. In these are also found the great symbolic panels that depict the conveying of the prophetic commission to the church to be a witness and the struggles with Judaism and Paganism that are the result of a faithful execution of the commission. This vital part of the book is framed in two Heavenly Scenes, one concluding the series of Seven Trumpets and the other opening the series of Seven Bowls. The former of these scenes is merely a brief verse (11:19), yet with a fivefold description of activities issuing forth from the opened sanctuary and the ark of the covenant. The latter of the scenes is longer, since it also contains the introduction to the series of Seven Bowls (15:1, 5-16:1), a description of the seven angels. But here also we are dealing with the opened sanctuary (15:5); yet it was so filled with smoke from the glory of God that no one could enter it (vs. 8). These are both heavenly scenes, and they may not in any sense be regarded as part of the two series of visions, since, in the one case, the Trumpet-visions have been concluded and, in the other, the Bowl-visions have not yet begun. They contain, like all frame-passages, messages of consolation, strongly reaffirming the presence of divine power soon to be manifested in behalf of the church. Such an assurance of divine aid could never be placed to greater advantage than before and after the four great panels that depict the struggle of the church with the world.

A closer study of the Comparative Outline will bring out several important facts concerning the structure of the two series. The Trumpet-visions proceed to the fourth, affecting in turn earth, sea; rivers and fountains of water; sun, moon, and stars. At this point the series is suddenly interrupted by an eagle (or an angel, if another reading is accepted) flying in mid-heaven and crying, "Woe, woe, woe for them that dwell on the earth." Each of the following three trumpets is identified with one of these woes. By this interlude in the series two results are achieved: (1) the interest of the reader is stimulated to a very high degree in the last three trumpets; (2) the series of Seven Trumpets is broken up into a four-three arrangement. The first four trumpets deal with *things*, but the last three affect *men*. The latter are also much longer and more gruesome in every respect, thus bringing the series to a great climax in the seventh member.

The Bowl-visions are briefer, covering the same ground in the same sequence as the Trumpet-visions; but they are by no means a mere echo of them. The agents that figure conspicuously at the blowing of the trumpets are all missing in the Bowl-visions, probably because the bowls themselves are conceived as containing the various afflictions that result (cf. 15:7). The symbolic numbers which were very conspicuous in the Trumpet-visions are nearly always absent in the Bowl-visions (cf. 16:13, 18, 19). In the former series they are mostly employed in a restrictive sense, for the results are often confined to "one third" of the spheres affected by the judgment. The removal of these restrictions from the judgments in the Bowl-visions render these highly climactic.

There are many other evidences of a climax in the construction of the Bowl-visions. The fire from heaven affects only *things* in one vision but *men* in the other (cf. 8:7; 16:2); a similar result is seen in two other visions (cf. 8:12; 16:9). These are the two instances in the Bowl-visions in which the first and the fourth panels introduce *men* in the effects of the judgments; this is not true of the Trumpet-visions. In one vision the sea becomes like blood and a third of its life dies; in the other the sea becomes like blood *of a dead man* and every living thing in it dies (cf. 8:8; 16:3); whereas in one the waters are made bitter, in the other they become blood (cf. 8:11; 16:4); in one men experience great pains, but in the other they gnawed their tongues for pain (cf. 9:5; 16:10); in one the horses of the cavalry are the synthesis of every harmful thing on earth, but in the other their place is taken by "the spirits of demons working signs" coming out of the mouth of the Dragon himself (cf. 9:12-21; 16:12-16); one vision merely announces the victory of Christ, with its accompanying rejoicing but the other gives a very detailed picture of the destruction of the arch-enemy of the church (cf. 11:14-18; 16:17-21).

The climax is extended also to the interludes. While one merely announces the three woes over them that dwell on the earth (8:13), the other is more specific, one might say, gloating over the impending judgment. "They poured out the blood of saints and prophets, and blood hast thou given them to drink. They are worthy!" (cf. 16:5-7). The interlude divides the Bowl series into a three-four arrangement, which is the inversion of the order of the Trumpet series. The arrangement of the two series into four-three and three-four groups is the writer's formal way of indicating that they belong together and are to be read with reference to one another. It is difficult to see how such an intention could be realized, unless we assume that the book was read as a whole at one time, and its parallel sections were rendered possibly antiphonally, however such rendition might be conceived.

We are told that with Seven Bowls "is finished the wrath of God" (15:1). Why such an announcement should be made about the Bowls and not about the Trumpets, when both series traverse the same territory, becomes clear in view of what has just been said in regard to the climactic nature of the Bowl-visions. In the writer's mind both series constitute a unity. There are other signs of the finality ascribed to the two series. The well-known formula, "who is, who was, and who cometh" (1:4, 8; 4:8), which recurs in the book, calling attention to the coming of the judge of all the earth, is changed in these two series. In 11:17 the third member is eliminated, and in 16:5 "thou holy one" is substituted. The reason for the change is plain, for each series brings the development to a close. The Lord is no longer coming; he has come! The kingdom of the world is now Christ's, and he shall reign for ever and ever. He has "taken his great power and didst reign" (11:15-17). The judgment is now come upon mankind. His servants are to be rewarded and his enemies destroyed (vs. 18). The elimination of the third term of the formula, however, shows us the exceeding great care with which the book is constructed. The distinction of being careful in the use of terms is not always accorded the author of this book!

The seventh bowl opens with "a great voice out of the sanctuary, from the throne" (observe the identification of the two), announcing, "It is done!" This announcement is immediately followed by lightnings, voices, and thunders (cf. 16:18 with 8:5). The earthquake, the like of which the earth has never seen, followed (here as in 8:5). This is the earthquake which we have previously identified with the *great* earthquake of the sixth seal (6:12-17). Babylon receives in full measure the divine wrath. The islands and the mountains fled (cf. 16:20 with 6:14). The judgment is now completed: "It is done!" The reign of Christ in his kingdom and the destruction of the kingdom of this world come before the readers of this book also in 17:1 and 21:9; these two panels serve to reaffirm the great contrast.

CHAPTER XXI

THE TESTIMONY OF THE CHURCH UNDER PERSECUTION

The four central main divisions of the book, designated EFF'E' in the General Outline, are the heart of the Book of Revelation. In these symbolic panels two great historic struggles of the church, the one with Judaism and the other with Paganism, are depicted. These struggles arose as the result of the function of the church as a witness in the world. To present to the world "the word of God and the testimony of Jesus Christ" is the great commission of its members (cf. 1:2, 9), and for this cause they are called upon to suffer (cf. 6:9; 12:17; 20:4). When the double vision in 10:1-11:13 is moved out of its present position between the sixth and the seventh trumpets and given the position indicated in the General Outline, it will be seen that those two panels in many ways are connected with the visions of the dragon in 12:1-17 and of the two beasts in 13:1-18.

With the origin of these symbols we are not now immediately concerned. Even if it could be established beyond doubt that these visions, or parts of them, are of Jewish origin and if the purpose they had served in the original apocalypse from which they are derived could be determined, such discoveries would have a certain historical interest but would add very little to the understanding of the visions themselves. The rule for interpreting words holds good for symbols also; for not only their derivation but their use in the context determine their meaning. And often the meaning derived from their context entirely departs from the meaning indicated by their derivation. Our reasons for treating these four sections as parallel, therefore, must be discovered within the sections themselves. In order to convey satisfactorily the symmetry with which these four panels are constructed it will be necessary to print the text and to indicate by italics and references the parallelisms that are to be found.

E *The Little Book: The Church's Testimony in the Roman Empire,* 10:1-11

A And I saw another strong angel coming down out of heaven - - -
arrayed with a cloud,
and the rainbow was upon his head, 1
and his face was as the sun,
and his feet as pillars of fire.

B
And he had in his *hand* a little book open, 2
And he set his right foot upon the *sea,* and this left upon the *earth;*

And he cried with a great *voice,* as a lion roareth, 3
And when he cried, *the seven thunders* uttered their voices.

And when *the seven thunders* uttered, I was about to write. 4

And I heard a *voice* from heaven, saying,
Seal up the things which *the seven thunders* uttered, and write them not.

And the angel that was standing upon the *sea* and upon the *earth* 5
Lifted his right *hand* to heaven.

C
And he sware by him that liveth for ever and ever, 6

Who created
the *heaven* and the things therein,
and the *earth* and the things therein,
and the *sea* and the things therein,

That there shall be delay no longer.

But in the days of the voice of the seventh angel, 7
When it is about to sound,
Then is finished the mystery of God,
According to the good tidings which he declared
To his servants the prophets.

B′
And the voice which I heard from heaven, again speaking with me, 8
And saying, Go, take the book which is open,
In the hand of the angel
That standeth upon the *sea* and upon the *earth,*
And I went to the angel, 9
Saying unto him that he should give me the little book.
And he saith unto me,

Take it and *eat it up,* and it shall *make bitter thy belly,*
But in thy *mouth* it shall be *sweet as honey;*
And I took the little book out of the angel's *hand,* and *ate it up.* 10
And it was in my *mouth* sweet as honey,
And when I *had eaten it,* was *made bitter my belly.*

A′ And they say unto me, thou must prophesy again over
many peoples,
and nations,
and tongues, 11
and kings.

Chapter ten depicts in a symbolic scene the prophet receiving his commission to witness for the truth. There is nothing new in this procedure itself, for similar scenes are related in the lives of the prophets of the Old Testament (cf. Isa. 6; Ez. 2:8-3:3). Neither should the similar commission in Rev. 1:9-20, which may be paralleled by 22:16-21, be regarded as a disturbing factor. The new representation of the commission to the prophet in the central part of the book is merely another instance of the law of distribution at the centre and the extremes of parallel material. There have been many instances of this law of structure in both longer and briefer portions of the book.[1]

The revealing angel bears the features which are commonly associated with the Lord himself in this book.[2] The writer has no intention of identifying the Lord with an angel; he merely hopes to convey the general idea that the angel in the scheme of the vision represents the Lord himself. The authority of the one who gives the commission is conveyed by vs. 1, and the scope of the testimony is indicated in vs. 11, both instances being in the form of a symbolic four. This is merely a way of stating in symbol liturgically what is given in the Great Commission (Matt. 28:18-20) in plain words.

Section B sets forth the first half of the action in the scene. The symmetry of this passage is perfect, the seven thunders, thrice repeated, forming the central triplet and the first and last couplet of the structure describing the angel with the book. The fact that the angel places his right foot upon the *sea* and his left foot upon the *earth* is twice repeated in the two extreme couplets. This statement recurs in vs. 8, but this time in the centre of the structure. When it occurs the third time it had become a kind of tag for the angel of vss. 2, 5. Evidently the actions of the angel, who is of gigantic proportions, are emphasized, and the meaning of the emphasis is made clear in 13:1, 11 when the two beasts are introduced, one coming out of the *sea* and the other out of the *earth*. The witnessing church is here told that its victorious Lord has

[1] Cf. 10:9b-10, "eat it up."

[2] Cf. 10:1 with 1:15, 16; 14:14; and 10:3 with 5:5.

trampled upon her enemies from whatever quarter they may appear (John 16:33).

The second half of the action in the scene is set forth in section B′, which contains two structures, the first describing the prophet's request for the book from the angel and the second the effects of eating it. Line by line these two chiastic structures offer parallels. We have already mentioned the fact that the reference to the sea and the earth is central in the first structure; the angel's hand, which also occurs in the two extremes in B, is found in the centre of B′.

To venture any opinion about the meaning of the little book may appear to be presumptuous. The fact that it was a small book and that it was open sets it immediately in contrast with the book of the fifth chapter that was sealed with seven seals. That nothing is said about the proclamation of its content to the world, but that its contents seem to affect only the seer himself, may be intended to convey the general idea of a mystic message intended for the church only (cf. 4 Esdras 14:44-48). If this book could be thought of as relating only to believers and their mystic experiences with Christ, a fine balance would at once be established between these two books and the two kinds of books in the judgment scene in 20:12; for there also one kind is of judgment and the other of life. If the little book relates to believers only, it would go far to explain why "the Lamb's book of life" (13:8) should appear in the scene which is parallel to chapter ten. The first sweetness would be a symbolic expression of the eagerness and anticipation attendant upon all reception of new truth,[3] and the later bitterness, of the temptation to unfaithfulness when the far-reaching implications of the truth are disclosed in conflict with the environment.[4] No group could better appreciate these common aspects of human experience than a martyr church on the eve of a great persecution.

Between the two sections BB′ which deal with the seer, the angel, and the book, a brief section appears depicting the angel's

[3] Cf. Jer. 15:16; 20:9; Job 23:12 with John 4:31-34.
[4] Cf. Jer. 15:17, 18; Matt. 10:34-39.

affirmation by solemn oath that there shall be delay no longer (vs. 6). The oath is sworn by God, who is presented as the creator of all things in a central triplet that has been injected between the two halves of the sentence. Whether the purpose of the oath is to emphasize the urgency of the testimony or the brevity of the persecution is difficult to say. It would not be beyond the range of possibility that both of these purposes could be served. They are certainly given prominence in the Missionary Discourse.[5] The great oath forms a fine central climax in the scene which certainly is not enhanced by the presence of vs. 7. This verse has no definite literary structure in keeping with the rest of the chapter, and its content is of the nature of stage directions in a drama. It has meaning only as long as the chapter is retained between the sixth and the seventh trumpets, for it looks forward to the sounding of the seventh trumpet. It was probably introduced by the editor who placed the two visions between the trumpets for the purpose of obtaining an episode; or, if the hypothesis of projections is accepted, by one who misunderstood the original writer's purpose of introducing the two visions between the trumpets.

The next phase of the testimony concerns Judaism. Historically, the testimony to Judaism precedes that to the Roman empire, but we are not concerned with historical sequence in symbolic visions. Dramatically, there is a very good reason for placing the testimony of the church to Judaism and the victory over the dragon in connection with this early chapter of Christian history in the centre of the book. Since the purpose of the book is to comfort and sustain the church that is soon to undergo a severe trial, no better method could possibly be devised than to recall the earlier trial of her faith and her victory in that great struggle.

[5] Cf. Matt. 10:7-10; 22-23.

F *The Two Witnesses: The Church's Testimony in Judaism*, 11:1-13

A
And there was given me a reed, like unto a rod, 1
And one said, Rise and measure — the sanctuary of God,
and the altar,
and them that worship therein.

And the court which is without the sanctuary cast without, 2
And measure it not, for it hath been given unto the nations.
And the holy city shall they tread under foot *forty and two months*.

B
And I will give unto my two witnesses, 3
And they shall prophesy *a thousand two hundred and threescore days*, clothed (in sackcloth.
These are the olive trees and the two candlesticks, 4
Standing before the Lord of all the earth.

And if any man desireth to hurt them, 5
Fire proceedeth out of their mouth and devoureth their enemies.
And if any man shall desire to hurt them,
In this manner must he be killed.

These have the power to shut the heaven, 6
That it rain not during *the days of their prophecy;*
And they have power over the waters to turn them into blood,
And to smite the earth with every plague, as often as they shall desire.

C
And when they shall have finished their testimony, 7
The beast that cometh out of the abyss — shall make war upon them,
and shall overcome them,
and shall kill them.
And *their dead body* (shall lie) in the streets of the great city, 8
Which spiritually is called Sodom and Egypt,
Where also their Lord was crucified.

And from among — the peoples, 9
and tribes,
and tongues,
and nations.

Do they look upon *their dead body three days and a half*,
And they suffer not their dead bodies to be laid in a tomb.
And they that dwell on the earth — rejoice over them,
and make merry, 10
and they shall send gifts to one (another,
Because these two prophets tormented them that dwell on the earth.

B′
And after *the three days and a half* a breath of life from God entered into (them, 11
and they stood on their feet.
And a great fear came upon them that *beheld them*.
And they heard a great voice from *heaven*, saying unto them, 12
Come up hither.
And they went up into *heaven* in a cloud.
And their enemies *beheld them*,
And *in that hour* there was a great earthquake. 13

A′
And the *tenth part* of the city fell,
And there were killed in the earthquake *seven thousand* persons
And the rest were affrighted and gave glory to the God of heaven.

In chapter seven we became familiar with one type of symbolic action, sealing; here we have another, measuring. The purpose of the measuring is to insure the safety of the thing measured (Zech. 2:5). That only the inner part of the temple is measured, while the court and the city are eliminated, indicate a distinction in Judaism itself (vss. 1, 2). This distinction is again brought home to us in the concluding words of the vision, where the references contrast the seven thousand persons that were killed and "the rest" that gave glory to the God of heaven (vs. 13). The severe censure of apostate Judaism which had refused to accept the Christ, given earlier in the book (2:9; 3:9), is still maintained. The holy city is ironically called holy; for it is "the great city," a name only applied to Babylon in this book;[6] it is also called "Sodom and Egypt," names which in the Old Testament are synonyms for all that is perverted and vile (Isa. 1:9, 10).

When the testimony of the church to Judaism is to be depicted, the symbols are derived from ancient prophetism.[7] The reason for this is not difficult to understand. The witnesses in the church were regarded as the legitimate successors of the ancient prophets (Matt. 5:12; 23:37), just as the church itself was regarded as the only legitimate Israel, since the Jews had rejected Christ. They were not only their successors but also heirs of all their persecutions (Matt. 5:12). The number *two* is in conformity with the ancient demand for "two witnesses or three" (Matt. 18:16), a demand that Jesus himself had granted in the days of his flesh (Mk. 6:7). In the symbolic language of the book "my two witnesses" are not two men that have been or are to come, but the whole witnessing church as its testimony relates to Judaism in the early period.

While the church performs its task, it is made invincible by divine protection. That is the substance of section B. When its mission has been fulfilled, it will share in the ordinary fate of mankind, including suffering and death (C). The witnesses are now overcome and killed by the Beast (cf. 11:7 with 13:1). They

[6] Cf. 18:2, 10, 16, 18, 19, 21.

[7] Cf. 11:4 with Zech. 4:1-14; vs. 5 with Jer. 5:14; 2 Kings 1:10-12; vs. 6a with 1 Kings 17:1; 18:1; Luke 4:25; Je. 5:17; vs. 6b with Ex. 7:17-ff.

are not even given a decent burial—the most sacred of all obligations in Judaism (cf. Tobit 1:17; 4:3, 4). Their enemies gloat over their dead bodies. We are probably not to look for any specific event in the encounter of the church with Judaism in order to satisfy the requirements of this passage. Paul's words in 1 Cor. 4:9-13 show that such figurative language may be employed in a letter; it is even more to be expected in an apocalyptic writing. After the suffering comes the reward (B′). The witnesses are now resuscitated and exalted. Just as the previous scene did not convey the idea of literally unburied corpses in the streets of Jerusalem, so this scene does not convey the idea of a literal resurrection of dead persons. The same apostle who described the sufferings of Christians in these words, "For thy sake we are *killed* all the day long; we are accounted as sheep for the slaughter," could also describe the restoration of his own confidence in these words: "For now we live, if ye stand fast in the Lord" (cf. Rom. 8:36; 1 Thess. 3:8). This vision, then, whatever previous use might have been made of it, is to be regarded as a symbolic canvas, depicting in greater detail the substance of the promise in 2:10, words which were spoken with reference to "the Synagogue of Satan."

When the Book of Revelation was written the struggle with Judaism was almost over.[8] For their encouragement Christians could be told that members of the Synagogue of Satan would come and worship at their feet (3:9). This statement should be read together with the promise that "the rest" would give glory to the God of heaven (vs. 13). There is a striking contrast between this remnant of Israel that becomes submissive through suffering, and the unrepentant "rest of mankind" of the Trumpet-and-Bowl-visions who persisted in their idolatry and blasphemed God because of their torments (9:20; 16:9, 11). What the struggle with Judaism was and how it was won is the topic of chapter twelve.

[8] Cf., however, *The Ignatian Epistles*, Magnes. X; Phila. VI; Justin Martyr, *Dialogue with Trypho the Jew*; Origen, *Against Celsus*, Bk. I, chap. 55; Bk. IV, chap. 52.

F′ *The Woman and the Dragon: The Church Persecuted by Judaism*, 12:1-17

A

And a great sign was seen in *heaven:* 1

A woman

Arrayed with the sun,
and the moon under her feet,
and upon her head a crown of twelve stars.

And she was with child, 2
And she cried out, travailing in birth,
And in pain to be delivered.

B

And there was seen another sign in *heaven:* 3

And behold, a red dragon, having
seven heads,
and ten horns,
and upon his heads seven diadems.

And his tail draweth the third part of the stars of *heaven*, 4
And did cast them to the *earth*.

* * *

X

And the dragon standeth before the woman that is to be delivered,
That when she is delivered he may devour her child.

And she was delivered
of a son,
a man child, 5
who is to rule the nations with a rod of iron;

And her child was caught up unto God,
And unto his throne.

And the woman *fled into the wilderness,* 6
A Where she hath a *place* prepared of God,
That there they may *nourish* her
A thousand two hundred and threescore days.

And there was a war in heaven: 7
Michael and his angels
Going forth to war
With the dragon;
And the dragon
Warred
And his angels:
And they prevailed not. 8
B
Neither was their place found any more in heaven.
And was cast down 9
The great dragon,
The old serpent,
He that is called Devil,
And Satan, the deceiver of the whole world:
He was cast down to earth,
And his angels were cast down with him.

And I heard a great voice from heaven, saying, 10
Y
C Now is come the salvation,
And the power,
And the kingdom of our God,
And the authority of his Christ.

For the accuser of our brethren *is cast down,*
Who accuseth them before God day and night.

And they overcame him because of the blood of the Lamb, 11
And because of the word of their testimony;
And they loved not their life even unto death.

Therefore rejoice, ye heavens, 12
B′ And they that tabernacle in them.
Woe for the *earth,*
And for the *sea.*

For the devil *is gone down* unto you, having great wrath,
Knowing that he hath but a short time.

And when the dragon saw that he was cast down to earth, 13
He persecuted the woman that brought forth the man child;
And there were given to the woman the two wings of the great 14
(eagle
That she might *fly into the wilderness,*
A′ Unto her *place,*
Where she is *nourished*
For a time, and times and a half time,

X′

Before the face of the serpent,
And the serpent cast out of his mouth after the woman, 15
Water as a river, that he might cause her to be carried away by the stream.
And the earth helped the woman, 16
And the earth opened her mouth,
And swallowed up the river,
Which the dragon cast out of his mouth,
And the dragon waxed wroth with the woman. 17

And he went away to make war with the rest of her seed,
That keep the commandments of God,
And hold the testimony of Jesus.
And he stood upon the sand of the sea. 13:1a

The structure of this chapter is most regular, even in its many minor details. In a prelude (vss. 1-4a) we have the *dramatis personae* introduced, namely, the woman in royal splendor about to give birth to her child (A) and the dragon, who is to play the part of the opponent (B). Interpreters have always had trouble with the sequence in these visions; the reason is that the woman, whose encounter with the dragon begins in X, is seen in safety in Y (cf. AA′) and again in X′ is seen engaged in a struggle. If, however, the hypothesis proposed in our arrangement is accepted, namely, that the material has been arranged in panels which are parallel, the thought of chronological sequence must be given up altogether. We have, then, a series of symbolic canvasses which are painted to match one another whose contents are quite clear. With this situation in mind we shall attempt to describe the relations of the various sections.

In X the birth of the man child is described in terms which identify him with Christ (cf. 12:5 with 19:15), and the encounter evidently terminates when Christ is removed from the earth. The attempt is made to "devour" the child, the woman being helped by heaven. In X′ we have again an encounter between the dragon and the woman described; this time "earth" helps the woman and "swallowed" the water from the dragon. Not only by the general theme of the two sections but by an adroit choice of synonymous and antithetic terms are the relations between the two sections kept before the reader.

In the central part of the chapter (Y) the symmetry is maintained in spite of a great deal of variation. We have the two frame-passages (AA′) with alternating lines which encase the whole. The flight of the woman, her place of refuge, her nourishment, and the prophetic time designations are all details of an orderly scheme. In B we have the war in heaven and in B′ the war on earth. In the first system in B (vss. 7-8a) the war in heaven is described in a perfect chiasmus, and in the following system (vs. 9) the result of the combat is given in the two couplets that encase the whole system, while the two couplets at the centre identify the great opponent of the woman as Devil and Satan. Turning now to the counterpart B′ we find an alternating structure, but the fact that the devil is "cast down" is mentioned in two parallel couplets, while in two sections of three lines each his struggle with the church on earth is set forth. The blood of the Lamb helps the church to overcome, and she is given "the two wings of the great eagle"—a symbol which evidently was conventional and needed no defining. In the centre of B′ we have an invitation to the godly to rejoice with an accompanying woe over the earth and the sea, i.e., the special dominion of the beast (cf. 13:1, 11). In BB′, then, we have not only a presentation of the struggle in heaven and on earth, but we have also a comforting account of the final outcome of the struggle. The note of final victory, however, is reserved for section C which is the heart of the whole structure. The futility of introducing chronology in the vision is definitely disposed of by vs. 10. There the great voice from heaven proclaims the ultimate victory in that the kingdom of God is come and the authority of Christ established. The presentation of a scene like this must be explained on the basis of such sentiments as those expressed in Acts 4:27-29. In the contemplation of past difficulties that have been overcome the church has often girded herself for future struggles.

We shall now undertake to delineate the features of the greatest opponent of the church, namely, Roman imperialism. The red dragon having discovered that the early attempts through Judaism had been frustrated, now makes a fresh start (cf. 12:17b-13:1a). There is a great deal of dramatic suspense in the simple statement, "and he stood upon the sand of the sea," that sea which soon would yield up a more formidable ally to the dragon than any one that had as yet appeared.

Before we enter into the detailed study of this ally we should recall that chapter thirteen is the literary counterpart to chapter ten.[9] The symbolic features of that chapter should be recalled before we take up its counterpart. The angelic messenger, we recall, is adorned by those symbols which in the book are related to the Lord of the church (10:1). The message is given to be delivered to all the world (10:11). The universal scope of the message is paralleled by the universal features describing the authority of the angel, whose feet are resting on both *earth* and *sea* (10:2, 5, 8).

The real significance of all these details does not become apparent until we reach the counterpart (E′). Here we discover that the important features of chapter ten are paralleled in an unmistakable manner. The quarters over which the angel had planted his feet are those from which the two great enemies of the church go forth. The first beast, Roman Imperialism, issues forth from the sea (13:1b), and the second beast, representing the Caesar cult, comes out of the earth (vs. 11). We understand now the accumulation of symbols indicating the authority of the Lord in the description of the messenger angel. Their meaning is, no doubt, that supporting the testimony of the church is the full authority of her Lord, a consideration which is all important to her witnesses in view of the authority of the pagan state which is opposing her. A greater array of symbols is hardly conceivable than that which describes the authority of the first beast (13:1-8).

[9] Cf. EE′ in the General Outline.

E′ *The Two Beasts: The Church Persecuted by the Roman Empire*, 13:1-18

The First Beast*

A And I saw a beast coming out of the sea. 1b
Having ten *horns* and seven *heads*,

B And on his horns ten *diadems*, and upon his heads names of *blasphemy*.

C And the *beast* which I saw was like { unto a leopard,
and his feet were as the feet of a bear. 2
and his mouth as the mouth of a lion. }

D And the *dragon gave* him { his power,
and his throne,
and great *authority*. }

And I saw one of his heads as though it had been slain unto death; 3
E And his *death-stroke* was healed:
And the whole earth wondered after the beast.

D′ And they worshipped the *dragon*, because he *gave* his *authority* to the 4
(beast.

C′ And they worshipped the *beast*, saying, { Who is like unto the beast?
And who is able to make war with
(him? }

B′ And there was given to him a mouth speaking *great things* and *blasphemies*; 5

A′ And there was given to him *authority* to continue forty and two months.

* * *

A And he opened his mouth for blasphemies against God *to blaspheme* - - - - - - - - - - { his name, 6
and his tabernacle,
them that tabernacle in the heavens. }

B And it was given him to make war with the saints, and *to overcome* them. 7

C And there was given to him authority over *every* { tribe
and people
and tongue
and nation. }

And all that dwell on the earth shall *worship* him, 8
D Every one whose *name* hath not been written from the foundation of the
In the book of life of the Lamb that hath been slain. (world

If any man hath an ear, 9
Let him hear;
E If any man is for captivity, 10
Into captivity he goeth;
If any man shall kill by the sword,
With the sword he must be killed.

F Here is the patience
And the faith of the saints.

*Every section of the second part of this chapter (vss. 11-18) should be compared with every corresponding section of the first part, and the terms that are underscored should be particularly observed. There are a great number of parallels in the description of the activities of the first and the second beasts.

The Second Beast.

And I saw another beast coming up out of the earth, 11
And he had horns like unto a lamb,
And he spake as a dragon,
And he exerciseth all the authority of the first beast in his sight. 12

And he maketh the earth and them that dwell therein
A To worship the first beast,
Whose *death-stroke* was healed.

And he doeth great *signs,* 13
B That he should even make fire come down out of heaven upon the earth
In the *sight* of men.

And he deceiveth them that dwell on the earth 14
B′ By reason of the *signs* which it was given him to do
In the *sight* of the beast;

Saying to them that dwell on the earth,
A′ That they should make an image to the beast,
Who hath *the stroke* of the sword and lived.

* * *

A And it was given him to give breath to it, even the image of the beast, 15
That even the image of the beast should *speak.*

B And he shall cause that as many as should not worship the image of the beast *should be killed.*

C And he caused *all* { the small and the great, and the rich and the poor, and the free and the bond, } 16

D {
That there be given them a *mark* { on their right hand, or on their forehead; }
And that no man should be able { to buy or to sell, } 17
Save that he hath the *mark,* { the name of the beast or the number of his name. }
}

F For here is the wisdom. 18
He that hath understanding

Let him count the number of the beast;
E For it is the number of a man,
And his number is six hundred and sixty six.

The panel that describes the first beast is very elaborate in its symmetry. It is made up of two halves, one describing the beast (vss. 1b-5), and the other his activities (vss. 6-10). The one is chiastic and the other is alternating. The second panel has also two halves with a similar arrangement. Although separate, it is, nevertheless, interlinked in various ways with the first panel. In the description of the first beast the death-stroke is mentioned in the central section E, but in the panel dealing with the second beast the death-stroke is alluded to in the two extreme sections (AA′). This is the law of the shift from centre to the extremes of parallel sections. Likewise in the latter halves we have in the first the words, "Here is the patience" (13:10). The words in this case refer to the principles of resignation and non-resistance to which the Christians were committed (EF). In this case it should be observed that the statement is *preceded* by the two principles (E) which each Christian is called upon to obey. In the sections dealing with the second beast, however, this order is reversed. We have a statement, "Here is the wisdom" (13:18), but it is not preceded but *followed* by the words to which it has reference, namely, the mysterious identification of the beast (FE). These operations of the laws of chiasmus serve to link the two descriptions of the beasts. The two panels are to be regarded as two phases of the same thing which together convey the whole message concerning the great enemy of the church, Rome.

The portrait of the first beast is painted in a lengthy chiastic structure, which is somewhat irregular, since triplets that occur in some lines are not balanced in the parallel lines. The authority of the first beast is expressed by horns and heads in A, and by the term "authority" in A′. The forty-two months, while indicating a time limit, are nevertheless to be synchronized with similar terms in the eleventh and twelfth chapters, where they express both the length of her witnessing period and the duration of the martyrdom of the church. For this writer does not comfort the church by promising a cessation of the trouble, but by holding out the possibility of her remaining faithful even unto death (13:7, 15). From the beast no quarter will be asked and none will be given; for the release from the war will come only with the Lord's return and the destruction of Rome. The beast is adorned with diadems on the horns (satire?) and names of blasphemy (B); he is speaking "great things" (boastfulness) and blasphemies (B′). The beastly nature is seen in the combination of leopard, bear, and lion (Dan. 7:4-6), which are the three beasts of Daniel in reverse order (C). Well may the world ask of such a monster, "Who is like unto the beast?" and, "Who is able to make war with him?" (C′). The source of his power is the dragon (DD′), who "gave him" whatever authority he possesses. Such is the description given of Roman imperialism. It is personified in the Caesars. They come and go, as expressed in the head that received the death-stroke. But the death-stroke is healed; the system continues, whatever may happen to its individual representatives on the throne. There is a majesty and solidity in Roman imperialism which even its enemy must admit excites the admiration of the world. Some such interpretation, it would seem, would satisfy the words in vs. 3; for even if *Nero redivivus* is seen behind this imagery, the meaning of it in this context, no doubt, is more general.

If Roman imperialism is designated by the first picture, its religious phase, or the emperor cult, is symbolized by the second beast. That this beast had horns "like unto a lamb" sounds like a contradiction, until we remember the description of the Lamb with the seven horns (5:6). This gives us the religious and sacrificial aspect of the second beast. Now and then we meet with an element of parody in this book. There are little touches of description which have been used of the Lord and his church which recur in connection with the enemy, and its total effect is a strong feeling of contrast. Although the beast is in some respects like a lamb, it speaks like a dragon, which is the ultimate source of its authority. In two sections (AA′) we learn that the second beast makes the world worship the first beast and make an image to it. This has reference to the cult of the emperors and of Dea Roma. The cult arose in 29 B.C. in the response of Augustus to a request from cities in Asia Minor for permission to erect temples in honor of the emperor.[10] The hierarchy in the prosecution of its interests often resorted to trickery with which they duped the worshippers. These practices are described objectively in BB′ without any attempt at condemnation; yet one cannot fail to sense the undercurrent of indignation in the introductory words contrasting the Lamb and the dragon (vss. 11, 12).

If we now take the latter halves of the two pictures and com-

[10] S. J. Case, *The Evolution of Early Christianity* (Chicago: 1914), pp. 195-238; for a satire on the deification of emperors, cf. Seneca, *Apocolocyntosis*, *Loeb Classical Library*.

pare the sections of alternating order, we shall obtain a very clear picture of the activities of the two beasts, i.e., of the civil and religious powers of Rome, co-operating to crush the nascent church. The two parallel sections deal with Rome's sins of speech (AA), her violence (BB), and the scope of her power (CC). In the one section (D) we learn that only those whose names are written in the Lamb's book of life will be able to resist Rome's claims to worship. Those "that dwell on the earth," in contrast to those who "tabernacle in heaven" (cf. 13:6 and vss. 8, 12, 14), will comply with the demands of the beast. The description of the privileges obtained by submission are elaborated in a triplet of statements which branch off into pairs in the parallel D section (vss. 16, 17). We thus obtain a symbolic six which is reminiscent of the number of the beast. But the privileges are only bought at the price of complete enslavement. The picture, no doubt, is intended as a warning to those who would be inclined to follow some middle course. The result of such compromises would be that the mark of the beast would be substituted for Christ's "new name"; Rome's name would supplant "the name of the city of my God." No compromise, no resistance against the violence of the state, and no false hopes of cessation of the persecution—such is the message of these symbolic panels. All these things are to be endured, but the church is assured that her Lord dominates the sea and the earth (10:2, 5, 8), out of which come the two beasts. The encounter with Judaism is to a large extent a thing of the past, and whatever opposition may arise from the Roman empire will be overcome and the church will ultimately triumph. The continuous care of God for his church under all conditions is an assured fact (12:6, 14).

Before leaving the four central panels of the book (EFF'E') one more detail must be considered, namely, the allusion to the Seven Thunders in 10:3, 4. These thunders were "uttered," but they were "sealed up." What could have been more appropriate than a description of Seven Thunders at the *centre* of the book in view of the fact that this would have made the *seventh* series.[11] One gets the impression that the author has anticipated an expecta-

[11] BCDD'C'B' in the General Outline.

tion of the Seven Thunders at this point, for he hastens to assure his readers that there shall be "delay no longer" (10:7).

The reader, no doubt, has already asked the question why we have taken the liberty of synchronizing the prophetic designations of time that have occurred. The answer is that the writer himself has taken pains to guide us in this matter, for there is certainly a discernible literary pattern in his employment of these terms.[12] Taking them as they now stand in the text we obtain the following list:

42 months	11:2
1260 days	11:3
3½ days	11:9
3½ days	11:11
1260 days	12:6
42 months	13:5

From this list we gather that chapters 11, 12 and 13 are part of the scheme, while chapter ten has no part in it. If we therefore feel inclined to regard the Seven Thunders as the centre of the original work and chapters 11, 12, and 13 as representing a stage of later editing, there is much against this view. The most obvious objection to it is the author's way of introducing and disposing of the enemies of the church. This is done after a definite chiastic pattern which is as evident as his arrangement of the designations of time.[13] A second objection would be the fact that many details in the panel depicting the destruction of Babylon depend on the picture in chapter 13 in order to become intelligible. Any hypothesis of later editorial additions of substantial portions of the book is likely to raise more questions than it solves. The facts that have given rise to such hypotheses may well be taken care of by assuming the original author's employment of sources. Yet his use of these sources is not a mechanical pasting together of fragments but is rather a process of assimilation. He is using Old Testament sources throughout the book, and we know how they are used. At some points he also touches common ground

[12] The 1260 days and "a time, and times, and a half time" are parallel in 12:6, 14 (AA'). The latter expression originates in Dan. 7:25, a symbol of troublous times.

[13] Cf. outline on p. 354.

with Fourth Esdras (either directly or indirectly through some writing unknown to us) and we know how these sources are used.[14] We see how he has studded his pages with allusions, but hardly ever without an individual touch, a new combination. These combinations are of such nature that they may best be explained as the outpouring of a mind that is already saturated with such imagery and such terms. When a creative mind lays hold of these materials they are fused into a new unity, they take on new combinations, and they yield up their former identity.[15] No amount of research into their origin can recover for us their meaning, for the meaning is only the one which the author assigns to them in their new context in his book.

The purpose of the book is practical. The author sees the impending clash of the church with Rome. To stiffen the morale of the Christians is his great task. How admirably he performs his duty! Our own unfamiliarity with his symbols, our misplacement of the climaxes, and our general disregard of structure has often obscured for us the great dramatic power of the book. Among early Christians, who were used to apocalyptic imagery and who had also preserved their Old Testament literary heritage of chiastic forms, the book doubtless had a wide appeal. We need only to bring vividly into our imagination an assembly of such Christians awaiting the outbreak of persecution. With solemnity and fervor the reader would recite the scenes in this book, and the courage of the assembly would be restored. The message of the book is timeless. No greater indictment has ever been written against unholy alliances of the church with essentially pagan states.

After surveying, if ever so hurriedly, the details of this book and after attempting to see its parts in relation to each other, one is left with a deep impression of the unity of the book. Tiny threads of phraseology are picked up in one end of the book, only to be dropped for a while, until they appear once more toward the

[14] Fourth Esdras 6:17, 18; 7:26; 8:52; 10:27, 42, 43, 44; 13:44; (2:42-45 cf. Rev. 7:9-10), the latter a Christian addition in the Latin.

[15] Cf. J. L. Lowe, *The Road to Xanadu.* Boston, 1927. An illuminating study of the workings of the creative imagination in the production of S. T. Coleridge's poem *Kubla Khan.*

close of the book. The great enemies of the church are brought on the scene with a vivid display of their dignity and power only to be removed, in the inverse order of their appearance, with strokes of judgment that follow one upon the other with surprising swiftness and thoroughness. Striking contrasts are drawn in canvasses of large dimensions, though far removed from one another by intervening panels, as in the case of Babylon the great and New Jerusalem. There is something gigantic in the whole plan of the book which taxes our imagination almost to the breaking point. In some instances effective climaxes are achieved between parts that are far removed in the text, as in the case of the Trumpet and Bowl series.

We are compelled to ask whether, after all, such features could have become intelligible to and effective in an audience unless the book were rendered *in toto*. May it not be possible that we have before us an early liturgical document of the church which was used in solemn assembly during times of great trial for the purpose of strengthening the faith and hope of its members? It would seem that both the exquisite artistry of some of the smaller panels as well as the perfect balance of the parallel series would favor the theory of some such liturgical function of the book. And the various literary devices that recur again and again in the book (like the eagle's three woes)—each of which serves to make emphatic the approach of the end—help to sustain the interest and to create suspense until the climax finally is reached. In a liturgical rendering of the book such features would become perfectly intelligible, but it is difficult to see how they could be made meaningful by reading the book merely in detached longer or shorter sections.

In the absence of any direct information concerning the order of worship in the apostolic church we are not in the position to say definitely how its public or private worship was conducted.[16] Much would be determined by the number and character of the worshippers and by the place and circumstances in which they met.

[16] L. Duchesne, *Christian Worship* (transl. by M. L. McClure, Ed. 5), pp. 46 ff.; A. E. Burn, "Worship," in *Hastings Dictionary of the Apostolic Church*, Vol. II, pp. 697 ff. cites all pertinent passages from the earliest times.

There was probably no universal order which was followed by all churches. But the presence in our New Testament of documents like the Gospel according to Matthew and the Book of Revelation would seem to indicate that some of the formalities of the Temple and the Synagogue, not to mention the aesthetic features of Greek and Roman worship, must soon have passed over to the church.

BIBLIOGRAPHY

BIBLIOGRAPHY

Albertz, Martin. *Die synoptischen Streitsgespräche*. Berlin, 1921.

Alford, Henry. *The Greek New Testament*. 4 Vols. New York, 1859.

Bassett, Samuel E. ὝΣΤΕΡΟΝ ΠΡΟΤΕΡΟΝ ὉΜΗΡΙΚΩΣ (Cicero, Att. 1, 16, 1) *Harvard Studies in Classical Philology*. Vol. XXXI, 1920.

Beckwith, Isbon T. *The Apocalypse of John*. New York, 1922.

Bengel, J. A. *Gnomon novi testamenti*. Tübingen, 1742. Translated by C. T. Lewis and M. R. Vincent. Philadelphia, 1860-62.

Bertram, Georg. *Die Leidensgeschichte Jesu und der Christuskult*. Göttingen, 1922.

Blass, Friedrich. *Grammar of New Testament Greek*. Translated by Henry St. John Thackeray. 2d ed. London, 1905.

——— *Die Rhytmen der asianischen und römischen Kunstprosa*. Leipzig, 1905.

Bousett, Wilhelm. *Die Offenbarung Johannis neu bearbeitet*. 6th ed. Göttingen, 1906.

Boys, Thomas. *Tactica Sacra*. London, 1824.

——— *Key to the Book of Psalms*. London, 1825. Revised and enlarged edition by E. W. Bullinger, London, 1890.

Breasted, J. A. *Ancient Records of Egypt*. 4 Vols. Chicago, 1906-7.

Briggs, C. A. *Biblical Study*. New York, 1883.

——— *The Book of Psalms* (ICC). 2 Vols. 1906-7.

——— *The Messiah of the Apostles*. New York, 1895.

Bullinger, E. W. *The Companion Bible*. Oxford University Press.

Bultmann, Rudolf. *Der Stil der paulinischen Predigt und die kynisch-stoischen Diatribe*. Göttingen, 1910.

——— *Die Geschichte der synoptischen Tradition*. Göttingen, 1921.

Burkitt, F. C. *The Gospel History and its Transmission*, 3d ed. Edinburgh: T. & T. Clark, 1911.

Burney, C. F. *The Aramaic Origin of the Fourth Gospel*. Oxford, 1925.

——— *The Poetry of Our Lord*. Oxford, 1922.

Case, S. J. *The Evolution of Early Christianity*. Chicago, 1914.

Charles, R. H. (ed.). *The Apocrypha and Pseudepigrapha of the Old* Testament. 2 vols. Oxford, 1913.

Cheyne, T. K. (ed.). *Encyclopedia Biblica*, New ed. New York, 1914.

Cobb, W. H. *A Criticism of Systems of Hebrew Metre.* Oxford, 1905.

Colwell, E. C. *The Greek of the Fourth Gospel.* Chicago, 1931.

Crum, J. M. C. *The Original Jerusalem Gospel.* London, 1927.

Dalman, Gustaf. *Jesus-Jeshua.* Translated by Paul P. Levertoff. New York, 1929.

Davidson, Samuel. *An Introduction to the New Testament.* 2 Vols. 1868.

Delitzsch, Franz. *Biblical Commentary on the Prophecies of Isaiah.* Translated by James Martin. 2 Vols. Edinburgh, 1886.

Dibelius, Martin. *Die Formgeschichte des Evangeliums.* 2d ed. Tübingen, 1933. Translated by Bertram Lee Woolf under the title, *From Tradition to Gospel.* London, 1934.

——— *Handkommentar zum Neuen Testament: An die Kolosser.* Tübingen, 1927.

Driver, S. R. *An Introduction to the Literature of the Old Testament.* New ed. New York, 1910.

Duchesne, L. *Christian Worship.* Translated by M. L. McClure. 5th ed. London: S. P. C. K., 1923.

Easton, Burton S. *The Gospel before the Gospel.* New York, 1928.

——— *Christ in the Gospels.* New York, 1930.

Fascher, Erich. *Die formgeschichtliche Methode.* Giessen, 1924.

Fiebig, P. W. J. *Der Erzählungsstil der Evangelien.* Leipzig, 1924.

Forbes, John. *The Symmetrical Structure of Scripture.* Edinburgh, 1854.

——— *Analytical Commentary on the Epistle to the Romans,* Edinburgh, 1868.

Goguel, Maurice. *Life of Jesus.* Translated by Alice Wyon. New York, 1933.

Goodspeed, E. J. *The Meaning of Ephesians.* Chicago, 1933.

——— *New Solutions of New Testament Problems.* Chicago, 1928.

——— *An Introduction to the New Testament.* Chicago, 1937.

Grant, F. C. *The Growth of the Gospels.* New York, 1933.

Gray, G. B. *A Critical Introduction to the Old Testament.* New York, 1917.

——— *The Forms of Hebrew Poetry.* London, 1915.

Gunkel, Hermann. *Schöpfung und Chaos.* 1894.

——— *Genesis übersetzt und erklärt.* Göttingen, 1901.

——— *The Legends of Genesis.* Translated by H. Carruth. Chicago, 1901.

Harnack, Adolf. *The Sayings of Jesus.* Translated by J. R. Wilkinson. London, 1908.

Harper, W. R. *A Critical and Exegetical Commentary on Amos and Hosea.* (ICC) New York, 1905.

Hastings, James. *Dictionary of the Bible.* New York, 1911.
——— *Dictionary of Christ and the Gospels.* New York, 1917.
——— *Dictionary of the Apostolic Church.* New York, 1916.
Heinrici, D. C. F. *Der literarische Character der neutestamentlichen Schriften.* Leipzig, 1908.
Herder, J. G. *Vom Geist der ebräischen Poesie.* Translated by James Marsh. 2 Vols. Burlington, Vt., 1833.
Hicks, E. "Saint Paul and Hellenism," in *Studia Biblica et Ecclesiastica.*
Horne, T. H. *An Introduction to the Critical Study and Knowledge of the Holy Scripture.* 3 Vols., 11th ed. London, 1860.
Houghton, Louise Seymour. *Hebrew Life and Thought.* Chicago, 1906.
Jebb, John. *Sacred Literature.* London, 1820.
——— *Thirty Years of Correspondence between John Jebb and Alexander Knox, Esq.* Edited by Charles Forster. Philadelphia, 1835.
Josephus, Flavius. *The Antiquities of the Jews.* Translated by Henry St. John Thackeray. (Loeb's Classical Library), 8 Vols. 1926.
Jülicher, Adolf. *An Introduction to the New Testament.* Translated by Janet Penrose Ward. New York, 1904.
Kirschmaier, G. W. *Parallelismos Novi Foederis et Polybii.* Wittenberg, 1725.
Knox, John. *Philemon among the Letters of Paul.* Chicago, 1935.
Kraeling, Carl H. "The Jewish Community at Antioch," in *Journal of Biblical Literature,* Vol. LI, Part II, pp. 130-160.
Lake, Kirsopp. *Landmarks in the History of Early Christianity.* New York, 1922.
——— *The Apostolic Fathers.* (Loeb Classical Library), 2 Vols. London, 1925.
Langdon, S. *Babylonian Wisdom.* London, 1923.
Lehmann-Haas. *Textbuch zur Religionsgeschichte.* 2d ed., 1922.
Lohmeyer, Ernst. *Kyrios Jesus: eine Untersuchung zu Phil.* 2:5-11. Heidelberg, 1928.
Lowth, Robert. *De sacra poesi Hebraeorum praelectiones academicae.* Translated by G. Gregory. New edition with notes by Calvin E. Stowe. Andover, Mass., 1829.
——— *Isaiah, A New Translation with Notes.* 1778.
Luckenbill, D. D. *Ancient Records of Assyria.* Chicago.
Lund, Nils Wilhelm. "The Presence of Chiasmus in the Old Testament," *American Journal of Semitic Languages and Literatures.* Vol. XLVI, No. 2, January, 1930.
——— "The Presence of Chiasmus in the New Testament," *Journal of Religion,* Vol. X, No. 1, January, 1930.

——— "The Influence of Chiasmus upon the Structure of the Gospels," *Anglican Theological Review,* Vol. XIII, No. 1, January, 1931.

——— "The Influence of Chiasmus upon the Structure of the Gospel according to Matthew," *Anglican Theological Review,* Vol. XIII, No. 4, October, 1931.

——— "The Literary Structure of Paul's Hymn to Love," *Journal of Biblical Literature,* Vol. L, Part IV, December, 1933.

——— "Chiasmus in the Psalms," *American Journal of Semitic Languages and Literatures.* Vol. XLIX, No. 4, July, 1933.

——— *Outline Studies in the Book of Revelation.* Chicago, 1935.

Macdonald, Duncan B. *The Hebrew Literary Genius.* Princeton University Press, 1933.

Meyer, H. A. W. *Critical and Exegetical Handbook to the New Testament.* American Edition. New York, 1884.

Milligan, William. *Lectures on the Apocalypse.* 3d ed. London, 1892.

——— *Discussions on the Apocalypse.* London, 1893.

——— *The Book of Revelation* (Expositor's Bible). New York, 1902.

Moffat, James. *An Introduction to the Literature of the New Testament.* New York, 1921.

Möller, H. "Strophenbau der Psalmen." *Zeitschrift für die alttestamentliche Wissenschaft,* IX, Heft 4, 1932.

Montefiore, C. G. *The Synoptic Gospels.* 2d ed. London, 1927.

Montgomery, J. A. "Ras Shamra Notes IV: The Conflict of Baal and the Waters," *Journal of American Oriental Society,* Vol. LV, No. 3, September, 1935.

Moore, G. F. *Judaism.* 3 Vols. Harvard University Press, 1927-1930.

Moulton, R. C. *The Literary Study of the Bible.* Boston, 1889.

——— *A Short Introduction to the Literature of the Bible.* Boston, 1901.

Nöldecke, Theodor. "Aramaic Language" in *Encyclopedia Biblica,* 1914.

Norden, Eduard. *Die antike Kunstprosa.* 2 Vols. Leipzig-Berlin, 1918.

——— *Agnostos Theos,* 1913.

Olrik, Axel. "Folkedigtningens episke love," in *Folkelige Afhandlingar.* Edited by Hans Ellekilde, Copenhagen, 1919.

Overbeck, Franz. "Über die Anfänge der patristischen Litteratur," *Historische Zeitschrift,* N. F. XII, 1882.

Paley, William. *The Works of William Paley.* Philadelphia, 1831.

Philo. *The Works of Philo Judaeos.* Translated by C. D. Yonge. Bohn Edition, London, 1854.

Ramsay, William M. *The Letters to the Seven Churches of Asia.* 1904.

Riddle, Donald W. *Early Christian Life.* Chicago, 1936.

Roberts, Alexander (ed.). *The Ante-Nicene Fathers.* Buffalo, 1885.

Sanday, William (editor). *Oxford Studies in the Synoptic Problem.* Oxford, 1911.

Schaff, Philip (editor). *The Nicene and Post-Nicene Fathers.* Buffalo, 1887.

Schmidt, Karl Ludwig. *Der Rahmen der Geschichte Jesu.* Berlin, 1919.

——— *Die Stellung der Evangelien in der allgemeinen Literaturgeschichte,* in *Eucharisterion.* Göttingen, 1923.

Skinner, J. *The Book of the Prophet Isaiah* (Cambridge Series). 2 Vols. 1915.

Smith, G. A. *The Book of Isaiah.* 2 Vols. London, 1888-90.

Smith, J. M. P. (editor) *The Old Testament, An American Translation.* Chicago, 1927.

Streeter, H. B. *The Four Gospels.* New York, 1925.

Strobach, Z. B. M. *De eruditione Pauli.* Leipzig, 1708.

Stummer, Fr. *Sumerisch-Akkadische Parallelen zum Aufbau alttestamentlicher Psalmen* (in *Studien zur Geschichte und Kultur des Altertums,* XI½, 1922).

Swete, H. B. *The Apocalypse of Saint John.* London. 1907.

Taylor, Isaac. *The Spirit of Hebrew Poetry.* New York, 1872.

Tholeman, Chr. *De eruditione Pauli Judaica non Graeca.* Leipzig. 1769.

Torrey, C. C. "The Aramaic Origin of the Gospel of John," *Harvard Theological Review,* Vol. XVI. 1923.

——— *The Four Gospels: A New Translation.* New York, 1933.

Trench, R. C. *Synonyms of the New Testament.* 11th ed. London. 1890.

——— *Notes on the Parables of our Lord.* London, 1841.

Vischer, E. "Die Offenbarung Johannes eine jüdische Schrift in christlicher Bearbeitung," in *Texte und Untersuchungen,* 1886.

Völter, Daniel. *Die Entstehung der Apokalypse.* 2d ed. 1885.

Walker, H. H. "Where were Madmenah and Gebim?" *Journal of the Palestinian Oriental Society,* Vol. XIII, 1933.

——— "The Literary Structure of the Book of Habakkuk" (in collaboration with N. W. Lund), *Journal of Biblical Literature,* Vol. LII, Pt. IV, 1934.

Weidinger, Karl. *Die Haustafeln.* Leipzig, 1928.

Weiss, Bernard. *A Manual of Introduction to the New Testament.* Translated by A. J. K. Davidson. 2 Vols. London, 1887-88.

Weiss, Johannes. "Beiträge zur paulinischen Rhetorik," in *Theologische Studien* in honor of Bernhard Weiss. Göttingen, 1897.

——— *Das Urchristentum*. Translated under the editorship of Frederic C. Grant under the title "*The History of Primitive Christianity*. 2 Vols. New York, 1937.

——— *Die Aufgaben der neutestamentlichen Wissenschaft*. Göttingen, 1908.

——— *Die Offenbarung Johannes*. Göttingen, 1904.

——— *Der Erste Korintherbrief*. Göttingen, 1910.

Wernle, Paul. *The Sources of Our Knowledge of the Life of Jesus*. Translated by Edward Lummis, Boston, 1907.

Wilamovitz-Moellendorff, Ulrich von. *Die Kultur der Gegenwart*. Teil I. Leipzig-Berlin, 1905.

Wilke, Christian. *Die neutestamentliche Rhetorik*. Leipzig: 1843.

Zahn, Theodor. *Introduction to the New Testament*. Translated by M. W. Jacobus and C. S. Thayer. 3 Vols. Edinburgh, 1909.

INDEX

INDEX OF SUBJECTS AND AUTHORS

INDEX OF PASSAGES CITED

Made in the USA
San Bernardino, CA
29 January 2020

63778761R00280